KINSHIP NOVELS OF EARLY MODERN KOREA

Premodern East Asia: New Horizons
A Center for Korean Research Book

PREMODERN EAST ASIA: NEW HORIZONS

This series is dedicated to books that focus on humanistic studies of East Asia before the mid-nineteenth century in fields including literature and cultural and social history, as well as studies of science and technology, the environment, visual cultures, performance, material culture, and gender. The series particularly welcomes works with field-changing and paradigm-shifting potential that adopt interdisciplinary and innovative approaches. Contributors to the series share the premise that creativity in method and rigor in research are preconditions for producing new knowledge that transcends modern disciplinary confines and the framework of the nation-state. In highlighting the complexity and dynamism of premodern societies, these books illuminate the relevance of East Asia to the contemporary world.

Becoming Guanyin: Artistic Devotion of Buddhist Women in Late Imperial China, Yuhang Li

Kinship Novels
of Early Modern Korea

BETWEEN GENEALOGICAL TIME
AND THE DOMESTIC EVERYDAY

Ksenia Chizhova

Columbia University Press
New York

This work was supported by the Core University Program for Korean Studies through the Ministry of Education of the Republic of the Korea and the Korean Studies Promotion Service of the Academy of Korean Studies (AKS-2016-OLU-2250006).

Columbia University Press
Publishers Since 1893
New York   Chichester, West Sussex
cup.columbia.edu
Copyright © 2021 Columbia University Press

Cataloging-in-Publication Data available from the Library of Congress.
ISBN 978-0-231-18780-0 (cloth)
ISBN 978-0-231-18781-7 (paper)
ISBN 978-0-231-54747-5 (ebook)

Columbia University Press books are printed on permanent and durable acid-free paper.
Printed in the United States of America

Cover image: Kim Hongdo 金弘道, Illustrations of Hong I-sang's Life, one of the eight panels from silk folding screen, courtesy of the National Museum of Korea
Cover design: Chang Jae Lee

For Anton and Daehwan, in honor of the complexities of kinship and in acknowledgment of my perpetual inability to achieve a semblance of work–life balance.

Contents

Acknowledgments

Now finished, this book appears to have so little that belongs to me only. Rather than a monograph, it is a web of connections and relationships, chance encounters—with written sources and people—that coalesced into a bound volume with physical proportions. These notes of gratitude chart the moments of reciprocity so fundamental to academic writing and all the more poignant at the time of the COVID-19 outbreak, social distancing, and canceled events.

I am deeply grateful for my time at Columbia University's East Asian Languages and Cultures Department, which changed me as a person and as a thinker. I still revisit the conversations I had with the late professor JaHyun Kim Haboush, surprised by how little I understood back then and how much her words can still teach me in the time to come. Dorothy Ko has been a truly enchanting mentor, showing how scholarship can be fun and elegant and deeply personal. Theodore Hughes was always there in times of trouble, and his unfailingly astute advice made all the difference. Jungwon Kim's friendliness and care made everything better. Particia Dailey was a guide to a sophisticated world of ideas, which I can only ever hope to be part of. Eugenia Lean's incisive feedback taught me a great deal. I am also very grateful for the company of Dajeong Chung, Shing-ting Lin, Sixiang Wang, Jenny Wang Medina, Mi-Ryong Shim, Jae Won Chung, and Jon Kief, who made Kent Hall feel like home.

My research in Korea was supported by the unbelievable generosity of local scholars. This project would have been impossible without Professor Im Ch'igyun of the Academy of Korean Studies, who extended his time and knowledge so unsparingly, patiently walking me through the intricacies of vernacular Korean manuscripts. Professor Jung Byung Sul of Seoul National University balanced encouragement and caution at the commencement of my research and has been a reliable guide throughout. Professor Han Kilyŏn of Kyŏngbuk National University gave me the most generous of gifts, sharing her reading notes of *The Pledge at the Banquet of Moon-Gazing Pavilion*, which served to abate my initial fear of dealing with this impossibly long and difficult text. Professor Pak Chŏngsuk taught me vernacular Korean calligraphy, leading me into the exciting practical dimension of handwriting that had fascinated me for years. Professor Sŏ Insŏk opened the treasures of the Yeungnam University Archive and was a wonderful host during my visit. I am deeply grateful for the hospitality of the Kyujanggak Institute, the Research Institute for Korean Studies at Korea University, the Academy of Korean Studies, and the National Library of Korea, which provided spaces for reading and writing at different points of my work.

The year in Canberra that I spent as a postdoctoral fellow at the Australian National Unviersity was filled with sunlight and fond memories. I can never give enough thanks to my colleagues there for their warm welcome, encouragement, and advice. Hyeaweol Choi was a generous mentor and a most hospitable friend; I am forever grateful for our walks to the National Library of Australia and our delightful winery trip in Adelaide. Ruth Barraclough has taught me a most precious life lesson: to make space for family in my academic life. Roald Maliangkay—along with his fun collection of office toys—was a cheerful, neighborly presence in my daily university routine. The friendly company of Narah Lee, Orion Lethbridge, Jeong Yoon Ku, Yonjae Paik, Hea-Jin Park, Qin Yang, McComas Taylor, Mark Strange, and Shameem Black made the year truly enjoyable.

The collegial Department of East Asian Studies at Princeton University made me a more mature thinker and teacher. The many conversations and coteaching opportunities I shared with my colleagues taught me so much, and the friendly atmosphere of the department made all the difference in the years I spent on the beautiful Princeton campus. As department chairs, Martin Kern and Anna Shields were remarkably forthcoming with their advice and encouragement through the years. My warmest thanks go to my colleagues Steven Chung, Paize Keulemans, He Bian, Erin Huang, Brian Steininger, Franz Prichard, Atsuko Ueda, Federico Marcon, David Leheny, Tom Conlan, Amy Borovoy, CP Chou, Willard Peterson, Benjamin Elman, Xin Wen, Susan Naquin, Nicola di Cosmo, Stephen Teiser, Sheldon Garon, Andrew Watsky, and Janet Chen. I thank the staff at the department office—Donna Musial-Manners, Jeff Heller, Margo Orlando, and Sean Miller—for their reliable support.

The feedback I received during my manuscript workshop was vital to the development of this book. I thank Yoon Sun Yang for honestly sharing her own writing experience, being straightforward in her critique, and suggesting a title that put everything in place and saved me from confusion. Maram Epstein's insights, acknowledged in so many notes of this book, have been eye-opening, and her sharing of her latest book ahead of its publication was incredibly generous. The strong voice of Ellen Widmer grounded my own way of thinking in times of doubt. Thanks to these three amazing participants, the manuscript workshop was the most exciting academic event I have ever been part of; it could never have come together without Steven Chung's encouragement and help, which over the years extended far beyond this project.

Sun Joo Kim, the convener of the annual New Frontiers in Premodern Korean Studies Workshop, and Si Nae Park, the workshop's cohost, have created a home ground for premodern Korea scholars, where different drafts of this book were presented. The friendly group of New Frontiers Workshop participants—Jungwon Kim, Maya Stiller, Seong Uk Kim, Hwansoo Kim, Eugene Park, Sixiang Wang, and Hyun Suk Park—made the gatherings truly stimulating and enjoyable. I am grateful for Sun Joo Kim's meticulous reading of this work at its various stages and her constant insistence on clarity. Martina Deuchler was an attentive and enlightening interlocutor during the conversations we shared in Seoul, Prague, and Rome.

At Columbia University Press, I was lucky to work with Christine Dunbar. This book owes much to her energy, her faith in this project, and the impeccable timeline she architectured. I thank Mary Severance for dealing with my tangled writing, making it so much better. Annie Barva's sharp eye and dexterous hand added clarity and polish at the stage of final editing. The deep, intuitive, and encouraging reading by the three anonymous reviewers gave me confidence in my ideas.

An earlier version of chapter 2 appeared in the *Journal of Asian Studies* 77, no. 1 (2018): 59–81. Some of the translated passages from *The Pledge at the Banquet of Moon-Gazing Pavilion* appeared in *Premodern Korean Literary Prose: An Anthology*, edited by Michael J. Pettid, Gregory N. Evon, and Chan Park (New York: Columbia University Press, 2018), 123–32. This project has been supported by a series of Princeton University summer salaries and two Korea Foundation Fellowships for Field Research. The Academy of Korean Studies Manuscript Completion Grant (Project Number AKS-2018-P14 (18P14)) was absolutely crucial for the final stages of my work.

This book is a product and a reflection of the exciting journey that carried me from Nizhny Novgorod to Seoul, Blagoevgrad, Frankfurt, New York, Canberra, Nagoya, and Princeton, introducing me to so many places and people who taught me how to feel at home in the world. Daehwan and Anton often begrudged but still followed my peregrinations; they are my kinnest kin.

KINSHIP NOVELS OF EARLY MODERN KOREA

Introduction

The Lineage and the Novel in Chosŏn Korea, 1392–1910

Vernacular Korean lineage novels (*kamun sosŏl* 家門小說) begin in exactly the same way. These texts, which elaborate the intricacies of the kinship system of late Chosŏn Korea (1392–1910), open with the unveiling of the genealogical subject—an emotional self socialized within the structures of prescriptive kinship. Unfolding the genealogical context of the lineages they center on, these novels connect the familial and the political: the hereditary moral excellence of the lineage members and the security of the dynastic royal house, which they serve. The status attributes—proximity to the affairs of the court and absolute dedication to moral virtue—are pinned to the figure of a notable ancestor:

> During the reign of Yŏngjong[1] [Ch. Yingzong, r. 1427–1464] of the Great Ming, the Imperial Grand Mentor (K. *hwang t'aebu*, Ch. *huang t'aifu* 皇太傅), the Grand Secretary (K. *sugangno*, Ch. *shoukolao* 首閣老) Lord Chin'guk Chŏng Han's courtesy name was Kyewŏn, and his nom de plume was Munch'ŏng. He was the descendant of Songhyŏn, Master Myŏngdo. This glorious lineage (*sŏngmun* 聖門) stretches to the Yuan dynasty [1271–1368], when the lineage descendants distinguished themselves from the ordinary folk: they loved learning and read books, possessed benevolence, wisdom, filiality, and brotherly love. Their virtues and sagely conduct were never marred by the ways of the world. With no desire for worldly fame, they were

inconspicuous as dust that covers all four directions. After T'aejo of Ming [Ch. Taizu, r. 1368–1398] unified the realm, and all under heaven came together, they did not leave their dwellings in deep mountains and remote abodes, thinking wealth to be no more than grass and dust. But when it came to the sagacious reign of Emperor Mun [Ch. Wendi/Yongle, r. 1402–1424], in his quest for virtuous officials immediately after enthronement, the emperor followed the examples of King Mun (Ch. King Wen), who finally met Yŏ Sang (Ch. Lu Shang/Jiang Ziya)[2], and Yu Bi's [Ch. Liu Bei] three-time visitation to the grass-thatched cottage.[3] Therefore, he recruited Lord Munch'ŏng [Chŏng Han] into his service and treated him with utmost decorum so that no one dared turn against him. Lord Munch'ŏng's loyalty to his sovereign and ability and virtue in all manners of conduct were unparalleled in the world.[4]

Like many other Chosŏn-dynasty novels, *The Pledge at the Banquet of Moon-Gazing Pavilion* (*Wanwŏl hoemaeng yŏn* 玩月會盟宴) is set in Ming China but unmistakably elaborates Korean historical realities. *The Pledge* begins with an account of the Chŏng lineage. In just a few lines, we learn all we need to know about the lineage's distinctness from those who seek power and recognition and its intimate connection with the emperor, who seeks the wise council of the patriarch Chŏng Han.[5]

Notably, however, the towering figure of the patriarch is never at the center of a lineage novel's narrative. The patriarch hovers above the described events: he presides over family banquets, issues wise words of warning, and dispenses punishment for his especially unruly children. Together with the earlier generations of the lineage, signaled in the genealogical opening, the patriarch remains on the narrative horizon, never directly involved in the protagonists' adventures, passions, and actings out. The patriarch is a living, even if formal link between the accumulated ancestral virtues, which constitute a social and familial legacy and define the structure of kinship obligation, and the lives of the young lineage members, whose journey through life is charted by their predecessors' example.

The genealogical subject[6] foregrounded in the lineage novel embodies the process of socialization of the emotional self through the structures of patrilineal kinship. This book contends that the lineage novel is integral to our understanding of the Chosŏn kinship system, which determined the aspects of political, social, and cultural life of the period. In the lineage novel, the genealogy embodies the incontestable kinship values embedded in the prescriptive social positions of patriarch, mother and child, husband and wife, step-parents and stepchildren, father-in-law and son-in-law. A person's correct fulfillment of these roles, which remain unchanged from generation to generation, guarantees domestic harmony and secures the smooth functioning of society and the state, conceived—in the lineage novel and in the political ideology of late Chosŏn—as a moral project of bringing correct order to human relationships. The genealogical opening of the lineage novel is matched by the genealogical closure, which enumerates the generations of the lineage that spring forth after the novel's narrative reaches conclusion. This generational framework establishes the timelessness and stability of kinship.

Lineage novels appeared on the literary stage just as the Korean patrilineal system was taking shape in the late seventeenth century and continued to circulate until the first decades of the twentieth century. The Confucian vision that underlies the Chosŏn kinship system "naturalizes the family as the site in which ethics are established."[7] In this moral scheme, familial bonds constitute the essential matrix for social architecture and emotional performance, stretching outward to the totality of social interactions. The hierarchy and affection of the father–son bond serves as a model for the relationship between ruler and subject. The husband–wife bond is fundamental for gender politics, mandating separate realms of activity and identity—domestic and public—to men and women. The Confucian moral framework that traveled from China to Korea was not just a philosophical system but also a practical tool of interstate relations during the long-standing alliance with China, a framework for institutional construction, and a foundation for political culture. The kinship system that took the form of patrilineal lineage in the late seventeenth century was key to the proliferation of Confucian ethics at the everyday level; the Chosŏn elites (yangban 兩班) used these precepts to buttress their social privilege, negotiating Confucian ideals against the configurations of Korea's local social and cultural terrain.

Martina Deuchler's principal works on the history of Korean kinship—The Confucian Transformation of Korea and Under the Ancestors' Eyes—trace the interlinked development and proliferation of kinship ideology and the Confucian culture that during the Chosŏn dynasty acquired a distinctive Korean interpretation and interacted with local ways of life.[8] As Deuchler details, lineage in Chosŏn "emerged above all as [a] social and ritual entit[y] that fused agnatic kinsmen into groups for worshipping their ancestors. . . . By celebrating their ancestors in grand ritual displays in front of graves, in domestic shrines, and in memorial halls, the lineage members invoked ancestral blessings and put themselves under ancestral protection. A lineage lived literally 'under the eyes of its ancestors.'"[9]

Kinship ideology was intimately linked with the Chosŏn state's project of ordering society according to the models outlined in the Confucian classics. This moral vision of the state became the source of ascriptive empowerment for Chosŏn elites, who aspired to be the most upright moralists. The fleshing out of the patriline transfigured the social structure formed during the preceding Koryŏ dynasty (918–1392). The changes largely concerned the lives of elites, and their effect on women was especially dramatic. During the Koryŏ dynasty and early Chosŏn period, women were free to divorce, inherit property, and reside in their natal households after marriage. Starting in the late seventeenth century, however, elite women began to lose these social freedoms,[10] and their lives became enclosed in the domestic space of their husbands' families, where their primary responsibilities included domestic work, household administration, filial service to parents-in-law, and child rearing. Although women could still petition the courts on behalf of family members,[11] they no longer had legal and social autonomy, and their mobility outside home was restricted. These changes were intended to weaken women's natal affiliations, which were further diluted by the lowering of the mourning grades for affinal kin. Patrilineal succession was secured by designating one primary consort as the legitimate mother of status-eligible issue. After more than two centuries of change, the patrilineal lineage system of Chosŏn took shape in the late seventeenth century.[12]

The lineage structure was socially exclusive and hierarchical, and one's kinship standing determined how—and often whether—one participated in the key aspects of social life: education and scholarship, officeholding, court politics, agriculture, burial practices, daily life in the rural society, and interaction with the variegated local population.[13] Social histories of Chosŏn convey an important lesson: kinship organization is the key to nearly all levels of social and cultural life of the period. Any discussion of Chosŏn Korea is incomplete without the knowledge of its kinship system, and the kinship system, as this manuscript contends, is not intelligible without its aesthetic archive, which extends beyond ideological and institutional frameworks.

The populous domestic communities of Chosŏn Korea had a rigid structure. They embodied a moral, state-endorsed vision of idealized human bonds and regulated the exclusivity of the status system. Viewed from the perspective of institutions and ideology, the kinship system that emerged in seventeenth-century Chosŏn Korea is understood in terms of patrilineality, primogeniture, virilocal marriage, and ancestor worship, all of which are elaborated in some detail at different points in this book. But kinship is what people do in their everyday life, how they view the world, and how they perceive the meaning and ground of social relations. How did people of Chosŏn do kinship? And how can we access its everyday affective content from the vantage point of the twenty-first century? This book addresses the question of Chosŏn kinship from the perspective of nascent affective responses to established ideological structures by tracing the structures of feelings embodied in the aesthetic archive of kinship, conceived dynamically but centered on the lineage novel.

Framed by a genealogical, multigenerational structure, the gist of the lineage novel is constituted by plots of unruly feelings, which follow the struggles of young protagonists with kinship norms. Feelings (K. *chŏng*; Ch. *qing* 情) in the lineage novel are the materials of social cohesion and intelligibility. When aligned with the objective rules of moral conduct (K. *kong*; Ch. *gong* 公), feelings enable the sincere (K. *sŏng*; Ch. *cheng* 誠) performance of prescribed relationships. Transformed into private selfish (K. *sa*; Ch. *si* 私) urges, feelings threaten to undermine the smooth relational fabric. Performed, exteriorized emotions constitute the system of social intelligibility, within which unruly, selfish feelings mark the most problematic junctures of kinship. This tension between objective rules and private feelings constitutes the ground for the articulation of genealogical subjectivity that implies negotiation and the coming to terms with the norms of kinship that are foundational to social order.[14] Lineage novels, however, show that the plots of private, unruly emotions are not just impediments to social harmony; indeed, they are integral to personal life stories. The lineage novel is in this way a discursive site where the genealogical subject of patrilineal kinship is articulated from a perspective that affirms the significance of private emotions.

The genealogical resolution of lineage novels creates a teleological horizon of monumental time, which ultimately mandates the sincere convergence of the person with the social norm. The narratives of rebellion as socialization—the microcosm of the protagonists' personal life stories—create a temporizing opening in the monumental fixity of the timeless lineage structure. By introducing the private life history—a process of contestation and negotiation of the social norm—the lineage novel problematizes the norms of kinship but ultimately endorses them as the valid ethical form of social life. The genealogical and the private temporalities not only coexist on the pages of the lineage novel but are inseparable.

More than a genre study, this book uses the aesthetic archive centered on the lineage novel in a historical sense as a site that illuminates socially productive notions of literacy, gender roles, and boundaries of domestic culture while also revealing the imaginative ordering of the contemporary historical milieu. Chosŏn kinship was as much a textual as a practical reality because social status was derived from cultural capital and public memory. Moving away from ideological and legal formulations of kinship, this analysis pays attention to the genres that focused on the domestic life. These genres reveal the domestic everydayness that remained outside the purview of public-oriented kinship textuality.

Lineage novels are vernacular Korean texts transcribed by elite women and circulated through kinship networks. Neither the authors nor the details of the manuscripts' circulation are known, which means the history of the lineage novel can be conveyed only in broad brushstrokes. Dozens of titles and thousands of surviving manuscript volumes capture the epic of Chosŏn kinship life.

The lineage novel captures the structures of feelings that embedded the ritual, economic, and moral imperatives of Chosŏn kinship in a life world, a space for living. This aesthetic archive provides a glimpse of the symbolic dimension of kinship that guided and embodied the affective itineraries of men and women who navigated this system. It illuminates what Lauren Berlant has called "the conventions of reciprocity that ground how to live and imagine life."[15] By capturing the structures of feelings,[16] the "method[s] of comprehending reality,"[17] and the "imaginary solutions to existing social contradictions,"[18] this aesthetic archive prompts us to rethink the space of kinship in terms of affective contours, domestic intimacies, and the centrality of women's bodies, work, and writing for the operations of the domestic realm. Centering kinship textuality on the lineage novel allows this book to explore the women-centered, domestic, vernacular Korean culture of the Chosŏn elites; connecting the lineage novel to other genres of kinship writing, such as funerary texts and family tales, opens up the trajectories and exchanges that shaped the centuries of the lineage novel's history.

Several preliminary highlights arise from the study of the aesthetics of Chosŏn kinship life. First of all, the historical dimension of Chosŏn kinship captured in lineage novels draws attention to the misalignment between blood-based filiation and the moral vision of human bonds that conceives them as transposable.[19] Two fundamental but problematic relationships—between father-in-law and son-in-law as well as between stepmother and stepson—are uniquely elaborated in the lineage novel and rarely mentioned elsewhere in Chosŏn-dynasty sources. Marriage required the redirection of a woman's allegiance from natal family to in-law family and a transfer of her obedience from father to husband. Lineage novels show how this relocation of patriarchal authority, which hinged on a woman's transition from her status as daughter to that of wife, was fraught with contradiction. Although adoption was meant to guarantee the uninterrupted succession of title and property in families that failed to produce a male heir, it nevertheless resulted in a relationship that was not built on the foundations of "natural," blood-based affinity. In this context, it is important to note that lineage novels are to a large extent preoccupied with reconciling the moral vision of kinship with the tenacity of "feelings of flesh and blood" (*kolyuk chi chŏng* 骨肉之情) that did not easily yield to ethical reformulation.[20]

Second, as the quintessence of women-centered elite vernacular Korean culture, the lineage novel allows us a glimpse of the domestic culture of the time. Lineage novels' texts feature encyclopedic accounts of domestic life cycles and relationships as well as vivid presentations of bedroom scenes, childhood, domestic gatherings, and intimate conversations. Of course, these accounts are not factual; rather, they are imaginative renderings of domestic life. But the massive span of lineage novels allows these texts to delve into the minutest gestures of domestic intimacy; although private emotions in these texts are placed on the horizon of kinship obligation, they are recognized as objectively conditioned and inalienable. Lineage novels' manuscripts, too, capture the sentimental fabric of kinship. Carefully transmitted through generations, these manuscripts are mementoes of deceased women's brushwork, treasured by descendants for their lasting affective value.

Third, the lineage novel captures the aestheticization of vernacular Korean writing and the emergence of early modern vernacular Korean fictional prose,[21] fueled by the narrative desire of kinship. After the promulgation of vernacular Korean script in the mid–fifteenth century, its use remained mostly functional until the late seventeenth century, when elite women appropriated vernacular Korean culture as the domain of their learning and creativity. The lineage novel marks the emergence of elite vernacular Korean literary tradition, which predates the popularization of vernacular Korean fictional prose among broader audiences in the eighteenth century. The emergence of early modern Korean fictional prose was fueled by the intense narrative desire produced by the Korean kinship system, which directed creative energy toward the elaboration of its main premises. The structural mirroring of the norms and aesthetics of kinship allowed lineage novels to grow like trees as they traced the ever-expanding generations of the central lineage. These kinship origins of early modern Korean fictional prose, in turn, offer a suggestive angle upon the global history of the novel.

The Novel in the Early Modern World

The emergence of the lineage novel in the late seventeenth century was coeval not only with the formulation of the Chosŏn patrilineal kinship system but also with the so-called rise of the novel—a global proliferation of fictional prose. No longer understood as the mirror image of European literary modernity, the global story of fictional realism receives a unique elaboration in a recent study by Ning Ma. In *The Age of Silver*, adopting an approach of "anthropocenic realism," Ma links the development of fictional realism in England, Spain, China, and Japan to the global flows of silver from Spanish colonies in South America to the Pacific trade network from the 1500s to the 1800s. Her approach disenchants and historicizes the central analytical terms developed by scholars of European fiction and uncovers a broader aesthetic movement from epic to biographical narrative facilitated within a network of horizontal monetary connections that disaggregated the junctures between state, society, and the person in different corners of the world.

The novel's "feminization" and "interiorization," Ma contends, register the unmooring of traditional hierarchies by the dynamic of money flows.[22] The prominence of female audiences, protagonists, and manuscript makers in the history of the lineage novel's development as well as its focus on private feelings warrant a closer look at the issues of feminization and interiorization in global perspective. A thorough historical comparison is not possible here, but an outline of the European and Chinese contexts will set into relief the historical contours of the Korean novel's development. China had long been a source of literary and philosophical influence for Chosŏn Korea, which is revealed in the aesthetic idiom of the lineage novel. The unfolding of the lineage novels' massive discourse of feelings, moreover, coincided with a growing philosophical and aesthetic preoccupation with the problem of emotions—the so-called cult of *qing*—in China during the late Ming (1368–1644) and Qing (1644–1912) dynasties.

The European novel, however, has been at the theoretical center of cross-regional literary studies; its central terms, in particular interiority, require historicization. The story of the Western novel's "rise" has been tied to the spread of capitalism and the transition of power from the aristocracy to the bourgeoisie. Bourgeois cultural politics sought to replace the aristocratic culture of inbred social distinction with a vision of the human being pure and simple. The novel foregrounded the image of a monadic individual with interiority and feelings, "transforming the body from an indicator of rank to the container of a unique subjectivity."[23] The English novel is thought to inherit John Locke's vision of rationalized individual efficiency in controlling networks of social and economic value, with an interior dimension providing a space for compromise between private desires and social expectations.[24] This notion of the interiorized, private being is indebted to an older philosophical tradition that draws boundaries between the body and the soul, inner and outer realms that foreground the self as the source of truth, rational order, and political accountability.[25] The bourgeois novel, which narrates social contradictions in the guise of personal encounters, finds its most powerful representation in the domestic woman: excluded from the political realm, she embodies affective domesticity and the socially exfoliating power of bourgeois love.[26] This shrinking of the novel's chronotope from the castle and the road of medieval romances to the eighteenth-century parlor and the salon,[27] centered on affective and intellectual autonomy, connects novelistic writing to female narrative authority.[28] The rise of the European novel, therefore, is inextricably linked to the emergence of female novelists and female readers.

The rise of the novel in seventeenth-century China, as scholars suggest, takes place against the monetization of the economy and the increased mobility of people and things, which severed the connection between moral norms and their social fulfillment and prompted significant changes in social structure and intellectual culture.[29] Chinese literati, whose social status was validated by the Confucian scholarship they pursued, grew increasingly disenchanted with the corrupt civil service examination and the system of knowledge that relied on the study of the external world to uncover the moral rules of the universe. The abundance of commodified things inspired mistrust of objective knowledge. Wang Yangming (1472–1529), whose name is habitually connected with the inward turn in philosophy and scholarship, was responding to the excesses of commodity culture when he posited the self as the source of philosophical insight and paved the way for the radical rethinking of private insights and desires.[30]

The eleventh-century institutionalization of Neo-Confucianism in China introduced a division of human nature into an ideal, heaven-endowed form and its worldly, material emanation. Following Zhu Xi (1130–1200), emotions became connected with material, subjective nature (K. *sa*; Ch. *si* 私), which explained their susceptibility to unrest and subversion. In order to follow the objective (K. *kong*; Ch. *gong* 公) rules of human conduct captured in ritual (K. *ye*; Ch. *li* 禮), feelings had to be brought under the control of the moral will. This public–private distinction that turned feelings into an object of concern for the Neo-Confucian thinkers is not discernible in the earlier philosophical formulations of emotion, which treat feelings as integral to human nature, neither good nor bad. Wang Yangming and such proponents of the Taizhou school as Wang Ji (1498–1593) and Li Zhi (1527–1602) reintegrated the self as the ground of valid knowledge and desire, critiquing the primacy of totalizing objective prescriptions. Li Zhi, who is often referenced in late Ming fiction colophons, bridged the realms of philosophy and fiction; his interpretation of desire was a major literary influence at the time.[31] The vibrant printing industry further stimulated the circulation of books and ideas, which reached new audiences—including women, especially in the wealthy Jiangnan region, where affluent families began to educate their daughters, who were becoming avid readers.[32]

Probing into the grounds of personal authenticity and the validity of feelings, late imperial Chinese novels rely on a feminized vocabulary premised on women's distance from the political realm, even when issues of male identity are at stake.[33] After the emergence of this literature of emotion, Chinese women did not begin to write novels en masse, like their

European counterparts. However, the so-called cult of *qing*, the centering of cultural production on feelings and on the interior, domestic spaces of women's everyday life, did spark a creative impulse in female circles. The appearance of Tang Xianzu's (1550–1616) play *The Peony Pavilion* (Ch. *Mudanting* 牡丹亭) fueled women's enthusiasm for reading, engaged them in manuscript making and circulation, and spawned a vast number of narratives that centered on *The Peony Pavilion* as well as on its readers.[34] Later on, Cao Xueqin's (1715/1724–1763/1764) novel *The Dream of the Red Chamber* (Ch. *Hongloumeng* 紅樓夢) inspired female writers to compose sequels.[35]

Feelings—especially desire and eccentric self-fashioning—are the focus of intense narrative desire in late imperial Chinese novels,[36] which unfold in the architectural inner realms of the boudoir and the garden, locations that mark the shrinking of the novel's chronotope from the battlefield setting of historical romances.[37] Although the Chinese novel's refiguration of narrative architecture is analogous to the European novel's domesticization, the architecture of the self in the Chinese context is distinct from the Western subject of interiority. Ling Hon Lam usefully reminds us that in pre-twentieth-century China emotions were spatial and inherently social and were necessarily shared with others and with the world.[38] Or, to borrow Angela Zito's observation about eighteenth-century China, "What we interpret in philosophical texts as the privileging of interiority, an inner self, could be understood as valuable proof of boundary creation and control."[39] In other words, the self is instantiated in the performative management of the boundary between private and public meaning. The late imperial Chinese novel, with its interest in emotion, was not attempting to focus on the interior space circumscribed by those boundaries but tried to manage the boundary between the private and the public in a different way.

Both the interiorization of the novel's chronotope and spatialization of the individuated self in the case of the European novel as well as the shift from objective norms to feelings in the context of late imperial Chinese literature coincided with economic development and women's increased participation in cultural production. European women emerged as readers and writers of fiction just when novels began to fashion their female protagonists as "specialists of the heart." In late imperial China, women emerged primarily as readers and commentators with a shared cultural idiom, although their participation in the writing of novelistic prose remained limited. Fiction in both Europe and China relied extensively upon a feminized vocabulary in creating narratives that articulated a distance between social politics and personal subjectivity. In both contexts, a commercialized literary market played an important role in the wide circulation of fiction.

In Chosŏn Korea, the development of fiction, feminine tropes, female cultural agency, and the discourse of emotions followed a different path. The lineage novel, with its inquiry into unruly feelings, was not immediately shaped by the monetized economy, and its aesthetic program aligned with the kinship ideology of the Chosŏn elites. Coeval with the cult of *qing* in late imperial China, the lineage novel was influenced by the Chinese philosophical rethinking of feelings as well as by the Chinese scholar–beauty novel (*caizi jiaren xiaoshuo* 才子佳人小說), with its aestheticized sensuality. But lineage novels inscribe all feelings, including desire, in a structure of kinship obligation, so that narrative resolution is capped by a genealogical record that affirms the endurance of the lineage through time. The commercialized book market notably played no role in the proliferation of lineage novels, which circulated in tight networks of kinship and acquaintance until the nineteenth century.

Ning Ma's horizontal hypothesis that links the privatization of the epic narrative to commercialization via global silver flows obtains a curious perspective in the context of the lineage novel. What was Korea's place in the global money infrastructure? Scholars still debate the issue of economic development in Chosŏn Korea. Korea's first large-scale influx of silver appears to have taken place during the Imjin Wars (1592–1598), when the entry of the Ming army as a relief force against the Japanese invasion inaugurated silver as the currency for transactions between Ming soldiers and the local population.[40] The Chosŏn state, however, did not patronize commerce and limited its foreign trade to the diplomatic channels it shared with China and Japan. Korea's place within the global trade infrastructure in the seventeenth and eighteenth centuries was therefore mediated by its relations with these two neighbors.[41] Even though Chosŏn played a crucial role as a conduit of Japanese silver to China between the late seventeenth and the early eighteenth centuries,[42] silver did not circulate widely within the country, and the scope of the Korean economy's monetization remained limited.[43]

At the same time, the emergence of markets and of an urban economy in Seoul and other Korean urban centers around the eighteenth century produced a new population marked by a "hunger for culture" that fueled the growth of the entertainment industry and the sudden appearance of the so-called town literature that zoomed in on the lives of these lower classes.[44] This localized urbanization, however, did not undermine the pivotal role of kinship in the articulation of status distinctions until the nineteenth century.[45] The lineage novel registers the emergence of a commodity economy but hardly contextualizes it as a threat to the traditional status system.[46] Although the precise geographical reach of the lineage novel remains to be identified, these texts appear to have circulated in Seoul and in the Andong area of Kyŏngsang Province, a stronghold of elite lineages whose ascriptive privilege enabled their economic domination of the countryside.

The lineage novel's beginnings in the late seventeenth century coincide with the emergence of Korea's lineage structure and with the rethinking of Korea's place in the reconfigured East Asian context. Defeated in the Manchu invasions (1627, 1636), the Chosŏn court was forced to pledge allegiance to the newly established Qing dynasty. Viewed as a barbaric usurpation of the center of civilization, this dynastic transition prompted the Korean court to see itself as the last bastion of Confucian orthodoxy in East Asia.[47] The concern with Confucian orthodoxy at the state level was an important horizon for philosophical and literary developments, including the lineage novel. This conservative political and intellectual climate provides an important perspective on the lineage novel's discourse of unruly emotions, which unfolded at the time when the so-called cult of *qing* was sweeping through late imperial China, placing feelings at the center of the intellectual and aesthetic agenda. Despite the Chosŏn court's conservative outlook, the more frequent interaction with Qing China in the late seventeenth century facilitated the flow of ideas across the Qing–Chosŏn border.[48] Lineage novels depict feelings as facilitators of choice, self-interpretation, and the loosening of the kinship prescriptions. In this way, these texts resemble the philosophy and literature of emotion in late imperial China. At the same time, the lineage novel encapsulates its privileging of unruly feelings within an overarching concern for the continuity of the fundamental social structure—patrilineal kinship.

Early Korean scholars raised the question of private insight in scholarship, which was central to Wang Yangming's intellectual program, but the proponents of this view—Yun Hyu (1617–1680), Pak Sedang (1629–1703), and Ch'oe Sŏkchŏng (1648–1715)—were put on trial, which left little doubt about the conservative stance of the Chosŏn court. These scholars disavowed their affiliation with Wang Yangming's ideas, but his influence on their work cannot be entirely ruled out.[49] Wang Yangming's philosophy was introduced to Chosŏn in the early sixteenth century, but the state agenda founded upon Zhu Xi's teaching made Confucian orthodoxy a matter of grave importance and strict control,[50] especially in the aftermath of the Ming–Qing transition. In addition, the imbrication of intellectual debates with factional politics at court meant that a revisionist philosophical approach would clash with the views of conservative power holders. An outlawed figure, Wang Yangming is rarely referenced directly in the sources from this period. Nevertheless, his notions of personal authenticity and interpretive variance as well as his critical approach to totalizing orthodox discourses are discernible in Korea's intellectual and literary landscapes.[51]

Chosŏn scholars were generally reticent about their allegiance to Wang Yangming's philosophy, which took the form of family learning, but his influence became discernible in the scholarly circles formed around Chŏng Chedu (1649–1736) of the Yŏngil Chŏng lineage, Chŏng Tongyu (1744–1808) of the Tongnae Chŏng lineage, as well as the Tŏgon branch of the Chŏnju Yi.[52] Wang Yangming's influence on literary discourses about personal creativity and the search for a time-specific literary idiom—in the writings of Hŏ Kyun (1569–1618), Chang Yu (1537–1638), Pak Chiwŏn (1737–1805), and Pak Chega (1750–1805), among others—appears to have been especially strong.[53]

The Chosŏn literati's increased interest in the reinterpretation of *The Book of Songs* (K. *Sigyŏng*; Ch. *Shijing* 詩經) in the seventeenth century exhibits the power of Wang Yangming's ideas. The erotic verses of *The Book of Songs* prompted an exegetical controversy in twelfth-century China over the proper reading of these texts. Zhu Xi, who stood behind the solidification of the Neo-Confucian corpus, articulated a moralistic approach, categorizing the erotic verses as "depraved" or "improper."[54] This interpretation dominated the intellectual culture in Korea until the seventeenth century, when dissenting voices attempted to read *The Book of Songs* outside of a didactic interpretation, disputing, among other things, Zhu Xi's classification of some of the poems as depraved.[55] Interest in emotion, linked to the change in the perspective on scholarship, was widespread in seventeenth-century Korea, when the lineage novel emerged.

The direct link between the lineage novel and the broader cultural interest in emotion is, however, hard to establish, given the absence of a single known author of a lineage novel. In her study of *The Remarkable Reunion of Jade Mandarin Ducks* (*Ogwŏn chaehap kiyŏn* 玉鴛再合奇緣), Yi Chiha uses the marginalia to connect this text to the household of the Chŏnju Yi lineage, which was associated with Wang Yangming studies in Chosŏn. The focus on the life of a poor scholar's household, the pointed interest in personal histories and feelings, and the criticism of court factionalism in *Jade Mandarin Ducks* further align its sensibility with the outlook of scholars of the Wang Yangming School in Chosŏn.[56] Although we cannot assume that the majority of lineage novels were composed by authors who shared this intellectual and aesthetic sensibility, we can establish the intellectual and aesthetic horizon of the lineage novel's formation. The lineage novel, in short, appeared at a time when Wang Yangming's discourses of personal authenticity rippled through the intellectual and literary culture of Chosŏn. These connections require further elaboration from the perspective of the contemporary philosophical engagement with feelings and lineage novels' circulation history, but such an elaboration at this moment remains beyond the scope of this study because these texts' authors remain unidentified. Although textual analysis reveals the main coordinates of lineage novels' symbolic field, further historical connections require some knowledge of the specific social context of these texts' circulation.

The lineage novel was certainly a product of the circulation of ideas that connected Korea to the intellectual culture of late Ming and early Qing China. While a direct materialist link with silver flows and economic development remains tentative at best, the early modern movement from the epic to the biographical is very much discernable in the lineage novel. This movement, however, has to be situated within the kinship culture of Chosŏn Korea, which provided the narrative material and social context for the creation and circulation of lineage novels.

The Vernacular Korean Novel

The proliferation of fictional prose in Korea coincided with the spread of vernacular Korean literacy among the elite women of Chosŏn in the seventeenth century. Although fiction had been written and read in literary Chinese script earlier in Korean history, it began to thrive in the vernacular Korean script, which was promulgated in the mid–fifteenth century. Both men and women wrote and read in vernacular Korean, but women's literacy and cultural activity relied heavily on vernacular Korean scriptural practices, whereas educated men focused on literary Chinese learning. With their identities growing increasingly domestic as patrilineal kinship took hold, elite women became excluded from multiple public domains, including literary Chinese education—which in terms of its ultimate horizon was linked to the processes of statecraft, social ordering, and moral self-cultivation.

Women's vernacular Korean literacy was linked to the performance of domestic work: as chapter 2 shows, orderly vernacular Korean brushwork and the exchange of letters in vernacular Korean were understood as extensions of the bodily discipline prescribed by women's roles within the kinship structure. But elite women were also among the earliest patrons of fiction, which began to circulate extensively in vernacular Korean script.[57] The two most famous Chosŏn novelists, thought to have authored the early vernacular Korean novels—Kim Manjung (1637–1692) and Cho Sŏnggi (1638–1689)—are said to have created their works as filial offerings to brighten their mothers' pastime.[58]

Elite, learned men of Chosŏn generally held fiction in low regard. They tended to bemoan Chinese novels' licentiousness even as they admired the refined Chinese vernacular prose.[59] But vernacular Korean fiction did not contribute much to the development of literary Chinese composition skills. Although men likely read vernacular Korean novels, they did not deign to write about these texts, brushing them aside as the domain of women's interest. Vernacular Korean fiction was nevertheless implicitly divided into higher and lower registers in the minds of both men and women of Chosŏn, and within this two-partite division lineage novels commanded special treatment.

The higher register—which Im Hyŏngt'aek calls the "boudoir novel" (*kyubang sosŏl* 閨房小說)—achieved a delicate balance between entertainment and conduct-book moralism. Lineage novels—as well as such shorter texts as Kim Manjung's *Madame Sa's Conquest of the South* (*Sa ssi namjŏng ki* 謝氏南征記) and *The Praise of Goodness and the Admiration of Righteousness* (*Ch'angsŏn kamŭi rok* 彰善感義錄),[60] attributed to Cho Sŏnggi—circulated among elite women and were considered worthy of their attention because they propagated the norms of kinship and gender performance. Moreover, texts associated with the elite vernacular Korean canon had a distinctive material form: they circulated in manuscripts executed by women in impeccable vernacular Korean calligraphy. Novels in the elite vernacular canon served as conduct manuals, reading textbooks, and calligraphic primers while also entertaining their readers.[61] Unlike late imperial China, where the monetization of the economy prompted the emergence of a separate group of itinerant female teachers, Chosŏn Korea's tradition of female learning was cultivated internally in select families that encouraged it. These were the households of the Andong Kwŏn, Ŭnjin Song, and Chŏnju Yi.

As Pak Yŏnghŭi has shown, an established familial tradition of female learning was instrumental to the emergence of the first known lineage novel: *The Record of So Hyŏnsŏng* (*So Hyŏnsŏng rok* 蘇賢聖錄), which was referenced in external sources in the late seventeenth century. This novel, transcribed by Lady Yi of Yongin (1652–1712), who married into the Andong Kwŏn lineage, was later conveyed to the family shrine. Its place in the domestic culture of Andong Kwŏn highlights the prestige associated with the creation and preservation of vernacular manuscripts. The case of this novel, which constitutes the earliest known reference to vernacular Korean fiction writing, also suggests that the lineage novel inaugurated the literarization of the Korean vernacular, which until the seventeenth century was used most frequently in translations of practical manuals and correspondence.[62]

Here, it is useful to note that the terms *elite* and *vernacular Korean* are certainly porous. On the one hand, although lineage novels were written in vernacular Korean, their diction and literary idiom were heavily indebted to literary Chinese texts. On the other, although they circulated among elite audiences, lineage novels incorporated cultural elements associated with a more demotic stratum of culture. Still, the notion of elite vernacular Korean culture allows us to stake out the women-centered culture of writing and reading in the Korean vernacular that commanded significant prestige and recognition in Chosŏn.

In addition to reading lineage novels, elite women in Korea also read translations of Chinese novels, especially historical romances such as *The Romance of the Three Kingdoms* (K. *Samgukchi yŏnŭi*; Ch. *Sanguozhi yanyi* 三國志演義), *The Water Margin* (K. *Suhoji*; Ch. *Shuihouji* 水滸志), and *The Romance of the Western Zhou* (K. *Sŏju yŏnŭi*; Ch. *Xizhou yanyi* 西周演義).[63] These texts were considered appropriate for elite female readers because they contained no frivolous "love" plots and because they imparted knowledge of Chinese historical dynasties. The main avatars of the cult of *qing* in late imperial China—*Peony Pavilion*, *The Plum in the Golden Vase* (K. *Kŭmpyŏngmae*; Ch. *Jinpingmei* 金瓶梅), and *The Dream of the Red*

Chamber—appear to have had limited circulation in Chosŏn.[64] The Yuan-dynasty drama that heavily influenced Tang Xianzu's work, *The Romance of the Western Wing* (K. *Sŏsang ki*; Ch. *Xixiang ji* 西廂記) was imported to Korea in the first part of the sixteenth century but did not become popular among male literati until the eighteenth century, and the first vernacular Korean translations of the text were not made until the late eighteenth or early nineteenth century.[65] Scholar–beauty novels, which dealt with companionate marriages between persons of shared refined sensibilities and education, were read widely.[66] Some of these texts were licentious due to their preoccupation with love and desire, but Chosŏn women appear to have read the more conservative texts of this tradition. Kwŏn Sŏp (1671–1759), for example, mentions that his mother transcribed *The Fortunate Union* (K. *Hogu chŏn*; Ch. *Haoqiu zhuan* 好逑傳), a notoriously moralistic and dramatically de-eroticized text.[67]

The influence of the scholar–beauty novel is discernible in lineage novels. In fact, *The Record of So Hyŏnsŏng* actually uses the phrase "a scholar and a beauty (K. *chaeja kain* 才子 佳人)" to describe an amorous encounter.[68] In line with the aesthetic idiom of the scholar–beauty novel, most lineage novels present their female protagonists as beautiful, educated, and skilled in calligraphy. The male protagonists are unrivaled in their handsome appearance and equally excel in battle. Encounters between male and female protagonists are often romanticized: female protagonists, usually fleeing adversity in male disguise, encounter their prospective or actual husbands fortuitously on the road. This gender-leveling logic of beauty and mutual attraction, however, always ends with marriage. Quite in contrast to scholar–beauty novels, marriages in the lineage novel are distinctly hierarchical. Patriarchal authority manifests itself through scenes of physical violence, including rape, which help bring delicate but stubborn spouses into submission. In the lineage novel, desire is coded as exclusively male: it is inconceivable that a female protagonist of the lineage novel could be both desirous and decent. Moreover, desire is hardly central to these texts, which explore a much wider array of feelings within the context of kinship obligation.

The relationship between high and low literary registers as well as between lengthy lineage narratives and shorter vernacular Korean fiction is subject to numerous hypotheses. Some scholars believe that the lineage novel represented a critical coalescence of literary energy that spawned shorter literary forms. Other scholars conjecture that the lineage novel absorbed shorter and more demotic literary genres, such as the popular battlefield novel (*kundam sosŏl* 軍談小說), and positioned them in elite culture by taming them within a more regimented canon.[69] Although the lineage novel has a dynamic relationship with "lower" literary forms,[70] it is important also to recognize its self-conscious affiliation with the highest register of Chosŏn literary culture.

Lineage novels often attempt to heighten their veracity by dissolving the boundaries between their own narratives and other prestigious literary genres. One text concludes the description of a poetry competition with the following remark: "The poetry is certainly worth recording, but it is already included in the [authors'] literary collections (*munjip* 文集), and thus there is no need to record it here."[71] Lineage novels often refer readers to family histories and biographies allegedly written for their protagonists. *The Pledge*, for instance, directs its readers to turn to such texts as *The Record of the Rewarded Filial Piety of the Chŏng Lineage* (*Chŏng ssi hyohaeng poŭng rok* 鄭氏孝行報應錄), *The Record of the Yang Lineage* (*Yang ssi ka rok* 陽氏家錄), and *Later Record of the Chŏng Lineage* (*Chŏng ssi hurok* 鄭氏後錄).[72] These references to allegedly extant texts that extend the story line connect the lineage novel to the prestigious documentary genres of kinship writing.[73]

Lineage Novels and Their Readers

Lineage novels constituted a massive vernacular Korean tradition—dozens of extant titles and thousands of manuscript volumes amply attest to this fact. Nevertheless, there are very few references to these texts in contemporary Chosŏn sources. The majority of pronouncements on the culture of the time were authored by elite men, most of whom were steeped in literary Chinese learning. The four appraisals of lineage novels discussed in this section virtually circumscribe the external visibility of these texts. These four readers' responses importantly allow us to link lineage novels to the sociolinguistic compositions of their audiences and to establish a general chronology of the lineage novel's evolution. These four readers include a scion of a prominent though not affluent lineage, a royal consort, one of the most prominent scholar officials and courtiers of his time, and an educated though unsuccessful man of obscure life history: Kwŏn Sŏp, Lady Hyegyŏng (1735–1816), Pak Chiwŏn, and Hong Hŭibok (1794–1859).

To proceed according to the chronological order of these notes that afford mapping points for the large-stroke history of the lineage novel, we must begin with Kwŏn Sŏp, who captures his mother's legacy:

Among the books that were directly transcribed by my late mother, Lady Yi of Yongin, *The Record of So Hyŏnsŏng* (*So Hyŏnsŏng rok* 蘇賢聖錄), a great novel (*taesosŏl* 大小說) in fifteen volumes is to be given to the first grandson, Choŭng, and stored in the family shrine (*kamyo* 家廟). *The Record of the Seven Sons of Minister Cho* (*Cho sŭngsang ch'ilja ki* 趙丞相七子記) and *The Record of the Three Generations of the Han Lineage* (*Han ssi samdae rok* 韓氏三代錄) are to be given to my younger brother, Taegan'gun [Kwŏn Yŏng]. Another copy of *The Record of the Three Generations of the Han Lineage* and *The Record of the Three Generations of the Sŏl Lineage* (*Sŏl ssi samdae rok* 薛氏三代錄) are to be given to my younger sister married into the Hong lineage. *A Fortunate Union* (*Ŭihyŏp hogu chŏn* 義俠好逑傳) and *The Record of the Three Rivers and the Sea* (*Samgang hae rok* 三江海錄) are to be given to the second son, Tŏksŏng. *The Record of the Three Generations of the Sŏl Lineage* is to be given to my daughter, married into the Hong lineage. It is then possible to preserve these books through the generations of each of the households.[74]

Kwŏn Sŏp's note details the distribution of the novels hand-copied by his mother among her descendants. Some of the volumes in Kwŏn's list have not been identified, but the titles of the bequeathed texts, which refer to lineages, households, and generations, suggest that many of them are lineage novels. Another marker of distinction is the texts' length—Kwŏn notably calls *The Record of So Hyŏnsŏng* "a great novel," referring to the length and perhaps also to the importance of this hand-crafted manuscript.

Kwŏn Sŏp's mother, Lady Yi of Yongin (1652–1712), appears to have been an avid reader and transcriber of novels. Kwŏn Sŏp, for instance, records the compliments his mother received from Queen Insŏn (1618–1674) for a novel manuscript she created and presented at court.[75] Kwŏn Sŏp's note on his mother's vernacular Korean legacy, situated in the broader context of this family's status and cultural outlook, indicates that lineage novels were essential to elite women's learning and cultural activity. Given that his mother made her bequest prior to her death in 1712, Kwŏn Sŏp's note—the earliest known reference to this group of texts—suggests that lineage novels were in circulation by the late seventeenth century.

Beyond their value as tokens of learning, the manuscripts bequeathed by Kwŏn's mother appear to have had intimate significance for Kwŏn's family. It is worth noting that Kwŏn Sŏp creates a separate, meticulous record of his mother's scribal efforts. Moreover, the manuscripts are deposited in the most revered space—the family shrine—in recognition of the sentimental value of his mother's handwriting. It would have been much more common for Chosŏn dynasty references to women's learning, reading, or calligraphic practice to appear passim in the funerary texts that celebrated the life and memory of the deceased. Kwŏn Sŏp's literary collection includes, along with the record of his mother's literary bequest, a short description of the literary activity of his grandmother, Lady Yi of Hamp'yŏng (1622–1663). "A Note on the Text of *The Romance of the Three Kingdoms* Transcribed by My Late Grandmother" ("Che sŏnjobi susa *Samgukchi* hu" 題先祖妣手寫三國志後) is the story of a manuscript lost and found. After a relative borrows *The Romance of the Three Kingdoms*, two of the manuscript volumes disappear. With great effort, Kwŏn Sŏp retrieves one volume, has its cover refurbished, and deposits it in the family shrine alongside the volumes his mother made.[76]

Kwŏn Sŏp's family clearly valued female learning. But while Kwŏn Sŏp reflects on his mother's scribal activities with reverence, he says nothing at all about the contents of the books she bequeathed. Similarly, when noting the compliments his mother received from Queen Insŏn, he offers details about the calligraphy but does not mention even the title of the book his mother presented at court. He writes that the text she offered to the queen was visually impeccable, its letters "like stringed pearls with not one askew (*kwanju muilch'ak* 貫珠無一錯)."[77] As chapter 2 shows, women's calligraphic practice in Chosŏn was validated as a gendered repertoire of bodily discipline and work prescribed within the kinship system. This validation helps explain why the visual aspect of the books merited Kwŏn Sŏp's comments but the vernacular Korean fiction did not.

Unreserved praise of a lineage novel's text appears in the memoirs of Lady Hyegyŏng, however. A member of an illustrious P'ungsan Hong lineage, Lady Hyegyŏng became the consort of Prince Sado (1735–1762), the son of King Yŏngjo (r. 1724–1776), and left a total of four memoirs capturing her journey from home to the palace and the hardships she endured along the way. The tragic story of Prince Sado overshadows the entire narrative. Prince Sado died in July 1762 after spending eight days trapped in a rice chest, being punished by his reigning father for a long history of manic behaviors deemed unacceptable for a crown prince. In narrating her own story and the story of the royal family, Lady Hyegyŏng crafts her narrative with utmost self-awareness and caution, balancing her feelings with ethical impartiality. Her language and sensibility are carefully controlled to ensure that nothing undermines her authority to narrate this personal cataclysm with dimensions of state importance.[78] This broader context for Lady Hyegyŏng's memoir—the fullness of feeling it seeks to convey and its concern with the author's voice—provide a setting for her reference to a lineage novel entitled *The Record of the Three Generations of the Yu Lineage* (*Yu ssi samdae rok* 劉氏三代錄).

As JaHyun Kim Haboush notes in her introductory study of Lady Hyegyŏng's memoirs, each of the four volumes follows a different generic convention. The first, from 1795, is written in the form of family instructions at the request of Lady Hyegyŏng's nephew Hong Suyŏng (?–1798), who wishes to keep some of Lady Hyegyŏng's writings within the family. Lady Hyegyŏng produces a narrative of her journey from home to the palace, describing in great detail the warm affection she shares with her parents. The scenes of parting are especially poignant, as is the scene of final farewell, when Lady Hyegyŏng recalls the lingering effects of her mother's death:

At the age of nine my sister lost her mother. . . . After the funeral, Grandmother took care of the boy, and my older sister-in-law looked after my sister. So as far as their daily needs were concerned, they were in good hands. But the image of these lonely and motherless children never really left me. My sister learned to read at a very young age. She was fond of reading and always carried books around with her. She often wrote to me and her letters were so sad and full of remembrances of Mother that for each word I shed one tear. In the winter of *chŏngch'uk* [1757], my sister came to the palace to see me for the first time after Mother's death. She brought our youngest brother with her. We spoke of Mother and our sadness over losing her. On this visit my sister read the novel *The Record of the Three Generations of the Yu Lineage*. She was strangely affected by the sadness of the book. I attributed her response to her general melancholy.[79]

The reference to *The Yu Lineage* is woven seamlessly into the account of a family event. We see layers of relationships: the tender bonds between Lady Hyegyŏng, her sister, and their mother are activated by a lineage novel, which allows mourning and aestheticizes the sensibility of loss. Although Lady Hyegyŏng's restrained praise of her sister's abilities shows that learning has worth in and of itself, she also highlights how *The Yu Lineage* moves its readers, a comment that speaks volumes about the place of lineage novels in elite women's lives. A careful, self-reflexive writer, Lady Hyegyŏng allows no misstep to undermine her narrative authority, and she maintains neutrality and refinement of feelings, thoughts, and expression throughout her text. *The Yu Lineage* apparently fits her exacting conception of style.

The third lineage novel commentator, Pak Chiwŏn, was an illustrious, reform-minded scholar, statesman, and writer of fiction. Pak Chiwŏn's diary, which describes his trip as an envoy to Qing China, also includes a reference to *The Yu Lineage*. On its journey through Qing, the legation is accompanied by a certain Li Shuanglin, a Chinese–Korean interpreter, whose obsequious ways and greed for gifts Pak Chiwŏn immediately dislikes. Most disappointingly, Li Shuanglin's Korean is faulty. Eager to show off, Li invites a Korean servant to share a carriage ride and carries on a conversation in which Li speaks Korean and the Korean servant speaks Chinese. Overhearing the conversation, Pak Chiwŏn notes with unconcealed satisfaction that the Korean servant's linguistic skills are far superior to Li Shuanglin's, which leads him to conclude that Chinese must be much easier than Korean to master.

To further test the impudent interpreter, Pak Chiwŏn pulls out a vernacular Korean volume and asks him to read it aloud:

The carriage was covered with a blanket, and somewhere underneath it were several volumes of *The Record of the Three Generations of the Yu Lineage* in vernacular (*tongŏn* 東諺). Not only was the vernacular writing (*ŏnsŏ* 諺書) rather coarse, but the book binding itself was worn. I made Shuanglin read the text. Shuanglin began to rock his body and pitched his voice high, all without having the slightest understanding of the text. The sounds of his reading were confused and muddled. It was almost as though his mouth were full of thorns and as if his lips were frozen: jumbled sounds came from his lips with no end. I listened for a while but could not get a faintest notion of what he was reading. Were I to listen to his reading until the end of my days, still it would seem to be of no use.[80]

Lineage novels, noncommercial texts that were reproduced exclusively in manuscript form, generally circulated through kin networks, within which the manuscripts, as Kwŏn Sŏp's note suggests, had emotional significance as their scribes' mementoes. Here, a lineage novel reaches a foreign audience, although the reader, Li Shuanglin, is hardly up to the task. What was *The Yu Lineage* doing in Pak Chiwŏn's cart? Who put the manuscript there? Pak Chiwŏn knows nothing about the volume, but it seems that others in the legation might have read lineage novels like this one to while away the time on their official journeys.

Li Shuanglin's reading of the text is curious. In the conversation that Pak Chiwŏn records, Li Shuanglin and his Korean interlocutor exchange a few sentences on rather mundane matters: marriage, the beauty of Korean female entertainers, and the appearance of Li's father, who is also accompanying the Chosŏn legation. Li Shuanglin, in other words, appears comfortable with everyday conversation. The language of the lineage novel proves too complex for him, however. Written in vernacular Korean, lineage novels include an abundance of Chinese loan phrases in an irregular Korean transcription. These transliterated phrases had to be matched with the Chinese characters and their literary context, a task that required considerable literary knowledge. Even if we assume Li Shuanglin's literary Chinese erudition, reading the Chinese characters in Korean phonetics and following the novel's complex, overflowing language would be much too taxing. Li Shuanglin's attempt to read a lineage novel aloud thus defamiliarizes the appearance of a vernacular Korean text and emphasizes its distance from the spoken register. The sophisticated literary vernacular would certainly be inaccessible to a reader who lacked literary proficiency in both literary Chinese and the overflowing vernacular Korean prose.

The final reference to the lineage novel to be discussed here appears in the preface to a vernacular Korean translation of *Flowers in the Mirror* (K. *Kyŏnghwa yŏn*; Ch. *Jinghua yuan* 鏡花緣) by Li Ruzhen (ca. 1763–1830). The translator, Hong Hŭibok, an educated and attentive though critical reader of vernacular Korean fiction, offers a detailed observation that captures not merely the structural characteristics of vernacular Korean novel but also the ambivalence of these texts, which seek to elaborate fundamental moral precepts while depicting unruly passions. Hong writes:

After Pokhŭi [Ch. Fuxi 伏羲] created writing and down through the ages until the present, there existed classics, histories, philosophies, and belles lettres. The books that claimed the name of the nine traditions of philosophy and hundred schools of thought (*kuryu paekka* 九流百家) filled the world; they were transmitted through generations, multiplied every year and increased with each day. . . . Among them, there is a category of novels (*sosŏl* 小說). Originally, these texts collected and recorded the information absent from the historical record that was transmitted in the world. Hence, some call them "unofficial histories" (*yasa* 野史). . . . In China, scholars who pursued studies but were unable to pass the civil service examination, showed off their literary artistry; if their families were poor, they took the sale of novels at the marketplace as the source of their livelihood. Because of this, strange and fantastic tales (*kidam koesŏl* 奇談怪說) spread in all directions.

The writing and speech of our Eastern Country are profoundly different. Because of the intention to create writing for the spoken language, we now have separate colloquial script (*ŏnmun* 諺文). The true script (*chinsŏ* 眞書) and colloquial writing (*ŏnmun* 諺文) are completely different. The common writing gives detailed representation to speech and is easy to learn. Women take up learning vernacular Korean script and stop there [without learning the true script], which is unfortunate. The classics of the sages and the biographies of wise people as well as *The Book of Rites* [K. *Yegi*, Ch. *Lizhi* 禮記] and *Elementary Learning* [K. *Sohak*, Ch. *Xiaoxue* 小學] are translated into colloquial writing and called "vernacular explications" (*ŏnhae* 諺解). Although many people aspire to learn and follow them, those who read them find them insipid and unpalatable, so instead they only clamor to enjoy reading the fanciful and strange novels and tales (*sosŏl sinhwa* 小說神話). So idle scholars and women of talent take to translating every single of the famed novels from old times to our days, and on top of that they compose empty tales (*hŏŏn* 虛言) so that idle talk is flourishing and overflowing. There are several thousand volumes that are devoted solely to the fantastic and the entertaining.

I abandoned my studies early on and failed to pass the civil service examination. Attending to my mother, I had a lot of leisure time, so I was able to read almost all of the vernacular Korean novels. Among them, texts such as *The Romance of the Three Kingdoms, Journey to the*

West [K. *Sŏyugi*; Ch. *Xiyouji* 西遊記], *The Water Margin, Romance of the Warring States* [K. *Yŏlgukchi*, Ch. *Lieguozhi* 列國志], *Romance of the Western Zhou*, and down to the *Romance of the Historical Dynasties* [K. *Yŏktae yŏnŭi*, Ch. *Lidai yanyi* 歷代演義] have already been translated and adopted from the true script; they are easy to read, and they are quite similar in content.

Apart from that, there are novels such as *The Record of the Three Generations of the Yu Lineage*, . . . *The Record of the Three Generations of the Cho Lineage* (*Cho ssi samdae rok* 曺氏三代錄), *Mirror of Loyalty and Filial Piety* (*Ch'unghyo myŏngam rok* 忠孝明鑑錄), *The Reunion of Jade Mandarin Ducks* (*Ogwŏn chaehap* 玉鴛再合), *Master Im and His Three Wives* (*Im Hwa Chŏng Yŏn* 林花鄭延), *The Record of the Virtuous Lord Ku Rae* (*Ku Rae kong chŏngjung chikch'ŏl ki* 寇萊公貞忠直節記), *The Record of the Two Households: Kwak and Chang* (*Kwak Chang yangmun rok* 郭張兩門錄), *The Record of the Immortal Realm of the Hwa Mountain* (*Hwasan sŏn'gye rok* 華山仙界錄), *The Record of the Illustrious Deeds and Righteousness* (*Myŏnghaeng chŏngŭi rok* 明行正義錄), *Dream of the Jade Kirin* (*Ongninmong* 玉麟夢), *Discourse That Dispels Illusion* (*Pyŏkhŏdam* 碧虛談), *The Pledge at the Banquet of Moon-Gazing Pavilion, Bright Pearls and a Precious Crescent Pendant* (*Myŏngju powŏlbing* 明珠寶月聘). . . . They amount to about thirty titles. . . . Among the readers [of these vernacular Korean novels], those who delight in the exemplars of virtue will greatly profit [from reading], but those who are bemused by the crafty plots of the wicked will be debauched beyond measure. This is deeply worrisome and lamentable.

Accidentally in recent days, I was looking at a novel composed by a Chinese scholar. Its narrative is amply beneficial for the readers, and its intent is to enlighten the world. It goes beyond the frame of vulgar novels, extending distinct ideas and incorporating histories and classics. With books of the strange in mind, this text does unfold the fiction of the fairy world, but it frequently has foundations in reality. It discusses the strangeness of foreign lands, but it provides details. This book expounds the classics and lays out moral precepts, catechizes the histories, and distinguishes the true from the false. It outlines the structure of heaven and earth, and reaching out for medicine, divination, and other crafts it explains their intricacies and fundamentals. Truly, this is a text of a great writer, most fit for reading far and wide.[81]

The preface, devised to praise *Flowers in the Mirror*, sets it against the entire literary field: it is better than classics and histories for its entertaining value and far superior to other types of fiction because of the useful knowledge it imparts. For all its merits, Hong bestows an outstanding title on Li Ruzhen's work, *The Book of Books in the Vernacular* (*Cheil kiŏn* 第一奇諺), in reference to the fact that this novel appears in Korean script for the first time in Hong's own translation. Hong's description of the literary field is remarkably detailed, and it is useful to note those of its features that are most pertinent to the contextualization of the lineage novel.

First of all, worth note is the translator's self-portrait. Hong was well educated but unsuccessful in office, and the time he spent in women's company led to his immersion in vernacular Korean culture. He reports that he reads all vernacular novels he can find and even decides to translate a Chinese text for the benefit of his female kin. Despite his knowledge of vernacular Korean literature, Hong maintains the traditional hierarchy between the four-partite Confucian canon and the idle prose of the novel as well as between the literary Chinese and vernacular Korean literary realms. In the closing lines of the preface, Hong, not without self-irony, admits that he does not discern any grand purpose behind the translation of Li Ruzhen's text; he only wants to read it in the company of his aged mother, sick wife, daughters, and daughters-in-law. Hong's disparaging view of vernacular Korean fiction, including lineage novels—which are, here again, identifiable through their distinctive titles—and the fact that he dictates his family's vernacular reading tastes distinguish his relationship to lineage novels from what we are able to glean from Kwŏn Sŏp's and Lady Hyegyŏng's accounts. The latter two praise women's vernacular Korean literacy and recognize the prestige of the lineage novel. Could Hong's humble background explain his strikingly different attitude? This is possible because women's vernacular Korean learning flourished in elite households.

Second, it is useful to reflect on the reasons why *Flowers in the Mirror* receives such enthusiastic praise. Li Ruzhen wrote *Flowers in the Mirror* in the early nineteenth century, when Qing China was undergoing a variety of changes, including an increase in women's participation in the realms of education, writing, and publishing. Scholars have scrutinized *Flowers in the Mirror* for "feminist" tendencies, homing in on phantasmagoric scenes of women's empowerment, such as the notorious women's country (K. *yŏin'guk*; Ch. *nüerguo* 女兒國) that reverses men's and women's roles in public and domestic spaces.[82] In Li Ruzhen's novel, women's talents are used for the betterment of society. Hong Hŭibok produced his translation between 1835 and 1848.[83] This was a time of nepotistic court politics centered on the powerful Queen Sunwŏn (1789–1857)—acting regent for two of Chosŏn's kings, Hŏnjong (regency 1834–1841) and Ch'ŏljong (regency 1849–1852)—and her kin, against growing discontent over court corruption and the dynasty's economic and political decline. Hong may have translated Li Ruzhen's vision of social renewal to express his discontent with the state of affairs in Chosŏn.

Curiously, Hong makes a critical revision to Li Ruzhen's text. *Flowers in the Mirror* begins with a moralistic roster of normative femininity—womanly virtues, womanly speech, womanly comportment, and womanly work—and a promise that female readers will emerge from the text better equipped to perform these roles. This cautious introduction, of course, does not reflect the entire scope of Li Ruzhen's work, but Hong entirely omits this preface. In his own introduction to the translation, Hong juxtaposes the overly dramatic domestic stories of vernacular Korean fiction with *Flowers in the Mirror* and its capacity to enlighten the reader. In this way, Hong appears to be quite reformist in his understanding of the social order and the significance of fiction. It might be useful to remember that he belonged to the secondary son's branch of his family; sons born of secondary consorts faced significant discrimination in the Chosŏn society. Hong's humble origins, coupled with his education and travel to China, could have pushed his imagination to new horizons,[84] making him more critical of the literary canon that perpetuated the value system of the Chosŏn elites.

These four references to the lineage novel, divided by time, circumstance, and social identity, reveal a perceptible split. For Kwŏn Sŏp and Lady Hyegyŏng, lineage novels embody the sophistication of the women-centered vernacular Korean tradition, whereas Pak Chiwŏn and Hong Hŭibok do not assign much value to these texts. Indeed, Pak Chiwŏn appears to be unfamiliar with the novel he asks his Chinese companion to read, and Hong Hŭibok makes an unfavorable comparison between Korean vernacular fiction and the text he is offering in translation. Chŏng Pyŏngsŏl, a Korean literary scholar, interprets Hong's preface, written in the early nineteenth century and inspired by a vision of social reform, as a statement of the lineage novel's misalignment with the realities of the nineteenth century and therefore a sign of its decline.[85]

Each commentator uses different terms to describe lineage novels. Kwŏn Sŏp designates *The Record of So Hyŏnsŏng*, transcribed by his mother, as a "great novel (*taesosŏl* 大小說)," emphasizing the length of the text, his mother's efforts, and the value of the manuscript for the ensuing generations of the family. Lady Hyegyŏng merely calls *The Record of the Three Generations of the Yu Lineage* "a book (*ch'aek* 冊)." Pak Chiwŏn, displaying no interest in the novel, characterizes it as "several volumes in Eastern vernacular (*tongŏn sugwŏn* 東諺數卷)." Finally, Hong Hŭibok speaks of "vernacular" or "colloquial fiction (*ŏnmun sosŏl* 諺文小說)" in generally disparaging terms and does not distinguish the lineage novel from shorter literary forms that had a distinctly inferior status in Chosŏn society.

Needless to say, *lineage novel* is a modern academic term conferred on a collection of texts that are hardly identical. Scholars have used a variety of terms for this group of texts: *Naksŏn Library novels* (*Naksŏnjae bon sosŏl* 樂善齋本小說), *lengthy lineage novels* (*changp'yŏn kamun sosŏl* 長篇家門小說), and *romans de fleuve* (*taeha sosŏl* 大河小說).[86] I find that the term *lineage novel* best reflects the main properties of these works: their immersion in the private culture of elite lineages, their central focus on the maintenance of the lineage structure in the face of external threats and unruly feelings, and, finally, their length, which is intimately related to their multigenerational structure. These features, in fact, allow us to draw the boundaries of this genre, even if these boundaries are not absolute.

Lineage novel titles reveal some distinctive features of these texts. As mentioned earlier, the titles most often identify the narratives as "records" (*ki* 記 or *rok* 錄) rather than as "tales" (*chŏn* 傳), thereby claiming a connection with the prestige of historical annals.[87] The titles often underscore the validity of kinship as a moral and social institution. Lineage novels' titles often refer to the narrative's multigenerational span, which is synonymous with the uninterrupted perpetuation of moral tradition and social system—for example, *The Record of the Three Generations of the Yu Lineage*. References are frequently made to an encounter that brings two outstanding individuals together and results in a marriage that perpetuates the lineage. A prime example is *The Remarkable Encounter of Pearls* (*Myŏngju kibong* 明珠奇逢). Lineage novels' titles also emphasize the exceptional moral qualities of their protagonists: titles such as *The Record of Loyalty and Righteousness of the Yang Lineage* (*Yangmun ch'ungŭi rok* 楊門忠義錄) convey the link between moral refinement and heredity.

Because of their anonymous authorship, lineage novels cannot be dated precisely, and their history, done by necessity in large brushstrokes, yields the following picture. The emergence of the lineage novel in the seventeenth century coincided with the rise of women's vernacular Korean literacy, which was fostered in select elite families. *The Record of Sŏ Hyŏnsŏng* is among the earliest known lineage novels to be mentioned by title in Kwŏn Sŏp's note. The lineage novel reached its zenith in the eighteenth century, when lineage ideology was in its prime. During the nineteenth century—a period of social unrest and dramatic realignment of Korea's geopolitical environment in the context of East Asian colonial politics and social change—the lineage novel lost its connection to elite women's culture and exhibited uncertainty about its cultural adequacy.[88] These texts nevertheless continued to circulate until the 1930s, interacting in a limited way with the commercialized literary marketplace.

Synopsis: Sources and Chapters

The gender identities, status distinctions, and patterns of filiation produced by the Chosŏn kinship system shaped all areas of life at the time. This study adds dimension to social, economic, and intellectual histories of the late Chosŏn by foregrounding the genealogical subject articulated in the aesthetic archive associated with Korean kinship. Producing more than a commentary on the institutional and social history of Chosŏn kinship, this book looks into the contours of historical experience that are left out of the hegemonic archive, probing into the domestic and everyday aspects of life in this kinship community. Centered on the lineage novel, my analysis crosses genre boundaries and traces exchanges, intersections, and genealogies of kinship imagination, closing with an investigation of the moment, the mid–nineteenth century, when kinship practice and imagination began withdrawing from the center stage of Korean society and culture. This book views the culture of late Chosŏn Korea through the lens of vernacular Korean writing, which thrived in the domestic space, to illuminate this little-studied area of life and culture.[89] At moments, vernacular Korean sources are intersected with literary Chinese genres of kinship textuality that are similarly focused on the domestic space and female protagonists.

Although patrilineal genealogy is usually assumed to represent the gist of kinship obligation and the main structuring principle of the Korean lineage, I explore a vast array of kinship writings that reveal alternative dimensions of generational continuity. Funerary genres, written in literary Chinese but centered on women, depict the domestic space as a site of intimacy and affective narratives that involve all family members, including secondary mothers and daughters, whose lives and memories are integral to the affective generational continuity. Lineage novels expand the generational structure that underlies the architecture of the novelistic space to include secondary family members and plots of unruly feelings that threaten to undermine the streamlined generational succession. A vernacular family history, *The Record of the Three Generations of the Yi Lineage from the East of the Sea* (*Haedong Yi ssi samdae rok* 海東李氏三代錄)—a documentary account of the three generations of the Chinsŏng Yi lineage—although centering on the careers of its prominent male members, configures the family as a confluence of the sociolinguistic idioms of its members, interweaving magistrate records, travelogue, and novelistic descriptions of the domestic space. These modes of entextualizing the kinship system capture alternative visions of familial domestic life.

The six lineage novels treated in this book embody the central features of the lineage novel genre—the length of the narratives, the significance of manuscript making in the lives of women and elite families, and the multigenerational sequel structure. These texts, especially *The Pledge at the Banquet of Moon-Gazing Pavilion*—were among the earliest to be studied precisely in relation to these features. *The Pledge at the Banquet of Moon-Gazing Pavilion*, with its 180 manuscript volumes, is the longest known novel in the Chosŏn literary canon.[90] Its length and its depiction of a particularly refined household—although it does include the violence of internecine domestic conflicts—make it a prime example of the elite vernacular Korean tradition. This is also one of the texts that makes a few appearances in both Chosŏn-dynasty and colonial-era sources. The attribution of *The Pledge* to the authorship of Madame Yi of Chŏnju (1694–1743) invited speculations about women's participation in fiction authorship in late Chosŏn, and it is the first among the lengthier lineage novels to have been published in typeface.

The two-novel sequence *The Remarkable Reunion of Jade Mandarin Ducks* and *The Commentary to Jade Mandarin Ducks* (*Ogwŏn chŏnhae* 玉鴛箋解)[91] has the most immediate connection to the manuscript-making culture of elite women. The margins of these two novels' manuscripts are palimpsests of intrafamilial memories centered on the figure of Madame Chŏng of Onyang

(1725–1799). The manuscripts were written mostly by Madame Chŏng, although several other hands can be identified throughout, showing at a glance that manuscript making was a communal, familial enterprise. The margin notes written by nieces, daughters-in-law, and granddaughters praise Madame Chŏng's skill and dedication and urge that the precious volumes be carefully transmitted to posterity. These novels' manuscripts, like no other known textual artifact from this tradition, refine our understanding of lineage novels' elite readers. *The Commentary*, in turn, is a remarkably self-reflective meditation on the main principles of the lineage novels' composition.

The three novels of the Hyŏn lineage sequel cluster—*The Record of Two Heroes: Brothers Hyŏn* (*Hyŏn ssi yangung ssangnin ki* 玄氏兩雄雙麟記),[92] *The Remarkable Encounter of Pearls*,[93] and *The Remarkable Reunion of Pearls and Jade* (*Myŏngju ogyŏn kihap rok* 明珠玉緣奇合錄)[94]—are illustrative of a more extended, tripartite, sequel growth. In addition, these novels evince a curious manuscript and print itinerary. Uniquely popular in Chosŏn Korea, *Brothers Hyŏn* has a connection to *The Tale of Hyŏn Sumun* (*Hyŏn Sumun chŏn* 玄壽文傳), a later hybrid narrative that transplants the eponymous protagonist from the lineage novel and amalgamates a number of other generic forms. *The Tale of Hyŏn Sumun*, also discussed in this book, represents the nineteenth-century hybridization of the literary market in the wake of the development of commercial book circulation that carried lineage novels to broader, more mixed audiences. The third novel in the sequel cluster, *Pearls and Jade*, highlights the connection between the lineage novel and the royal palace audiences. One of its manuscripts is recorded on the reverse side of palace letters of greeting, which suggests that palace ladies were the transcribers of this text.

This book is divided into three parts. Part 1 traces the refractions of kinship imagination and kinship ideology of Chosŏn in different realms of cultural production. Contending that kinship is a textual as much as a social practice, chapter 1 traces the aesthetic metamorphoses of the central figuration of kinship—patrilineal genealogy that mandated the perpetuity of the lineage institution. Coeval with the emergence of patrilineal kinship in the late seventeenth century, the lineage novel, commemorative texts written for female kin, and family tales, all set in the domestic space, expand the figure of male-centered genealogical continuity and use generational reciprocity to map alternative temporalities, sensibilities, and relationships.

If generational architecture structures the narrative space of the lineage novel, vernacular Korean calligraphy, practiced by elite women in the domestic space, adds volume to the text of kinship. Never deemed calligraphic in the contemporary male-authored sources and hardly ever discussed strictly in terms of its aesthetic merit, elite women's practice of vernacular Korean brushwork was grounded in the register of gendered, corporeal performance linked to women's domestic identities within the lineage structure. Unraveling the cultural contours of vernacular Korean calligraphic practice, chapter 2 draws attention to elite women as important producers of culture and foregrounds the lineage novel as the sensuous surface of women-centered domestic memories, where manuscripts served as tangible mementoes of deceased kinswomen, transmitted through generations.

In part 2, I turn to the affective contours of kinship that constitute the crux of lineage novels' narratives. A product of the Chosŏn patrilineal kinship system, the lineage novel foregrounds the genealogical subject— the emotional self socialized through the structures of prescriptive kinship. The lineage novel's affective coordinates include ethical feelings, feelings of flesh and blood, and unruly feelings—sentiments that are distinguished according to the degree of their socially productive potential. Suspended between antisocial, selfish urges and the prescribed ideal of ethically balanced feelings, the lineage novels' protagonists traverse the landscape of emotions that chart their social belonging. Following their trajectories, chapter 3 analyzes emotional performance as a system of social visibility, defined by its negative limit—dissimulation, which produces a socially illegible subject of negative interiority. In the lineage novel, it is the negative interiority, not the defiance of the social norm, that constitutes the most problematic subject position. While laying out the affective coordinates of the lineage novel, this chapter ponders the alternative topography of subjectivity, which elides the interior/exterior division of the Cartesian subject.

Chapter 4 uses the lineage novel as a roadmap of the most problematic junctures of patrilineal kinship that are indexed in these texts through unruly feelings, which mark the misalignment of the person and the kinship norm. Relationships between stepmothers and stepsons, fathers-in-law and sons-in-law, as well as spouses are among the problematic junctures of kinship that lineage novels recurrently highlight. All of these relations center on the problematic co-optation of ethical norms and blood connections of kinship. Female protagonists, problematized in these instances, suggest that the issue of women's position within patrilineal kinship became a subject of intense imaginative scrutiny, even if that scrutiny centered mostly on women's relationships with men.

Part 3 focuses on the fading away of patrilineal kinship from the center stage of cultural and social life in Korea. Chapter 5 casts a look back at the history of the lineage novel from the beginning of its decline in the middle of the nineteenth century, when cultural, economic, and social developments decentered elite lineages from their social prominence. The breaking up of the lineage novel's generational chronotope and kinship audience, its disappearance from cultural memory, and its exclusion even from the academic definitions of Korean literary canon offer important insights into the unraveling of the grand narrative of kinship that sustained the lineage novel through the centuries of its history. Stepping away from the teleological frame of cultural renewal, this chapter views the period of cultural hybridity in Korea at the turn of the twentieth century from the perspective of the disappearance of kinship narratives, offering additional insights into the reformulations of fiction's narrative aesthetics, the operations of the book market, and the academic history of national literary studies in South Korea.

PART I

Figurations of Chosŏn Kinship

CHAPTER I

The Structure of Kinship

Generational Narratives

The lineage novel is conspicuously coeval with the emergence of patrilineal society in Chosŏn: these texts started circulating in the late seventeenth century just as patrilineality became formalized in social life. Lineage novels unfold in a genealogical fashion. Rather than telling the stories of single protagonists, these narratives trace the lives of numerous family members living in populous domestic communities. These lives unfold in the process of maturation—as the characters at first contest and then grow into the social roles prescribed by the kinship system. In this way, the genealogical subject is constituted at the intersection of kinship obligation and personal choice to embrace it. Although violent plots of unruly emotions and behavior punctuate the characters' life trajectories, the novels' opening with the vitae of notable ancestors constitutes a framework of moral and social expectations, and the records of the ensuing generations are proof of happy resolutions. This generational framework extends the ramifications of the protagonists' actions far beyond their own lives. This chapter reconstructs the genealogical imagination embedded in the lineage novel's aesthetic program by setting it alongside other generational narratives of early modern Korea.

Like the lineage novel, shorter Chosŏn-era fiction also brings the generational horizon into its narrative architecture. For example, hero novels (*yŏngung sosŏl* 英雄小説) and battlefield novels (*kundam sosŏl*) cover a protagonist's rise from obscurity to greatness through feats of military prowess that reassert the lineage's glory.[1] Battlefield successes and subsequent renown are often celebrated by a visit to ancestral graves.[2] This chapter traces the generational aesthetics across a variety of genres in Chosŏn: funerary texts, lineage novels, and family tales. This allows us, first of all, to approach Korean patrilineal kinship as a massive aesthetic project of textual iteration that took a variety of shapes and, second, to set into relief the narrative conventions of the lineage novel against the broader literary field of late Chosŏn Korea.

The Korean lineage system took shape in the late seventeenth century as perpetuation of status through patrilineality and primogeniture. The state agenda of Confucian orthodoxy recognized this social form as appropriate to its larger ethical goals. Chosŏn elites (*yangban*), by declaring themselves to be the most upright moralists, used the exclusivity of the lineage system to derive "their *social* empowerment and identity from the aggregate power of close-knit agnatic groups of kin whose cohesion was supported by an elaborate ancestral cult."[3] By perpetuating the distinctions between elite and nonelite, these agnatic groups acquired and maintained an array of social, economic, and cultural privileges.[4] Status, however, was confirmed, not conferred, by the state; it relied on social recognition, which was obtained through various demonstrations of lineage prestige.

Lineage to a great extent was a representational, textual entity. The most authoritative text of kinship connections was of course the genealogy. Genealogies defined the shared belonging of a willfully manipulated kinship group. The China historian Michael Szonyi calls genealogies "strategic text[s], which [are] intended to produce and [do] produce certain social effects."[5] Although the earliest known extant Korean genealogies date back to the fifteenth century, it was only around the seventeenth century that the creation of a genealogy became a lineage-wide effort.[6] Around this time, women were marginalized in the genealogical records, which began to document a strictly patrilineal descent.[7] Genealogies selectively reconstructed the past of a given kinship group and embellished the facts of the kin group's social prestige—suppressing, for instance, the lineage's connection to local gentry, or *hyangni* (鄉吏), who used to be provincial powerholders in Koryŏ but had been gradually downgraded to inferior status in Chosŏn. In some cases, spurious connections were made to the leaders of the celebrated righteous armies (*ŭibyŏng* 義兵), who during the Imjin Wars (1592–1598) raised popular resistance to invading Japanese forces.[8] Genealogies also cut off branches of the lineage that were deemed less illustrious.[9] This skillful manipulation ensured the continuity of a male-centered tradition of social excellence and impeccable descent. Both men and women were expected to be familiar not only with the history of their own kin but also with the most notable male representatives of other illustrious lineages.[10]

Another crucial textual practice directly linked to the kinship-based status system was Confucian scholarship. The public memory of lineages centered on the figures of illustrious male members who held office in the civil bureaucracy and distinguished themselves through their writing. Whereas genealogies captured the principle of father-to-son succession of property and ritual roles, literary collections (K. *munjip*, Ch. *wenji* 文集) anthologized a man's lifelong scholarship. Published posthumously by descendants or disciples, literary collections preserved the literary legacy of the deceased. In some cases, the memory of an especially outstanding ancestor was perpetuated through architecture: prominent lineages sought to construct shrines and Confucian academies dedicated to notable ancestors, even erecting these edifices with unlawfully procured state assistance in the form of corvee labor and thus generating discontent among competing social groups.[11] Genealogies, literary anthologies, and architecture turned notable male figures into highly visible tokens of prestige in order to garner social recognition for the associated kinship group.[12]

Leaving aside the public facade of the lineage, which projected a monumental male-centered narrative of hereditary eminence, this chapter focuses on what happened in the interior, domestic space, to which women were integral. The meaning of kinship was entirely different in the context of densely populated domestic communities, which included those members who were necessarily left out of the grand narrative of prestige. This chapter attempts to access the domestic space through the texts written about and for women in both literary Chinese and vernacular Korean scripts. These texts include funerary texts written in vernacular Korean and literary Chinese for the deceased female kin as well as vernacular narratives of kinship, such as lineage novels and family tales.[13]

An extended discussion of the Chosŏn scriptural culture in chapter 2 shows that literary Chinese was the script associated with Confucian scholarship, status, and political culture. It was the script of the legislature, the legal sphere, and erudite men's writing. Vernacular Korean script, promulgated in the mid–fifteenth century, was used mostly in the domestic setting by men and women alike. This domestic setting to a large extent determined the genres of vernacular Korean writing: correspondence, fiction, women's conduct books, and women-authored manuals that perpetuated useful knowledge. Like lineage novels, funerary writings and family tales pay pointed attention to everyday domestic life. They also forge an alternative perspective of generational continuity that allows space for a more complex fabric of kinship links than given in the male-centered genealogy.

A variant of the following sentence prefaces a great number of lineage genealogies: "If there are people, there is kinship; if there is kinship, there are genealogies, and genealogies have been made since time immemorial."[14] Poetic as it is prescriptive, this turn of phrase marks the emergence of a narrative pattern that embeds individual lives in the structures of kin obligation. Following Lauren Berlant's imaginative definition of genre as "the nameable aspiration for discursive order through which particular life narratives and modes of being become normalized as the real, the taken for granted,"[15] we can thus evaluate the narrative conventions of commemorative texts, lineage novels, and family tales side by side. What was being taken for granted in these texts? What angles of kinship life did they develop? And where does the lineage novel's vision intersect with or diverge from these discursive elaborations of kinship?

The Familial Palimpsests: Funerary Writings

In Chosŏn Korea, the instance of a person's death marked the beginning of extensive textual commemoration, and a variety of textualized kinship links were woven around the memory of the deceased. The significance of a life was captured in a posthumous textual portrait that was either composed or commissioned by the surviving kin. Funerary writings served a variety of purposes. They fulfilled the filial duty of mourning, gave expression to feelings of loss, and perpetuated the code of normative conduct among the living, who were to be inspired by the virtue of the deceased. Some of the many surviving artifacts of funerary writing amount to nothing more than a few formal lines, while others give poignant articulation to grief and mourning. Commemorative texts have an extended history in East Asia; in Chosŏn Korea, texts focusing on women began to be produced in great quantity after the seventeenth century.[16]

Commemorative writing existed in a variety of forms and scriptural spaces. The most standardized and detailed narrative was articulated in the posthumous biography (*haengjang* 行狀), which provided an extended account of a person's life. These texts sometimes relied on vernacular Korean writings by women, who were privy to the daily routine of the deceased; these writings served as the source material for the final draft written in literary Chinese.[17] The record of the deceased person's speech and conduct (*ŏnhaengnok* 言行錄) was more attuned to everyday comportment and conveyed a few characteristic examples. Eulogies (*chemun* 祭文), often more poetic in nature, would be read out loud at the gravesite. Tombstone inscriptions (*myojimyŏng* 墓誌銘), written in prose (*chi* 誌) and verse (*myŏng* 銘) and sometimes appended with a preface (*myojimyŏng pyŏngsŏ* 墓誌銘幷序), were carved on durable materials and placed above or below the ground at the gravesite.

In some families, it was an emphatic rule that funerary texts for the deceased should be written by the family members.[18] But these texts, published in literary anthologies and therefore highly visible, were also oftentimes solicited from acclaimed writers, who drew from life narratives composed in the family. For some writers, this became a burdensome chore. Kim Ch'anghyŏp (1651–1708), famous for his literary compositions, regretted the duty of commemoration he undertook at the request of some families in detriment to his own studies. Writing to a friend, Kim Ch'anghyŏp complains:

What do I study? . . . During an illness that lasted nearly half a year, I could not read at all. Several of my old friends are here, at the academy, but they are so occupied with the [examination] essay composition that we cannot hold leisurely discussions to our hearts' content. Sitting despondently, I have no means of distraction. Recently, I planned to pull myself together [for studying], but I took the trouble of agreeing to compose commemorative texts (*myodo munja* 墓道文字) for a few families, so all my efforts go there. My abilities do not follow my heart. Truly, this is what the Buddha calls "unwholesome deeds" (*agŏp* 惡業) [that perpetuate retribution]. Originally, I wanted to pause my studies for one or two months, finish this business, and then wholly devote myself to my own studies. This did not work at all, and, unknowingly, I continue in the same way, having trouble keeping the schedule. Indeed, this is lamentable.[19]

As much as commemorative writing was prized in the families of the deceased, it was a burden for those who agreed to lend their brushes to the filial enterprise.

The original writings for the deceased produced within the family were sometimes composed in vernacular Korean before they were synthesized into literary Chinese texts, which would also be included in their authors' literary collections. These literary Chinese texts were in turn translated back into vernacular Korean for the benefit of the female audience within the family. Writing about his mother, Madame Sin of P'yŏngsan (?–1763), in *The Biography of My Late Mother* (*Sŏnbuin kajŏn* 先婦人家傳), Hong Nagwŏn (1743–1775) clearly recognizes the pedagogical value of commemorative writing:

> I, Nagwŏn, have already written *The Biography of My Late Mother* (*Sŏnbi kajŏn* 先妣家傳) and *Separate Record of Speech and Conduct* (*Ŏnhaeng pyŏllok* 言行別錄). Then the eulogies composed by young and old members of the family were collected and compiled into one volume and translated into vernacular Korean (*ŏnmun* 諺文). All this was transmitted to the young sisters, so that all women can read this text day and night and be moved [by it]. We, the worthless (*pulch'obae* 不肖輩),[20] follow, admire, and imitate [the wise exemplar], but our bodies can barely endure the enormous sorrow that is about to break the sky.[21]

Hong's note captures the mixed scripts, authors, and audiences of funerary compositions. Alongside the posthumous biography, Hong's volume contains the account of Madam Sin's life, *Separate Record of Speech and Conduct* (*Ŏnhaeng pyŏllok* 言行別錄), and the eulogies that the members of Madame Sin's family composed for her. The biography describes conventional female virtues: her dexterous performance of practical tasks, such as sewing and household administration; her love of learning, though it is circumscribed to the appropriate womanly repertoire; and the earnest instruction Madame Sin gave to her sons, Hong Nagwŏn and Hong Naksul (1745–1810). Like other funerary texts, this account combines the normative narrative of virtue with an evocative testimony of grief. As Maram

Epstein notes in her study of the affective contours of Qing filial discourse, funerary writings reveal "discursive traces of the private selves of highly ritualized subjects."[22] Korean funerary texts likewise reveal the affective contours of kinship that crisscross the normative fabric of kinship ideology.

A curious note at the end of the biography attempts to exonerate its seemingly trivial domestic focus: "Among the boudoir affairs, many are delicate and small, but as days and months flow by, the memory of them wanes, little by little. Concerned, lest the descendants have no exemplar to emulate, and, furthermore, [realizing that] delicate affairs build up to great ones and finally reach the affairs of the state, I am writing this original biography."[23] Hong Nagwŏn belonged to the illustrious P'ungsan Hong lineage, and so the lives of this family's members were indeed inseparable from the affairs of the state. Madame Sin's biography, for instance, records the exceptional honor she had in 1762 as a participant in the royal wedding of Chŏngjo (r. 1776–1800), then the crown prince (wangseson karye 王世孫嘉禮).[24] Hong Nagwŏn's cousin Lady Hyegyŏng (1819–1895) was the wife of Chŏngjo's father, the unfortunate Prince Sado (1735–1762), who was executed by his father, King Yŏngjo (r. 1725–1776), for his unruly behavior. Lady Hyegyŏng's father, Hong Ponghan (1713–1778), and her uncle (and Nagwŏn's father) Hong Inhan (1722–1776) actively participated in court politics and were embroiled in a number of highly charged political controversies. Both Hong Nagwŏn and his father, Hong Inhan, were ultimately executed for treason, one year apart from each other.

In her memoirs, Lady Hyegyŏng reveals that no detail of domestic life is too small. She recalls with fondness and pride the days she spent with her parents before leaving for the palace at the age of eight. Her vernacular Korean record was written at the request of her nephew and the Hong lineage heir, Hong Suyŏng (?–1798): "If your ladyship could write something for us, then we would treasure and transmit it to the family."[25] Although not strictly of the funerary genre, this memoir commits to memory the textual portraits of Lady Hyegyŏng's parents.[26] The P'ungsan Hong were a prominent lineage, and their commemorative tradition created a thread of intrafamilial memories that captured the family's proximity to court politics, the family members' high moral standard, and the affective contours of this family's life, punctuated with loss and grief.

Funerary texts demonstrate most vividly the affective entanglement of lives in the domestic space, in which it is impossible to narrate one life apart from the others. Sŏ Yugu's (1759–1824) funerary texts illustrate this fabric of domestic reciprocity. The first tombstone inscription, written for his wife, Lady Song of Yŏsan, effortlessly encompasses an address to his young son:

On the twenty-sixth day of the seventh month of the *kapchin* year [1820], which marks the sixtieth anniversary of my wife's birth, our son Ubo has tidied up the sacrificial vessels and made an offering at the grave. Then he turned to me in tears, "I lost my mother at such an early age and know nothing of her virtue. Moreover, there is no record left that could be passed on to posterity." Grieving, my heart rose [at these words]. I asked [Ubo] to sit down and told him the following. "You were only around five years old when you lost your mother, and you can remember only faintly her voice and her smiling face. As to her beautiful conduct, if I do not tell you, who else will be able to do it?"

. . . "We begot you at an old age and loved you dearly, like a pearl treasured in one's palms. Indigent, we could not afford a wet nurse, and your mother always nursed you. In the cold, when the water was freezing, your mother, with a bucket to her side, washed your clothing and swaddle cloths. The appearance of her ten fingers, frozen, crooked and twisted, pained everyone who saw it. Two years before her death, [your mother] suffered from consumption, and her condition was grave. I left office [to visit her] and saw her lie weak and unconscious on her bed. She only responded to my third call. Then she noticed you crawling in front of her and pointed at you with the following words: 'After I die, you will remarry, so who will this baby have to look to? When I am no longer alive, Matron Pak could take proper care of him. The late grandfather cherished the child dearly, and Matron Pak served grandfather and knew [of his love for the child].' After your mother died, I thought about her words and decided against remarrying, consigning the children to the care of Matron Pak. Matron Pak did her utmost to take care of the children and stepped back only when all of you reached maturity. People around knew about Madame Pak's efforts to bring you up but knew nothing about the foresight of your mother's words that extended to you. That was your mother's motherly way."[27]

The story of Lady Song's life is refracted through the eyes of her devoted son, who feels incomplete without the knowledge of his mother. The commemoration that was due to the deceased is offered in the manner of a testimony heard by an eager listener—Ubo. And it is not just the mother's and son's life stories that are unthinkable one without the other. Matron Pak's story is similarly impossible to disentangle from the memories of Ubo's early childhood. Lady Song's commemoration in this way provides an occasion for a retrospective glimpse of the family's affective fabric.

The eulogy for Matron Pak, Ubo's devout caregiver, proceeds according to similar logic. After the death of her master (Ubo's grandfather), Sŏ Myŏngǔng (1716–1787), Matron Pak stayed in the Sŏ household despite continuous encouragement to return to her native place. She wanted to witness the birth of a male heir so desired by Sŏ Myŏngǔng. After Ubo was born, she took the utmost care of him, and later Ubo, together with his wife, happily paid his respects at the celebration of his faithful nurse's sixtieth birthday. At this point, the narrative shifts its focus to Matron Pak's tombstone inscription:

> Ubo asked my permission for the making of the tombstone inscription [for Matron Pak], and I gave my consent, saying, "Wait until you rise in the world,[28] and then, in your full glory, it will not be too late for you to offer libations at her grave and make an inscription for her." Alas! While twelve years (*ilgi* 一紀) have not even passed, my son has followed the matron and left me—who could foresee this! Woe! The inscription reads: "Glory to the eldest grandson, raised by Matron [Pak]. A lonely, orphaned child, for him I cry. Sorrow that fills all under heaven—this inscription is written to express it."[29]

Here, Sŏ Yugu's effortless transition is even more striking than the one in his wife's inscription. The story of the matron is encapsulated by the grief he feels for the untimely death of Ubo, whose life provides a hermeneutic of Matron Pak's virtue.

Concubine mothers, grandmothers, and wet nurses are featured with striking regularity in funerary texts. Coming from a lower socioeconomic background, these women are described with ironic warmth. They are crude yet sincere, uncouth yet uncompromising in their devotions. Although concubine women occupied the lowest position in the status-conscious society of Chosŏn, and their progeny faced lifelong discrimination in terms of service appointments and marriage prospects, they earned high praise from some of the most notable representatives of the Chosŏn male elite. In this way, funerary genres conferred visibility upon those members of the domestic communities who were marginalized in the conspicuous, self-fashioning kinship textuality. Their presence, moreover, was deemed essential to the affective fabric of the domestic space.

Chŏng Yagyong (1762–1836), for instance, fondly remembers his concubine mother: "When she first came to our house, I was twelve years of age, and my head was full of lice, and I also often had boils [on my scalp]. Concubine mother always combed my hair and cleaned away the pus and blood. She washed and mended my undergarments, pants, jackets and socks. She only stopped doing this when I married. Among all my brothers and sisters, the two of us had special affection."[30] In similarly warm terms, Hong Sŏkchu (1774–1842) recalls his deep connection with his concubine great-grandmother, who held him on her knees when he was a child, played shadow theater with him when he got bored over his books, and took him to gaze at the river boats, pointing out their names. Sitting at her deathbed, the now thirty-two-year-old Hong remembers that his concubine great-grandmother continued to treat him as though he were a child.[31] Sŏng Haeŭng (1760–1839) offers a more lively depiction of his concubine grandmother: gaudy, loud, and eager for luxury at the time she enters the household, she softens under the relentless guidance of her husband, becoming "smooth as polished wood." From then on, her life-long services relieve the hardships of those around her.[32] Women of no importance, concubine mothers and grandmothers secured lasting gratitude and affection from the primary descendants left in their care. Sometimes these grateful memories yielded practical returns: it was not uncommon for elite men to leave some property for secondary descendants and mothers.[33]

In addition to the visibility gained by women of secondary importance, what becomes strikingly noticeable in funerary texts is the role of bodily intimacy in the constitution of domestic interactions. This element adds nuance to the bird's-eye view of kinship provided by the genealogical chart: it allows us to see the thick, entangled presence woven by the bodies dwelling in the kinship community. The commemorative texts written for women chart the flows of a precious substance—breast milk. In this way, they reveal the contours of what I call the "milk family"—a kinship group centered on the crucial services performed by nursing mothers, who shared the flows of this precious liquid not only with their children but also with others who needed it.

Kim Ch'anghyŏp, for instance, writes about his mother's careful rearing of his maternal uncle: "Mother in her own person took care of her brother, feeding him rice congee. She prepared the rice and the congee and fed my uncle with a spoon. [Too weak], he was unable to eat anything. Then, Mother expressed the milk that was meant for me and nursed her brother as though he were a small baby."[34] A similar story appears in Im Hŏnhŭi's (1811–1876) remembrance of his mother:

In the year 1796, in the fourth month, my mother's brother was suffering from smallpox. The illness grew only worse, and for a long time there was not a sign of relief. My mother was the one who took care of him. Because uncle was lying down all the time and had continuous diarrhea, and the dampened clothes caused rashes [on his skin], mother constantly carried him on her back. . . . In the middle of winter, because uncle was still nursing, Mother carried him to her cousin's house twice nightly [to procure breast milk from her cousin's wife]. The ground was covered in ice and snow, and for fear of tripping and thereby hurting or startling Uncle, Mother would take off her shoes and even socks and walk barefoot.[35]

A life-saving substance, breast milk would be distributed in the circle of closest and neediest kin. Did the circulation of this liquid create alternative bonds within the carefully delineated kinship system? This certainly seemed to be the case for Im Hŏnhŭi's secondary daughter, Ŭnghŭi—who, he notes, is extremely selective as to the source of her sustenance. Thoughtful and bright, Ŭnghŭi shows great discernment: "She loved her primary mother as if she were her own and never nursed at anyone else's breast."[36] Layered into this eulogy are Im Hŏnhŭi's tender feelings for his deceased secondary daughter. But this text, echoing other references to mothers' milk, also charts microaffiliations within the hierarchized domestic community—the milk family, a present-tense, fleeting, yet fundamental filiation of nourishment, constructed around the intimate, centering presence of women.

In his study of medieval Chinese Buddhist writing, Alan Cole notes that Buddhist authors disarticulate the father–son dyad. Whereas Confucianism viewed the father–son bond as pivotal to social organization and mentioned nothing at all about men's relationship with their mothers, Buddhist texts "stressed the deep emotional ties between mother and son and identified the mother, not the father, as the primary source of a son's being."[37] The cultivation of mother–son bonds and the representation of sinful mothers who required their sons' assistance for salvation insinuated the Buddhist community—which maintained that monastery patronage produced Buddhist merit—into this reconceived familial relationship. In a structurally similar manner, Chosŏn funerary writings created a textual space for the celebration of nonnormative intimacies with female kin, which were left out of the purview of hegemonic kinship writings. What's more, the existence of the vernacular Korean realm of funerary writing indicates the importance of female audiences, who learned about the family history and familial exemplars from these texts, which were in turn based on the memories communicated by women.

Funerary writing highlights an intriguing aspect of the Chosŏn kinship system. Just as physical bodies dwindled away, they were replaced by textual memories, which added up into multigenerational palimpsests of textualized, crisscrossing gazes structured by kinship duty and emotional investment. The accounts of women's lives, inextricable from the life narratives of their nearest domestics, male and female, depict the intimate links of kinship.

Although women's lives receive recognition in commemorative texts, it is important to note the gendered imbalances in these texts' narrative structure. Men control the narrative idiom of the deceased women's lives. The roster of virtues, intended to perpetuate the moral message to the living, is normalized according to the patriarchal vision. These post mortem accounts include little that is subversive. Whatever rough spots might have been present during the life of the deceased are at the end of that life smoothed out. Lineage novels, to which I now turn, expand the aesthetic notion of the kinship fabric, making it amenable to contradictory emotions that disarticulate and expand the streamlined generational ordering of kinship.

Growing Trees: Lineage Novels

If funerary writing creates a palimpsest of kinship intimacies, what happens when kinship imagination makes its way to the pages of lineage novels? In other words, what does the fictionalized kinship of the lineage novel add to the textual field of Korean kinship narratives? One of the lineage novel's most remarkable features is its genealogical architecture of narrative space, which I call "textual filiation."

Like genealogies, lineage novels expand along with the lineages upon which they center. A single linage novel can cover several generations of protagonists, but there are also sequel clusters—independent texts that continue with the descendants of the parent novel's protagonists.[38] The textual filiation of the three novels centered on the Hyŏn lineage—*The Record of Two Heroes: Brothers Hyŏn*, *The Remarkable Encounter of Pearls*, and *The Remarkable Reunion of Pearls and Jade*—is captured in the closing paragraph of the last novel in the sequence, *Pearls and Jade*:

> Originally the story of Hyŏn Sumun and Hyŏn Kyŏngmun is recorded in *The Record of Two Heroes: Brothers Hyŏn* and that of Hyŏn Ch'ŏnnin and Hyŏn Ungnin in *The Remarkable Encounter of Pearls*. The rest of the history of the Hyŏn lineage is recorded in *The Record of Eight Hyŏn Dragons* (*Hyŏn ssi p'allyong ki* 玄氏八龍記). However, since the story of the remarkable reunion of jade and pearls of Princess Okhwa is so amazing, the stories of Hyŏn Hŭibaek and Hyŏn Hŭimun are recorded here under the title *The Remarkable Reunion of Pearls and Jade*. May [this text] be transmitted to later generations, illustrating the rewards for good and evil deeds, and may later generations continue the records of the Hyŏn lineage.[39]

The allegedly four-partite sequence still has a missing element, though: the novel about the eight dragons of the Hyŏn lineage is yet to be discovered, and we can only wonder if it ever existed. This passage, however, registers the lineage imagination that underlies sequel creation and produces a narrative with perpetually open horizon. A lineage novel is potentially an infinitely writeable text: the endurance and continuity of the generational kinship structure perpetuates narrative desire. Generational succession here provides a frame and a structure for the stories of individual lives: it embodies the generational continuity of normative social values and the structure of time, which runs through the expanding, growing branches of the family tree.

Although the Hyŏn lineage sequel cluster follows the lives of the lineage males presented in direct patrilineal succession, these novels also undermine the notion of a streamlined genealogy, thus problematizing the power of unruly feelings. The memory of the protagonists' struggles with norms of kinship becomes integral to the family history. In the Hyŏn lineage sequels, the two Masters Chang—brothers-in-law of the lineage patriarch Hyŏn T'aekchi—are endowed with a crucial function: to remember the plots of feelings that delay the fulfillment of perfect lineage vision. The Masters Chang, who appear in all three Hyŏn novels, offer their own recollections of the family's past, dismantling the air of infallible moral authority that the family patriarchs come to assume with age. In *The Remarkable Encounter of Pearls*, when Ungnin, Hyŏn Sumun's son, berates another youth's lovesickness in the company of Ungnin's brothers and cousins, the Masters Chang suggest that such speech comes from ignorance of the elder generation's adventures:

> The two Masters Chang said with a big smile, "Ungnin can speak like this only because he seems to know nothing at all about his own father and uncle's behavior in the old days. But we will tell their stories especially for your ears." Clearing their throats and assuming a pathetic tone, the two Masters Chang told everyone how Sumun first saw Madame Yun and beleaguered her and how Sumun and Kyŏngmun's secret council [on this matter] was overheard in the backyard, which made their father [Hyŏn T'aekchi] give both a serious beating. Then they told how Kyŏngmun abused Madame Chu and also about his stubborn irreverence toward [his father-in-law], Master Chu, and how Master Chu, securing the support of Hyŏn T'aekchi, made sure that Kyŏngmun received a flogging. After that the two Masters Chang recounted how Sumun first lost sight of Madame Yun and went everywhere to look for her and after finally finding her gave way to his rage at the tricks she had played on him earlier, so that he commissioned ten servants to create a commotion on the big road [wrecking Madame Yun's sedan chair on her return journey to the Hyŏn mansion]. They also told how Kyŏngmun later had to beg his wife [Madame Chu] to forgive him. Recounting all the details and embellishing them, [the two Masters Chang] told a truly entertaining tale. . . . All the young boys sitting around could not help but be amused by the stories told about their father and uncle, and everyone burst out laughing without restraint. Sumun and

Kyŏngmun lowered their heads; their faces grim, they did not join in the shared merriment.[40]

This account registers socialization as a contested process. Although the Masters Chang are comical figures, their asides place the figure of the patriarch against his own youthful history and thereby institute the moment of conversion from reckless youth to morally sound patriarchal authority as the explicit link between generations.

Another kind of sequel creation can be seen in the two-partite composition of *The Remarkable Reunion of Jade Mandarin Ducks* and *The Commentary to Jade Mandarin Ducks*. Instead of progressing down the patriline, *The Commentary* makes a lateral move, shifting attention to the affinal kin of the family presented in the parent text. Whereas *Jade Mandarin Ducks* describes the marital struggles of So Segyŏng and Yi Hyŏnyŏng, *The Commentary* moves on to the stories of Hyŏnyŏng's father, Yi Wŏnŭi, and brother, Yi Hyŏnyun.[41]

In a preface by Sŏk Toyŏn (a protagonist in the parent text), *The Commentary* begins by retelling the story of jade mandarin ducks featured in the title of the parent novel. The ducks have a remarkable history of transmission, stretching to the Tianbao era of the Tang dynasty (742–756), but the introduction warns the reader not to read only for the plot.

The Commentary looks back at the history of the composition of the parent novel, *Jade Mandarin Ducks*, to derive a reading strategy for the latter text. One of the important messages is that *Jade Mandarin Ducks* is a documentary account, recorded from the words of a household servant—not just "vulgar talk (*kujŏn chungsŏl* 口傳衆說)" or a "compilation of groundless rumors (*puŏn chŭngik* 浮言增益)" or even a "beautiful story with no substance (*kahwa musil* 佳話無實)," it is a "chronicle of the So lineage (*So ssi sega* 蘇氏世家)," which at its core is "a record of conduct of gentlemen and ladies (*kunja sungnyŏ sohaeng ki* 君子淑女所行記)."[42] The narrative, moreover, is verified by eyewitness accounts.

Jade Mandarin Ducks focuses on the long-standing conflict between Yi Wŏnŭi—a petty, weak-willed, and corrupt man—and his virtuous son-in-law, So Segyŏng. *The Commentary* describes Yi Wŏnŭi's disheartening encounter with this biographical text. Yi Wŏnŭi's son, Yi Hyŏnyun, is married to Kyŏng Pinghŭi. Her father, Kyŏng Naehan, has witnessed Yi Hyŏnyun's mistreatment of his daughter. Thirsting for revenge, Kyŏng

Naehan comes across the *Jade Mandarin Ducks* manuscript and decides to pass it on to Hyŏnyun's father, Yi Wŏnŭi, to embarrass him. Yi Wŏnŭi reads the text and feels such powerful shame and remorse that he becomes seriously ill. Yi Wŏnŭi insists on keeping the record as a moral warning for his descendants. Sŏk Toyŏn, the alleged writer of *Jade Mandarin Ducks*, decides to write a sequel, *The Commentary*, in which Yi Wŏnŭi's virtues shall be praised:

> In the end, Toyŏn composed *The Commentary* (*Chŏnhae sŏ* 箋解書), continuing the narrative. As a result of this virtuous influence (*sŏnghwa* 聖化), good and evil became clearly distinguished in the world, and all the gentlemen of prominent houses (*myŏngmun kunja* 名門君子) took this book as a guide. That volume (*ki* 其, i.e., *The Remarkable Reunion of Jade Mandarin Ducks*) conveys the original story (*ponmal*), and this volume (*si* 是 i.e., *The Commentary to Jade Mandarin Ducks*) gives rise to satisfaction.[43]

The Commentary traces Yi Wŏnŭi's transformation and his subsequent mediation of his son's tormented relations with his father-in-law. In essence, the sequel praises the moral virtue of the originally corrupt protagonist who follows a path to moral transformation.

The structure of the two novel sequels discussed here, the one centered on the Hyŏn lineage and the other on the family of Yi Wŏnŭi, is quite different. The Hyŏn lineage sequels follow the patriline, which is quite common. In the jade mandarin ducks sequence, Yi Wŏnŭi becomes the connecting figure between the two novels—which, instead of generational succession, present mirror images of a father's and son's struggles. Through his moral transformation, Yi Wŏnŭi assumes the role of a patriarch, able to transmit kinship values to his son. The two sequences illustrate the process of moral conversion, which is pivotal for the transmission of kinship ideology and institutions.

The growth of kinship links in the treelike sequence of generations is captured in *The Book of Rites*: "He is in his person a branch from his parents; can any son but have this self-respect? If he is not able to respect his own person, he is wounding his parents. If he wounds his parents, he is wounding his own root; and when the root is wounded the branches will follow in the dying."[44] Growing like trees, lineage novel clusters capture two principles of generational reciprocity: the injunction that moral norms are to be reinscribed by the new generations and the necessity of coming to terms with prescriptive social roles. Moral precepts in these texts are viewed from two different angles: from the vantage of the multigenerational macrostructure of the lineage and from the particularity of a single person's life. The zooming into the process of personal negotiations establishes the conflict with the norm as a worthy narrative focus, which is particular to the lineage novel.

The genealogical sequel structure of the lineage novel raises two questions: Were all the novels in a sequel cluster composed by the same author(s)? And what kind of narrative desire prompted sequel composition? Stylistic differences between the novels of the Hyŏn lineage sequels suggest that the texts were written by different people. First of all, the three novels appear quite different in tone and style. Compared to the fast-paced, often bawdy plot of *Brothers Hyŏn*, which includes scenes of rape and open confrontation between the man and the object of his desires, *Pearls* is more subdued and less original, and the same can be said about the third novel, *Pearls and Jade*. Whereas the first two novels focus mainly on marital problems, *Pearls and Jade* places much greater weight on magic and female lust: the lineage and the realm are besieged by vengeful female magicians, who are enthralled by the beauty of the Hyŏn males.

Pearls and Jade also evinces a remarkable degree of social awareness; it documents the emergence of a monetized economy and the blurring of class boundaries. The text notes: "Even metropolitan elites (*kyŏnghwa sadaebu* 京華士大夫) are treated as slaves when they are out of money."[45] The narrative also hints at the development of a commodity market, and a conflict between a man and his concubine is resolved with the concubine receiving a "hundred silver coins to be used for adornments."[46] The majority of lineage novels center on established and prosperous lineages and pay no special attention to money. *Jade Mandarin Ducks* depicts the story of a noble but impoverished lineage that eventually gains good fortune; the protagonists' lack of money highlights their moral qualities and reconfirms their elevated station. In *Pearls and Jade*, money appears to circulate and create meaning—it confers status, resolves conflicts, and procures pleasure.[47] We can hence surmise either that this novel was composed at a much later date than the two preceding texts or that it reflects the distinctive social awareness of its writer(s).[48]

The case of the jade mandarin ducks sequel cluster is quite different again. The two narratives are very closely aligned, and there are no striking differences in style.[49] A margin note on one of the leaves of *The Commentary*, moreover, indicates that the two texts were transmitted together in the family of Madame Chŏng of Onyang (1725–1799),[50] which further emphasizes the close relationship between these two texts and, perhaps, their shared authorship.

A comparative look reveals that Korean lineage novel sequels are structurally different from novel sequels in China—in particular, from China's most famous sequel cluster centered on Cao Xueqin's (1715/1724–1763/1764) *Dream of the Red Chamber*. Both Keith McMahon and Ellen Widmer note that this text's sequels seek to "improve" the original narrative.[51] In contrast, lineage novel sequels never encroach upon the narrative space of the source novel; they are instead extensions that perpetuate the story of the lineage.

Another striking difference between Korea and China lies in the different developments of book culture in each place. In their prime during the eighteenth century, lineage novels circulated in manuscript form, and Korea did not have a booming publishing industry to distribute them to wider audiences. Some lineage novels were much more popular than others. *Brothers Hyŏn*, for example, comprises an extensive number of editions—around seventy identified so far.[52] These editions include rental library manuscripts and printed texts, embodiments of the commercialization of the lineage novel in the late nineteenth and early twentieth centuries.[53] One edition of the second novel in the sequence, *Pearls*, is believed to be associated with a commercial rental library.[54] However, with only nine surviving editions, this second novel was clearly not as popular as the parent text. The third and final novel in the sequence, *Pearls and Jade*, has just two extant editions. Similarly, one of the editions of *Jade Mandarin Ducks* appears to be a rental library manuscript.[55] The emergence of rental libraries and the provenance of the lineage novel manuscripts therein are discussed in chapter 5, but I will note here that commercial book circulation did not become widespread until the nineteenth century. Before then, lineage novels were hand-reproduced in familial circles, and so commercial considerations can hardly account for sequel creation.

The narrative desire that drives sequel composition is instead attributable to the structure of kinship imagination that plays out in literary production. This genealogical imagination institutes an expandable horizon in lineage novels that can continue indefinitely through many generations of protagonists.[56] It ultimately affirms the perpetual validity of the institution of kinship and creates a stabilized narrative pattern.

By the nineteenth century, the lineage-based imagination saturated the literary field of Chosŏn, stretching beyond the genre of the lineage novel. A testimony to the genre's pervasiveness appears in Nam Yunwŏn's (dates unknown, second half of the nineteenth century) preface to *The Record of the Jade Tree* (*Oksugi* 玉樹記): "As to this novel, I think if the stories of the descendants of its four families—Ka, Hwa, Wang, and Chin—were continued, it would make a novel equal to *Master Im and His Three Wives* (*Im Hwa Chŏng Yŏn* 林花鄭延) or *The Record of the Illustrious Deeds and Righteousness* (*Myŏnghaeng chŏngŭi rok* 明行正義錄)."[57] Both of the novels Nam names are lineage novels. His note underlines both the prestige of the lineage novel and the idea that any text could expand like a branching-out generational tree.

A similar belief in narrative expansion appears in a manuscript edition of *The Tale of Ch'oe Hyŏn* (*Ch'oe Hyŏn chŏn* 崔賢傳). The copyist's note suggests that the novel was handwritten in 1891 by a girl from the So family, eleven years of age: "If descendants continue in generations and emulate [virtuous deeds], there is no need to worry about loyalty and filial piety. Having copied the entire narrative, I am sad and amazed. The narrative is very appealing from the beginning until the end, and it seems to have deep meaning. However, since there are so many fantastic words in the world, no one can really know what is true and what is false. If the narrative were to be continued, it would make another volume, but I will just stop here."[58] The idea that almost any narrative can continue through the life stories of succeeding generations appears to have been shared by very different personae, attesting to the pervasiveness of the genealogical imagination.[59] Nam Yunwŏn's note indicates that the lineage novel came to be seen as the quintessence of generational textuality.

What the lineage novel contributes to the field of kinship narratives in late Chosŏn Korea is the aesthetic internalization of generational figuration: the lineage structure—the genealogy—generates an unending narrative. This infinite horizon valorizes and glorifies kinship ideology. But the lineage novel also rearticulates the genealogical vision. Rather than narrating a seamless succession of male protagonists captured in the genealogical chart, lineage novels zoom in on the messy details of everyday life, turning generational succession into a contested process of socialization.

The domestic space in the lineage novel is very different from the space depicted in funerary texts: as chapter 4 shows, fictional family relations involve a great deal of disagreement and even violence. What brings lineage novels and funerary texts together is that they are not gender exclusive, giving equal focus to men and women.

A Family of Genres: The Family Tale

In posthumous life narratives, kinship is a fabric that encompasses the affective intricacy of familial relationships in excess of streamlined male descent. In the lineage novel, generational succession constitutes a narrative carcass that is filled with everyday conflicts that problematize and delay the fulfillment of the kinship norm. The third type of generational figuration considered in this chapter—the family tale[60]—affords yet another vision of Chosŏn kinship.

Family tales were a popular genre of kinship writing in Chosŏn. Writing in the eighteenth century, Kim Sangch'ae (dates unknown) notes: "People make family records (karok 家錄), in which they capture the affairs of their household. All the prominent houses keep chronicles (ilgi 日記) or family accounts (kajang 家藏) in order to reflect the virtue [of their ancestors] and impress other people with their ancestors' benevolence and longevity."[61] Much like funerary texts, family tales were compiled from extant family writings. The main difference was, however, that these tales spanned the life of several generations,[62] and this required alternative narrative strategies to flesh out. *The Record of the Three Generations of the Yi Lineage from the East of the Sea*, a vernacular Korean family tale composed in the late nineteenth century, stands out because of its remarkable intertextuality, which incorporates elements of novelistic style. This tale construes kinship as a convergence of textual idioms that reflect the sociolinguistic identities of this family's members. These idioms include travel writing that documents a diplomatic trip to Qing China, officials' notes on local life, and the lineage novel.

The Yi Lineage traces the lives of three men from the eponymous household, each with an illustrious career in civil officialdom. Yi Ŏnsun (1774–1845) served in various prestigious positions, including minister of personnel, and traveled to Qing China in 1835 as an envoy. His son, Yi Hwijŏng

(1799–1875), served as a magistrate in Ch'ungch'ŏng Province. Yi Ŏnsun's grandson, Yi Manun (1815–1887), served as a secret royal inspector.

Ying Zhang has noted the emergence of what she calls "Confucian family tales" in seventeenth-century China "as a result of people's amplified interest in politics, the negotiation of Confucian values, and the immense popularity of historical novels, crime-case fiction, and god-and-demons fiction."[63] Against the backdrop of an expanding print culture and the deepening of factional politics at court, carefully crafted family narratives that highlighted hereditary virtues were used to boost the political prestige of the literati elites; accounts of depravity, on the contrary, could dampen the reputation of factional opponents. Although image politics was similarly important for the elite lineages of Chosŏn, Korean family tales were quite different from their Chinese counterparts. As noted earlier, Chosŏn Korea did not have a comparable print culture, so Korean family tales circulated mostly through family networks rather than in the commercialized book market, as in China. Moreover, there was no comparable use of politically inflected family tales in the Korean court. These differences notwithstanding, Zhang's term *family tale* evokes the entanglement of kinship image politics and fictional idiom and offers a suggestive lens upon Korean family narratives.

The Yi Lineage appears to have circulated extensively in the Andong area of North Kyŏngsang Province.[64] This area has been the provincial base of the Chinsŏng Yi since the lineage founder, Yi Chasu (dates unknown), migrated to Andong during the late Koryŏ dynasty. The Chinsŏng Yi of Andong were a prominent lineage that produced one of the most revered philosophers in Chosŏn—T'oegye Yi Hwang (1501–1570). The cultural capital generated by this luminary gave his descendants a strong foothold in the Kyŏngsang region; they dominated the local society by a variety of means, including the administration of Tosan Sŏwŏn, a local academy erected in honor of the great ancestor, which became the major intellectual center of Andong elites.[65]

The composition, transcription, and circulation of *The Yi Lineage* were embedded in the fabric of kinship. The narrative was transcribed with reverence for the ancestors' lives, and it traveled along matrimonial links. Its composition appears to have been a collaboration among men and women of the Chinsŏng Yi lineage. In particular, Hyoam Yi Chungch'ŏl (1848–1938), a nephew of Yi Hwijŏng (whose life is covered in the second of the tale's three generations), appears to have collaborated with his niece Madame Yi. The daughter of Yi Chungch'ŏl's cousin Yi Chunggo, Madame Yi achieved literary fame in her home region for her skillful composition of prosimetric verse, *kasa* (歌辭).[66]

Margin notes in the extant editions of *The Yi Lineage* suggest that the text was dutifully transcribed by female kin (see figure 1.1). One note reads: "Hujodang. Miss Kim, twelve years of age, [copied this book] in clumsy handwriting. But because this volume [records] the illustrious deeds of the maternal great-grandfather, it had been pledged to be preserved among descendants. Therefore, all those who read it do so with care."[67] "Hujodang" is the name of a pavilion that was erected by Kim Pup'il (1516–1577) of the Kwangsan Kim lineage in Kunja village in Andong and that carries Kim Pup'il's own courtesy name. Kim Pup'il and his adopted heir, Hae, accumulated considerable wealth in the Andong area, and this prominent family was linked by marriage to the Chinsŏng Yi, whose lives *The Yi Lineage* records.[68] Kim Pup'il, moreover, was an enthusiastic disciple of T'oegye, and Yi Ŏnsun, whose life is the first one narrated in this family tale, petitioned King Sunjo (r. 1800–1834) to grant Kim Pup'il a posthumous title for his dedication to T'oegye scholarship.[69] Given that the young scribe mentions that the story captures the memories of her maternal great-grandfather, it appears that this family tale was transmitted to the Andong residence of the Kwangsan Kim lineage through a marital connection. Yet another manuscript includes a reference to the efforts of a certain Madame Yi, who copied the text ("*puin Yi ssi tŭngch'o*" 夫人李氏謄寫). Another note on the same volume cover, written with a different brush, reveals that the tale is in the possession of Yi Hwang's descendants ("*T'oegye kamun kajang*" 退溪家門家藏).[70] Two things become apparent from these notes: *The Yi Lineage* circulated in tight kinship networks in the Andong area, and women played an important role in its manuscript transmission.

As befits a Confucian family tale, *The Yi Lineage* glorifies the elevated status of the members of the Chinsŏng Yi. When Yi Ŏnsun receives an unspecified book gift from the king, the text comments: "Such a graciously bestowed heavenly volume (*ŭnsu ch'ŏnch'aek* 恩授天冊)—one could hardly find anything like this in Yŏngnam."[71] At another point, in celebrating the appointment of Yi Ŏnsun as magistrate of Kaesong, the narrative notes that such a coveted position is not available to "just any person from Yŏngnam."[72] The three generations of the Yi lineage whose lives are described in the account did indeed have illustrious careers. Their careers, in turn, are

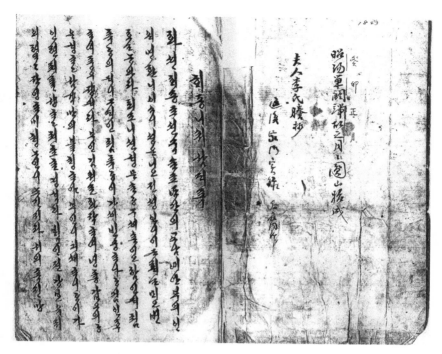

Figure 1.1 Leaf from *The Record of the Yi Lineage from the East of the Sea* (*Haedong Yi ssi samdae rok*).

Source: Courtesy of the JaHyun Kim Haboush Archive.

closely related to specific genres of writing, such as travel notes and observations of local life in the provinces. These different sociolinguistic idioms are woven together in this three-generation account.

Part of the narrative is composed of a travelogue that records Yi Ŏnsun's journey to the Qing in 1837 as the deputy envoy of gratitude for the imperial grace (*saŭn pusa* 謝恩副使). The travelogue's documentary desire is revealed in a list of tributary items, a roster of legation members and their titles, as well as the Korean cities on the itinerary, which offer farewell banquets to the legation. In line with the anti-Qing attitudes that were widespread if not universal in late Chosŏn, the narrative remarks bitterly upon the crossing of the border, labeling the Qing as a "desolate barbaric land (*such'am hoji* 愁慘 胡地)."[73] Yet this negative attitude coexists with admiration of breathtaking views and the sheer vastness of the state the envoys traverse; these descriptions are steeped in the idiom of envoy poetry. The register is lowered when the figure of the Daoguang emperor (r.

1820–1850) is described: "In his dragon robe, the emperor is laughable like a sitting yellow dog. There is nothing worth looking at. At the sight of this pathetic figure of the emperor, one cannot but succumb to resentment."[74] The insults directed at the Chinese emperor symbolically redress the imbalance of power between the suzerain and the tributary state, China and Korea. The cultural space of the Chinsŏng Yi family, then, incorporates the intimate knowledge of the diplomatic culture and foreign lands, and this knowledge is embedded in the memories assiduously transmitted by female scribes through generations and kinship ties.

Yi Ŏnsun's son, Yi Hwijŏng, serves as a magistrate of Kŏch'ang, and the record of his life sheds light on local politics. When Yi Hwijŏng uncovers manipulations by lower officials that produce tax deficits, he recovers the stolen funds from the culprits. The text depicts the pathetic and discomfited clerks fearing for their lives: "All the lower clerks feast on the people's blood and meat, having plentiful dress and food. Now that their crimes warrant definite punishment, each of them is scared and earnest. The yamen is like a pot of boiling water."[75] The account is in line with the habitual depiction of lower functionaries in Chosŏn-era sources, in which lower clerks, *hyangni*, "emerge . . . as a faceless mass of undisciplined and greedy, yet indispensable underlings running the day-to-day local administration."[76] The magistrate's righteous conduct, offset by the clerks' iniquities, reinforces his status superiority.

The narrative's observation of local lives continues when Yi Manun, the third-generation descendant of Chinsŏng Yi, is appointed as a secret royal inspector. During his visit to Ch'ungju, Yi Manun tours the villages in the scorching summer heat, forgetting food and rest. At one point, Yi Manun comes across two fields: a well-irrigated one above and a scorched one below that is cut off from the waterway. Having cleared the second one's conduit to the waterway, Yi Manun is indecorously scolded for his efforts by a "ruffian monk (*sŭngnom*)" who suddenly appears on the road. Later, in his lodging in one of the local houses, Yi Manun hears loud voices in the middle of the night. The "ruffian monk" has come to collect his debt from the wife of the housemaster's brother; he threatens to take the wife in exchange for the forfeited loan. The monk is eventually caught and punished, and the owner of the house later explains that his impoverished family is unable to repay the loan, which they took to cover his younger brother's wedding expenses. The narrative comments that this case should be a warning for those who would dare torment "an impoverished scholar."

The hierarchies of the countryside, which had been endangered by unequal economic status, are thereby restored. These scenes show how the stories of the three illustrious members of the Chinsŏng Yi family are elaborated in the vocabulary of their experience, steeped in relevant textual traditions that pertain to their government service.

The overarching framework that welds together the narratives of excellence over the span of three generations draws heavily from the lineage novel, which pays close attention to the details of everyday domestic life. For instance, the narrative opens with a genealogical summary and lays out the political, local, and ancestral contexts of the events:

> In the country of Chosŏn to the East of the Sea, during the reign of King Sunjo, in the village of Yean in the Kyonam region,[77] there lived an illustrious official. His last name was Yi, and he was a man of Chinsŏng. His courtesy name and his taboo name were X,[78] and his nom de plume was Nongwa. He was the ninth-generation descendant of T'oegye Yi Hwang Lord Munsun and the son of Haminje Lord Ch'ŏmch'u.[79] His father, Lord Ch'ŏmch'u, had a poor household, but he was modest, benevolent, and generous, and he was the oldest son of P'ungu.[80] Lord Ch'ŏmch'u lived in harmony with his wife, Madame Kim. In the *kabo* year during the reign of Yŏngjo [1774], they gave birth to [Yi Ŏnsun]. But in just three months, haplessly, Madame Kim left this world, and Lord Ch'ŏmch'u lost his beautiful companion and wise wife. The lord's sadness and the loneliness of the newborn child, not even a hundred days old, could be felt even by passers-by. At that moment, among Lord Ch'ŏmch'u's nephews there was Lord Mangch'ŏn,[81] whose wife, Madame Kim, an outstanding person slightly over thirty, was unable to conceive. The couple spent their days in sadness because of this. A child's misfortune became this couple's happiness, and they brought [Yi Ŏnsun] into their house to raise him. The milk started to flow from [Madame Kim's] breasts by itself to nourish [Yi Ŏnsun]. Is this not a miraculous happening, indeed?[82]

As is typical of the lineage novel, this novelistic opening names the country and the reign era in which the tale takes place. (Of course, *The Yi Lineage* is set in Chosŏn Korea, whereas lineage novels are without exception set in China). Together with its narrativization of the geopolitical context, this opening features a dramatic moment, depicting the rescue of a bereft child and suggesting that the lineage is in crisis[83] Novelistic idiom is discernible in other instances of the text as well.

The text's title and three-generational structure emulate the narratives and titles of lineage novels, which often include three generations of a given lineage.[84] Another affinity with the lineage novel can be seen in *The Yi Lineage*'s use of formulaic phrases—such as *hwasŏl* (話說), an opening line that resembles "once upon a time," and *chaesŏl* (再說), "to speak of this again," which signals a shift to a previously discussed topic.[85] In addition to novelistic features like these, *The Yi Lineage* includes a much more striking aesthetic affinity with the lineage novel: a thick everydayness, where kinship is greater than the vitae of its outstanding representatives; in this text, domestic kinship life emerges as a spatiotemporal continuum. The domestic space is fleshed out with consistent chronological detail, comparable with the narrative of the lineage novel.[86] While the three successive generations provide the temporal macrostructure, the flow of everyday time is organized around central life events and associated rituals—birth, marriage, and death. Chapter 3 shows how all of these elements are constitutive of the lineage novel's chronotope.

For a glimpse of the architecture of daily life depicted in *The Yi Lineage*, we can turn to the scene of a banquet in honor of the sixtieth wedding anniversary of the patriarch, Yi Ŏnsun, in 1872:

> The first son, when the time approaches, offers his bows for longevity and prosperity. Then, the four sons and two daughters together offer their congratulations. The grand banquet unfolds, with colorful pillows filling every courtyard. Colorful clouds shine in the brilliant strings of beads and copious golden carafes. On this glorious day, white clouds gather, people from all around fill the mountains and cover the fields, thousands of kin and friends from the capital and the countryside, and more than half of the district magistrates gather. All kinds of musical instruments are prepared everywhere, so, at a close distance, one cannot tell apart the tunes that are played. The flowery red chariots, horses and carriages, and attendants are coming and going in every corner. Spectators, gathered everywhere, clamor to offer their congratulations until their mouths go dry. The delicacies are piled up in the inner court. The patriarch straightens his cap. The matriarch, in a red top and green skirt, with a flower-embroidered

cap sitting upright on her head, has phoenix pins fixed in her hair, and her white temples glimmer brightly. The patriarch, with his cranelike, immortal-like air, is all the more stately in his appearance. The couple sit next to each other and receive the wishes of longevity from their sons, daughters-in-law, daughters, sons-in-law, and all the grandchildren. Guests, numerous as clouds, and the magistrates of every town enter in multitudes. From all four directions the musical rhythms echo the fragrant laughs and piercing songs of the exquisite maidens in red skirts and colorful jackets.[87]

This banquet scene does not fail to draw attention to the opulence and social recognition that this family enjoys—the family's excellence is witnessed by a multitude of guests, some of whom are particularly eminent. In its rich detail, the description of this family celebration is strikingly similar to a banquet scene in *The Pledge*, a lineage novel discussed in chapter 3.

The Yi Lineage includes many scenes that hardly belong to the register of memories appropriate for a glorious ancestral portrait and evoke novelistic idiom. Depictions of eroticized bedroom conversations, the lineage members' social anxieties, and secondary household members' misbehavior bring the narrative of social excellence—that runs like a red thread through the record—to the level of everyday experience.

As Yi Ŏnsun's son, Yi Hwijŏng, prepares to marry a woman from the wealthy Inch'ŏn Ch'ae lineage, their enviable union prompts evil tongues to spread a rumor about the bride's hopeless illness, which causes Yi Ŏnsun and his wife, Madame An, to worry about the couple's ability to conceive. Yi Ŏnsun approaches his wife with the following words: "Marriage is a great matter in human relations (*illyun taesa* 人倫大事), and you cannot go about it carelessly. I want to ask [our son about his opinion on the matter], but as it is unseemly for a man to do this, why don't you do it yourself?" Yi Hwijŏng, after his mother conveys this parental concern, repeats his father's words almost verbatim but gives them a different interpretation: "Marriage between man and woman is the foundation of human relations (*illyun ch'odan* 人倫初段). Therefore, a pledge once made cannot be changed even in one hundred years. If the bride is deformed, this too is our family's lot. Could we really go against the old agreement now? If our house defaults on the promise, the bride will become a castaway [unable to marry again]. Would this not be the accumulation of evil deeds [for us]?"[88] This insistence on the inviolability of the marriage pledge is a common motif in the lineage novel: the ability to honor these arrangements even in the face of adversity that threatens to turn the nuptial union into a mésalliance reflects the morality of the lineage. Only characters unworthy of respect refuse marriage pledges. *The Yi Lineage* balances this idealized perspective by depicting a prominent lineage's concern about its future.

On the wedding night, Yi Hwijŏng laughingly tells his wife about the rumors of her alleged sickness. He teases her, "Now that we have met this night, how does it feel?" After some hesitation, she responds: "This is not for me to say. Find the answer in your gentleman's heart." The groom is "laughing to himself and stroking his jade hands; his exquisite feelings are like a great mountain, making deep rivers and seas seem shallow in contrast."[89] Here, we do not see the patriarch from the apex of the genealogical chart: he is in bed on his wedding night, and he is making a joke. The portrait of a great ancestor in bed is striking. The scene is highly eroticized even as it leaves out sexualized details. The tension between the groom's direct, playful question and his wife's reticent rejoinder generates arousal, which the text drapes with gender-specific vocabulary that interpellates patriarchal power—to question and to let feelings encompass a realm that is vaster than mountains and seas—into the bedroom scene.

The thick everydayness of domestic life also emerges in scenes of emotional upheaval, though such scenes are not prevalent in a text that aims to memorialize the ancestral glory. The violent side of family life surfaces in a curious incident during Yi Hwijŏng's magistracy. At night, he goes to bed with one of the courtesans, Ch'aebong. His concubine, Changsŏng, sees them through the side door: "Unable to restrain her ignorant jealousy, [Changsŏng] started to bang on the side door with the words, 'Ch'aebong, you vixen, how is it that you dare encroach upon my life?!' Her vulgar and unrestrained words cannot be described here. The yamen attendants were deep asleep, but Changsŏng's shrieks startled them. Wondering if anything was amiss in the government hall, they lit candles and rushed to the scene."[90] Beside himself with anger, the magistrate nearly expels his concubine, but she is allowed to stay after all of the domestics out of pity plead on her behalf. The depiction of this self-forgetful concubine offers intimate insight into the household's daily routine and conforms closely to descriptions of secondary household members in funerary texts as crass but endearing in their sincerity. Needless to say, no unseemly outbursts of emotion are attributed to the thoroughbred members of the Yi clan. However, their misgivings about marriage arrangements and their playful bedroom conversations are hardly imaginable in the more formal genres of funerary writing.

Although we cannot trace the authorship of *The Yi Lineage* to a concrete historical person or persons with absolute certainty, the familial nature of this text's composition is noteworthy. Ellen Widmer raises an intriguing question in her study of the familial literary space shared by men and women from the provincial family in Qing-dynasty Quzhou: "Why study family and fiction side by side?" Widmer's answer is that the "conceit of describing sets of genres as a family brings out other correspondences,"[91] so that the textual experience of a family provides a microcosmic, close-up view of late nineteenth-century provincial Qing society, which was affected by the dramatic aftermath of the Taiping Rebellion (1850–1864), the emergence of print culture, and the changes in gender roles and state identity. Literacy and affinity to a certain type of literary idiom, in Widmer's view, are embedded in the structure of historical-familial experience.

In *The Yi Lineage*, a coalescence of genres constitutes the dimensions of this family's lived experience, the horizons of family learning, and the idioms of writing about the activities of various family members throughout their lifetime. Family as a space of linked narratives is captured in the text. For example, in recounting his return from Beijing, Yi Ŏnsun "detailed the affairs of the heavenly court to gathered relatives and friends, also telling them about things Chinese. His narrative was dignified."[92] Here, we get a visceral sense of the family circle fascinated by tales about experiences that few domestics could ever hope to witness firsthand. The family banquet scene that closes the narrative also produces narrative desire, with the patriarch, Yi Ŏnsun, instructing his descendants to keep a faithful record of all important family ceremonies and transmit them through generations.[93]

If funerary texts point to the family as a palimpsest of filial, intergenerational memories, records such as *The Yi Lineage* reveal another dimension of the domestic space, where texts as genres of experience, perception, and narrative idiom intersect on the home stage. The lineage novel's chronotope, which accommodates the narrative of domestic everydayness, provides a unifying background to this hybrid familial textual space.

In Conclusion

Kinship in Chosŏn Korea was mediated by writing: the documentary genres of kinship textuality, such as genealogies and literary collections, helped perpetuate a lineage's ascriptive privilege. The genres of kinship writing that focus on the domestic space—funerary texts, lineage novels, and family tales—foreground the affective centrality of the domestic space woven from the lives of family members who are marginalized in the hegemonic, male-centered texts of Korean kinship. In their different ways, these genres of kinship writing decenter and expand the male-centered verticality of a genealogy. Funerary texts reveal the palimpsest-like proliferation of ancestral memories encompassing kinswomen and secondary-status family members. Lineage novels narrate the personal life stories of protagonists who are misaligned with the kinship norm, marking problematic junctures in generational continuity. Fictional writing, then, circles back into documentary kinship writing, as is illustrated by the curiously hybrid narrative of *The Yi Lineage*, which intersperses the record of kinship excellence with the flow of domestic time and everyday interactions.

The textual dimension of Chosŏn kinship—and here I refer to elite lineages of the Chosŏn era—was exceptionally diverse, and the emergence of the lineage novel in the late seventeenth century is inseparable from the wider current of kinship textuality that swept through Chosŏn cultural production as lineage society took shape. The lineage novel appears on the literary stage of Chosŏn as part of this massive current, and its disappearance is marked by the demise of kinship narratives and kinship-centered audiences in the nineteenth century, as discussed in chapter 5.

These different forms of kinship writing are not merely coeval; they interact constantly. As I note in the introduction, lineage novels often refer to other allegedly existing documentary narratives of kinship life.[94] More broadly, from their position within elite reading culture, lineage novels frequently attempt to claim the prestige of documentary genres of kinship writing. The incorporation of novelistic elements in a family tale such as *The Yi Lineage* has a reverse effect: it lowers the narrative's register to allow figurations of domestic life in which even the patriarch is depicted from an everyday angle. These interactions and influences show that Chosŏn-dynasty kinship writing was a dynamic space that incorporated both the monumental and the everyday.

Another striking feature of the three narrative types discussed in this chapter is the intermeshing of different authors and narrative modes. The multilayered narratives of funerary texts are composed by different authors in entangled kinship contexts: life narratives and modes of remembering are inextricably interlinked. Although lineage novels' authors are unknown, chapter 2 shows that their manuscripts were created collectively by men and women of elite families. The different sociolinguistic idioms embedded in the composition of *The Yi Lineage*—magistrate's notes, envoy diary, and lineage novel—furthermore point to the entanglement of learning, literacy, and experience within the domestic space. Women—as sources of familial memories, as objects of remembrance in funerary texts, and as scribers who create manuscripts of lineage novels and family tales—are notably central to this textual realm.

The polyphony of domestic life, however, is organized according to clear, kinship-based notions of value. One of the central figurations in these genres is generational reciprocity: a common ground articulated through a shared set of values and a bond that is cemented by filial piety, or reverence for the lives and legacy of the deceased elders. Downward generational flow is disrupted in funerary texts written by parents grieving for their children. At the same time, funerary texts are created with a generational audience in mind. The lives of the deceased are committed to memory and transmitted forward, so that no one is forgotten and virtuous exemplars live on. Lineage novels temporize generational continuity, showing that adherence to ancestral example involves a conflicted process of socialization, and yet the perpetuity of the lineage as an institution and a site for the reinscription of moral ideals defines the horizon of the lineage novel's vision. Like funerary writing, the family tale records the family excellence that is sustained across generations, but this record is texturized by means of the aesthetic devices of fiction.

Generational temporality constitutes the macroarchitecture for kinship writing, organizing its narrative space and coordinating its expected audience. Chapter 2 explores how lineage novels, like funerary texts and family tales, were transmitted through generations. Although lineage novels were fictional, the manuscripts testified to the intricate calligraphic skills of actual elite women of Chosŏn. They were also mementoes, preserving embodied traces of their deceased scribes for familial audiences over many generations.

CHAPTER II

The Texture of Kinship

Vernacular Korean Calligraphy

Compared to standardized modern typefaces, the texture of a book leaf in Chosŏn Korea was exceptionally diverse, and this diversity betokened the different reading experiences and the variation in readers' socioeconomic backgrounds. Vernacular Korean fiction circulated in woodblock editions and manuscripts, which looked strikingly different. Coarse woodblock editions sold at the marketplace were densely printed on grayish paper and peppered with mistakes and omissions. Manuscripts produced for the rental libraries were often executed by professional scribes in regulated, practiced brushstrokes. Oftentimes, however, rental volumes could be written in haphazard brushwork squeezed between wide margins that lengthened the volume and inflated the rental charge. Readers filled these margins with often immodest commentary and illustrations pertaining to the owner of the rental shop, the daily rental price of the books, or the books' contents. Manuscripts that circulated in the palace featured meticulously executed calligraphy on solid white paper, with wide margins and a single blank leaf at the front. Such unsparing use of paper was a luxury at a time when paper prices were relatively high.[1] Volumes crafted in elite families also featured exquisite vernacular brushwork, though their binding and paper were not as luxurious as those of the palace volumes. Unlike the palace manuscripts, which reveal little about the history of their creation and circulation, vernacular Korean lineage novels produced in elite families are palimpsests of kinship connections. They often record the history of the manuscript's production and its journey through many hands and generations.

In many ways, the materiality of lineage novels is as important as their content: it provides a clue about the pervasiveness of vernacular Korean calligraphy in the elite women's culture of the time. A simple fact calls attention to the lineage novels' material form: whereas not a single author is known with certainty, the names of the scribers who produced lineage novels' manuscripts are sometimes mentioned on the novels' margins and in external sources. Needless to say, calligraphic training—an activity that required a significant amount of leisure time—was the prerogative of elites, and my discussion of the development of vernacular Korean calligraphy focuses on the elite women who cultivated this practice. As this chapter shows, vernacular Korean calligraphy constitutes a vantage point not only for the history of the lineage novel's circulation but also for the domestic lives of elite women and the role of patrilineal kinship in the shaping of vernacular Korean cultural space.

The fashioning of the lineage structure in the late seventeenth century had a significant impact on women's lives, and these changes were felt most acutely by elite women. Patrilineality resulted in elite women's economic and social disempowerment as their lives gradually transitioned to the domestic space of their husbands' households. Elite Korean women lost the right to inherit property, to divorce, and to move freely outside their homes. Although Korean women had depended on their relationships with men throughout history, the distinctive ideal of female domesticity that emerged in the late seventeenth century had profound implications for women's identity: women's bodies and the productive corporeal work they performed became central to their social visibility.

In the domestic space, women's bodies created a dense fabric of habitation, attachment, and care. This chapter shows how dexterous female bodies produced objects of everyday use and enacted relational hierarchies of the patriarchal kinship system. More importantly, it examines an aspect of women's lives that has long been obscured: their role in the creation of a sophisticated vernacular Korean canon of calligraphy and literature that thrived alongside literary Chinese culture, the prerogative of educated males. The history of the lineage novel is inconceivable apart from the trajectory of its material transmission: women's carefully cultivated calligraphic skills and the prestige associated with manuscript transmission enshrined lineage novels in the elite culture of late Chosŏn.

This chapter traces the boundaries of the cultural space constituted at the intersection of women's legislated corporeality and their creative engagement with the world of letters. It demonstrates that the gender politics of Chosŏn society and the dynamic vernacular Korean culture, hitherto understood mainly through the lens of male-authored sources, can be observed from the perspective of women's lives and activities.

Although the lineage's cultural eminence depended on the prestigious office appointments and literary fame of its male members, life in populous domestic communities was sustained by so-called womanly work. Women brewed soy sauce, prepared meals for ancestral worship ceremonies, and supplied seasonal outfits to the entire family, while also attending to a variety of domestic bodies: growing bodies, decaying bodies, and dead bodies. In a detailed instruction, Kim P'yŏngmok (1819–1891) offers the following advice to future mothers: "Say, if a woman is with a child, [she] does not sleep askew, nor does she lean to one side while sitting or put her weight on one leg while standing."[2] Women were also intimate with decaying bodies. Sŏng Haeŭng (1760–1839) writes that his mother took utmost care of her own mother-in-law on the latter's deathbed: "When my grandmother suffered from dysentery and her symptoms grew worse, Mother tasted her excrement in order to obtain a diagnosis for her illness. But my grandmother was ultimately unable to recover."[3] The bodies of the deceased were similarly entrusted to women's hands. According to a testimony of her husband, Hŏ Chŏn (1797–1886), Madame Cho of Hanyang (1794–1852) dressed the remains of her mother-in-law with great care: "When it came to funerary preparations for Mother, of combing the corpse's hair, holding of the funerary shroud, and washing the corpse, my wife handled everything herself. The dressing of the corpse, too, was handled by her alone. She did not let any female servants near."[4] Hŏ's emphasis on his wife's dedicated performance of the necessary rites for sending off the deceased highlights the value of women's bodily devotion.

Women's diligent bodies of devotion, always at the service of their household members, are often celebrated in male-authored commemorative texts that appeared in quantity after the seventeenth century. These texts provide perhaps the most extensive view of women's everyday experience while outlining the repertoire of prescriptive womanly conduct. Importantly, in addition to celebrating a variety of embodied skills, commemorative texts often praise women's ability to write vernacular Korean in a well-trained hand. Women's writing, however, is never called calligraphy (sŏ 書),

an artform reserved for men; at best, the strokes of a woman's brush are said to be orderly and vigorous.

In excess of its aesthetic aspect, calligraphy in literary Chinese was a mode of self-cultivation and even statecraft. As John Hay, a historian of Chinese art, has noted, calligraphy was traditionally viewed as an emanation of moral character.[5] A vigorous, unclouded spirit revealed itself in measured, powerful brushstrokes, a comparison that placed the bodily act of writing at the center of an evenly ordered macrocosm. The link between the personal and the political embodied in calligraphic training prompted King Chŏngjo (1752–1800, r. 1776–1800) to reform the calligraphic styles of his time, thus standardizing this scriptural medium of governance. Aesthetic and moral cultivation were central to the learning and careers of elite men. Although women were held to rigorous standards of comportment based on various forms of bodily discipline—chastity, circumspection in speech and conduct, and diligent application to variegated household tasks—education for its own sake was never a priority in their lives. Therefore, when women's regular brushstrokes are mentioned in male-authored sources, they are neither said to reveal the scribe's moral character nor seen as having public valence. Yet the elegant latticework of vernacular Korean letters was a product of ambidextrous women's bodies, able to master patriarchal corporeal normativity while also venturing into the space of aesthetic training.

Instead of mapping the multilayered sociolinguistic practices of Chosŏn—a vast ground for theoretical study—this chapter outlines the historical process through which vernacular Korean culture acquired connotations of social prestige and thus became stratified. To this day, vernacular Korean writing is linked largely to unsophisticated popular literature or to mundane scribal practices, such as note taking and correspondence, that had very little aesthetic value. This chapter shows that vernacular Korean calligraphy and lineage novels became ingredients of the cultural proficiency of the most exclusive elites—women who were educated if not always affluent.

The term *vernacular* here means two things. Quite literally, it designates writing in the Korean script—a vernacular development within the culture of Chosŏn, which prioritized literary Chinese scriptural practices. More broadly, "vernacular" connotes the local and therefore circumscribed cultural domain. Far from asserting an obviated male-elite-Sinographic and female-colloquial-Korean binary, this chapter treats the scriptural sphere of Chosŏn as a heteroglot mixture of sociolects organized around the use of two scripts: literary Chinese and vernacular Korean. Neither practice was homogeneous. Sixiang Wang shows in his recent study that the script of a literary Chinese play, *Story of the Eastern Chamber* (*Tongsang ki* 東廂記/東床記), exhibits the concern of elite male literati about the way "language was bound with time, location, and social level," or, to put it differently, with "local difference and cultural divergence."[6] The Korean vernacularisms in the play's literary Chinese text decentered the literary language of the timeless classics and imbued it with local and temporal specificity. Chosŏn literati, in other words, *vernacularized* literary Chinese works along the lines of the cosmopolitan–local paradigm developed by Sheldon Pollock.[7] At the same time, the *vernacular* Korean language of the lineage novel includes a great number of literary Chinese loan words and phrases. These two- or four-character compounds are transliterated in vernacular Korean, but this graphic homogeneity belies the extent of heteroglossia and literary influence.

A distinction between the *vernacularization* of literary Chinese writing and writing in the Korean *vernacular* is useful in that it highlights the graphic difference of *vernacular* Korean script that set it apart from *vernacularized* literary Chinese writing, which meant that no vernacular Korean texts would be included in elite men's literary anthologies. Vernacular Korean practices, in other words, did not merely localize and *vernacularize* the high cosmopolitan language—literary Chinese—but were founded on radically different premises. In China's case, as Patrick Hanan notes, "the critics who praised vernacular works praised them, generally, in elegant Classical Chinese; their concern was with literary merit, not with the literary medium, or if with the literary medium, then only as used in that genre."[8] In Chosŏn Korea, vernacular Korean fiction was hardly ever praised in literary Chinese—on the contrary, male literati either ignored vernacular Korean novels altogether or characterized them as a dangerous enchantment for weak minds. As this chapter shows, lineage novels were exempted from this strict hierarchical vision. At the same time, handwriting in vernacular Korean was denied aesthetic value precisely because it was executed in a script that did not command any prestige. In Japan, some vernacular literary practices, such as *waka* and *monogatari*, were canonized,[9] but in Korea the vernacular script was usually designated as "colloquial" (*ŏnmun* 諺文) in contradistinction to the "true script" (*chinsŏ* 真書), literary Chinese.

The material difference of vernacular Korean contextualizes its different *affordance*. Defined by Caroline Levine as "the potential uses or actions latent in materials and designs,"[10] *affordance*—a term brought into cultural analysis from design theory—refers to the enabling and constraining properties of the materials of culture. The radically different graphic materiality of vernacular Korean script prevented it from occupying the same cultural register as literary Chinese writing. Notably, even those Chosŏn-era intellectuals who were interested in vernacularization as a mode of grounding the cultural identity of Chosŏn in its own time and space never considered the use of vernacular Korean.[11] Although the heteroglot composition of linguistic practices of Chosŏn must be acknowledged, it is also important to understand the radical difference—grounded in the affordance of each script—between vernacular Korean and literary Chinese writing.

The firm boundary between vernacular Korean and literary Chinese scriptural practices afforded women greater creative freedom. Because women's domestic identities were just as circumscribed as the cultural connotations of vernacular Korean script, they were free to appropriate the vernacular domain for their use. This chapter shows how the aesthetic value of vernacular Korean writing became closely intertwined with women's identity in the kinship system.

In the argument that follows, I first outline the politics of gender that orchestrated the disparate visibility of men and women in the society and culture of Chosŏn, ponder the striking similarities in the calligraphic training of men and women, and foreground the calligraphic significance of women's vernacular Korean handwriting. Finally, I pinpoint the intersection of vernacular Korean calligraphy and the lineage novel, showing how women's manuscript making generated the cultural prestige of a literary genre that elaborated the major historical transformation of early modern Korean society: the establishment of patrilineal kinship that took place around the late seventeenth century.

The Womanly Art of Vernacular Korean Calligraphy

In the late eighteenth century, Yi Tŏngmu (1741–1793), a prolific scholar and writer, ventured an explanation of the glaring silence surrounding women's scriptural practice. In a short essay, "Women Calligraphers of the Eastern Country" ("Tongguk puin nŭngsŏ" 東國婦人能書), Yi wrote:

"Before the promulgation of the *Correct Sounds to Instruct the People* (*Hunmin chŏngŭm* 訓民正音), many women were able to write in a good hand, methinks. However, beginning with Sejong's reign [1418–1450], even if some women are famed for their poetry, hardly any woman is known for her calligraphy."[12] Revealingly, Yi's understanding of calligraphy is limited to writing in literary Chinese. After the promulgation of the Correct Sounds to Instruct the People (the name given to the Korean alphabet at the time of its creation) in 1446 during the reign of King Sejong, women began to write almost exclusively in vernacular Korean. Yi Tŏngmu and his educated male contemporaries saw little value in vernacular Korean culture: the only aesthetically significant compositions and calligraphy were written in literary Chinese, which was monopolized by elite men.

Chosŏn society comprised an array of sociolinguistic practices, two of which are central to this discussion: the high literary Chinese canon and the elite vernacular Korean culture, which were interrelated in practice even though they had different levels of prestige. Unspoken but written literary Chinese was the language of legislation, official histories, government bureaucracy, and educated men's writing. Men resorted to vernacular Korean when exchanging letters with the women in their families[13] and when they composed conduct books for the benefit of their marrying daughters.[14] Writing in vernacular Korean, however, did not contribute to men's cultural capital. Literary collections compiled posthumously to preserve a learned man's legacy never included fiction or any texts in vernacular Korean. Women, in contrast, wrote letters, poetry, and miscellaneous practical tips in vernacular Korean freely and not without pride; they also copied books of fiction.

The edict promulgating the Korean alphabet reveals that the script was devised to reflect Korean phonetics and provide a medium for learning and communication to all those who could not master literary Chinese—including women and the lower classes.[15] Whether truly demotic in design or not,[16] the Korean alphabet might well have been easier to master than the Chinese logographs, but this alone cannot explain its lower cultural status. The politics of gender adopted by the Chosŏn state was layered into the distinction of prestige accorded to literary Chinese and vernacular Korean written realms.

Before women began writing exclusively in vernacular Korean, they were often well versed in literary Chinese, but references to women's Sinographic literacy gradually disappear after the seventeenth century—though a few maverick females continued to compose poetry and even Confucian treatises in literary Chinese.[17] As women's identities grew increasingly domestic after the seventeenth century, their access to education and their pursuit of knowledge for its own sake became limited.[18] Women's use of vernacular Korean writing, distant from the realm of literary learning par excellence, appeared consonant with their domestic lifestyle.[19] Moreover, women's use of vernacular Korean script acquired an array of useful connotations, the practical value of which was underscored by women's roles in the kinship network.

Yi Tŏngmu and his male contemporaries' refusal to apply the term *calligraphy* to women's vernacular handwriting is another token of the overarching scriptural hierarchy mapped upon the Confucian gender norms. Yet, at the same time, male-authored records do capture the aesthetic and social significance of women's handwriting, even if they do not explicitly acknowledge the cultural prestige of the vernacular Korean canon on its own terms.

When women's cultivation of vernacular Korean handwriting came to the attention of Yi Tŏngmu's slightly older contemporary Yi Ok (1760–1815), he accorded women's vernacular Korean brushwork a name with particular attention to style. In his literary Chinese poem "Maxims" ("Yiŏn" 俚諺), among the etudes on marriage preparations, women's life after marriage, and the relationship between husband and wife, Yi writes:

> Since you learned the palace style calligraphy early on,
> You crown the round letter with a handsome sharp stroke.[20]
> Your parents-in-law delight in your writing;
> "It is that of a female scholar-official!" they say.[21]

Yi Ok renders a woman's writing prowess as a desirable and reputable achievement from the perspective of her parents-in-law, who embody ultimate authority in the life of a married woman. The poem's use of the specific term *palace style* (*kungch'e* 宮體) is, moreover, a rare characterization of women's handwriting as aesthetic.

The so-called palace style of vernacular Korean writing is believed to have been created by palace women.[22] It was the first truly aestheticized form of vernacular handwriting to emerge after the square vernacular graphics of the fifteenth-century state-sponsored print publications were appropriated for daily epistolary use and thereby softened and rounded.[23]

Having entered royal service as young girls, palace women who belonged to the secretariat received rigorous calligraphic training so that they could write the letters of greeting that were exchanged between royal family members (*munan* 門安), keep royal household registries (*palgi* 件記), and copy books for the palace readers.[24] There are virtually no records of the lives and work of Korean palace women, but the latticework of linked cursive letters they created quickly spread outside the palace and became a necessary ingredient in the education of girls in upper-class families.[25] Calligraphy was a task and a skill, a livelihood for palace women—as professionalized subjects who were not allowed to marry, they existed outside kinship networks. Palace women's calligraphy traveled outside the palace walls in the letters they sent[26] and in the volumes of palace manuscripts— including lineage novels—that royal princesses took with them as part of their dowry upon marriage.[27] Elite women were expected to marry, and their lives, including their calligraphic practice, were determined by the structures of kinship obligation. Thus, once the first aestheticized form of vernacular handwriting had transitioned from the semiprofessionalized activity of palace women to the practice of elite women, vernacular Korean calligraphy became tightly interlaced with women's role in kinship networks.

Although records show that elite women received an education, book learning was never a priority in their upbringing. Rather, productive work, such as brewing soy sauce and wine, as well as proper bodily comportment, such as chastity and circumspection in speech, defined women's identity in Chosŏn. Francesca Bray defines this "womanly work" (K. *yŏgong*; Ch. *nügong* 女工) as a technology of "shaping and transmitting ideological traditions" through bodily habit that produces objects with social meaning and embodies human relations.[28] Womanly work, hence, is a cultural symbol, a code that identifies the subject's position in the gendered system of intelligibility.

References to women's vernacular calligraphy in commemorative genres place writing, bodily discipline, and women's work on a semantic continuum. Yi Chae (1648–1746) writes the following lines about his aunt, Madame Yi of Yŏnan: "[Lady Yi] took pleasure in every kind of womanly work (*yŏgong* 女工), doing everything with great dexterity and bringing each task to perfection. Moreover, she wrote in elegant hand. To all the women of the house, a piece of her writing was a treasure."[29] In an epitaph for a girl who died in her youth, Song Siyŏl (1607–1689) notes, "You learned all womanly work (yŏgong 女工) by eight years of age, and there was nothing you could not do. You wrote letters instead of your mother, and she was never dissatisfied [with your writing]."[30] According to Madame Yi's son An Chŏngbok (1721–1791), she had "at six years learned the vernacular script that records the sounds of our language; at seven wrote letters instead of her elders, writing with great affection, beyond the mere officious greetings, which pleased each [addressed] person. Her skills of womanly work (yŏgong 女工) surpassed those of everyone else."[31] A woman's ability to write, one of the practical skills collectively termed "womanly work," fell within the repertoire of gender-marked bodily competence.

Women's epistolary calligraphy (see figure 2.1) was similarly linked to the maintenance of their families' immediate social circle. In a tomb inscription for his aunt Madame Yi of Hansan, Kim Chusin (1661–1721) writes: "Lady Yi was extremely diligent, and even in her advanced age she never put away her weaving instruments. When exchanging letters or sending food or clothing to someone else, she would always write the notes herself. The strokes of her brush were vigorous and upright, with not a single letter askew. Sometimes she would spend days on end [writing notes], but without ever showing so much as a sign of fatigue."[32] This praise for Madame Yi's calligraphy notably comes after a comment about her dedication to weaving; it is also linked to her social prowess—she takes utmost care to remember and maintain her immediate social network by sending gifts and writing accompanying notes in beautiful calligraphy.

Women's writing, a laborious and consuming activity, could also serve as a tangible token of filial piety or devotion to their parents-in-law. Of the various performances of filial piety, bodily offerings that inflicted harm on the filial subject were the most convincing.[33] In a tomb inscription for his aunt Madame Min (1678–1741), Min Usu (1694–1756) draws a connection between women's writing and filial piety:

> Master Yi [Madame Min's husband] in his late years retired to the countryside to take care of his elderly parents. [Madame Min's] mother-in-law, Madame Hwang, in her advanced age suffered from insomnia and thus took to vernacular fiction. Master Yi would not leave her side even for a moment, reading aloud for Madame Hwang. Madame Min took his place a number of times and then completely replaced him in this task. Later, if there were books that were of

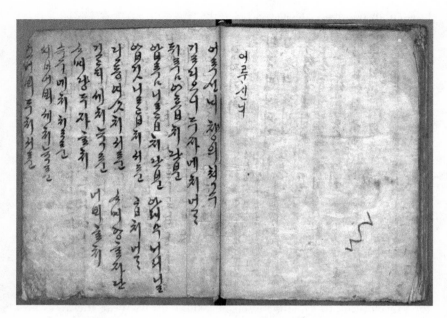

Figure 2.1 Posthumous biography of Madame Yun (Yun ssi haengjang).
Source: Courtesy of the Kyujanggak Archive, Seoul National University.

interest to Madame Hwang, Madame Min would do her best to
borrow them. Since she could not keep the borrowed books too long,
Madame Min would spend long nights copying them herself. In the
end, her eyes were so worn that a few times she was on the verge of
going blind. In this way Madame Min made utmost effort to please
Madame Hwang.[34]

Min Usu's note as well as the references to women's handwriting discussed
earlier show that the semantic range of women's vernacular Korean brushwork was distinct from the connoisseurship and self-cultivation achieved
in the male-centered practice of literary Chinese calligraphy.

As has been noted, much of our knowledge about women's lives in
Chosŏn Korea comes from male-authored sources that reveal considerable
ambivalence. Men propagated the womanly ideal of cultivated corporeality and domesticity, but they also registered the aesthetic and social value
of women's training in vernacular Korean handwriting. These sources
reveal the tension between the validated cultural significance of women's
vernacular brushwork and the status of the literary Chinese as the script of

high culture. The term *calligraphy*, retroactively applied to women's refined handwriting, consolidates the contours of women's culture hinted at in the surviving articles of women's calligraphy and in men's reticent praise of women's handwriting. In the next section, I examine the three aspects that allow us to speak of vernacular *calligraphy* rather than simply of handwriting: the meticulous process through which it was learned, its aesthetic dimension, and its social value.

Learning to Write: Men and Women

In adulthood, men and women were supposed to inhabit distinctive areas of society—public and domestic—and the meaning of calligraphy in their lives differed. Whereas for men calligraphy in literary Chinese became a means of moral self-cultivation and the highest aesthetic achievement, for women writing in elegant hand was a form of bodily discipline and an activity with practical social value. However, in the early stages of their education boys and girls acquired literacy in environments that were mixed in terms of gender and script, even using similar learning practices. Boys learned their first letters, both literary Chinese and vernacular Korean, from their mothers, while doting fathers and grandfathers often taught their daughters and granddaughters literary Chinese and poetry composition.

Madame Yun of Haep'yŏng, mother of the famed Chosŏn novelist Kim Manjung (1637–1692), was a well-known figure during her time. Kim Manjung's "Posthumous Biography of My Honorable Late Mother" ("Sŏnbi chŏnggyŏng puin haengjang" 先妣貞敬夫人行狀), a celebration of Madame Yun's exceptional virtues, circulated widely outside Kim Manjung's household. Kim Manjung recollects the difficulties his mother endured in order to educate her sons after her husband's death:

> Not much time has passed since the disaster [the Manchu Invasions (1627, 1636)], and no matter how hard one tried, books were difficult to come by. My mother exchanged grain for books such as *Mencius* (K. *Maengja*; Ch. *Mengzi* 孟子) and *The Doctrine of the Mean* (K. *Chungyong*; Ch. *Zhongyong* 中庸). My elder brother was particularly fond of *The Zuo's Commentary* (K. *Chwa ssi chŏn*; Ch. *Zuozhuan* 左氏傳/左傳), and when he heard that someone was selling this book and saw that it came in many volumes, he agreed to the purchase even before asking

the price. Mother then cut a bolt of silk in order to pay for the books—we really had nothing else to offer as payment. If some of our neighbors worked at the Office of Special Counselors, Mother would ask them to borrow the vernacular exegeses to the Four Books and *The Classic of Poetry* (K. *Sigyŏng*; Ch. *Shijing* 詩經), which she would then copy by hand. Her letters were like stringed pearls—exquisite and delicate, with not a single stroke remiss.[35]

Here, Kim Manjung highlights the decisive role Madame Yun played in her sons' early education during a time when books were scarce: she transcribes books by hand, cuts a bolt of silk to organize a payment for books, and uses the network of her connections to procure learning materials for her sons. He also praises Madame Yun's calligraphy, the first model for her sons' own handwriting.

Madame Yun's calligraphy is revisited in another biography composed by her grandson Kim Chin'gyu (1658–1716). Kim Chin'gyu recollects the words of his father (Kim Manjung's brother), Kim Man'gi (1633–1687): "Having lost his own father as a child, my father learned letters directly from my grandmother [Madame Yun], and in his late years he would ask his own grandchildren, 'If you had learned calligraphy from a woman, like I did, would your brushstrokes be the same as mine?'"[36] It is likely that Kim Man'gi is referring here to literary Chinese calligraphy because writing in vernacular Korean was never considered a great accomplishment for a man of letters; he also takes apparent pride in the fact that even though he learned it from a woman, his calligraphy lacks nothing in comparison to the handwriting of his male peers. Madame Yun's aptitude as a calligrapher and educator was cherished by her family across several generations. The fact that Madame Yun was able to develop a fine hand in both literary Chinese and vernacular Korean can be explained through numerous references to girls receiving instruction in literary Chinese from elder male members of their families. Pak Sedang (1629–1703), in the tombstone inscription for his granddaughter, notes that her father, while suffering from a protracted illness, taught his daughter literary Chinese calligraphy, and as a result "her brush was forceful and vigorous, unlike the writing of other women's small and weak hands."[37]

For men and women alike, family instruction was a crucial resource for calligraphic training. Yi Tŏngmu, for instance, recalled fondly how his own father copied *The Thousand-Character Classic* (K. *Ch'ŏnjamun*; Ch. *Qianziwen*

千字文) for him and his younger brother, Yi Kongmu.[38] Yi Tŏngmu then perpetuates calligraphic knowledge within his own family by constantly commenting on his nephew's calligraphy. Responding to one of his nephew's epistles, written in grass script, he writes, "The letter I just received is extremely difficult to read, and although [the writing style] is intricate, [looking at it] one feels as if one has fallen into a bush of thorns, and one cannot understand anything." Yi Tŏngmu cautions his nephew against unnecessary displays of calligraphic prowess: the harmony and simplicity of brushstrokes, not forced artistry, are the most convincing proof of one's skill.[39] In addition to family instruction, men turned to their intellectual networks in order to benefit from the advice dispensed by expert calligraphers. Kim Chŏnghŭi (1786–1856), perhaps the most renowned calligrapher of late Chosŏn, writes that he received numerous requests for letters from those who wanted to emulate his hand and thus hoped to secure his written response.[40] Kim Chŏnghŭi even conducted calligraphy contests among his disciples, where he corrected and commented on their brushwork.[41]

Careful attention to calligraphic training put under scrutiny the bodily comportment that accompanied this practice, and writing implements became objects of connoisseurship. Yi Tŏngmu, in his manual for daily comportment *Fine Manners for Gentlemen* (*Sasojŏl* 士小節), strongly discouraged men from spitting onto their ink stones instead of using water when making ink.[42] Yi also revealed his fascination with writing implements in such poems as "Ode to a Bamboo Brush Holder" ("Chuk p'ilt'ong myŏng" 竹筆筒銘) and "Ode to the Ink-Stone Case of Old Wood" ("Humok yŏn'gap myŏng" 朽木硯匣銘). In the latter poem, the worn exterior of the old wooden ink-stone case is unappealing to vulgar people, but to a knower it signifies a lifetime of calligraphic training.[43] Men's prowess in literary Chinese writing was an important part of their public identity, and it was interlaced with moral cultivation, etiquette, and connoisseurship.

The aesthetic dimension of women's practice of vernacular calligraphy was similarly imbued with moral and social significance, although of a different kind. Importantly, womanly work, or gender-marked productive bodily discipline, was a category with moral valence that generated self-worth and social respect. And although women's calligraphic connoisseurship might not have involved an extensive list of objects and manners, we can see that women relied on aesthetic circles, sharing letters and sketchbooks, and created intrafamilial lines of manuscript transmission that perpetuated the memory of skilled calligraphers across multiple generations.

Like men, women relied on their domestic networks to learn vernacular Korean calligraphy: familial letters and books were their main learning primers. Sin Kyŏng (1696–1766) writes the following about his mother: "My mother's brush strokes were elegant, firm, and measured, so all women at that time sought to emulate her hand. In writing letters, she focused on communicating just the gist without wasting paper for artful verbiage. All who received her letters relished them and longed to model them, but my mother had not the slightest liking for boasting about it."[44] Along with the reticent appreciation of his mother's beautiful handwriting and stylish prose, Sin Kyŏng reveals that women's epistles, as artifacts of fine vernacular calligraphy, were appreciated and used as style guides in women's circles.

Another way for women to learn calligraphy was by copying out fiction. One undated sketchbook includes carelessly copied excerpts of fiction and poetry alongside some items of practical advice, such as the most auspicious dates for placenta burial (see figure 2.1).[45] The text in this sketchbook is written in different hands, and along with letters traced in well-trained cursive brush there are jottings made with uncertain, childish brushstrokes. On page after page, wobbly brushwork patiently follows the playful, flowing letters of a skilled tutor; it is apparent at a glance that the cultivation of vernacular Korean writing was a much-desired skill that was acquired through assiduous application. The texts that were chosen for brushwork practice—a woman's posthumous biography and practical advice for placenta disposal—hint at the activities of female scribers, while the varying levels of skill illuminate a paradigm of communal learning.

As the following section shows, men and women were also wont to copy vernacular Korean novels together, practicing vernacular Korean handwriting in the circles of women of their household. Although Chosŏn society prescribed strict gender segregation from the age of seven forward, numerous extant records intimate that boys and girls often participated in the same activities in the domestic space: some girls learned to read and compose poetry in literary Chinese by listening to their brothers' lessons, and boys would often join in their sisters' pastimes.

The pride women took in vernacular Korean culture becomes apparent in a letter from Madame Kim of Andong to her son, Song Ikhŭm (1708–1757): "What is so hard about writing three–four letters in vernacular

Korean that you have to write your letter in literary Chinese?"[46] Kim Hoyŏnjae (1681–1772), Madame Kim, left a sizable body of literary Chinese poetry, but her epistles are masterpieces of vernacular Korean brushwork. Although she is amply proficient in literary Chinese, in urging her son to use the vernacular Korean script, Madame Kim also stakes out a cultural space, which is proudly acknowledged as the domain of women's choice and making. This exposes the gendered logic of representation that underlies men's references to women's vernacular Korean calligraphy as "orderly brushstrokes"—a term that downplays and marginalizes the aesthetic valence of vernacular Korean culture, which became a unique organizing pole for an array of women's aesthetic, moral, social, and embodied practices.

Despite the evident multidirectional exchanges between male and female scribers and between vernacular Korean and literary Chinese calligraphic practices, it is useful to map the scriptural economy of Chosŏn along the lines of its gender politics. Vernacular Korean and literary Chinese—it must be emphasized—acquire gendered connotations not at the level of practice but at the level of social visibility, as part of normative gender identities. Vernacular Korean proficiency garnered little prestige for men, and women's literary Chinese learning, although not unusual, was not on the spectrum of desired womanly accomplishments.

Vernacular Korean Calligraphy and the Lineage Novel

In the space of literary production, women's vernacular Korean calligraphy played an important role in defining the cultural prestige of the lineage novel, which constituted the vernacular canon of elite literature beginning in the seventeenth century. Chapter 1 has shown how the narrative space of the lineage novel is organized around generational succession, which embodies the perpetuity of kinship values. Lineage novels' manuscripts also capture the generational structure of kinship, but in a different way. The manuscript volumes, transmitted within the lineages in which they were created, accumulated numerous margin notes made by the generations of readers who encountered these familial manuscripts and expressed appreciation for their ancestors' handwriting. These manuscripts embody the affective texture of kinship as the somaticized brushstrokes of the deceased are contemplated by their descendants with filial reverence.

Hong Hŭibok's (1794–1859) preface to his translation of Li Ruzhen's (ca. 1763–1830) novel *Flowers in the Mirror* includes a note on the material properties of fiction circulating in late Chosŏn. Although Hong uses the term *vernacular fiction* (*ŏnmun sosŏl* 諺文) in his preface without distinguishing the lineage novel from other vernacular texts, he delineates the material textures of different types of books:

> [Lineage] novels are of massive size, some longer than a hundred volumes, other ones a few tens, the shortest being around ten volumes in length. The number of these novels must be thirty or forty. Indeed, there are other, lowly novels—the kind of *The Tale of Sukhyang* (*Sukhyang chŏn* 淑香傳) or *The Tale of Wind and Rain* (*P'ungu chŏn* 風雨傳). They are written in the common vulgar language, carved in lowly clumsy letters in woodblock, and sold at the market. I will not be able to record the titles of all of them.[47]

We know that Hong's general conception of vernacular fiction includes lineage novels because he mentions several titles earlier in the preface, also noting these texts' exceptional lengths. Although Hong refuses to distinguish between the contents of lineage novels and shorter vernacular Korean fiction, he marks their difference in terms of the mode of circulation, length, and material quality. Hong's dismissal of the variety of fiction written in "crude letters" and sold at the marketplace suggests that he and his contemporaries were wont to distinguish crude letters from refined handwriting.

Because lineage novels were too long and complex to be reproduced in woodblock editions, they were products of women's scribal activity, and kinship networks were responsible for their circulation. In the absence of a single known author, the names of women calligraphers are frequently recorded on the novels' margins alongside praise of their skill and work. This recording underscores the prominent role that women played in establishing the cultural prestige of the lineage novel and, more broadly, their role as calligraphers and readers in the culture of Chosŏn.

Collectively produced by and circulated among kinswomen, lineage novel manuscripts were regarded as valuable tokens of family refinement. As noted in the introduction, Kwŏn Sŏp (1671–1759) made a careful record of the books that his mother, Madame Yi of Yongin (1652–1712), copied in her own hand and consigned to the care of her family members. The

Andong Kwŏn did not have great wealth or social prestige, but they were a family of learning, and the tradition of copying and reading lineage novels was continued by generations of women who were born or married into the Kwŏn lineage. Kwŏn Chinŭng (1711–1775), Kwŏn Sŏp's grandson, eloquently records the esteem that lineage novel manuscripts continued to command in his family. For example, he writes the following about his mother, Madame Song of Onp'il (1676–1737):

At the time when I was six or seven years of age, my sisters and I stayed together with our mother. Dabbling with our brushes, we nearly spoiled one book. Snatching the book away, Mother scolded us: "This is *The Record of the Three Generations of the Han Lineage* (*Han ssi samdae rok* 韓氏三代錄), an old volume that I hand-copied in my childhood to practice writing. The story is not entirely proper, and my handwriting is childish, so there is hardly any worth to this book except that it has the letters of my deceased younger brother, which I cannot let perish." At that point, my sisters and I were prostrate at our mother's knees in fear. We were glad to have come off without punishment and took no note of the sadness that permeated my mother's words. We also had little idea of the value of that volume that has been transmitted through generations. Alas! Twenty years have passed since—how extreme are the changes of human affairs! Heaven! Oh, this sadness! In the summer of Kimi year, my wife, Madame O, sent me an old book with a boy servant. She implored, "This is the book that remains after your mother. How could you neglect your filial duty?" After this, I conducted a commemorative service twice, and these words forever remained in my heart. In a fit, I reached for the book and opened it to read. Before I even read until the middle, tears were streaming down my face, without me knowing. Alas! There remained letters of greeting written in my mother's hand, which she exchanged with my father, but *Record of the Three Generations of the Han Lineage* is the single book that survives. Sadly, the book has been damaged by mice, and more than half of it was ruined and torn beyond repair. Still, line after line of my mother's handwriting survive as mementos of the days now past. Alas! How dare I read this book again? And how could I shamelessly abandon this volume, even for a day, so that it came to this dire condition? Finally, after repairing the worn patches, supplementing the missing parts, and refurbishing its binding and cover, I wrote on the title page "Ink of the Deceased (Sŏnmok 先墨)." Now I am writing down these circumstances to reflect on my own stupidity and to give a warning to young children so that they refrain from repeating my foolishness of ruining a book.[48]

The ruined volume was even more precious to Kwŏn's mother because it contained the handwriting of her brother, Kwŏn Chinŭng's maternal uncle—the two siblings copied the volume together in their youth, a fact that underscores the fluidity of gender boundaries in vernacular Korean culture. Reproaching himself for the negligence that ruined the precious volume, Kwŏn Chinŭng importantly establishes the prestige of lineage novels' manuscripts over letters. His text thus highlights the intersection of women's vernacular calligraphy, literary production, and private memory making through the intrafamilial preservation of writings.

Among kinswomen, lineage novel manuscripts turned into special objects of intimate significance. The sequel cluster consisting of *The Remarkable Reunion of Jade Mandarin Ducks* and *The Commentary to Jade Mandarin Ducks* produced in the family of Madame Chŏng of Onyang (1725–1799) is a unique artifact of intergenerational readership. Although written mostly in Madame Chŏng's hand, the manuscript also contains margin marks by other women in her family, expressing their pleasure at beholding her brushstrokes after her death. One anonymous remark on the margin reads: "The handwriting belongs to Madame Chŏng of Onyang. This is a book that has been preserved and transmitted across several generations. If your hands are damp with sweat, do not just thumb through this book, but wrap [your hands] in something before holding it. The exquisite handwriting of Madame Chŏng of Onyang" (see figure 2.2).[49]

The Commentary is written on the reverse sides of letters exchanged within this family. The letters, written in literary Chinese and vernacular Korean by writers of different genders, ages, and calligraphic skills, constitute an added layer of calligraphic texture. The volume covers were reverently refurbished in 1847, about sixty years after the manuscript's creation, by Madame Yun of Haep'yŏng, wife of Madame Chŏng's great-grandson.[50] To borrow Reginald Jackson's words from his study of *The Tale of Genji* (J. *Genji monogatari* 源氏物語) scrolls, "calligraphy produced for the reader the sense of corporeal closeness."[51] In lineage novels, the encounters happen within the space of kinship. The manuscripts of the

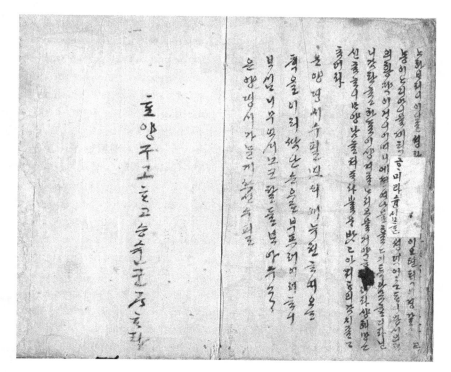

Figure 2.2 Leaf with a margin note from *The Remarkable Reunion of Jade Mandarin Ducks (Ogwŏn chaehap kiyŏn)*.
Source: Courtesy of the Kyujanggak Archive, Seoul National University.

Jade Mandarin Ducks sequel cluster coordinate the encounter—as aesthetic and affective connection—between several generations of Madame Chŏng's kinswomen. This manuscript is unique in the amount of information its margin notes supply, but similar margin notes commemorating the scribal efforts of deceased kinswomen can be found in other lineage novels' manuscripts. In an undated and anonymous manuscript of *The Record of Two Heroes: Brothers Hyŏn*, a margin note reads: "This tale contains my eighty-year-old mother's writing, combined with the gemlike, exquisite handwriting of my nieces and my nephews' wives. Will anyone recognize their writing later? It is unfortunate that the pearl-like letters of the mothers are so scarce."[52] Notes such as this one illuminate the sentimental value of lineage novels' manuscripts in the culture of the Chosŏn elites; the irreducible materiality of the ancestral brushwork warranted the filial preservation of these texts across generations.

Although manuscript culture was clearly linked to women's practice of vernacular Korean calligraphy, which was embedded in the repertoire of productive corporeal work that women performed in their households, the question of lineage novel authorship remains unanswered. Contemporary records seem to suggest that women were not merely the calligraphers but also the authors of lineage novels, yet not a single woman novelist can be definitively named for the Chosŏn period. In his encyclopedic miscellany *The Miscellaneous Records of Songnam* (*Songnam chapchi* 松南雜識), Cho Chae-sam (1808–1866) notes: "It is said that *Moon-Gazing* (*Wanwŏl* 玩月) is written by the mother of An Kyŏmje (1724–1791)—she wanted to circulate it inside the inner palace to increase her fame."[53] *The Pledge at the Banquet of Moon-Gazing Pavilion,* with 180 manuscript volumes, is the longest novel in the early modern Korean canon; such an abbreviated reference to the author of this massive work is intriguing. However, the miscellany's imprecision in making other attributions casts doubt on the credibility of its identification of Madame Yi's authorship.[54] Madame Yi of Chŏnju (1694–1743), the mother of An Kyŏmje, is indeed a historical person who grew up in an elite household and married into another, somewhat less prominent lineage. Her class and education make her authorship plausible,[55] but Cho Chaesam's note remains unverified.

A similar intimation of a woman's authorship is inscribed in a margin note that appears at the end of the *Jade Mandarin Ducks* manuscript transmitted in Madame Chŏng of Onyang's family. The note reads: "It is a pity that the literary talent and erudition of the person who composed *Jade Mandarin Ducks* (*Ogwŏn* 玉鴛) is buried in the inner quarters (*kyubang* 閨房) and used for such useless miscellaneous writing (*chapchŏ* 雜著)."[56] The note, then, proceeds to attribute other novels to the same author. It is unclear who wrote the note or who is being identified as the author of *Jade Mandarin Ducks.*[57] Chosŏn-era sources referring to women's literary ability—often using the term *female scholars*—also lament that such talents have no application in women's lives. Although *Jade Mandarin Ducks* is called "useless miscellaneous writing," this remark has to be contextualized by the ultimate prestige of literary Chinese composition at the time and not as a necessarily derogative attitude toward the lineage novel. The fact that literary talent is said to be wasted in female quarters points to a female author, although the veracity of this statement is likewise impossible to confirm. We might surmise that many of the lineage novels' authors were men because it was not uncommon for men to write fiction in both

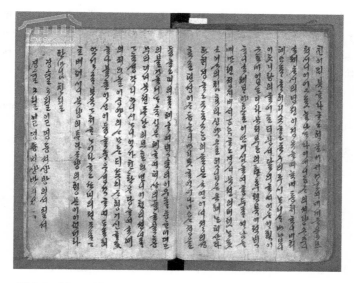

Figure 2.3 This leaf from *The Remarkable Reunion of Jade Mandarin Ducks* showcases the calligraphic skills displayed in this manuscript.
Source: Courtesy of the Kyujanggak Archive, Seoul National University.

literary Chinese and vernacular Korean. These notes, however, suggest the possibility of women's creative engagement with the world of vernacular writing. Given the communal mode of manuscript production, intimated in Kwŏn Chinŭng's note, collective authorship of lineage novels by men and women of the same family appears especially likely.

After decentering the contested issue of authorship, a privileged notion of textual creativity, we can discern the register of corporeal discipline and aesthetic cultivation of Chosŏn elite women behind the creation of intricate lineage novels' manuscripts (see figure 2.3). For much of their history, lineage novels circulated exclusively in the form of family-transmitted manuscripts,[58] and through women's skilled handiwork these manuscripts became specimens of fine calligraphy as well as objects of sentimental value. The materiality of the lineage novel is highlighted in men's writing—both Kwŏn Sŏp and Kwŏn Chinŭng focus on the process of transcribing and transmitting the novels but mention nothing at all about their narrative content. Women scribers of Chosŏn were recognized for their aesthetic training and for the effort they put into the creation of lineage novels' manuscripts. Their calligraphic work, just like the embodied womanly work discussed earlier in the chapter, was evaluated in the context of kinship roles and appreciated for the affective texture of domestic life it created. We can also see that these elite female calligraphers skillfully navigated the gender norms of their time, carving out a space for aesthetic cultivation within the prescriptive repertoire of femininity, focused on corporeal domestic work. As the center of elite vernacular Korean culture, women's quarters produced an extensive cultural realm of reading, calligraphic training, and, possibly, novelistic composition.

In Conclusion

In South Korea's contemporary scholarship and cultural projects, vernacular Korean or palace-style brushwork has long been accepted as a full-fledged calligraphic practice,[59] celebrated for its indigenous origins. We can certainly see this view as part of an extended decolonizing project that stretches from Japan's annexation of Korea in 1910 to the post-1945 South Korean historical scholarship. On the verge of colonization, it became the primary task of Korean nationalist intellectuals to disentangle the indigenous culture from the Confucian system founded upon the literary Chinese canon, seen as a foreign "borrowing" that stifled "native" creative impulse.[60]

This chapter has traced the contours of elite vernacular Korean calligraphy, which became the domain of elite women's creativity and which was shaped by the kinship system that prescribed domestic lives and embodied work for Chosŏn women. The aesthetic aspect of vernacular Korean calligraphy, notably, is distributed across the register of bodily discipline. Far from asserting the separation of the female cultural realm from male aesthetic practices, I have mapped a series of vital links between them and have shown that elite men were versed in vernacular Korean, and elite women could read and write literary Chinese. The repertoire of women's work, conceived in accordance with women's roles in the kinship system, clearly provides a framework for understanding cultivated vernacular brushwork as part of women's productive social identities. The vernacular Korean cultural realm, therefore, cannot be treated as an oasis of absolute creative freedom. The emergence of vernacular Korean calligraphy, in short, is directly linked to the rise of Chosŏn's kinship structure and the domesticization of women's lives and identities.

Women's vernacular writing was implicated in the creation of the palimpsest of intrafamilial memories. The sentimental significance of vernacular Korean calligraphy lends an extra layer of meaning to lineage novels. Thomas Lamarre reminds us that in Heian manuscripts inscription has a range of meaning that exceeds signification. Calligraphy and the texture of the inscribed page are balanced on the boundary between the cosmological and the social, with calligraphy akin to a corporeal performance of a text.[61] In a similar way, lineage novels' manuscripts capture corporeal performances of kinship-based aesthetics. Just as the narratives of these texts grew to include ever new generations of protagonists, their manuscripts also had an infinitely expandable structure: notes upon notes in the margins captured encounters between the new generations of the lineage and the brushstrokes of their ancestors. Notably, this vernacular kinship culture is configured around female figures, the principal makers and readers of lineage novels' manuscripts.

The scope of elite vernacular Korean culture and the prestige it had in Chosŏn society make its obscurity all the more striking: it remained unknown to broader academic and general audiences until the 1990s, and I remark on the itinerary of elite vernacular Korean culture in twentieth-century scholarship in chapter 5. Much in excess of its purely demotic connotations that predominate in historical thinking—certainly under the influence of the highly visible promulgation edict for the Korean script—vernacular Korean culture of late Chosŏn was a sophisticated and lively domain with clearly distinct elite and demotic layers.

The prestige of literary Chinese learning in Chosŏn society obscured the contours of women's elite vernacular Korean culture to latter-day historians. Reconstructing the contours of this space requires archaeological engagement with the gendered logic of representation that predominates in the male-authored sources of the period. Although male writers of Chosŏn refused to designate women's vernacular Korean brushwork as calligraphy, they were wont to praise women's vernacular Korean handwriting. My reading of women's creative presence beneath the script of patriarchal authority is inspired by Hui-shu Lee, a China historian who has unraveled the gendered system of representation in Song-dynasty art. Lee shows how through a series of fellowships and negotiations women carved out a space for their own creative practice—for example, the palace women who acted as ghost scribes for Emperor Gaozong (r. 1127–1162) entered the aesthetic space under his name.[62] Similarly, the gendered logic that governs men's representations of women's lives—if deciphered—reveals that the Confucian patriarchy of Chosŏn was a carefully and rigorously constructed model of people's relationships that was open to maneuverability—an advantage that elite women, as we see, freely availed themselves of to become active producers of culture.

Last, a note is due on the nature and the historical fate of the vernacular Korean canon. Canon formation is commonly understood as a process of exclusion and empowerment that perpetuates the cultural capital of a particular group of people. According to this view, Korean vernacular practices did not coalesce into a canon because they were circulated in narrow, familial groups of women who did not have access to the public space of connoisseurship and exchange outside the domestic realm. John Guillory, however, suggests a compelling redefinition of canonicity; he argues that "the most socially consequential process of exclusion occurs primarily at the level of access to literacy."[63] In other words, canonicity inheres not in the relationship between canonical and noncanonical works but in the sociohistorical aspect of writing, which includes some groups but excludes others.

The rise of an elite vernacular Korean canon in Chosŏn should be understood precisely in terms of the access to literacy and aesthetic cultivation that it opened up for women, whose social identities were based on the productive bodily work they performed and on the stratified social system that relied on cultural capital for the articulation of status distinctions. The emergence of the lineage novel and vernacular Korean calligraphy expanded the range of women's bodily competencies to include aesthetic cultivation, which in turn contributed to their families' prestige. Quite unlike the Chinese vernacular, which was monopolized by elite men, or the vernacular literary forms that were canonized early in Japanese history and were practiced by both men and women, vernacular Korean cultural production was entangled with the Chosŏn kinship structure as well as with the ideal of women's domesticity and bodily discipline that structure prescribed.

PART II

The Affective Coordinates of Kinship

CHAPTER III

Feelings and the Space of the Novel

T he narrative architecture and the manuscript form of the lineage novel reflect a genealogical principle of operation. The narratives have an open horizon that can expand indefinitely with the new generations of the central lineage. The manuscripts, carefully transmitted through generations of kinfolk, accumulate an ever-expanding paratext of encounters with the brushstrokes of the deceased kinswomen transcribed on the novels' margins. Generational reciprocity perpetuates kinship ideology and culture. But lineage novels also chart the struggles and contradictions that are central to this reciprocity and perpetuity. Their narratives center on the process by which unruly feelings are brought into alignment with social norms.

In the lineage novel, feelings are visible and legible indices that chart a variety of significant boundaries for human reciprocity. Drawing on lineage novels of late Chosŏn Korea, this chapter examines the capacity of emotions to define the structure of the larger world, kinship, and self. Lineage novels elaborate a major historical transformation of early modern Korean society that occurred in the seventeenth century: the emergence of patrilineal kinship. In these texts, the contradictions and values of this process are rendered on a scale that is at once massive and intimate. Lineage novels inscribe kinship in the context of world significance, and the boundary between kin and nonkin assumes a fundamental, world-structuring function. When it comes to the problematic junctures of personal and social meaning, the lineage novel looks into the space of the self, which becomes the site of complex negotiations among duty, self-perception, and self-expression. This chapter outlines the way world, kinship, and self in the lineage novel are charted through affective coordinates.

Scholars agree that feelings are neither disorganized spontaneous emanations opposed to reason nor intensely private experiences that occur in the mysterious realm of interiority detached from the social.[1] Barbara Rosenwein, a historian of medieval Europe, makes a case for taking emotions seriously in historical inquiry.[2] For Rosenwein, emotions are acts suspended between normative social structures and strategic identity taking. As junctures of the social and the personal, emotions are historically conditioned; this is why Rosenwein foregrounds the idea of "emotional communities" in which emotions provide "shared vocabularies of thinking that have a controlling function."[3] Anthropologists similarly recognize patterns of social life in expressions of emotion. In her classic study of a Micronesian atoll, Catherine Lutz concludes that feelings function as the "index of social relations," an indication that "a cultural knowledge system for interpreting self and other is at work."[4] Feelings, in other words, are historically contingent vocabularies of social relations, and these shared vocabularies constitute theories of the social world and practical guides for action therein.

In the Confucian culture of Chosŏn Korea, family was understood as a microcosm of fundamental relationships that radiated into the larger world. In the words of Mencius, "The root of the kingdom is the state. The root of the state is the family. The root of the family is the person of its head."[5] Family facilitates the central affective dispositions, which Mencius describes as "love between father and son, duty between ruler and subject, distinction between husband and wife, precedence of the old over the young, and faith between friends."[6] The hierarchy and affection of the father–son bond notably served as the model for the ruler–subject relationship. Radiating from the space of the home, these relationships extended as far as imperial frontiers: the sovereign's virtue was expected to exert moral influence over his subjects.[7] The important requirement of this system of ordering is that persons be capable of bringing their feelings into convergence with the objective system of order (K. *kong*; Ch. *gong* 公), thus preventing selfish (K. *sa*; Ch. *si* 私) attachments and desires from obscuring and upsetting the harmonious flow of feelings through ethically prescribed social bonds.

Bringing order to human emotions and relationships was the Chosŏn state's fundamental political and social aim, conceived and proclaimed under the auspices of the Confucian moral vision. As shown in the introduction and chapter 1, the creation of the lineage structure was central to this vision, and its emergence dramatically altered the social and cultural landscape in Chosŏn Korea as well as the everyday experience of all who lived in populous domestic communities. Martina Deuchler has noted that the main issue for the Chosŏn dynasty's founders was giving appropriate forms of expression to human sentiments. The state adopted the rituals of ancient China, which were created, it was believed, "after closely evaluating human nature and matching social institutions to human needs" in order to provide people with "suitable models for correcting their feelings." Grounding the practice of filial piety in ancestral worship ritual—a vehicle for the expression of ethical human feelings—the lineage streamlined generations of descendants according to the logic of patrilineality and primogeniture to secure the correct configuration of descendants for ancestral service. The marginalization of affinal links through the lowering of mourning grades for maternal kin and virilocal marriage arrangement was also a matter of affective reorganization. In Deuchler's view, the reforms were an "attempt to create a new social milieu in which sentiment and allegiance would shift from matrilateral to patrilateral kin and the married couple would reside virilocally."[8]

In the ideology and institutions of Korean patrilineal kinship, feelings had a fundamental, practical function: kinship hierarchies and practice demanded that each person fulfill his or her prescribed social role(s) with absolute sincerity (K. sŏng; Ch. cheng 誠). The lineage novel takes us beyond normative ideology and institutions, outlining a theory of practice refracted in this aesthetic archive. The system of affective coordinates in the lineage novel is multilayered. First of all, these texts operate with the major Confucian concept of human feelings (K. injŏng; Ch. renqing 人情), or ethically ordered sentiments that are integral to human nature and essential to social cohesion. Human sentiments signify the fulfillment of fundamental human bonds. Second, lineage novels capture the historical details of Korean kinship, which—though configured according to the Confucian model—carried its own distinctive traits. One of the most conspicuous idiosyncrasies of the Korean kinship system was "the continued strength of the maternal line of descent in determining and reproducing elite status."[9] The resilience of affinal connections was a direct violation of the prescription that ethical sentiments be transposable and centered on the patriline. Of particular note is the lineage novel's valorization of "feelings of flesh and blood" (*kolyuk chi chŏng* 骨肉之情),[10] which violate the ethical norm of kinship and have incontrovertible power.

The lineage novel overlays these two types of kinship community: the one based on the objective ideal of human feelings and the one that recognizes the persistence of inalienable blood bonds, such as those between parents and children or between siblings.[11] Although human feelings are posited as the incontestable ideal, feelings of flesh and blood are also acknowledged as powerful affective foundations of human relationships that cannot be disarticulated through ritual prescription. In the lineage novel, the dissonance between the contours of ritual kinship and blood kinship produces unruly emotions that erupt in unruly conduct. These unruly emanations do not have a productive social function but instead serve as indices of the most problematic aspects of the norm, with which lineage novels' protagonists are at odds. Highlighting situations that are out of joint, unruly feelings call for moral effort to repair the rift within the relational network.

Unruly feelings are pointedly visible in the lineage novel—they are always a matter of exteriority and witnessing. Protagonists speak profusely to a listener about the origin and vagaries of their feelings. A listener might be taciturn, adding little and provoking no further thought. Nevertheless, the protagonists are always *seen* and *heard*. Their unruly feelings are always social—interpreted in front of and in relation to others. Although these feelings trace the unique personal trajectory of a protagonist's life experience, they must always be situated within the concatenation of human bonds. When unruly feelings are unexteriorized, unexpressed in the social context, they constitute a troubled, negative interior, a configuration that is in striking contrast to the modern Western identification of interiority with personal depth. In short, in the lineage novel the exteriority and visibility of feelings constitute boundaries of affective reciprocity and define the grammar of sociality.

Centered on the main patrilineal household, the lineage novel's expansive geocultural terrain comprises the domestic space, with its rich texture of daily interactions; the royal court of Song or Ming China, which provides the habitual setting for Chosŏn novels; and the barbaric lands of Mongols, Vietnam, and Parhae, located on the fringes of the civilized realm. The domestic space of the lineage is the aesthetic center of the narrative: it anchors the civilized world. This patrilineal household is represented as the source of hereditary dedication to moral virtue that is maintained with great effort against malignant, disruptive forces. The domestic space is also center stage for tumultuous negotiations between the protagonists' unruly feelings and their prescribed roles in the kinship structure. This placement of the domestic realm within the larger geocultural context places the problem of affective order on the horizon of world significance. The well-ordered home, in short, guarantees the stability of the world.

In the lineage novel, kinship encompasses the totality of human relationships. Curiously, among the most prominently displayed feelings in the lineage novel is the so-called longing for one's parents (sach'in chi sim 思親之心). A particular type of speech always accompanies separations and reunions. Protagonists who set out on expeditions to barbaric lands or are thrown into circumstances beyond their control—ranging from kidnappings to travel accidents that produce involuntary separations from their kin—lament profusely the loss of the familiar kinship context. The emotions that connect these protagonists to their kin—the most immediate domain of a person's belonging—are viscous like honey, and separation is construed as a physical sensation of being "pulled out" of affective kinship bonds. Reunions similarly are accompanied by manifestations of joy. Feelings of longing for one's kin mark the boundary between affective kinspace and the world outside that forecloses emotional reciprocity. When the lineage novels' protagonists are outside the civilized space of kinship, they exude a benevolent influence—a hierarchical, downward-working moral power—but no affective reciprocity.

What are the boundaries of social reciprocity in the lineage novel? And how are the contours of the kinship community drawn across the two relational structures—one based on blood and the other on ritual? In this chapter, I outline the dramatized distinction between the space of affective kinship and its negative outside. I look into a taxonomy of feelings organized according to their productive social function—human feelings, feelings of flesh and blood, and unruly feelings. And, finally, I show how lineage novels, in tracing the boundaries of the self, locate an area that has the potential to remain foreclosed to reciprocity.

The Home and the World

Korean lineage novels are tens and even hundreds of manuscript volumes (kwŏn 卷) long, capacious enough for a vast imaginative geography that spans from the court of the Chinese Son of Heaven—in Song or Ming China—to the barbaric realms of Yunnan, Mongols, and Parhae. These unstable lands on the periphery of the Confucian empire are prone to rebellion and unrest but are quelled in due course by the representatives of the main lineage. Nestled in the middle of this vast geographical expanse, the domestic space is its cradle of refinement; it produces Confucian gentlemen who spread the civilization outward. This is what Nicola di Cosmo describes as "a radiating civilization, shedding its light in progressively dimming quantity on the surrounding areas."[12] Because civilization in the lineage novel radiates from the home space, the domestic realm acquires world-constituting significance.

Taking into account what Franco Moretti calls "the place-bound nature of literary forms," it is important to reflect on the spatial arrangement of the lineage novel—"its peculiar geometry, its boundaries, its spatial taboos and favorite routes," which "reveal the internal logic of the narrative."[13] Rather than delineating the geocultural conception of self and other that unfolds in Confucian rhetoric,[14] my goal is to canvass the conceptual horizon of the discourse of feelings in the lineage novel. What are the boundaries of the space in which emotions are transacted? And why is the domestic realm, described through the intimate texture of touch and gaze, situated in a world that extends far beyond it? In other words, what stands behind the juxtaposition of these spaces, and how is the boundary between them articulated?

Each lineage novel focuses on one prominent lineage, the first among equals. The domestic quarters of this lineage constitute the spatial center of the narrative, and the lineage's offspring guarantee an uninterrupted supply of protagonists. The main household's ritualized propriety and prosperity—which is naturally allotted to an illustrious lineage (with one exception, all of the novels discussed in this book feature affluent households)—are captured in the banquet scenes. For example, the banquet at the Moon-Gazing Pavilion described in the first volume of *The Pledge* becomes an occasion for the arrangements of marriages and heir adoption:

On this day, the upper seats are arranged according to the royal decree, and the lower banquet is set up by the two Chŏng brothers, offering prayers for the Patriarch's longevity. Imperial relatives are present, and luminous clouds and auspicious energy permeate the place, while wine fumes cloud the minds. Precious gems are in abundance just like seashore pebbles, and beautifully made-up faces are everywhere, like common sand. There are maidens, tender and pure, and ladies, gentle and delicate. This truly is the congregation of honor, elegance, virtue, and sagacity. Bright jewels dangle over mistlike robes while cloudlike fans waver softly. Matriarch's dignified look is complimented by her daughters-in-law—with Madame Yang's wisdom, Madame Sang's cordiality, and the uprightness of Madame Hwa. All the guests' eyes are riveted upon them. Next enters Patriarch. All women retreat, and the guests rise from their seats in greeting.[15]

Honored by the imperial favor, Chŏng Han emerges to preside over a perfectly ordered household that appears ritually arranged, beautifully prosperous, and morally satisfying before his eyes, just as the banquet seats are taken. The banquet scene conveys a promise that the lineage will endure over time: the children of the Chŏng lineage and those in their closest social circle are pledged to marry. The pledges also signify the moral constancy of this household: "A gentleman's pledge is unchangeable for a thousand years and is unaffected by prosperity or misfortune."[16]

The refinement of the central lineage is emphatically connected to the status of civil elites—those who devote their lives to the study of Confucian classics, belles lettres, and service in the civil bureaucracy. The title used to designate Chosŏn elites—*yangban* (兩班), literally "two divisions"—points to the dual composition of the Chosŏn aristocracy, comprising the civil branch (*munban* 文班) and the military branch (*muban* 武班). Although in reality the two branches were closely affiliated through intermarriage and adoption,[17] members of the civil branch occupied major government positions and enjoyed greater social prestige. Lineage novels mark the superiority of their protagonists, who belong to civil lineages, over members of military branches, who are uncouth and unrefined.[18] This is not to say that lineage novels completely disregard martial abilities: their male protagonists are highly capable generals who quell rebellions on behalf of the emperor. It is just that their skill in the art of war is counterbalanced by their civility, and the latter is a more important status marker.

Within the households of these civil elites, life is charted by the central Confucian rituals—capping, marriage, funeral, and mourning (*kwan hon sang che* 冠婚喪祭)—which are performed with impeccable regularity. Laid out especially carefully are the elaborate details of marriage ceremonies: the wedding conducted at the bride's house (*sŏnghon* 成婚), the bride's induction into her husband's household (*ch'in'yŏng* 親迎), and, finally, her appearance before the parents-in-law and the presentation of the dowry (*napp'ye* 納幣).[19] The novels also assiduously record the punctilious performance of daily decorum—morning and evening greetings from the younger members of the household to their elders. This focus on daily propriety and ritual is deliberate, conspicuous, and highly significant in the articulation of the domestic space. The carefully enacted life-cycle rituals constitute the rhythm that syncs the individual lifetime with the transition through crucial human relationships aligned with the ethical norm. This ritually ordered lineage home is presented in direct juxtaposition to the barbaric spaces that surround the civilized center and threaten to undermine it. The home extends its civilizing influence by producing upright gentlemen, who in turn spread civilization outward, quelling provincial rebellions; their military prowess is reinforced by the supreme morality they embody.

The home realm and outer spaces are intimately interlaced in the three-novel sequel centered on the patriline of the Hyŏn lineage: *Brothers Hyŏn*, *Pearls*, and *Pearls and Jade*. The pearls referenced in the titles of the second and third novels are used as betrothal gifts in the marriages of three generations of Hyŏn men. Hyŏn Kyŏngmun, protagonist of the first novel, receives the precious jewels from the king of Unnam (Ch. Yunnan 雲南) after his army quells a local rebellion. In the second novel, Hyŏn Kyŏngmun transfers the pearls to his son and nephew, and the pearls are passed down to the next generation in the third novel. These charismatic tokens are lost and found in a variety of convoluted circumstances, but over the life span of the three generations they keep coming back. In both good fortune and adversity, the pearls have a strong connection to the couples who exemplify the best moral qualities and hence are predestined to marry and continue the lineage. A gift from the subjugated king who recognizes the suzerainty of the Confucian empire, the pearls epitomize cultural conquest. They link the expanding Confucian civilization to marriage, a fundamental moral bond. This bond is also seen in the lineage novel as a highly privatized relationship that is threatened by the spouses' unruly feelings. Harmonizing the conjugal union against these unruly passions is an arduous task that lineage novels depict in great detail. As nuptial gifts, the pearls connect the outer and the inner boundaries of the ordered world and signal the constant need to uphold those boundaries.

The lineage and the civilized political center are often besieged by lecherous women, magicians, and rebellious rulers.[20] Practitioners of magic are among the most vicious adversaries. They embody the antithesis of Confucian culture in their amorphousness and disavowal of fundamental human bonds. In *The Pledge*, for instance, a Daoist practitioner, Yohwa, attempts to undermine the basic tenets of the Confucian world:

> Even a sage like Yo (Ch. Yao) of the Tang had said that having multiple descendants brings multiple worries, while long life engenders a multitude of desires. The sagacious Yo was warning against having multiple descendants. People of the world nowadays are ignorant and bankrupt. Overcome with greed for possessions, they fail to see that we live in a drifting world, just like mayflies. Men bedeck themselves in Confucian caps and robes, professing to be disciples of a certain Master Confucius; women don wedding outfits and rejoice in their virtue of producing multiple descendants. I simply laugh at this.[21]

In asserting the transience of earthly being, Yohwa attempts to entice the members of the Chŏng household to join her camp and abandon the Confucian ways that she says lead to nothing more than delusion. Not every magician in the lineage novel has such a clearly formulated philosophy. But by changing their appearance at will, impersonating lineage members, and generally wreaking havoc, all magicians undermine the clearly formulated underpinning of identities and relationships.

In *Pearls and Jade*, a lovelorn magician, Uhwa, steals into the chamber of the man she lusts after by turning herself into a butterfly. Naturally perspicacious, the unwilling lover immediately doubts the innocence of the insect on his wall and with a light swing of his hand tries to dislodge it. With a rather human cry—"Ouch! (*aego*)"—the butterfly soars into the air, leaving behind a human tooth, knocked out by the blow.[22] Magicians are the worst possible offenders; they have no kinship structure, no home, and not even a fixed form. With their power to metamorphose and traverse sweeping distances, they have nothing in common with the civilized human culture, and they are usually killed.

Barbarians, however, are amenable to moral influence. Barbaric lands, located on the fringes of civilization, represent a more stable outside to the well-ordered political and domestic space. Lineage novels sometimes capture the strangeness of life in the foreign lands. *The Pledge*, for instance, includes a brief description of Parhae (Ch. Bohai 渤海):[23]

> About five hundred *li* from the borders of Namwŏl (Ch. Nanyue 南越), there is a country of Parhae. Among all other barbarians, the appearance of its people is most frightening. [People of Parhae] clothe themselves in grass and leaves, and they do not cultivate land. Feeding mostly on wild beasts, herbs and fruits, cows, horses, chickens, and dogs, sometimes they also eat people. In their hideousness they are no different from beasts. Because human skin is tough and thick, they make their armor of human skin. In battle, even when swords and lances are hitting their bodies, their armor withstands the attack. Ferocious like flying birds, these people are tough like stone and metal. The skin of [Parhae people] is strangely oily, as if smeared with grease, so if caught on fire [they] would burn day and night. This seems to be the reason why they especially fear and avoid fire and do not eat cooked food. They are formidable warriors, ferocious in fight, and even when other barbarians fight each other, they cannot easily attack Parhae.[24]

In *The Pledge*, Parhae represents the proverbial antithesis to the civilized human life.

Constantly immersed in warfare, Parhae knows no technologies of everyday life, such as cooking and weaving. Residents of Parhae seem oblivious to the distinction between people and birds and beasts—they feed on animals and humans alike. Curiously, the novel does not dwell for long on the strangeness of Parhae. It only briefly describes the aftermath of an invasion: set on fire, the residents of Parhae burn day and night until the population is thoroughly decimated. The novel reveals no fascination with exotic detail—after marking the space of Parhae as radically alien, the narrative quickly moves on to the state that borders Parhae—Tongwŏl (Ch. Dongyue 東越).[25]

Tongwŏl merits a significantly longer and more engaging narrative because it offers a plot of feelings rather than mere exotic scene. The story of a young prince's grievance and his quest to redress it (sŏrwŏn 雪冤) is laid out in detail. Prince T'apt'al'yu is deeply disgruntled after his father, the depraved king T'apt'algye, dies at the hands of the Ming army under the leadership of the illustrious Chŏng Inung. King T'apt'algye's debacle is self-inflicted: he raised an unlawful rebellion against the Ming suzerainty. Nevertheless, for T'apt'al'yu, avenging the death of his father is a filial duty that he pursues passionately despite his conflicting loyalties—political and filial: "It is not my ambition to go against a great country and plot a rebellion. It is just that I cannot tolerate the pain of knowing that my father's name is tarnished for posterity and that he died to no good purpose. I need to cleanse this offense. As a son, I need to avenge my father's death, and if I fail and die on the battlefield amid the innumerable enemy army, I will have fulfilled my feelings and intent. Even if heaven does not help me, there is nothing else I can do."[26] Willing to sacrifice his life in order to redress his grievance (wŏnsa 怨死), Prince T'apt'al'yu cuts a poignant if not faultless figure. The sincerity of his grief is especially moving because he was unloved and unwanted by his father. The father's fondness for his younger offspring prompted him to resent T'apt'al'yu—indeed, he even attempted to remove his older son from the line of succession. Prince T'apt'al'yu is depicted as a noble savage: "among the barbarians, T'apt'al'yu is wise and eager to learn; he is loyal and filial, and his conduct extraordinary and without a fault."[27] The prince's life follows a standard Confucian course toward moral transformation and acceptance of Ming suzerainty. Importantly, his story's significance lies in its plot of feelings. Here the system of affective coordinates offers a rubric for comprehending and organizing the geocultural space of the narrative.

Namwŏl (Ch. Nanyue 南越) is the venue for another plot of feelings in *Pearls*. Two Namwŏl princes are involved in a bitter succession dispute. Of the same age but with different pedigrees, the princes have different mothers: one a queen, the other a concubine. Hyŏn Hŭngnin, at the head of the Song army that pacifies the realm, decides to pass the throne to the queen's son. The rejected prince comes to Hyŏn Hŭngnin's bedchamber one night with a dagger. Professing his anger (punham 憤) at the succession decision, he explains that he is in fact his father's beloved son (ch'ongaeja 寵愛子). He then promises to kill Hŭngnin first and then his own half-brother, who has been selected as the crown prince. Hŭngnin explains that the affection shared by those of the same flesh and blood is like "the precious feelings between hands and feet"—with hands and feet missing, a person is decrepit ("*pyŏngjan chi in*" 病殘之人).[28] This lesson in the proper ordering of feelings bears fruit, and the rebellious prince achieves correct understanding. This story, too, is noteworthy for its plot of feelings: the rebellious prince has unruly feelings of anger and vengefulness that are not aligned with the appropriate sibling affection described by Hŭngnin. Moreover, the prince comes to understand that his father's love for him plays no role in his succession decision, which is based on the appropriate order of descent.

In short, feelings rather than the exotic details of a foreign lifestyle command attention in the lineage novel. Observable, manifested feelings constitute the phenotype of a people, which is measured against the ideal of harmonious human bonds. What distinguishes those who live outside the civilized bounds of kinship from those who live in the domestic space of the central lineage is the dissonance between their feelings and correct moral norms.

The movement between civilized and barbaric spaces constitutes a rhythm that dramatizes the boundary between them. The vicissitudes of life—foreign expeditions, treacherous plots, travel accidents—lead first to the separation of kinfolk and then to reunions. This movement produces a profound emotional experience in which the palette of feelings stretches from grief and longing to joy and jubilation. As noted in the introduction, lineage novels incorporate martial motifs to enliven the narratives of domestic life. But unlike martial narratives, which are preoccupied with battlefield scenes and valiant heroes, lineage novels zoom in on the affective experience of such journeys of conquest, featuring barbarians who adjust their feelings in accordance with the ethical norm and lineage members who commence foreign journeys while displaying a rich palette of emotions.

In the lineage novel, the moment of crossing the boundary between the home space and the outer space is marked by feelings of longing. The experience of the borderlands, in other words, is foregrounded by the dramatized departure from affective kinship.[29] When Inung in *The Pledge* sets out on his first foreign journey, his longing for home is so intense that it stretches beyond this already sizeable excerpt:

Going beyond the border (*seoe* 塞外), Inung had to bid farewell to his father and part with his elder brother. The three of them growing distant [was] like having [one's own] flesh and blood (*kolyuk* 骨肉) divided across ten thousand *li*. East and west are far apart, and where is the northeast? Turning back, [Inung's] longing for his mother is fierce. No one else has experienced such a farewell.

On this long journey into foreign lands and being parted from his father, Inung is overwhelmed with longing and is wearing his eyes out by staring into distance. Lamenting the long separation, he recites, "I ascend that bare hill and look toward [the residence] of my mother."[30] Inung is content knowing that home is full of joy, with his siblings, older and younger, being close like branches of a tree. He alone is in the foreign land, and he is longing for his parents. He also knows that the sadness of his mother is great. Being different from others, Inung feels as though a day is longer than three autumns. Although he has no other worries, he is restless and has had no desire for food ever since he parted with his father. He is looking in the direction of the ancestral graves and in sadness speaks to himself: "The boundless sky has created things and placed them all over, having also provided each with a pair. It is the same for human beings. . . . This sorrow (*han* 恨)—what can I compare it to? Being born into this life brings much sadness and little joy." . . .

Being worried like this, Inung grows sick, ridden by his anxiety over separation and his unfilial nature. Despite his illness, every night he goes outside to observe his mother's constellations and check if all is well with her. In early spring, all of a sudden his body begins to shake, and his heart is upset. In vain tries Inung to calm himself, and his hands and feet grow numb, so he almost faints. These are the heaven-endowed emotions (*ch'ŏnsok chi chŏng* 天屬之情) that resonate in blood (*hyŏlmaek sangŭng* 血脈相應), and this is known even to ordinary people. Inung's filiality is such that he feels his mother's plight when he is thousands of leagues away.[31]

This effusive description of Inung's sentiments has been shortened by about a third, but the intensity of his longing remains clear. Looking back at his happy childhood, Inung laments his lengthy separation from his father: like himself, Inung's father is spending years in foreign lands at the service of the emperor. A filial son, Inung anxiously watches his mother's constellation: the celestial configuration augurs fortunes of the loved ones he leaves behind. In this way, Inung's experience in the foreign land revolves around his intense longing for his family. The last line of his lament invokes the physicality of the bond that allows him to feel from a distance his mother's precarious situation. The materiality of emotions that connect Inung with home is underscored by his longing-induced sickness. The physical distance from home is in a sense filled in by the emotional attachment that stretches forth.

Importantly, foreign sojourns always occur at an affective distance from the local populations. Neither disgust at the depraved ways of foreigners nor any positive feeling, such as sympathy, emanates from the lineage members when they are outside. During their journeys, the radiant, charismatic bodies of the lineage males are viewed as if from a distance; they attract but can never be approached. During Insŏng's sojourn in the Mongol lands in *The Pledge*, his very appearance transforms those who behold it: "Just a single look [at Insŏng] makes a person feel bedazzled, unable to comprehend his appearance and character [all at once]. With a second looking [at Insŏng], one's heart swells, and one realizes that one has lived in vain if one could not offer one's life [to Insŏng]. Looking [at Insŏng] for the third time, a person loses all debauched and unseemly thoughts and abandons all vicious tricks and inhumane thoughts, being overcome in a single glance."[32]

The power of Insŏng's appearance goes beyond its morally edifying function. Insŏng and other virtuous males provoke intense desire in women—their moral power is expressed through their irresistible charisma. When Insŏng and his father, Chŏng Cham, return home from a military expedition, women line up on the sides of the road to steal a glimpse: "Matrons and unmarried girls of several towns struggled with each other as they congregated to gaze at the stateliness of Chŏng Cham and stare at Insŏng's figure. [Women] forgot all shame and broke out of the proper distinctions between the inner and the outer. . . . Their mouths were dried, their throats were steaming, and their hearts were on fire. These women were like ten thousand monkeys unable to stay calm."[33] If cultural conquest occurs in tandem with erotic conquest, affairs of the heart between barbarian women and lineage males are never described in voyeuristic detail. If these affairs lead to marriages, the latter are conducted and consummated in the home space after the return from the frontier. Instead of grotesque erotic encounters with the barbarian women, which are abundant in late imperial Chinese novels, lineage novels focus on the irresistible attraction that emanates from the moral figures of the lineage males.

Venturing outside the cultured space of the home, lineage bodies act as physical markers of distance between the two realms. Some protagonists refuse local food, preferring to sustain themselves with their own encrusted blood[34]—a filial nourishment derived from the body one receives from one's parents.[35] While in Mongol lands, Insŏng refuses to leave behind even a piece of his handwriting. When the Mongol king's daughter, eager to improve herself, asks Insŏng to write down precepts for womanly comportment, he dictates the precepts so that his handwriting will not remain in the barbaric realm.[36] The nonreciprocal charisma of Insŏng's moral nature is inscribed on his body.

The return from the frontier conjures a rich palette of emotions, and the regaining of affective context at home is described in extended detail. When Inung's cousin In'gwang, also an accomplished and experienced general even though he is still in his teens, returns home after a lengthy absence, he cannot contain his joy:

> Seeing from afar the faces of his father and uncle, the filial son's heart is filled with glowing elation (*pan'gim*) and boundless delight (*kippŭm*) hardly comparable to anything else. On a day like this, when human joy (*in'gan ŭi chŭlgŏom*) is extreme, even if the affairs of the world are out of order, there is nothing one finds dissatisfying. At this moment, pondering over the past affairs and not knowing of his older brother's provenance, [In'gwang] is aching with sorrow (*sŭlp'ŭm*), and his grief only increases (*pihoe ch'ŭngik* 悲懷層益), but his steps are brisk, and his heart is aglow. Dumbfounded, he walks toward his father and uncle in bewilderment, and, taking them by the hem of their dresses, he offers his respects in prostration. . . . Overflowing with delight (*kippŭm*), he is also filled with sorrow (*sŭlp'ŭm*).[37]

In this scene, In'gwang nearly collapses with the joy of beholding his father and uncle. Emotions here are a contextual frame—they place a person in a network of relationships and connections deemed at once natural and ideal.

Writing about the affective turn in Chinese cultural production after the seventeenth century, Martin Huang notes that the preoccupation with feelings resulted in a shrinking of the chronotope of the novel. The space of the narrative, in his account, narrows from the battlefield and the court of *The Romance of the Three Kingdoms* to a privatized, domestic setting.[38] Although this observation is not entirely applicable to all of the novels Huang discusses, it holds for the most prominent literary avatars of desire: *The Peony Pavilion*, *The Plum in the Golden Vase*, *The Dream of the Red Chamber*. These texts unfold in boudoirs and gardens, which become the primary loci of connoisseurship, intimacy, and aestheticized sensuality. In the lineage novel, the space of the home is folded into the larger world, whose very stability depends on the lineage members' correctly ordered feelings. At the same time, the boundary between the home and the world is of fundamental importance because it separates the realm of emotional reciprocity from an unrelatable exterior realm.

The Taxonomy of Feelings in the Lineage Novel

The spatial logic of the lineage novel organizes the world around the boundary between the home space of kinship and the outside spaces, where emotions are out of joint and where one is dislodged from one's cognate affective context. The coordinates of feelings divide the world into these two realms. But what are the coordinates of the affective home space? What system of feelings organizes the fundamental human bonds? Within the boundaries of the home that circumscribe the community of affective reciprocity, the lineage novel distinguishes three types of feelings in terms of their capacity to constitute relationships: human feelings, feelings of flesh and blood, and unruly feelings.

Lineage novels describe "human feelings" (*injŏng* 人情) or "feelings mandated by heaven" (*ch'ŏnsok chi chŏng* 天屬之情) as natural, sincere, and ethically moderated. These feelings constitute the ideal and unfold exclusively in the space of kinship. The worst possible human condition is to lose or be oblivious of one's kin: "As people are born into the world, it is the worst of calamities not to know one's kin (*sŏngssi* 姓氏)."[39] Since kinship circumscribes the affective space of a person's life, to lose one's kin is to be cut off from fundamental human feelings. The loss of a child, in one instance, produces "this mighty human feeling (*injŏng* 人情) [that] cannot but follow the heavenly principle."[40] When in *The Pledge* a young boy delights in his parents' presence and attention, the scene manifests the spontaneity of human feelings: "A child's love (*sarangham*) for his parents is a heavenly mandated feeling (*ch'ŏnsok chi chŏng* 天屬之情); the awareness of it comes easily, and its knowing is not difficult."[41] Kinship, in this way, provides the ethical structure for the articulation of fundamental human feelings.

When human feelings are discussed in the lineage novel, they are rarely classified as nameable, concrete emanations. The narrative simply states that human feelings are revealed naturally as part of a sweeping human condition in which all people are presumably able to share. The notions of naturalness and spontaneity, however, require qualification. Lineage novels clearly show that human feelings are experienced and performed by those with an impeccable moral nature and that the process of bringing feelings into alignment with ethical norms is lengthy and trying.

Some blood-based kinship links came into profound conflict with Chosŏn's ritual-based patrilineality and status system. These contradictions became most apparent in the relationship between parents and children. Sun Joo Kim has shown that elite fathers used the notion of "my own flesh and blood" (*kolyuk* 骨肉) to express the extent of their compassion for concubine-born children. Despite their sharing of blood ties and affective links, such fathers and children were on the opposite ends of the social hierarchy because the children would inherit their mothers' abject slave status. Elite men not only wrote extensively about the feelings of flesh and blood but also sought legal remedies, trying to purchase higher status for their secondary, concubine-born children or bequeathing them property.[42] Lineage novels, curiously, never dwell on the status distinction between elite fathers and secondary descendants. Whereas secondary consorts of lower social status are often presented as gaudy and uncouth, sometimes even grotesque, their progeny inevitably carry on the illustrious patrilineal heredity.

Lineage novels problematize the misalignment between ritual and blood kinship that is manifest in the institution of adoption. A crucial means for sonless couples to continue their line through the transmission of property and ritual roles, adoption required that parents and children share ethical feelings not based on blood ties. *The Pledge* depicts an adoption that is initially a success. The affective bond between Chŏng Cham, Madame Yang, and their adopted son, Insŏng, is ethically sound and powerfully spontaneous already in their first encounter:

Insŏng is brought in to pay his respects. Insŏng and Chŏng Cham then proceed to perform the father–son rite. . . . Chŏng Cham and

Madame Yang receive Insŏng's bows with such a look that one cannot easily guess if they are his birth parents or adopted parents. The couple's love for Insŏng is so warm and their affection for him so overwhelming that it can hardly be eclipsed even by his birth parents' feelings. There hardly is a feeling at all that can surpass this profound affection that fills preordained human bonds. Chŏng Cham's bright eyes beam with gentleness of spring breeze, and his scarlet lips fail to conceal the dazzling whiteness of his teeth. The tormented expression of Madame Yang, burrowed with years of exacting illness, gives way with a slight tremor; her face glows anew with peaceful warmth that emanates from her eyes and reaches heaven itself. The two faces, like jades shining with morning glory, turn toward each other, issuing fragrance of a plum tree covered with snow. Like a lotus flower that rises on its emerald stalk above the stillness of an autumn pond, smiles ascend the two faces, tender as apricot flowers.[43]

Certainly, this rapport is due to the supreme moral integrity of Chŏng Cham, Madame Yang, and Insŏng, which allows them to fulfill the prescribed affective bonds to the fullest extent. When Insŏng at a very young age eagerly responds to his adoptive parents' warm affection, the novel comments: "This [situation] would have been impossible without heaven endowing these emotions (hanŭl i siginŭn chŏng)."[44]

Madame Yang is, however, prone to sickness, and after her early death Chŏng Cham's parents urge him to remarry. Eventually yielding to their gentle urging, Chŏng Cham marries Madame So, a beautiful and capable woman with a powerful temper. Insŏng's relationship with his stepmother turns out to be quite unlike the one he had with Chŏng Cham's first wife, Madame Yang. After Madame So gives birth to twin boys, Injung and Inung, Insŏng's presence compromises the succession privilege of Injung, Madame So's own first-born son. This prompts Madame So to take violent action, and she tries to arrange assassinations and kidnappings of Insŏng, his wife, Yi Chayŏm, and their young son. Chapter 4 discusses the violent excesses and complexity of Madame So's character more fully, but it is important now to take a closer look at the case she makes for the power of feelings of flesh and blood within the structure of ritual kinship.

The Pledge acknowledges in multiple instances that feelings of flesh and blood constitute natural and powerful foundations for human bonds even among people with inferior morals. Even the uncouth, who fail to establish proper moral hierarchies in their homes, respond spontaneously to "the resonance (sangŭng 相應) of blood (hyŏlmaek 血脈) in the emotions of those who come from the same womb (tongp'o 同胞) and share [the same] flesh and blood (kolyuk 骨肉)."[45] In contrast, the lack of even these blood-based emotions in those who are ignorant of ritual decorum is conceived as the final degree of degradation: "the obliviousness to the very resonance of blood (hyŏlmaek ŭi sangŭng 血脈 相應)."[46]

Madame So takes the idea of feelings of flesh and blood further, though, positioning them in direct contradiction to human feelings. She insists that feelings of flesh and blood constitute the grounding premise of affective kinship. Scornful of her husband's unabated favoring of his admittedly worthy adopted son, Insŏng, Madame So recasts human feelings as excessive in their disregard for fundamental, affectively powerful blood bonds. She says to her son Injung: "Your father is so biased, treating you like a base person and praising Insŏng like a sage. . . . Without your father's loving affection (cha'ae 慈愛) and guidance, your ways become ever more deviant."[47] In his wife's mind, Chŏng Cham is guilty of excessive love for his adopted son, which produces an affective lack in his relationship with his blood son Injung and thus makes Chŏng Cham accountable for the ruin that this dysfunctional relationship causes to Injung's person.

Seeing the destruction that his wife has wrought in his household, Chŏng Cham attempts to comprehend the nature of her passion. In a pensive mood, he says to his and Madame So's second son, Inung, "As though at her wits' end, your mother's love (saranghanŭn pa), without her own knowledge, turns into harm. This behavior arises from [her] confused nature. Now, our lineage's fortune is blocked, and our situation is grave like this. It is not that I blame your mother, but [I say these words] out of sympathy for you."[48] Chŏng Cham claims to withhold judgment for the benefit of his children, but he also affirms that his wife's actions are propelled by love, a natural though excessive feeling. In her husband's words and in her own, Madame So appears to be a person of excessive passion. The novel comments on the feelings Madame So has for her firstborn: "Her love (sarang) for this son, who resembled her so much, was extraordinary."[49] This love casts her wrongdoing in a different light, drawing attention away from the figure of the villain and toward the relationship between two types of feelings, both affirmed as valid: the ideal of ethical, heaven-granted emotions and feelings of flesh and blood that have undeniable power.

Certainly, Chŏng Cham is not indifferent to his son Injung: "Chŏng Cham regretted Injung's unworthiness and valued him less than Insŏng and Inung, but, nevertheless, Injung was his son. How could the working of the emotions of the heavenly bond (*ch'ŏnnnyun chi chŏng* 天倫之情) not be wondrous? Himself unaware, Chŏng Cham's heart moved for Injung."[50] Chŏng Cham's thinking about the relationship with his two sons—the adopted son Insŏng and the son by blood Injung—is guided by ethical sentiments, called "emotions of the heavenly bond" in the novel. These ethical sentiments allow Chŏng Cham to recognize the appropriate positions of the primary, adopted son and the second-born direct offspring. Having affection for both, Chŏng Cham is mindful of the appropriate distinction between the two as far as normative lineage structure is concerned. Even though her feelings are represented as excessive, Madame So gives voice to the powerful and controversial ties that are not easily disarticulated by the normative vision of kinship. As shown later in this chapter, Madame So's violence shakes up the Chŏng household, but she eventually settles into her prescribed position within the lineage, recognizing the moral superiority of Insŏng and his legitimacy as heir. Nevertheless, her powerful story is a reminder of the fundamental importance of blood bonds within the ideal configuration of patrilineal kinship structure of Chosŏn.

Despite their misalignment with the ethical fabric of kinship, the sheer power of feelings of flesh and blood inaugurates their constructive aspect. The system of affective coordinates in the lineage novel is therefore expanded to affirm the productive aspect of feelings of flesh and blood alongside ethical human feelings. This affirmation becomes apparent in the next chapter, which shows that lineage novels recognize and make amends for the inalienable blood links that are compromised in the patrilineal configuration.

Feelings of flesh and blood and human feelings represent competing hypotheses about the fundamental premise of human bonds. But lineage novels also consider feelings that work against the web of human relationships. I call these feelings "unruly" because they indicate that a person is out of sync with his or her relational context. Unruly feelings have an asymmetrical relationship with both human feelings and feelings of flesh and blood. Despite their veracity and necessity, feelings of flesh and blood tend toward the unruly because of their power to overflow the moderate ethical ideal. *The Pledge* nevertheless signals the possibility of interpretive variance with regard to human feelings, recognizing the imbalance created when feelings of flesh and blood are completely disregarded. Unruly feelings overlap with feelings of flesh and blood in their capacity for excess, but they do not arise exclusively from blood bonds. In more general terms, unruly feelings indicate a variety of tensions between a person's prescribed social roles and his or her self-perception.

Lineage novels do not designate unruly feelings as an explicitly defined category—these feelings are not encompassed by a cumulative term, such as feelings of flesh and blood or human feelings. Feelings such as hatred (chŭngbun 憎憤), resentment (nohan 怒恨), torment (pyŏnghoe 病懷), jealousy (t'ugi 妬忌), and sadness (p'ich'ang 悲愴) as well as feelings of excessive affection (chungae 重愛, sarang) and sexual desire (ŭmjŏng 淫情) cannot be productively incorporated in the system of proper human bonds. The feelings that escape the prescribed relational hierarchies and affective dispositions "stick out" from the relational framework. But in this capacity, they, as excess, become hermeneutical indices that signal the disharmony of the self, which then foregrounds a person's ethical program of bringing these unruly feelings under control. As chapter 4 shows, unruly feelings in the lineage novel are considered integral to private identity—they chart a person's trajectory within the highly regulated structure of kinship. The lineage novel acknowledges them as socially unproductive but objectively valid.

The most important aspect of unruly feelings is their visibility. From the perspective of Confucian ethics, the interpretation of manifest unruly feelings is a matter of both personal and state importance. Emanations of royal rage that did not serve any useful purpose prompted extended debates and exhortations in the Chosŏn court.[51] The feeling of grievance at unjust treatment was a sentiment that qualified for legal remedy among the representatives of all classes and genders.[52] As long as unruly feelings were manifest and visible, they could be incorporated into the moral program of the person and even of the state. A good example of this in the context of Chinese history is the ledger of merit and demerit of the Qing-dynasty Neo-Confucian Li Gong (1657–1733). Organized under the motto "Make the surface and inside consistent," Li Gong's diary offers a graphical chart where each hidden desire and urge, from a sexual drive to a tiny itch, leaves its mark—a horse eye, a circle, a square. Rather than a script of failures, these marks provide a road map for Li Gong's self-reforming efforts, which were so fervent that they became the stuff of jokes for his contemporaries.[53]

Turning back to the lineage novel, we can note that although the novelistic home space of the lineage is understood to create the natural and necessary environment for emotional reciprocity, it is also constituted by the complex entanglement of ethical sentiments considered ideal and powerful feelings of flesh and blood, which are recognized as an inalienable aspect of human bonds. The correct negotiation of these significant boundaries of kinship sociality actualizes the regenerative moral potential of the home space represented in civilizational conquest of the hinterlands and underscores the centrality of the domestic realm for social ordering.

The Negative Interiority

Deep self-reflection and the search for the causes and origins of unruly feelings set the protagonists of the lineage novel apart from the clear-cut heroes and villains that appear in other Chosŏn fiction. In the lineage novel, heroes are prone to self-doubt and despair, and even the worst villains are able to detail the journey that brought them to depravity, showing a self-reflective sensibility. All lineage novel protagonists speak profusely, exteriorizing everything that torments them, and every plot turn is accompanied by extended verbalization of the feelings it generates. In short, unruly feelings and actions are consistently and pointedly externalized.

In *The Pledge*, for instance, one of the most unruly protagonists is Chŏng In'gwang, Madame So's nephew. Disgruntled about having been tricked into an unwanted marriage, In'gwang repeatedly sends poison along with suicide orders to his wife, abuses his father-in-law, and whips all the household servants on a whim. Importantly, In'gwang rebels openly. His fits incur multiple floggings, but even though his stubborn and violent nature is known to all, he is not considered to be anything out of the ordinary. The case is similar with the unruly protagonist of *Brothers Hyŏn*, Hyŏn Sumun, who acquires a wife by raping a woman and leaving her little choice but to join his household. He, too, is known for his rash temper, but he is not described as a fundamentally problematic person. The exteriority of unruly feelings and of the unruly actions they cause points toward the social context of their interpretation. As visible manifestations of a person's misalignment with the regulation, these feelings and actions do not constitute inner truth or individual depth but are instead publicly manifest indications of such disagreement. Society and human bonds constitute the appropriate context for emotional expression, and emotions that misalign the appropriate relational context are positioned as opportunities for self-interpretation and harmonization.

What happens when unruly feelings are illegible, obscured, unexternalized? Madame So of *The Pledge* offers a prime example. The scenes in which she forces poison down the throat of her full-term pregnant daughter-in-law or sends her newly born stepgrandson floating down the river in a sealed wooden box filled with poison are outstanding. But, as I show earlier, these violent acts are not what make Madame So unique. The uniqueness of her case is that she does everything in secret, taking great care to conceal her true heart. In the novel, she is described as a person of doubleness; among the novel's extensive cast of protagonists, she is the only one endowed with this quality. The problem with Madame So, therefore, is not so much the disorder she creates and the violence she perpetrates—although these things certainly become a matter of concern to all around her—but the dissonance between her exterior and her inner intent.

Madame So's doubleness becomes apparent the moment she enters the Chŏng household as the new bride. Endowed with stature, beauty, discernment, and charisma, Madame So captivates the wedding banquet guests, but the third-person undertone to the presentation of the bride provides a warning: "Who could know how dissimilar she was on the inside and the outside?"[54] Over the course of the novel, Madame So's story is one of emergence—of making manifest and working through the dissimulation that constitutes her second nature. *The Pledge* notably emphasizes the uniqueness of Madame So's case: "Those who are conniving and artful by nature attempt to feign inner calm to conceal their ruthlessness and affect wisdom, but Madame So did not strive to appear wise. Her manner seemed unaffected, composed, and elevated. To someone's praise, she would offer a fervent rebuttal. . . . While she is thrice more atrocious than all the villains of the past, who can catch her shadow? Everyone is won over and impressed by her moral disposition and outstanding qualities, noting her purity and hardly considering her to be anything of the ordinary."[55] The problem with Madame So is that rather than affecting qualities she does not possess, she dissimulates, concealing her feelings. In this way, she withholds her unruly feelings from the interpretive horizon of human bonds; these feelings constitute a negative interior that is exempted from the realm of emotional reciprocity.

The novel suggests that because members of the Chŏng household possess superior understanding, they are not oblivious to the discrepancy between Madame So's inside and outside:

All men and women of the Chŏng household possess the acute ears of music master Gwang [Ch. Shi Kuang] and the power of vision of Yi Ru [Ch. Li Lou]. Therefore, they did not take Madame So to be a wise woman. . . . They also did not think Madame So was on par with Madame Yang, whose outside and inside (kŏt kwa an) were like clear frost on autumnal waters, with her [nature] from beginning till end being directed toward benevolence. But common people, especially those who saw Madame So for the first time—how could they help thinking that in her talent, comportment, refinement, and character Madame So was equal, even superior, to Madame Yang?[56]

The Chŏng lineage members' perspicacity leads them to initial suspicions. It seems, however, that even though they are able to grasp the inherent flaws of Madame So's character, they are oblivious to the true nature of her designs: "Even the acute ears of music master Gwang and the powerful vision of Yi Ru are insufficient to grasp her vile schemes and deception. . . . [No one] can see her shadow and grasp her true nature."[57] The meaning of discernment, which is emphasized in this passage, is multilayered: it exemplifies observant knowledge, but at the same time it represents dedication to perfecting the moral fabric of human bonds and to preventing the slightest indecorousness from entering that fabric.

The two ancient masters of discernment—the blind and powerful musician Shi Kuang and Li Lou, able to see the tip of a hair from a hundred-pace distance—are used in the Mencius to explain the inner origins of propriety and social harmony. Shi Kuang and Li Lou's skill is, after all, to discern and fulfill preexisting patterns with which a person must align herself. The inner intent and the relational context of one's life require reconciliation: "If a man loves others, and no responsive attachment is shown to him, let him turn inwards [K. pan; Ch. fan 反] and examine his own benevolence."[58] The inside and outside are configured as a result of introspection. In the words of Confucius, the interior constitutes the locus of moral scrutiny: "When we see men of worth, we should think of equaling them; when we see men of a contrary character, we should turn inward and examine ourselves (K. *nae cha sŏng*; Ch. *nei zi sheng* 內自省)."[59] Mencius notably does not designate the interior with the literally spatial term *inside* (K. *nae*; Ch. *nei* 內). When delineating the imperative of moral introspection, he prompts one to "turn to" or "to return" to oneself (K. *pan*; Ch. *fan* 反).

Although conduct can be cultivated through practice, the mind has to be constantly monitored to examine whether it aligns with one's performance. This alignment is achieved through sincerity, which guarantees that performance is grounded in feeling. Sincerity, or the coincidence of the inner intent and its outward manifestation, is achieved through introspection—returning to oneself from the perspective of relational order, viewing oneself from the position of cardinal human bonds. The self is inherently pervious to and mediated by the social realm. The requirement that one maintain the alignment of inner and outer in accordance with the moral norm makes the self one's "greatest charge" (K. *su*; Ch. *shou* 守).[60] When sincerity as inner–outer alignment is achieved, a person's outward emanations—speech, conduct, display of feelings—are spontaneously harmonious and unperturbed, and there is nothing that prevents sincere fulfillment of prescribed human relationships. In the Confucian view, the correct administration of the boundary between inner intent and its outer manifestation is what makes a cultivated human being.

Madame So skillfully manages this inner–outer boundary, which the novel repeatedly comments upon. Significantly, her exterior is not lacking in substance or truthfulness: in the eyes of others and in fact Madame So is a beautiful, accomplished, refined, and intelligent woman. The problem is that this exterior does not contain the entirety of Madame So's person. With part of her true nature concealed, she becomes an opaque, dark personality, distanced even from the one she loves most—her son Injung. Madame So and those around her describe her as a person with exceptional passions, chief among them her love for her children—the aspirations she has for Injung drive both her actions and her dissimulation.

Madame So's doubleness, however, eventually begins to work against the feelings of flesh and blood, creating a fissure in her relationship with Injung. As Injung eagerly participates in Madam So's plots, mother and son become united in crime but divided in their hearts. The novel dramatizes this division through a series of scenes of spatial separation between the two characters. At first, Madame So tries to keep her disgruntlement hidden from Injung. She opens her heart to her two servants, bemoaning her husband's endless suspicion of her animosity for Insŏng and deploring Injung's secondary position in the lineage. Injung, standing at his mother's bedchamber window, hears every word: "Having glimpsed his mother's doubleness (*naeoe tarŭm*) and also realizing that [she] purposefully withheld her intent from him, Injung became quite pleased, thinking that at some point he would attain the glory of becoming the lineage heir in his own person. Knowing [his mother's] true intent, Injung did not let it show, tempering his feelings. He offered [his mother] the evening snacks and wished her a good night. In this way, the mother and son were hiding their true hearts from each other."[61] Having overheard his mother's conversation with the servants through a window crack, Injung gains full knowledge of her, and this knowledge exacerbates the estrangement between mother and son. Injung continues to observe his mother's doings from a distance, all while condoning and even relishing her efforts to improve his fortune. When Madame So violently assaults her daughter-in-law, Yi Chayŏm, Injung is again a silent witness: "Injung was standing outside the window, having tucked up his sleeves [to refrain from making the slightest noise] and watching the night scene in elation, not averting his gaze. [All the while], he did not say a word."[62]

Injung, like his mother, masters the art of dissimulation: "He acted as though there were no artfulness between his inside and outside (*p'yori* 表裏),"[63] using his quick wit to conceal his thoughts and win everyone's favor. After realizing that his mother is trying to change the succession in his favor, Injung cautiously approaches her and says he has vaguely heard about her plans. Madame So, however, is far from being delighted; she scolds Injung for gathering rumors.[64] Even after Injung and Madame So become secret allies, Madame So cannot stop lamenting the fact that her first-born son lacks virtue. At some point, she even warns Injung that his behavior may destroy her affection for him altogether: "If you do not reform your ways quickly, I will cut off my feelings [for you] (*chŏng ŭl pŏhyŏgo*) and give up [on you] and will never forgive you."[65]

The novel notes that the relationship between Madame So and Injung, despite the love Madame So has for her son, is quite different from that between other parents and children: "The feelings between these two differ from those shared between other mothers and children. Without speaking, they know each other's designs at a glance, and at a wink of an eye they devise ingenuous schemes; putting their wits together, they are planning mischief. In their wickedness, they naturally resonate with each other, and their vicious minds are of the same kind."[66] Rather than aligning their hearts and deeds in the full realization of the appropriateness of correct human bonds, Injung and Madame So are pretenders who are cut off from the relational fabric that surrounds them and whose connection is based instead on the glances and observant concord that two evil minds share. Their relationship, rooted in constant watchful scheming, stands in sharp contrast to the intuitive, spontaneous affection between other parents and children.

The story of Madame So's doubleness prompts us to think about the historically specific boundaries of the self. Interiority—the locus of identity and affective experience that is central to the emergence of the modern Western subject and literature[67]—appears to have different coordinates in the lineage novel. To place Madame So within the system of affective coordinates articulated in the lineage novel, I propose a distinction between public interiority and negative interiority. *Public interiority*, a term invented by David Lawton in his study of late medieval English literature, represents an attempt to rethink the relationship between authority and voice by shifting attention to the "textual production of interiority by quotation." Lawton sees the practice of revoicing or using available Christian vocabularies of thinking—"a prayer, or a Psalm, or an *exemplum*"—as a way of staging voice in literature. What results is a voice that is "neither universal nor personal."[68] The public nature of this interiority inheres in the commonly available vocabulary of expression, accessible to all for interpretation and revoicing. But revoicing is an instance of inwardness: the voice is constructed through a reconfiguration of commonly available expressive sources.

The interiority that lineage novels depict is public in the sense that the moral conception of human bonds configures the relationship between a person's interior and exterior, between inner moral intent and outward conduct. Introspection—a mode of constructing a self that is aligned with the premises of ethical sociality—constitutes an instance of personal identity taking, but this identity taking is always already emplaced within the social, which makes the interiority public. Emphatically public is also the experience of feelings in the lineage novel. Feelings serve as indices of one's position within the relational fabric, and the fact that feelings are profusely displayed through exterior monologues suggests that the stage for the articulation of personal emotional experience is always already within the social. Manifestations or even protestations of feelings by the lineage novels' protagonists are acts of position taking in the context of surrounding relationships, which make the protagonist's position observable and interpretable by others.[69] The failure of human relationships, signaled by unruly feelings, becomes a hermeneutical imperative directed at the restoration of a harmonious social fabric.[70]

Madame So and her son Injung undergo this hermeneutical process. The difference between inside and outside, so frequently commented upon in *The Pledge*, first creates a self that I describe through the idea of *negative interiority*. This self is illegible vis-à-vis the social interpretive process. After Madame So's actions become known to all around her, she emerges from this negative interiority unwillingly at first. Once she is discovered, though, she becomes an eloquent speaker, reflecting on the journey that has brought her to the point of violence and dissimulation. The narrative of her unruly emotions—which ends with her eventual incorporation into affective kinship—is central to the story line of *The Pledge*.

In Conclusion

The lineage novel constructs narrative space in accordance with the Confucian vision of human relationships and relatability that radiate from the home. The domestic space in the lineage novel plays a central structuring role in that the well-ordered home guarantees the moral stability of the world itself. The domestic space, the imperial court, and the outer frontiers of the Confucian empire form a continuum of well-ordered human bonds, identifiable through the exteriorized manifestation of emotions, which, ideally, are in harmony with moral prescriptions. In other words, the emotions, flowing through this ordered concatenation of human bonds, are called upon to endow the human realm with stability, and the wise heads of the household make good generals who keep order on the outer frontiers of empire. The lineage novel modifies this understanding of the world by drawing an impenetrable boundary around the space of kinship. In the lineage novel, emotions experienced within the space of kinship differ radically from emotions experienced in the outer world. Outside the boundaries of the kinship space, lineage novels' protagonists exude the power of moral attraction but experience no emotional reciprocity with "barbaric" outsiders. The foreclosure of emotional reciprocity outside the kinship space dramatizes this boundary, and the boundary is further reinforced through the depiction of feelings of flesh and blood—innate, untransferable connections between parents and children and among siblings.

The affective coordinates of the lineage novel are a set of boundaries: between the domestic space and outside spaces, between feelings of flesh and blood and kinship norms, and between interior and exterior dimensions of the self.[71] The negotiation of these boundaries enables the creation of the genealogical subject, or the subject defined by the performance of ethical feelings within the normative structure of kinship. This subject is able to distinguish the spaces of emotional reciprocity and alterity and to align feelings with the ethical view of human relationships. As the China anthropologist Angela Zito has argued, subjectivity in the context of the Confucian moral system is distinct from the monadic Western Cartesian subject. The Confucian subject is embedded in a web of resonances, where the body functions as "interfacing membrane." Bodily traces left in the world through ritual performance (clothing, movement) and calligraphic practice are constitutive of the order performed by human society and essential to human culture. Performing these patterns out of chaos constitutes the quintessence of civilized human lifestyle: "subject positions (ruler, subject, father, mother, son, daughter, friend of higher status, friend of lower status, elder, younger) were practically embodied in a variety of ways that produced reciprocal hierarchical relations in a circulation of powers."[72] The embodied, exteriorized emotions performed by lineage novels' protagonists can similarly be understood as acts of subjectivation within this ethical order.

A product of the Confucian worldview, albeit in its historically specific Chosŏn inflection, the lineage novel thematizes a variety of boundaries that structure the emotional pattern of kinship life in Chosŏn. Having set the stage by examining the affective coordinates of the lineage novel, I devote the next chapter to a discussion of the feelings of kinship, with a focus on the role of unruly emotions in articulating kinship's problematic junctures.

CHAPTER IV

Feelings and the Conflicts of Kinship

A variety of significant boundaries for emotional reciprocity, discussed in chapter 3, lay out the grid for the formulation of the genealogical subject—a relational self embedded in kinship hierarchies, which are harmonized through the ethical ordering of emotions. The world, the home, and the self become the main spatial nodes for emotional performances, which form the grammar of intelligibility in the lineage novel. Taking the larger framework of the lineage novel's affective coordinates as its background, this chapter analyzes the role of unruly feelings in the articulation of the lineage structure, which is composed of multiple problematic junctures.

The lineage novel highlights several key relationships, including the bond between spouses, the ties between maternal and paternal sides of the lineage, and the affective ramifications of heir adoption. Marriage and heir adoption are the central institutions of lineage perpetuity, while the negotiation between the patrilineal and matrifilial legacy constitutes a crucial moment in the configuration of male descent. The problematic nature of these relationships is underscored by the fact that they produce a palette of unruly feelings and behaviors, which, as the previous chapter has shown, chart the course of the protagonists' moral transformation and integration into the kinship structure. This chapter shows that lineage novels do not treat unruly feelings merely as disruptive emanations of troubled protagonists. These feelings instead function as mechanisms that distance the person from the kinship norm, so that the norm is transformed into value as it is reapproached through choice and fulfilled through moral effort.

Marriage and the motif of the remarkable encounter that brings the spouses together are frequently featured in the lineage novel titles. All but one novel discussed in this manuscript—*The Pledge at the Banquet of Moon-Gazing Pavilion*, *The Remarkable Encounter of Pearls*, *The Remarkable Reunion of Pearls and Jade*, *The Remarkable Reunion of Jade Mandarin Ducks*, and *The Commentary to Jade Mandarin Ducks*—reference nuptial tokens and conjugal arrangements in their titles. Because marriages—their arrangement and consummation and the subsequent birth of descendants—are central to the perpetuation of the lineage, they come under intense scrutiny. Conjugal relationships in the lineage novel are controversial, even when concluded among descendants of illustrious lineages and lauded as fortunate matches. Spouses' tempers and the vagaries of desire—its lack or its excess—are two major causes of trouble, but another problematic aspect of marriage is the figuration of maternal and paternal kin into the structure of patrilineal kinship. If shorter Chosŏn novels, such as *The Tale of Ch'unhyang* (*Ch'unhyang chŏn* 春香傳) and *The Tale of Unyŏng* (*Unyŏng chŏn* 雲英傳), use plots of desire and upwardly mobile marriage as critiques of social hierarchies,[1] lineage novels inquire into the role of desire in the repertoire of normative gender identities. In this context, marriages—conducted between social peers—problematize the relationship between patrilineal and matrifilial kinship links.

Notably, the narrative of the contested relationship between maternal and paternal kin is unique to the lineage novel—other Chosŏn-dynasty texts neglect this crucial kinship juncture.[2] The attrition of women's natal kinship links—both affective and legal—was a prerequisite for the formulation of patrilineal kinship. A series of ritual and legal reforms stripped women of their right to inherit property and to divorce, which made them entirely dependent on their position within their husbands' families. Residing in their husbands' households, women were also expected to transfer their filial devotion to their parents-in-law. The ritual framework excluded women from direct participation and downgraded the mourning ranks for matrifilial kin. These reforms, finalized in the late seventeenth century, marked a significant departure from earlier marital practices, according to which women continued to live in their natal households after marriage and had the right to divorce and inherit property. These reform measures aimed to ensure women's complete transition into their husbands' households and to sever all natal ties. The reality of kinship, however, was far more complex. The state, for instance, recognized and rewarded women's filial violence on behalf of their fathers.[3] The relationship between the maternal and paternal sides of the lineage was, moreover, important for elite men: in their bureaucratic careers, fathers-in-law and sons-in-law were part of a network of connections.

Because wives were required to make a complete affective and practical transition to their husbands' households, lineage novels treat lingering affective links between women and their natal families as problematic. Lineage novels are wont to depict the moral imbalance between fathers-in-law and sons-in-law, with the young and virtuous son-in-law scorning the petty and depraved ways of his father-in-law, which leads to continuing conflicts between the two. This raises a question: Whose side should a woman abide by? The social prescription would make her unquestionably obedient to her husband's will, but the lineage novel complicates this view. Insisting that their husbands accord appropriate respect to their fathers, women in lineage novels act out their resentment of their husbands' authority on the figure of the (often hard-begotten) boy heir. The scenes of disconsolate, even abused children, calmly watched by their mothers, who offer no solace, not even a caress, are striking on the pages of lineage novels. By turning against their sons, who embody the future of the lineage, these women fight for their husbands' reconciliation with their fathers. The figure of a disobedient wife and frigid mother is a vivid embodiment not only of women's conflicted position within patrilineal kinship but also of the ultimate importance of honoring matrifilial affective links.

Female protagonists in the lineage novel essentially embody the conflict between the patrilineal norm, configured on ritual and ethical premises, and the blood-based kinship ties. This conflict is also acted out in the problematized relationship between adoptive parents and children. Ideally, they are expected to share spontaneous rapport, no different from the natural affection children have for their natural parents. Lineage novels, however, show that heir adoption, a crucial institution of lineage perpetuity, is fraught with contradictions.

The predominance of unruly emotions and behavior in the lineage novel drew the attention of contemporary critics. Hong Hŭibok (1794–1859), whose exposition of the lineage novel is quoted at length in the introduction, singles out its narrative excesses:

[Vernacular novels] are the amusement for women and the ignorant. The simple stories of their protagonists end with lifetime prosperity that follows the marriages made in the middle. Between these events, the plots depict stories of losing children and then finding them again and marrying them off, social advancements of treacherous subjects, households in disorder, wrought by jealous wives and concubines, with subsequent reconciliation. . . . It is not that [vernacular Korean novels] do not depict virtuous maidens and faithful wives. Their moral virtue and beautiful conduct are indeed powerful enough to move and educate the reader. Apart from this, however, [vernacular Korean novels] depict vile schemes and strife of treacherous subjects, jealous wives, and lustful women. They heap false accusations upon others and concoct disastrous conflicts, and their artifice and ill will, told in words never seen before, are astounding. Truly, even if such behavior actually occurred in real life, one would have to turn a deaf ear and a blind eye to it. Instead, all the fantastic details of married couples' struggles, intimate exchanges at the boudoir, or illicit thoughts of men and women are laid out in great detail, even praised, and overall relayed with such vivid realness—How could all this be appropriate for women's eyes? These stories can be beneficial if the reader appreciates and emulates the wise conduct of the good. However, if one perversely identifies with artful malignance, nothing can be more dangerous than that.[4]

It is noteworthy that Hong refuses to make a distinction between the lineage novel on the one hand and the shorter fiction of Chosŏn on the other. He instead refers to both as "vernacular Korean novels," even as lineage novels' titles are listed earlier in his piece.

The problem of feelings, for Hong, is placed within the horizon of moralistic reading, which constitutes the correct hermeneutics for the novel. In other words, the stories of unruly protagonists, for him, are meant to be read as negative examples. This chapter shows, however, that plots of unruly feelings in the lineage novel have an entirely different function: rather than instances of negative conduct, unruly feelings in these texts mark the trajectory of a personal life through systems of order. If classics and moral primers represent and prescribe the ideal of well-ordered feelings and clearly articulated human bonds, shorter vernacular Korean fiction offers negative plots of disequilibrium that result in the happy end of rewarded virtue and punished vice. Quite distinctly, the lineage novel eschews the depiction of clear-cut villains and heroes. Although well-ordered kinship constitutes the ideal of human sociality in these texts, unruly feelings are treated as integral to the process of personal socialization. The most willful of the lineage novels' protagonists command the greatest attention, which inaugurates defiance as a premise for subsequent reconciliation with kinship norms. In the discussion that follows, I explore the conflicting junctures of kinship: marriage, accommodation between the patriline and matrifilial kin, and heir adoption. The chapter closes with a meditation on the role of unruly emotions in the articulation of a personal life narrative.

Marriage and Desire

Chang Serin, a pining lover in *The Pledge* who is already married but love-sick and bed-ridden on account of another beauty, muses about the place of desire within the normative kinship structure: "How can something that originates in heavenly predestination (*ch'ŏnyŏn* 天緣) and remarkable encounter (*kibong* 奇逢) be considered as wantonness (*ŭmhaeng* 淫行) and charged as a crime?"[5] Expanding the notion of conjugal union, referenced as "heavenly predestination" and "remarkable encounter," Serin opens this normative relationship to choice and mutual attraction.

The relationship between husband and wife is one of three fundamental Confucian moral bonds. In Chosŏn Korea, marriage, signifying the passage to adulthood, actualized the repertoire of gender performances, which regulated sexuality, bodily comportment, and the relational hierarchies of kinship. Chosŏn gender politics operated through the category of separation (*pyŏl* 別): after the age of seven, women and men—with the exception of close family members—were prohibited from associating. Women's lives and duties were located in the domestic quarters of their husbands' families and were centered on the performance of womanly work—corporeal discipline that brought practical outcomes. Men led public lives, and their bureaucratic careers often entailed long absences due to official appointments. Women's chastity was a matter of family honor.[6] Men owed their loyalty to the sovereign, and although polygamy did not place explicit restrictions on male sexuality, the ideal of moral cultivation implied the desirability of control over sexual excess. For a woman, marriage signified a crucial transition through the chain of three obediences (*sam-jong* 三縱) owed to her father, husband, and son. Men, in contrast, assumed control over the moral discipline of their households, which hinged on their authority and ethical example. Over and above its importance to the system of gender differences, marriage was a crucial institution of status perpetuity because descent was based on both maternal and paternal pedigree.

In short, marriage in Chosŏn was a highly regulated institution of moral control and status continuity, but lineage novels reconceive this union as a matter of choice and attraction between spouses. Conjugal union became the site for the reconceptualization of human bonds in late imperial China, its voluntary potential seen as conducive to shared feeling, which eclipsed obligation. The influence of Chinese scholar–beauty fiction, which depicts couples united in their beauty, refinement, and mutual feeling, is discernible in the lineage novel, which romanticizes marriages that in reality were prearranged. Like late imperial scholar–beauty fiction, lineage novels emphasize the parity of the spouses' appearance and sensibility. The ubiquitous motif of male love sickness imprints deep sensitivity on men's very appearance,[7] presented to be as delicately beautiful as women's. Women are shown to be in possession of supreme calligraphic and poetic skills, which complement their elegance and upright character. In the lineage novel, some spouses meet by accident—they have a chance roadside encounter, or the man steals a glimpse of his future wife in the female quarters of relatives' or friends' households. Even virtuous maidens are afforded free-spirited rendezvous with their prospective or actual husbands. This usually happens when the cross-dressed woman escapes the domestic compound, fleeing from family discord or from an undesirable marriage. The novels comment on the ravishing beauty of this slender youth, which plants the seeds of doubt regarding her gender in all those who see her. The moment of exposure is an occasion for an unveiling of womanly charms. Flustered at having been discovered and at the immodesty of having male company, these women are transformed into objects of desire. Importantly, these cross-dressed female figures never embody seduction in their own person.[8] They are the objects of desirous gazes, but the tantalizing impropriety of the situation is appreciated only by the reader.

The ideal of female chastity that predominated in late Chosŏn society explains the anxiety about women's desire that lineage novels exhibit. There are two types of lustful women. Ugly dimwits who cannot withstand lineage males' powers of attraction are treated condescendingly: they usually succeed in becoming concubines of the object of their desires; thanks to the mediation of the lineage elders, these marriages are consummated, with the groom spending the wedding night in a state of high intoxication. Take, for instance, the figure of Yuk Ch'wiok, secondary wife of Hyŏn Kyŏngmun, in *Brothers Hyŏn*. Her ugliness, love of gaudy adornment, pettiness, and irascibility turn her lust into little more than a testament to Kyŏngmun's appeal; unable to seduce, she poses no threat. The case is different, however, when lustful women possess beauty and magical powers. Consort Hwang and her maid Sŏlmae in *Pearls and Jade*, the third novel in the Hyŏn lineage sequence, represent the dangers of female lust. They change their appearance and use magic potions to win over the men they desire. Their efforts result in their deaths—an outcome that tames the dangerous potential of female desire and powers of attraction.

The polarity of the chaste wife and the profligate shrew who seeks to subjugate the husband is a familiar trope in late imperial Chinese fiction, which explores polygyny by charting the flows of desire around the man's centrality. The dream of a benevolent and vigorous polygamist ensconced amid expendable females is augmented by representations of the dangers of polygyny in the figures of shrews, who seek to subjugate men.[9] Literati writings from the same period are similarly wary of the dangers posed by unbridled sensuality.[10] Desire was seen in the Confucian moral system as the most dangerous feeling that needed to be placed under constant watchful control. Lineage novels, hence, pose a question: Given that desire is integral to human nature, what forms of desire are permissible within the patriarchal order?

For male protagonists, the conjugal union becomes the site for the regulation of desire and enactment of patriarchal authority, which constitute the quintessential aspects of their socially productive identity. Whereas some men need to learn moderation, others have to learn their ways with women (i.e., put a lot of effort into consummating their marriages and dealing with their wives). Curiously, men's desire and sexual performance are directly related to their patriarchal authority. Lustful men have no lack of power, but abstemious men have trouble prevailing over their wives or even consummating their marriages. It is therefore no surprise that desire and sexual performance in the lineage novel are subject to keen domestic surveillance and control. Although there is a degree of gender fluidity in the commensurate distribution of beauty, education, and refinement among male and female protagonists of the lineage novel, the problematization of patriarchal control and male-centered desire upholds the incontrovertible centrality of male power.

Desire and marriage are the central themes in the trilogy focused on the Hyŏn lineage: *Brothers Hyŏn*, *Pearls*, and *Pearls and Jade*. The parent novel, *Brothers Hyŏn*, focuses on twin brothers who are quite unlike. Hyŏn Sumun, the older brother, is the quintessence of virility and lust. The younger brother, Hyŏn Kyŏngmun, is a scholar, uninterested in the affairs of the bedchamber. First, let us consider the relationship of Hyŏn Sumun and Yun Hyebing, who later becomes his wife.

Hyŏn Sumun notices Yun Hyebing performing household tasks in the Hyŏn mansion. With the help of his nurse, who claims Hyebing as her niece, he tricks Hyebing into a private chamber and rapes her. Hyebing later turns out to be a long-lost daughter of an illustrious lineage, and she eventually reunites with her parents. While Hyebing hopes to spend the rest of her life tending to her parents, Sumun presses her to enter his household, claiming that she has already become his de facto concubine. Hyebing's parents, too, support this arrangement, seeing it as a confirmation of Hyebing's deflowering and also believing that obedience is a woman's greatest virtue. Their emphasis on obedience might appear paradoxical against the background of the Chosŏn cult of female virtue, but it is important to note that Hyebing is raped *into marriage*, which constitutes the appropriate station for a woman. In this situation, all Hyebing can do is rely on her own wits. After a wedding ceremony is held with the approval of both sets of parents, Hyebing selects a disfigured servant and sends her to spend the wedding night with the drunken groom. It is only in the morning that the unsuspecting groom notices something is amiss, when he spots surprisingly coarse red hands sticking out from the blanket. After he struggles to pull the covers away from his bride, he sees "a face, plastered with generously applied powder that caked in patches; a broken ulcer right below the nose with the pus flowing down to the mouth—a dirty and unseemly sight that was hard to behold."[11]

Hyebing escapes to her relatives' house; Sumun soon finds her, but Hyebing again deceives her unwanted husband, sending forth a life-size doll in the sedan chair arranged for her to return to the Hyŏn household. This substitution transpires only when the doll is unable to pay respects to her parents-in-law, sagging on the floor instead of standing upright. But Hyebing's triumph ends abruptly and violently. If the tricks she plays on Sumun seem to represent a challenge to male desire, this challenge is ultimately invalidated. After the doll incident, Sumun forces Hyebing to return to the Hyŏn mansion. On the way, Hyebing is confronted by a brigade of servants who completely wreck her sedan upon Sumun's orders. The novel comments, "Although at first Yun Hyebing succeeded at deceiving Hyŏn Sumun with her little tricks, now, in front of the people of the world Sumun has cleansed his offense."[12]

Hyebing's rank is raised to primary wife after the discovery of her originally unknown aristocratic pedigree, but her troubles continue. After her return to the Hyŏn mansion, Hyebing whiles the time away in the company of her sister-in-law, sharing her grievances. In the middle of a comforting conversation, Sumun dispatches a servant with the following message: "Quickly, bring the bedding to the outer hall and attend to your lord."[13] Furious, Hyebing refuses to go, and Sumun, unable to restrain his desire, comes into her room and forces her to bed. Hyebing's frustrations and the discord between the two newlyweds become known to her father-in-law, Hyŏn T'aekchi. Calling her in for a conversation, Hyŏn T'aekchi lays out the situation. First of all, he admits that Sumun's rash temper is aggravated by his youthful recklessness. He notes that Sumun's offenses were committed before he was aware of Hyebing's status. He adds that Hyebing was able to have her revenge by playing tricks upon Sumun. Hyŏn T'aekchi concludes that although both sides are at fault, two decisive factors settle the matter: the first is that "it is [fit for] a woman to submit to a man (yŏja pok ŏ in 女子伏於人)," and the second is that the two "have already encountered each other through ritual."[14]

The finality of this prescription is underscored by the complexity of the situation, amply acknowledged by both Hyŏn T'aekchi and the narrator. Even though Sumun treats Hyebing badly, he is said to have "great affection (ŭnjŏng 恩情)" for her. Hyebing has no choice but to submit to her husband's authority, which has been reinforced by her father-in-law's incontrovertible injunction, so hers is a bitter lot: "The way Hyebing has become a woman of the world, obeying her husband's orders, is indeed pitiful."[15] The nuance in the relationship between Hyebing and Sumun is not settled in a manner of a personal score. Rather, the moment of social inscription—Hyebing's settling into the role of a wife, or "a woman of the world," which finalizes her social identity and belonging—arrests the violent development of this relationship. Set against the complexity of character and circumstance, the obedience required of Hyebing as wife is facilitated through her lustful husband's violence[16] and ratified by the kinship norm.

Whereas the first novel of the Hyŏn lineage sequel authorizes male desire and transforms it into a vehicle of control, the second novel, *Pearls*, seeks to stabilize male desire within the moral conjugal union. The amorous hero of *Pearls* is Hyŏn Ch'ŏnnin, Hyŏn Kyŏngmun's son and Hyŏn Sumun's nephew. Ch'ŏnnin marries Sŏl ssi, a beautiful if somewhat calculating woman. Soon, however, an itinerant monk divines that Princess Wŏlsŏng, the emperor's beloved daughter, is a more appropriate match for Ch'ŏnnin. At the emperor's insistence and in spite of the Hyŏns' unwillingness to break up the lawful marriage, Ch'ŏnnin is separated from his wife and married to Princess Wŏlsŏng. Before Ch'ŏnnin is married again, he visits Sŏl ssi to comfort her, and he is so moved by the sight of her grief that the two consummate their marriage despite Ch'ŏnnin's father's prohibition of it. Having become husband and wife in deed, Ch'ŏnnin and Sŏl ssi are inseparable: "Although Ch'ŏnnin was only twelve years of age, he was already knowledgeable about hundreds of affairs, so how could he be ignorant about the joy that arises between a man and a woman? He harbored the most tender affection in his heart, and Sŏl ssi's feelings were thrice as strong as Ch'ŏnnin's."[17] Ch'ŏnnin naturally neglects Princess Wŏlsŏng and uses every pretext to visit Sŏl ssi, and when his conduct ultimately becomes known to his father, he gets a hefty flogging.

Ch'ŏnnin cannot understand why he and Sŏl ssi, who were legitimately and happily married, had to be separated. Naturally, Ch'ŏnnin blames Princess Wŏlsŏng for his and Sŏl ssi's misery: "Who is this Princess Wŏlsŏng to intrude upon the harmony of a married couple?!"[18] he demands. Princess Wŏlsŏng has to withstand many violent episodes. At the peak of his rage, Ch'ŏnnin throws a letter case at the princess, severely cutting her forehead. When Princess Wŏlsŏng's maid rises to her defense, Ch'ŏnnin beheads the faithful servant and flings her bloody head at her mistress. Princess Wŏlsŏng maintains her equanimity though all these trials, offering proof of her exceptional virtue, and in time Ch'ŏnnin recognizes not only his forced wife's outstanding character but also her delicate beauty.

As a result of Ch'ŏnnin's unruly behavior, it is decided that Ch'ŏnnin and the princess should live apart. However, when Princess Wŏlsŏng falls ill and palace doctors prove powerless, Ch'ŏnnin rushes to her side. He admires the modesty of Princess Wŏlsŏng's room, filled only with books and calligraphy, a single court robe hung on the wall. Turning to his wife, Ch'ŏnnin notices her subtle charm:

> Ch'ŏnnin looked [at the Princess] again. Disheveled, her cloudlike hair was covering her jade face. Flushed, her cheeks seemed to possess all imaginable beauty. Her fragrant spirit emanated softly, like an autumn moon that is just about to conceal itself in a misty forest. . . . The Princess had just turned eleven years of age and she was extremely becoming. Of course, she could not help looking somewhat childish, but even then her dignity permeated the whole world, and her stature was radiant as sun and moon. If it were not for someone like Hyŏn Ch'ŏnnin, one could not easily prevail over her. Although Hyŏn Ch'ŏnnin has the power to shake the universe and tuck the sky and earth into his sleeve, he too has a body of flesh, and his heart is not made of metal or stone. Seeing this ravishing beauty, how could he help being moved?[19]

Ch'ŏnnin's change of heart, prompted by the alluring visage of his enfeebled wife, importantly comes with a forewarning: Ch'ŏnnin has to *prevail* over the princess. Although he is said to possess sufficient power of character for this task, it requires effort. Despite Ch'ŏnnin's approaches, Princess Wŏlsŏng cannot stop thinking about his earlier behavior: "The princess could not forget [Ch'ŏnnin's] mad fits and debauchery in the earlier days. When she thought of Ch'ŏnnin beheading her maid and tossing her blood-stained head, fear filled the entire body of Princess Wŏlsŏng."[20]

Enthralled by the princess's beauty, Ch'ŏnnin longs to be with her, but the cold treatment he receives throws him into love sickness. It is now the princess's turn to attend to her sick husband. Ch'ŏnnin seizes this opportunity to win her favor, but his feigned symptoms and straightforward invitations to join him in bed only make the princess more vigilant. The memory of the maid's beheading haunts the princess every time her husband makes gestures for conjugal rapport.[21] Frustrated with her stubbornness, Ch'ŏnnin even attempts suicide. After the princess snatches the knife from his hands and wounds herself, Ch'ŏnnin once again visits her bedside. Her disheveled appearance makes yet another striking impression on Ch'ŏnnin, and, despite her gentle remonstrations, he is finally able to get his way: "You have been unwell for only a day, and there is nothing particularly dangerous in spouses' sharing of the same bed. For a young woman, you are being excessively careful about your body," he says.[22]

The story of Ch'ŏnnin and Princess Wŏlsŏng's marriage reroutes the flow of desire from an erotic to a moral vein. After Princess Wŏlsŏng and Ch'ŏnnin reconcile and consummate their marriage, Sŏl ssi exposes her own evil nature by scheming against the princess. The novel confirms that although Ch'ŏnnin and Sŏl ssi's marriage is legally sound, it is inferior to his union with the princess, who in the end is given the rank of the first wife. The power of desire is channeled into an ethical bond: Princess Wŏlsŏng's beauty affirms her attractiveness, but it is her moral virtue that wins her respect and empowerment, underscoring the appropriateness of her position as first wife. Princess Wŏlsŏng's virtuous and uncompromising nature makes Ch'ŏnnin's conquest all the more rewarding. Lineage novels inevitably underscore the fact that no matter how hard dainty maidens try to ward off their husbands' desire, which is "extensive like mountains and seas," they have few resources for resistance.

In contrast to the first two novels of the sequel cluster, which articulate the patterns of male desire, the third novel examines the destructive power of female lust. In *Pearls and Jade*, female lust assaults not one but two households—that of Crown Prince Kwangp'yŏng, brother of Princess Wŏlsŏng, and that of Hyŏn Hŭimun, Princess Wŏlsŏng and Hyŏn Ch'ŏnnin's son. While Prince Kwangp'yŏng's concubine, Consort Hwang, tries to displace his virtuous wife from his affections, her faithful aide, palace lady Sŏlmae, longs for Hyŏn Hŭimun. Unable to get their way through their highly skilled use of magic, Consort Hwang and Sŏlmae gather a rebel army for a strike of revenge. At this point, the power of these women's lust endangers the entire realm, rendering Hyŏn Hŭimun and Prince Kwangp'yŏng, in charge of the imperial army, powerless. Just at this moment, Hyŏn Hŭimun's wife, Yŏn Hwaok, saves the day: she learns magic after Sŏlmae organizes her kidnapping from the Hyŏn mansion, and she ultimately defeats the two lustful women.

Yŏn Hwaok embodies patience: she is the ideal wife who does not attempt to seduce her husband but instead acts as a guardian to him and his family. At the end of the novel, the virtuous wife is recognized and praised at large: "The entire army learned that . . . it was the wife of Hyŏn Hŭimun [who helped them]; they clapped with happiness and spoke of it in amazement."[23] In short, the novel literally puts the virtuous wife in charge of an army that defeats the lust of other women.

It must be noted that in this novel female lust unfolds in parallel to the lustful escapades of a man, Hŭimun. If female lust is punished with death, Hŭimun's desire is instead subjected to another containment mechanism: domestic surveillance. Two cousins, Hŭimun and Hŭimyŏng, are wed on the same day, but the couples' young age procures a prohibition against the consummation of their marriages. Hŭimun, however, is too taken with his wife, Yŏn Hwaok, to comply. "On this wedding night, with not a soul around, who would hear and report the quiet words and deeds to Father?"[24] With these words, Hŭimun proceeds to make advances to Yŏn Hwaok, who flees the bedroom. What Hŭimun does not know is that he is acting in front of an audience: two maids have been dispatched to keep vigil under the windows of each newlywed couple. Over a late-night meal that follows, one of the maids complains:

"Hoping to hear something interesting I spent half the night eavesdropping by the back window. Having been on my feet all night, I am all sore and numb. I barely managed to stay awake, and I am extremely hungry. Finally, I have something to eat now. I do hope that my exploits get rewarded." [The second maid] replied with a smile, "Even though you say you had trouble for half of the night, you do not have anything interesting to tell, so why do you expect to receive prize wine? I myself have seen the curious act of Hŭimun. Tomorrow, I will go to our master and mistress and embellish this tale; if they are amused with this anecdote, would I not receive three cups of wine? When I receive my prize wine, I will be sure to share one cup with you!"[25]

Hŭimun's decision to defy his father's prohibition against the consummation of his marriage supplies an entertaining story to the lucky maid, who hopes to receive prize wine after relaying it to her masters. The other maid's labors are lost as Hŭimyŏng simply spends the night over his books. Martin Huang notes that in the late imperial Chinese novel "one peeps at what one is not supposed to see," meaning that secret witnessing enables the gratification of desire.[26] This instance of witnessing described in *Pearls and Jade* carries an entirely different function. Peeping does not gratify desire but rather opens the space of the matrimonial bedchamber to disciplining surveillance by the larger kinship structure.

The structure of desire traced in the lineage novel can be summarized as follows. Only men can figure as subjects of desire and still retain their productive identity within the kinship system. Lustful women are warded off by chaste wives, who are armed either with virtue and attraction or, alternatively, with martial powers that defeat lustful shrews. Male desire is affirmed as a source of patriarchal power, but it is contained within the conjugal relationship and distributed through the kinship network as spectacle.

It is, however, not just the ebullient sexuality that receives heightened visibility in the lineage novel. Desexualized couples also come under intense scrutiny within the domestic compound. Going back to the first novel of the Hyŏn lineage sequence, Brothers Hyŏn, we now turn to Hyŏn Kyŏngmun, who, unlike his lustful brother Sumun, has difficulty consummating his marriage. The trouble begins when Kyŏngmun is wed to a rather unattractive though virtuous woman, Chu Yŏgyo. After several ups and downs in their relationship, Kyŏngmun's affection for his wife grows, but he fails to sleep with Yŏgyo, who resists all of his advances. At one point, Kyŏngmun's maternal uncle, Master Chang, plays a trick on him by leaving a red mark on Kyŏngmun's hand.

The "red mark" (chup'yo 朱票), also termed "nightingale" or "parrot blood" (aenghyŏl 鸎血), appears in lineage novels as a virginity marker, which would disappear only after a woman's deflowerment. Traceable to a Jin-dynasty (265–420) practice of applying a paste made of cinnabar-fed gecko to women's bodies to detect virginity,[27] this sexual inscription appears frequently in Korean texts, especially lineage novels,[28] even though the practice did not appear to have a real-life parallel in Chosŏn.[29] Used exclusively on women's bodies, nightingale blood subjects Kyŏngmun's body to resignification. If female chastity constitutes cardinal virtue, the male chastity of the already married Kyŏngmun heightens the comic visibility of his paradoxical body, unruly in the view of gender norms. The domestics poke fun at Kyŏngmun, saying that from an able-bodied man he has been transformed into a boudoir woman.[30]

Kyŏngmun and his wife have a series of disagreements that further delay the consummation of their marriage. During an illness, Kyŏngmun reminds Chu Yŏgyo of his shame, and he is quite desperate:

Pointing at the red mark, [Kyŏngmun] said, "Just look at this! I am not a thirteen-year-old child. Not only can I not claim to be fully a man (*sunyang* 純陽),[31] but with this thing on my body I simply don't know where to turn to. Now, [this red mark] is not widely known among the people, but once even the ignorant come to see it, they will take me to be a woman and seek to take me in marriage. What would you think of such a scene? . . . I am especially worried about this blotch during this illness, for fear that I die childless, failing to fulfill a man's duty. Truly, you are doing things that no one else would dare to."[32]

Because his words are decorous, and because he has made amends for his earlier ill treatment of his wife, Yŏgyo has no further pretexts for resisting his demands, and Kyŏngmun finally succeeds in erasing the mark of shame. The next day Kyŏngmun's uncle, Master Chang, offers a humorous greeting: "This mark was so easy to erase, so why would you carry it on your body for so long, undermining your appearance as a man?"[33]

We must remember that Kyŏngmun's story unfolds in parallel with his brother's. Sumun's lustful and violent conquest of Yun Hyebing and Kyŏngmun's protracted courtship of Chu Yŏgyo are at opposite extremes of the conjugal spectrum, and each has to be brought into equilibrium. Of note is also the fact that Kyŏngmun's sexuality has to be claimed as a visible, bodily transformation that inaugurates him as a man, a husband, and future father. Although Chosŏn society sought to control women's sexuality, the male body, as shown in this lineage novel, is similarly subjected to a visible and highly monitored process of sexualization.[34] Women's chastity, curiously, is also treated as existing on a spectrum. Chastity constitutes a woman's chief virtue, but its excess—embodied in the figures of wives who deny bed to their husbands—is seen as problematic from the perspective of lineage continuity. Lineage novels suggest that a husband's inability to control an excessively chaste wife undermines his dignity. Whereas the classics and conduct books praise women's chastity and obedience and valorize men's patriarchal authority by providing moral guidelines or virtuous exemplars, lineage novels tell us that regulation of these identities and relationships occurs in a specific place—the matrimonial bed.

Maternal and Paternal Kin

A crucial relationship fleshed out in the lineage novel and rarely featured elsewhere in Chosŏn-dynasty sources is that between father-in-law and son-in-law. The father-in-law is usually presented as a petty, profit-seeking man, scorned by his upright son-in-law. I have already noted that when the two most important men in a woman's life fail to develop amity, the daughter-wife, resenting her husband's treatment of her father, becomes a frigid mother to her own son and lineage heir. This problematic figure demands resolution of a concatenation of entangled relationships.

I have also noted that sexuality is integral to the articulation of patriarchal authority within the matrimonial relationship. The man's sexual violence, in this scheme, actualizes the woman's transition through the structure of the three obediences. When she leaves the authority of her father, she is expected to transfer her deference to her husband; the failure to consummate a marriage in the lineage novel is coterminous with lack of patriarchal control. Sexuality, curiously, enters into the relationships between father-in-law and son-in-law in two novels considered here: *Jade Mandarin Ducks* and *The Pledge*.

In *Jade Mandarin Ducks*, Yi Wŏnŭi, a treacherous and greedy official, turns his back on the betrothal pledge between his daughter and So Segyŏng after learning about a downturn in the So family's political fortunes. Segyŏng eventually marries Yi Wŏnŭi's daughter, per the earlier agreement, but first So Segyŏng dresses as a maid and enters service in Yi Wŏnŭi's house to avoid political persecution. There, he encounters his future father-in-law in the most unexpected of circumstances, when Yi Wŏnŭi steals into Segyŏng's room in the middle of the night. In surprise, Segyŏng asks:

"My lord, why is it that you are here in the middle of the night?" How could Yi Wŏnŭi know that these were words of resentment. Laughing giddily, he closes and locks the door, saying: "My heart moved the moment I saw you (*ttŭsi kiurŏsidoe*), but my wife is old, and her jealousy is immense. There was nothing I could do, and I decided to place you at the service of my daughter. I can no longer wait, though. Do not worry about your lowly station. Because of my love for you, my wife will be unable to harm you. Do not think much about my age, either—even young boys could envy my energy (*kiryŏk* 氣力) and strength (*chŏnggangham* 精强)."

Although discomfited, Segyŏng could not hold back a smile. He replied with a laugh: "Having achieved a ministerial rank and wide renown, how is it that you could not acquire someone to attend to you? Now, you have to steal your daughter's maid. Being just ten years of age, I am quite confused. Why do you speak these indecent words to me?"

Yi Wŏnŭi looked closely at Segyŏng's delicate appearance in candlelight: the stature of Consort Yang (Ch. Yang guifei) and the daintiness of Empress Cho (Ch. Zhao Feiyan) paled in comparison. Such an alluring and beautiful [sight] bedazzled Yi Wŏnŭi and stirred him. How could he possibly accept those words? With an absent-minded laugh, he approached Segyŏng and took his hands, intending to coerce him to play. How could Segyŏng, deploring Yi Wŏnŭi's depravity but still youthful, pure at heart, and oblivious of desire, know that this debauched man was making advances? Frightened, Segyŏng tried to end this, but Yi Wŏnŭi was putting all his strength in the effort. When Segyŏng turned his body the wrong way, his natural form (*ponhyŏng* 本形) broke out. When Yi Wŏnŭi realized what happened, losing the color of his face, his eyes askew, and his head afloat, he was as if split in half with confusion.[35]

The aberrant sexual encounter between father-in-law and son-in-law problematizes their relationship along the axes of gender hierarchy and sexuality.[36] Like the red blotch on Hyŏn Kyŏngmun's hand, which is a deeply problematic bodily inscription, this encounter between father-in-law and son-in-law enacts a temporary gender reinscription, transforming the unwilling son-in-law into an object of male desire (although the reader is never led to read this encounter as homoerotic). As noted earlier, sexuality— that is, women's chastity and men's sexual dominance—constitutes the crux of gender roles and kinship hierarchies in the lineage novel. The sexual domination of women enables and signifies masculinity and patriarchal authority. The subversive gender hierarchy established in the amorous encounter between father-in-law and son-in-law ultimately pivots on the figure of the daughter-wife: the disgruntled husband maltreats her father, so she insists that the two reconcile, thus disobeying her husband's authority. The husband needs to prevail over his wife by winning her obedience.

Segyŏng and Hyŏnyŏng marry after many adventures, magical interventions, and reencounters. Even after marriage, Segyŏng continues to scorn and ignore Hyŏnyŏng's father, Yi Wŏnŭi. Hyŏnyŏng's resentment of her husband's treatment of her father then turns her into a frigid mother to their son. The lengthy excerpt from *Jade Mandarin Ducks* given here shows how the minutest details of everyday interactions are captured as they unfold between So Segyŏng, his wife, and their toddler son:

Just five months after birth, Ponghŭi appeared mature and percep- tive, already walking and trying to learn the sounds of language. He could already distinguish his parents and especially liked to follow his father. Seeing his father, Ponghŭi would cross his hands and imi- tate the posture assumed at reading. Sometimes he would even take the brush and pretend to be washing it. At moments, Ponghŭi would let go of the breast and look back at his father, clapping happily and then embracing his mother again. Then he would go down to the book case and take a book, giving it to his father and, lowering and nodding his head, imitating the sounds of reading and urging his father to read. . . . To Hyŏnyŏng, this was an unwanted child, and she did not rejoice in his outstanding behavior; being reserved, she did not express affection (*kach'aham* 假借). But Segyŏng, finally see- ing this much-awaited son, was astonished and amused. The boy was growing up so fast that Segyŏng often measured his height, asking, "When did you grow so?!" Every day Segyŏng played with the boy, feeling that in some mysterious way it was his own body, which just became divided into two. When Segyŏng looked at the amusing things the boy did, his face shone, and, embracing Ponghŭi, Segyŏng said, "Now my boy is encouraging me to study, but then he is dis- tracting me, so why don't I make him read instead!"

With these words, Segyŏng taught Ponghŭi the six characters for *heaven, earth, man, son, father,* and *mother.* Ponghŭi took the book right away and found these characters, one by one. Although he skipped over other characters written in the same way, finding only exactly the ones pinpointed by his father, and although he was still not good at speaking and therefore could not pronounce the sound of these characters, it was clear Ponghŭi knew them. In great surprise, Segyŏng said, "What an able boy! . . . Now that my son has already learned letters, what could I possibly worry about?"

With these words, Segyŏng raised his eyes. Hyŏnyŏng's expres- sion was cold like a crisp plum blossom. Her hands arranged orderly and her gaze lowered, she was not even looking at the tender amuse- ments of father and son. Finding Hyŏnyŏng so cold-hearted, Segyŏng

FEELINGS AND THE CONFLICTS OF KINSHIP [141]

said to her, "To me, the relationship of father and son is the most precious thing in the world. I have a father above me and a son below me, myself being in between; at the moment my heart is filled with joy. Is it not the same for you?" After pondering it silently, Hyŏnyŏng said, "Whose human feelings (*injŏng* 人情) are unaware of the precious bond between father and child (*puja* 父子)? For someone like me, cut off from my own heavenly essence from above (*ch'ŏnsŏng* 天性), what can I know about the heaven-mandated motherly love that continues below (*ch'ŏnsok chaae* 天屬慈愛)? In the same way, all people have children and raise them, but becoming unworthy of one's parents and thoughtlessly forgetting the boundless grace given by the parents, only caring for one's own progeny, are the way of birds and beasts. Although people are unsteady, they are different from birds and beasts, and seeing a young child fills their hearts with tremor. How can motherly love (*chaae* 慈愛) issue forth?"[37]

The domestic idyll is disrupted by the frigid mother: Hyŏnyŏng remains a distant onlooker, which prompts her husband to question her feelings for their son. Hyŏnyŏng explains that if she is unable to share a harmonious relationship with her father, how can she hope to become an affectionate mother? Having produced a male heir for her husband's family, Hyŏnyŏng is perfectly in sync with her position in terms of duty, but as an emotional subject she has no place within this domestic community. Her self-distancing is all the more striking because this passage depicts family as a zone of affection and intimacy, fleshed out in the minutest details: Ponghŭi's growth spurts, his childish gestures, and his first attempts to read. Insisting on honoring her own affective connection with her father, which would require Segyŏng to give his father-in-law due respect, Hyŏnyŏng is unable to fully transfer her affective allegiance to her son.

As time goes by, Hyŏnyŏng becomes ever more adamant in her refusal to be part of the family on emotional terms. Her last hopes are shattered when Segyŏng writes to announce that he has passed the civil service examination. The honors that Hyŏnyŏng receives as the wife of the examination laureate bring her little happiness; she is dismayed after finding not a single mention of her father in Segyŏng's letter. Thus, the news of success is transformed into a story of failure: "This was not what Hyŏnyŏng hoped for. Longing with all her heart to see the happy event in which her fundamental bond (*ch'ŏnnyun* 天倫) with her father is restored, Hyŏnyŏng wished that on the day of his success Segyŏng would reconcile with his father-in-law."[38] In her disappointment, Hyŏnyŏng ignores her crying daughter, and later she even announces to her son that she has no desire to live. Hearing the words of his despairing mother, Ponghŭi too confesses his feelings. Remembering his father's prolonged absences due to studies and service appointments, he says:

> "Ever since I was a baby and until now that I am four years of age, I have barely known my father—my longing grows stronger by day, and I am anguished. Although I should be a careless child, my feelings are so difficult to control when I hear other children call for their fathers. Awaiting the joy of reunion, I gaze into distant future, and this yearning becomes a disease. Mother, if now you harbor these strange thoughts, how can I go on living? Please put me to death first." Having spoken thus, Ponghŭi put his head into Hyŏnyŏng's lap and could not stop crying until the sleeves of his dress were moist with tears that were falling like rain.[39]

At this point, Hyŏnyŏng's unruly emotions pose a threat to the lineage. Should she decide to take her own life, the well-being of the hard-begotten heir of the So lineage would be endangered. Hyŏnyŏng's father-in-law calls her filial devotion to her father excessive ("*hyosŏng i kwainhada*" 孝性 過人) and her stubbornness inordinate ("*kojip i p'yŏnsaekhada*" 固執 偏色).[40]

Ultimately, Yi Wŏnŭi, Hyŏnyŏng's father, gets a chance to reform. In response to the protestations made by his virtuous son, he repents and decides to distribute his wealth to the poor. The story of his transformation is narrated in the sequel, *The Commentary to Jade Mandarin Ducks*. Now reformed, Yi Wŏnŭi has to mediate a conflict between his son and his son's father-in-law. The difficulty of this crucial relationship is featured in numerous lineage novels.

This relationship between father-in-law and son-in-law is even more dramatic in *Pearls*. Hyŏn Hŭngnin's reasons for despising his father-in-law, Hwa Chŏngik, are already well established: Hwa Chŏngik is petty, corrupt, and greedy. In one scene, Hyŏn Hŭngnin's son, Hŭimong, bears the brunt of the confrontation between Hŭngnin and his wife, Hwa Oksu, after Oksu yet again demands that her husband treat her father with respect:

Hŭimong woke up and started crying. Seeing Hŭngnin inside, the nurse went away, and Oksu did not pay any attention, while the crying grew only louder. Composing himself, Hŭngnin spoke, "It is because Hŭimong is of my blood that you hate him so. Did you not kill the baby while he was still inside you only to give birth to him and torment me with this piteous sight?" Oksu only smiled coldly and remained silent. Hŭngnin was already frustrated by the baby's desolate appearance, and now that the crying would not stop, his anger rose suddenly, and he pushed the baby with his hand. Crying, the baby rolled over, fell down, and his nose started to bleed. Hŭngnin only glared at Oksu angrily and did not move, while Hŭimong was crying desperately with red blood flowing profusely and covering his face. Though feigning nonchalance, Oksu was frightened by Hŭngnin's stubbornness and deplored it. Now that Hŭimong was in pain, she finally turned around, took the boy into her hands, put him in her lap, wiped his face, and comforted him. Hŭimong was a bright child, and now that he finally shook off his sleep, he realized that it was his own father who pushed him, and this terrified him. This was also the first time he was held by his mother, so he was satisfied and just clung quietly to her. Oksu saw that the boy was hurt and that his blood would not stop and also that he was so frightened he could no longer cry. She was too overcome with pity to hold back her own tears and just held Hŭimong until he fell asleep.[41]

Hŭimong fares even worse than Ponghŭi: his parents' discord brings him physical suffering. The text vividly captures Hŭimong's fright as he is pushed and hurt by his father. The startling admission that it is the first time Hŭimong has been held by his mother paints an even more dramatic image of emotional turmoil produced by the conflict in women's allegiance. Hŭngnin later regrets his outburst against Hŭimong, and the story of this family receives a rather formal resolution. The genealogy of new descendants that follows this scene of family discord suggests that the lineage is able to weather all calamities.

JaHyun Kim Haboush has identified the conflict between "filial emotions" and "filial values" in the short vernacular Korean fiction of Chosŏn, which depicted women as filial subjects, even after marriage. Filial emotions, in these texts, are considered to be more important than prescriptive values of kinship, and women's connection with their natal families is deemed inalienable and nontransferrable.[42] The treatment of women's natal affective ties is more complex in the lineage novel. These texts show that the price for severing women's affective connection with their native families is disobedience to their husbands and disaffection for their sons. This price appears too high to pay, and lineage novels ultimately allow fathers-in-law and sons-in-law to reconcile. The conflict in women's affective allegiance is notably treated as extremely problematic, even dangerous, in these texts, which show that these women fall short in performing their duty as wives and mothers. Despite—or perhaps because of?—their dangerous, disruptive potential, the affective connections women share with their natal families require nurturing, and the reconciliation between father-in-law and son-in-law takes the form of a difficult but necessary compromise.

Heir Adoption

The figures of abused children who are caught up in their parents' strife, which is a symptom of contested co-optation of matrifilial and patrilineal affective allegiance, draw attention to the complex relationship between parents and children even in families united by blood ties. The institution of heir adoption—through which sonless couples could transmit property and ritual roles[43]—further complicated this relationship. In *The Pledge*, the figure of an adopted son activates the tensions between blood-based affinities and ritual prescription. In chapter 3, I outlined the structure of this conflict vis-à-vis the tension between blood-based and ethically prescribed emotions. Now it is time to take a closer look at heir adoption as a problematic juncture of the kinship structure.

We are already familiar with the story of Chŏng Cham and Madame Yang's adoption of Chŏng Cham's nephew Chŏng Insŏng as their heir. Already at their first encounter during a family banquet when the adoption is arranged, the three are immediately linked by spontaneous and powerful feelings that are appropriate to the parent–child bond. After Madame Yang dies of illness, Chŏng Cham eventually marries Madame So. In due time, Madame So gives birth to twin boys, Injung and Inung. The scene of the children's arrival is depicted with attention to the minutest details of daily interactions characteristic of the lineage novel:

Madame So engages in lighthearted banter with the wet nurse, trying to decide which of the two children is better looking.[44]

The fact that Insŏng has already been designated as the lineage heir means that Madame So's firstborn son, Injung, loses the succession privilege. This prompts Madame So to devise kidnappings and assassinations of Insŏng and his family in the hopes of clearing the position of the lineage heir for her own son, Injung. One scene depicts Madame So's plot against Yi Chayŏm, Chŏng Insŏng's wife. Madame So forges a letter from Chayŏm to her parents, in which Madame So is accused of all manner of vices. Then, after Madame So "discovers" the letter, the following scene unfolds between mother-in-law and daughter-in-law:

Madame So folded the letter and threw it onto the table. Her clear eyes blazed coldly upon Chayŏm, as though hurling thousand arrows upon the girl. Venomous fire flashed in her gaze, when Madame So opened her lips:

"In your letter, you say that in my inhuman cruelty I am worse than any villain. Indeed, how could I ever measure up to your wisdom and virtue! What do I care if people call me a harpy—I will take your heart out to see what is truly on your mind."

With these words, Madame So came closer to Yi Chayŏm, who lay still on her bed. She straddled the girl, bringing into disarray her cloudlike layered coiffure. No matter how hard Madame So tried, the silk of Chayŏm's hair would slip away from her hands that ended up grasping only air. Then Madame So grabbed a golden pin and started lashing Yi Chayŏm's shoulders. Annoyed that a few layers of clothing still covered the girl's body, Madame So took a knife and cut the outer layers until only a single gauze blouse was left over Chayŏm's skin. Then Madame So lashed Chayŏm again. With every strike, crimson blood welled forth, staining white cloth with bright red flowers. Prostrate on her bed, Chayŏm stopped breathing and did not move at all, so who could know if she were dead or alive.

Succumbing to her frenzy, Madame So could not stop, and in a moment the girl's shirt turned crimson, with not a single patch of white left. Chayŏm herself lost her senses in a swoon. Facing such a sight, even one's mortal enemy could hardly forbear pity, but hatred permeated Madame So's very bones, and she could not restrain herself. After banging Chayŏm's head against the wall, she pulled the body to herself, rolled Chayŏm's sleeves, baring the jade hands, and plunged her teeth into Chayŏm's hand. The beautiful head was bruised, and the blood flowed; jade flesh tore off and was like shreds of lunchmeat in the teeth of Madame So. Madame So quickly reached for the knife and was about to cut Chayŏm's legs when a little maid stormed into the room and, risking death, grasped Madame So's knife and, clinging to her, prevented Madame So from going further.[45]

In this scene, Madame So would seem to be little more than the wicked stepmother (or stepmother-in-law): she literally feasts on the flesh of her breathless stepdaughter-in-law. But *The Pledge* adds dimension to Madame So's character and permits no easy judgment on the matter.

After an unsuccessful attempt to kidnap and kill Chŏng Insŏng and Yi Chayŏm's child, Madame So makes a confession to her son Inung, who is genuinely worried about his mother's reckless ways:

"In plentiful words you say that no one could match Injung and me in their atrocities, wondering how people like us could be tolerated by heaven and earth. If someone hears you say that it was so fortunate for a newborn child, tied and thrown outside in violent storm, to survive, they will either think this is empty talk or imagine some crafty spell-casting monster at work. It would be best not to speak of this at all, but you cannot stop, as if the affairs of the world were all entrusted to your care. It is absurd and futile to go around with cries like 'Unbelievable!' and 'Unnatural!,' so I did not want to listen to you from the beginning. . . .

"A while ago, in *chŏngmyo* year, your mother entered the Chŏng family. Although I lack virtue that other people possess, I was properly instructed by my parents and followed wifely ways with no fault, so while I cannot call myself a wise woman and a worthy person, I could be accused of no glaring misconduct. Suppose one is accused of a fault or some inhuman trait that one does not possess—what comes of it? Your father, since the very first day, considered our marriage a misfortune and ceaselessly suspected me, worrying that some trouble might be caused to Insŏng. Although I am not bright by nature, how could I not know his heart? Would I not be disturbed? Would I not be furious? My numerous virtues and great wisdom— even if I possessed those—would never be acknowledged or approved by my husband. So I decided that I indeed would live up to his suspicions and spare no effort in tormenting his beloved son. Once I made up my mind, there was no turning back. Insŏng is truly outstanding, and in vain could I wish that Injung were his match, but Injung too is his father's son, even if his father's cold-heartedness does not befit this cardinal human bond. And now, when Insŏng has a son of his own, your father is so overjoyed that he gives all his love to Insŏng's family. When I see this, my grief and regret know no measure, so I indeed do not wish any good to Insŏng and his wife. But while my hatred is a matter of a moment, with all my heart I know that Insŏng and his wife are very filial and virtuous, and I admire them for it, so one might indeed find it strange that I can commit all these atrocities and turn into a harpy."[46]

Here, Madame so speaks about her feelings with absolute sincerity. She is also quite objective in her judgment, noting Chŏng Cham's groundless early suspicions of her hostility toward Insŏng. Indeed, on their wedding night Chŏng Cham has a dream in which Madame So turns into a hideous beast and pursues Insŏng, who barely manages to escape with his life. Madame So explains that her violence was prompted by objective circumstances. And despite her animosity, she is able to acknowledge the superior moral qualities of Insŏng.

Madame So's character appears ever more complex when she is described from the perspective of her parents, who see her as a woman with many outstanding abilities, although matched, unfortunately, with a short temper. This combination of qualities appears fateful when Madame So assumes a decidedly unwanted role, entering a man's house to succeed to his deceased wife:

Lord So and his wife had no worries over their other children, but Kyowan, Madame Chŏng [Madame So],[47] was their late child and youngest daughter. It is true that all people love their youngest the most; Madame Chŏng, moreover, was truly unique and outstanding by nature. In their tender affection, how could her parents help loving and admiring her? Lord So, however, possessed outstanding wisdom, and his astuteness surpassed that of others. He did not rejoice in his daughter's extraordinary qualities and was concerned over finding her a fit husband. When Chŏng Cham sought marriage after the death of his first wife, Lord So had many concerns when sending his daughter over.

. . . Lord So's wife knew of her husband's concerns but chose to remain silent, harboring her regret. In this vast, vast world, should they search long enough, would they not find an excellent husband for their young daughter? Should they really commit their youngest girl to the unwanted lot of the second wife? Moreover, they knew all too well that their child's temper prevailed over her virtue and that her rage could never be tempered by her will: she prided herself in her abilities, while her virtue and benevolence were very far from proper wifely ways.[48]

Lord So, Madame So's father and a benevolent and wise patriarch, has a prescience of his daughter's future mishap, which is confirmed in the silent regret of Madame So's mother.

The story of Madame So, in short, is refracted through multiple perspectives, which emphasize the complexity of her relationship with her adopted son. This nuanced treatment transforms her story from an account of immoral conduct to an index of the complexity of kinship relations. Moreover, the novel positions the practice of adoption as highly problematic. Insŏng is Chŏng Cham's nephew, born to Chŏng Cham's brother, Chŏng Sam. When Chŏng Cham originally asks for his brother's consent for Insŏng's adoption, Chŏng Sam hesitates. The novel makes it clear, however, that Sam "does not have thoughts of blocking [the adoption] because, holding him dear, he wanted to spare his son. Rather, he was worried that, if arranged so early, this serious matter might pose difficulties (nanyŏn chi sa 赦然之事) in the future."[49] At first, Sam notes that Insŏng is only six years old, much too young to be adopted. He adds that Chŏng Cham's wife is still of child-bearing age, which makes the adoption decision preposterous. It is this second remark that reveals Sam's real source of concern: if Madame Yang were to have any children, Insŏng's life and fate within the Chŏng lineage would become precarious. Cham reacts to these arguments very quickly, saying that he, as the eldest son, is preoccupied with securing his line of succession, but he has no doubt that Sam is right in judging the case this way. Sam, in turn, offers profuse apologies, saying that he was inconsiderate in his reply. The matter is settled by their father, Chŏng Han, the lineage patriarch. Chŏng Han says that the succession issue is indeed a grave matter that should be settled according to Chŏng Cham's plan.

Although Cham and Sam settle the issue of Insŏng's adoption rather peacefully, the small ripple caused by Sam's hesitation points to the multilayered complexities that surround the adoption issue.

A second heir adoption occurs after Madame So gives birth to her twin sons. The second twin, Inung, is adopted by Chŏng Cham's nephew Chŏng Hŭm. The scene of Inung's adoption is quite peculiar. The matter of Inung's adoption is decided the moment he is born, and his adopted father is the one who names him. Chŏng Hŭm takes nightingale blood and writes the following on the boy's left arm: "On this day, month, and year, the adopted father (yangbu 養父), Mun'gye [Hŭm's courtesy name], gave the baby this name." Inung's name and courtesy name are then recorded on the boy's right arm.[50]

From the earlier discussion of Kyŏngmun's case, we remember that inscription of the male body with nightingale blood is a gesture of gender reversal, perceived as an affront to male dignity. Hŭm's sister makes a similar comment about the inscription on Inung's arms: "This child, having a man's body, has to endure the red mark, like a woman." She goes as far as to call Hŭm's gesture "ungainly (sohwalhada 疏濶)." To this, Hŭm replies: "For me, it is no small matter to establish the father–son [bond]. While I might be ungainly . . . I want to record that today the fundamental father–son bond has been settled."[51] Although the potentially subversive connotations of the inscription of the male body with nightingale blood are brought into the picture, Hŭm dispels such allegations. Throughout the novel, this marking never surfaces as an injury to Inung's virility, constituting instead a durable means of inscription that will stay on Inung's body until he reaches the age of maturity. Inung's flesh and body are claimed by his adopted father in a gesture that at once dramatizes and mitigates the anxiety about the power of feelings of flesh and blood in the structure of kinship.

After Chŏng Hŭm inscribes Inung's arm, the matriarch, Madame Chang, joyful about the conclusion of the adoption arrangements, reminds everyone that it is improper to keep Inung's mother, Madame So, in the dark. When Madame So appears in front of Madame Chang, she acts "as if she did not mind (korikkiji anin tŭt) the adoption in the slightest."[52] The concise "as if" carries dramatic weight in light of the love Madame So has for her children and in light of her doubleness and dissimulation, which is discussed in chapter 3.

It is important to note that the novel finds ways to circumvent adoption arrangements that are clearly deemed problematic. Even though Inung is adopted the moment he is born, his relationship with his blood mother, Madame So, continues to be extremely intimate. Take, for instance, the scene of this tender play:

> Lying down on his mother's lap, Inung was sucking her breast. Turning his head around while holding on to her nipple, he showed his white teeth. Stroking his shiny hair to arrange a strayed lock and straightening his headband, Madame So spoke, "When will I stop seeing your extraordinary ways? Even for an uncouth [child like you], sucking [your mother's] breast looks utterly silly." Inung, letting go of the breast, replied, "How much longer can I be doing this? If you see me doing this even after my capping ceremony, then you can be displeased. But now that I am not capped yet, why can I not have my mother's breast?"[53]

To comprehend the strength of this intimate connection between Madame So and Inung, we must remember that Inung is the first to hear Madame So's confession about her violent schemes against Insŏng. Also, as we saw in chapter 3, Inung's thoughts during a foreign expedition are so focused on Madame So, his birth mother, that her augured misfortune drives him to sickness.

Madame So's story highlights the powerful pull of feelings of flesh and blood, but she is not the only character who expresses these feelings. Insŏng, the adopted heir, and his own birth mother, Madame Hwa, share similarly strong feelings when Insŏng comes to bid her farewell before he departs on a journey:

> [Insŏng] put his head on the lap of Madame Hwa with these words: "Now that I am leaving your care, I will only return next year. When I imagine that you will think of me and worry for all this long time, my heart aches. . . ." With these words, taking his mother's hand, Insŏng was overcome with tender feelings. Madame Hwa slowly took off her outer garments and went to bed, asking her son to lie down beside her. Stroking his hair, she forced herself to smile, saying, "When I am beside you, ten years pass by as swiftly as one day's night,

and I realize that human life is but one brief moment. Nothing can be better than the two of us lying in the same bed this night."[54]

Insŏng's relationship with his birth mother, Madame Hwa, makes the story of his struggles with his adopted stepmother, Madame So, all the more poignant. Within the context of late Chosŏn social practice, the relationship between mothers and sons, which extends beyond these children's adoption by ritual parents, adds dimension to the intersection of social norms and everyday affective practices. The intimacy shared between sons and birth mothers even as they are separated through adoption "creates spaces and usurps places meant for other kinds of relation."[55]

The Pledge ultimately makes space for the blood-based bonds and affective links in the ritually sanctioned rubric of patrilineal kinship. The genealogy of the Chŏng lineage at the end of the novel begins with Chŏng Injung, Madame So's conniving son, and not with Insŏng, the virtuous stepson and the de jure lineage heir. Injung is described in the following terms: "The second son of Chŏng Cham is Minister of the Board of War Chŏng Injung. His courtesy name is Yibo, and his nom de plume is Chok'am. He is the firstborn of Madame So and the twin brother of Inung. During his youth, he gave himself to evil ways for a time but then changed his course, reformed himself, and fortified his character, emerging in his shining glory. His endowments are outstanding and ten times superior to those of the people who never erred."[56] Insŏng, in fact, is recorded third, after the twin sons of Madame So and Chŏng Cham. Although Insŏng's adoption is a necessary step, and although his moral worth is uncontested, The Pledge, in this gesture of veiled compromise, acknowledges the primacy of blood ties even as it expands the vision of the streamlined patriline to accommodate for other vital kinship links.

Emotions and Values of Kinship

The patrilineal kinship structure of Chosŏn was founded upon the belief that moral effort could bring feelings—which are integral to human nature—into alignment with moral prescription and that correctly ordered feelings would lay the foundation for ethical conduct. Lineage novels notably focus on troubled protagonists who because their feelings are not in harmonious order engage in unruly behavior. Powerful feelings and impudent actions are paradoxically a kind of mark of honor.

Looking back at *Pearls*, we see that its unruly protagonist, Hyŏn Ch'ŏnnin, who beheads his wife's maid and flings her head at the terrified mistress, is set apart from his brothers and cousins. When Ch'ŏnnin and his brother, Myŏngnin, are flogged for their escapades, Ch'ŏnnin withstands ninety sticks, while Myŏngnin can bear only sixty. This prompts the following comparison: "Although Myŏngnin is certainly strong and sturdy, his strength is still no match to Ch'ŏnnin's youthful and sturdy spirit."[57] Ch'ŏnnin becomes a legend for his brothers and cousins; his charisma to a large degree stems from his unruly and stubborn nature.

What to make of these stories? How are they situated in the narrative of normative kinship, which remains an incontestable value in the lineage novel? Madame So, the unruly heroine of *The Pledge*, devises a reading strategy for the narrative of her life in response to the incessant moralizing of her virtuous son Inung: "Do not tell me of my lofty station—all this murmuring only exasperates me. . . . After I die, in the very first part of my posthumous biography (*haengjang* 行狀) it shall be written that I excelled in tormenting my stepson and beating my daughter-in-law."[58] From the perspective of normative-conduct literature, of which posthumous biography is part, Madame So's story is a negative example and a warning. But *The Pledge* promotes a different reading of Madame So's life.

The Pledge ends with a banquet that celebrates the prosperity of the Chŏng lineage. Madame So has been appeased by Insŏng's filial devotion. Indeed, it is noted that Madame So and Insŏng have a karmic connection, and her hostility to her stepson is explained away by predestination. The Chŏng lineage is preserved, but the massive span of *The Pledge* lays out the scope of unruly feelings and the immense moral effort required to preserve the kinship order. The novel's final lines revisit the importance of emotion, invoking Madame So:

Even if the wise deeds of Chŏng Insŏng and his great filiality permeated the entire realm, without the moral transformation of Madame So and Chŏng Injung this story would not be possible, and the people of the world would know nothing about it. Now that Madame So and Chŏng Injung have been transformed, the life story of Chŏng Insŏng has been recorded in great detail, but without the atrocities of his stepmother and stepbrother, the story of his suffering in the spirit of filiality and brotherly love would not be the same; without the transformation of Madame So and Chŏng Injung, this story would not take shape. In human affairs, the old times and the present differ greatly, but it is pathetic (*kaso* 可笑) that good and evil continue to revolve.[59]

In these last lines, *The Pledge* confesses its own narrative desire: unruly feelings make this novel possible. *The Pledge* refers the reader to a biography of Chŏng Insŏng, but the story of Insŏng's virtue remains untold.[60] Madame So and Injung—not Insŏng—are central to the 180 volumes of *The Pledge*, and even though Madame So is ultimately reinscribed into the kinship fabric, the lengthy and nuanced portrayal of her character monumentalizes the discourse of feelings and establishes the autonomy of private emotional experience. In light of Madame So's ironic remark that a posthumous biography could not do justice to the narrative of her life, the focus on defiance and unruly emotion professed in the novel's closing lines sets it apart from other life narratives. Unruly feelings are integral to the lineage novel because they mark the trajectory of a person's socialization through structures of prescriptive kinship.

In her study of the expression of sentiments in Bedouin poetry, Lila Abu-Lughod makes a distinction between social norm and social value, noting that it is "a matter of self-respect and pride that the individual achieve the standards, not an obligation."[61] In other words, because in Bedouin culture the system of kinship relations constitutes the totality of the social world, with no conceivable outside, voluntarily belonging to the world of kinship obligation produces a sense of self-worth. And although individuals observe social norms in everyday life, Bedouin poetry recited in everyday situations valorizes defiance as choice in juxtaposition with unwitting submissiveness. Writing about the cult of *qing* in late imperial China, Haiyan Lee has noted that one of the most significant late Ming redactions to the orthodox Confucian view of human relations was "the shift from ethical imperative to voluntary choice," whereby human relationships were understood to be "fundamentally grounded in affect," which implied subjective choice and personal predilection.[62] Haiyan Lee is describing a cultural context in which the conjugal couple—an elective and deeply felt relationship—constituted a site for rethinking of the larger matrix of human bonds. This chapter has shown that desire and the conjugal relationship, although problematized, do not constitute the exclusive focus of the lineage novel. Instead, the lineage novels' accounts of the most troubled and defiant protagonists turn an array of problematic relationships—between spouses, between fathers-in-law and sons-in-law, and between stepmothers and stepchildren—into values reapproached as choice.

The distance that lineage novels introduce between the person and the social norm are reminiscent of Ning Ma's notion of unmooring, produced by global money flows in the seventeenth and eighteenth centuries and reflected in the shift from epic to individuated narrative, which constitutes a contingent phenomenon of the emergence of fictional realism across the world in the context of global commercialization and relaxation of the social structure.[63] As noted in the introduction, the lineage novel's place within the global age of fictional realism remains ambiguous. The influence of the scholar–beauty novel and Wang Yangming's (1472–1529) ideas, which emerged in the commercialized society of the late Ming, upon the lineage novel appears to have been significant. At the same time, Korea itself did not experience a comparable extent of commercialization, and the emergence of the lineage novel is very much embedded in the context of Korea's kinship structure and its ideology of patrilineality. Although lineage novels' protagonists navigate the distance between personal meaning and the social norm and narrate the vagaries of their unruly emotions, the teleological horizon of the lineage structure dominates their stories. The succession of numerous generations after the plots of unruly feelings are settled constitutes the ultimate happy ending of these texts. Nevertheless, genealogical imagination does not foreground an exhaustive reading strategy for the stories of the unruly protagonists. By exploring the distance between the person and the social norm, the lineage novel offers a vision of human sociality that delicately balances a prescriptive vision and an openness to the specific trajectories of lives that crisscross it.

In Conclusion

The problematic junctures of kinship discussed in this chapter are articulated in the lineage novel through the display of unruly feelings, which disrupt the harmonious performance of correct human relationships and upset the fulfillment of prescribed kinship norm. This is not to say that unruly feelings can be comprehended within the so-called hydraulic theory of feelings that foregrounds a clearly demarcated inner self delimited by the social order, always pushing against it, with feelings signifying transgressive overflow of the social norm. Against the context of Confucian moralism, in which the social order rests upon the alignment of feelings and social values, unruly feelings are hermeneutical indices for moral cultivation. They are always expressed and understood in their social context, and they do not constitute personal depth. In the lineage novel, unruly feelings identify the problematic junctures between the self and the social world, highlighting the most troublesome aspects of kinship and calling for moral effort to overcome them.

Read against the background of the Korean kinship system, the lineage novel can be seen as diagnosing the "hot" and "cold" spots of kinship,[64] identifying situations of affective lack and excess—unruliness that does not conform to the affective mean, envisaged as ideal. Along these lines, excessive desire and its gratification are just as dangerous as an untouched conjugal bed, and disproportionate love of one's progeny called forth by feelings of flesh and blood is just as immoderate as the frigidity of mothers and fathers who are locked in conflict.

The lineage novel reminds us that emotional complexity is not unique to the cultural logic of Western individualism. It presents a concatenation of human bonds that branch out into ever more tangled relationships—the conflict between father-in-law and son-in-law affects the bond of mother and son, creating the figure of the frigid mother. These conflicts are integral to the process of figuration of kinship.

The idea that emotional complexity was invented by the Western novel became the self-fulfilling prophesy of modernity, projected onto Korea's literary past through the rubric of "encourage goodness and warn against evil (*kwŏnsŏn chingak* 勸善懲惡)," which early twentieth-century Korean intellectuals attached to the moralizing canon of Chosŏn literature in a gesture of distancing that called for literary renewal. This hundred-year-old viewpoint lingers in modern Anglophone historical studies of Korea, which treat literary and cultural modernity as the ground zero of innovation and invention rather than a reformulation of essential cultural coordinates. *The Pledge* gives us not only the striking figure of Madame So but also a portrait of her husband, Chŏng Cham, the patriarch upon whom her temper leaves an indelible mark. After the trouble with Madame So becomes known to her natal family, Chŏng Cham's father-in-law, Lord So, observes the withered appearance of his son-in-law:

Chŏng Cham arranged his seat in front of Lord So. Lord So asked Chŏng Cham if he was comfortable after his long equestrian journey and after receiving Chŏng Cham's good-natured assurance, Lord So raised his eyes to look at his son-in-law. It had been a long time. Chŏng Cham's skin now appeared saggy, his once sturdy figure was gaunt, and his entire look changed. Chŏng Cham was not just lean: his once radiant appearance was dimmed, and his mighty spirit seemed tempered. Even if the mountain is great, a thin stream of water can slowly carve its way; although this man is mighty, the light frost in his black whiskers betrays the autumn of his days.[65]

From a third-person perspective, the change in Chŏng Cham's appearance is striking, and the subtlety of Lord So's mediating gaze makes it even more poignant.

It is, however, the conspicuous presence of female protagonists in the lineage novel that is most striking. In the context of the Chosŏn vision of femininity that pivoted on obedience, lineage novels certainly shatter the simplistic assumption that women's lives and voices did not amount to much in the patriarchal culture of the time. At the very least, lineage novels reveal that the complexity of women's position within the kinship culture was a major focus of imaginative scrutiny, even though this scrutiny was restricted largely to the culture of the elites. It would, however, be an oversimplification to read lineage novels as stories of women's empowerment. Although women voice the unruly feelings that arise within the gender politics of kinship, their voices are always contained within the rubric of patriarchal power. This power manifests itself most violently in scenes of rape, but it is also evident in the absence of a space in which women's lives and feelings can be discussed apart from their relationships with men.

Notably, the mother–daughter relationship is not featured in the texts discussed in this chapter. Whereas the mother–son bond is prominent in the lineage novel, the relationship between daughters and their mothers is rarely in the spotlight. In the conflicts between women's fathers and husbands, mother figures rarely offer comfort or council. On the contrary, they inflict the worst possible indignities upon their sons-in-law. In *Brothers Hyŏn*, Hyŏn Kyŏngmun's mother-in-law sends a servant to spew excrement upon him to avenge his ill treatment of her daughter. Afflicted women usually find solace in their wet nurses and maids, but the latter are excluded from the kinship fabric and therefore are seen as extensions of the heroines rather than persons with social power and character complexity. The need to balance patrilineal and matrifilial connections within a lineage may be represented by a woman's conflicted allegiance both to her natal family and to her husband's household, but this balance is achieved through the filial efforts of the son-in-law and the moral reformation of the father-in-law, assigning to women just the experience of this contradiction. Thus, although lineage novels signal importance of women's affective links to their natal families, the ramifications of this affective dissonance are contextualized through the centrality of the patriline, which frigid mothers threaten to undermine by maltreating their sons and lineage heirs in a desperate gesture to defy their husbands' authority. Moreover, women's excessive feelings for their blood children, their refusal to consummate their marriages, and their lust are depicted as threats to the perpetuation of the lineage that must be overcome.

At the same time, women are not depicted as exclusively prone to the experience of unruly feelings. Every lineage patriarch traverses a path of trial and error that lives on in the family memories. *The Commentary to Jade Mandarin Ducks* offers us a way to understand the balance of gender power within the structure of kinship. In that novel, Kyŏng Pinghŭi, whose relationship with her husband, Yi Hyŏnyun, has long been strained, falls ill, and her spirit travels to the underworld. She is called upon to adjudicate a trial over the souls of the dead, and her aptitude earns her the reward of being reborn as a man. As she drifts back to her senses and her female body, Pinghŭi faintly hears the following words: "Even men (*taejangbu* 大丈夫) who took over the world pay deference (*kyŏngŭi* 敬意) to the lord above them."[66] Pointing to shifting relational context of any person's life, this comment suggests that gender is relative within the larger system of hierarchies and compromises required by kinship and social norms.

PART III

Reconfiguration

CHAPTER V

The Novel Without the Lineage

Lineage novels' content and mode of circulation as well as the creation of their manuscripts were inextricably linked with the patrilineal kinship system of late Chosŏn Korea (1392–1910). Narrating the genealogical subject situated within the structure of kinship obligation, these novels laid out a temporal landscape and modeled family-based Confucian human bonds within a generational framework. Outlining the problematic junctures of the Korean kinship system, lineage novels treated the unruly emotions they caused as integral to the narratives of their protagonists' lives. Furthermore, the domestic identities of elite women, mandated by the gender logic of the kinship system, and the interior, familial location of vernacular Korean literary practices warranted the intrafamilial transmission of these novels in manuscripts created by kinswomen, whose embodied brushstrokes gained sentimental significance after their deaths.

This chapter examines the moment when the structures of social life as well as the aesthetic configurations that brought the lineage novel to the center of elite vernacular Korean culture were disarticulated. China's defeat in the second Opium War (1859–1860) and Western concession politics shattered China's centrality in East Asia, although Korea continued to appeal to China's authority until the 1890s. A series of French and American invasions into Korea in the 1860s and 1870s made the Chosŏn court mistrustful of the Western powers and led to conservative, inward-looking policies until Korea signed the Kanghwa Treaty with Japan in 1876 and opened its ports for trade. The assassination of Queen Min (b. 1851) by Japanese troops in 1895, Japan's victory over a European power in the Russo-Japanese War (1904–1905), and the Protectorate Treaty between Japan and Korea, signed in 1905 before Korea's ultimate colonization in 1910, redefined not only East Asia's geopolitical landscape but also Korea's notions of statecraft, civilization, and knowledge. The moral view of human bonds, which linked the familial and the political realms and defined inquiry into cosmological moral laws as the highest form of cultural competence, was no longer aligned with Korea's place in the changing world.

Within this larger geopolitical realignment, Chosŏn was also dealing with a number of domestic issues: a preponderance of consort families in court politics following the death of King Chŏngjo (r. 1776–1800), inefficient taxation, economic shortages, and popular discontent. Visions of an egalitarian society and political reform that developed from the 1850s to the 1870s appealed to elite and lower classes alike. On the one hand, the socially mixed followers of Tonghak professed an egalitarian vision founded on a mixed idiom of Christianity and local beliefs. The large-scale Tonghak uprising of 1894—before it was suppressed by the Korean and Japanese armies—pursued an agenda of local land reform and vented antiforeign sentiments. On the other hand, elite reformers, influenced by Western knowledge, attempted to enact their political vision through the Kapsin palace coup of 1884, the Kabo Reforms of 1894–1896, which abolished social distinctions, and the Independence Club Movement (1894–1896).[1]

Although the economic development, urbanization, and social change that occurred in Korea in the late nineteenth century remain debated issues in Korean historiography, it is clear that the position of the elite lineages was gradually decentered. Economic development endangered the elites' countryside estates. Geopolitical changes, Japanese influence in late nineteenth-century Korean politics, government reforms, and a shift in the conception of productive knowledge from Confucian learning to practical skills (language, science, and arts) that were historically cultivated by nonelites promoted the social advancement of secondary groups: secondary sons, local clerks or *hyangni*, and commoners.[2] The Kabo Reforms of 1894–1896, which officially abolished status distinctions, signified the official eradication of the link between Confucian learning, government service, and elite status.[3] This is not to say that the lineage system and the prestige associated with long-standing civil excellence disappeared in a moment. Descendants of Chosŏn civil elites retained their political power,[4] and in the variegated social scene of Korea in the late nineteenth and early twentieth centuries the empowerment of inferior social groups produced a desire for status accoutrements associated with elite culture.[5]

Lineage novels and their audiences registered these changes. A twenty-five-volume rental library manuscript of *The Record of Two Households: Ha and Chin* (*Ha Chin yangmun rok* 河陳兩門錄) is a case in point. The rental provenance of this novel is amply confirmed by the notes that pepper the manuscript's margin space. Derogatory characterizations and bawdy sketches of the rental library owner and the women of his house—the mimetic effort drawn to their lower parts—are common in the rental manuscripts' marginalia. One particular commentator, however, weaves the concern over the contemporary state of affairs into the attacks on the library owner. Penciled in the spare lower margin, the note begins in the second volume and continues through the entire third volume. As such, it represents a curious convergence of old media and new questions that arose at the turn of the twentieth century:

Library owner, son of a bitch! Can you read? Do you know what this age is like? It is the twentieth century, where strong prey on the weak (*yagyuk kangsik* 弱肉強食) and where the fittest survive (*usŭng yŏlp'ae* 優勝劣敗). You too live in this world, don't you know anything about the twentieth century? Living in this terrifying world, people applying their abilities to any occupation (*ŏp* 業)—agriculture (*nongŏp* 農業), commerce (*sangŏp* 商業), manufacturing (*kongŏp* 工業)—are on the verge of collapse. The power is in the hands of the strong. How is it that you neglect agriculture, commerce, and manufacturing and instead take up this useless book-lending trade to make a living? This is all to your own detriment. But because you too are a person of Korea, this is the country's misfortune as well. Now, what is the state of affairs in our country? Have you not heard about *The History of the Loss of Vietnam* [K. *Wŏllam mangguk sa*; Ch. *Yuenan wangguo shi*; V. *Việt Nam vong quốc sử* 越南亡國史]? It is the same in our country, where people abandoned practical occupations (*sirŏp* 實業), entertaining fanciful beliefs. Now they are ready to continue the destiny of Vietnam and Poland. Even those men whose fervor had been extinguished—if they put their thoughts to this situation—they would cry days on end, abandoning food and drink, and even then would fail to obtain relief. What about you? Do you still live in the dream world of the Peach Garden (*towŏn segye* 桃源世界) expecting to enjoy everlasting prosperity? . . . The rise and fall of states very much depend on whether their customs (*p'ungsok* 風俗) are sound or awry.[6]

The note introduces a dichotomy between the famed fable by a classical Chinese poet, Tao Yuanming (365?–427), *Peach-Blossom Spring* (K. *Tohwa wŏn ki*; Ch. *Taohua yuan ji* 桃花源記), which depicts a utopian space of harmony removed from the unrest of the world, and the work of a revolutionary Vietnamese intellectual, Phan Bội Châu (1867–1940), which describes the French occupation of Vietnam in the late nineteenth century. According to this reader, the lineage novel is closer to the fanciful tales that delude those who live in a world that operates according to the logic of social Darwinism. As the guns of the Japanese and European empires make their way to Korea, the harmonious arrangement of human bonds radiating outward from home to the society and empire that are depicted in lineage novels no longer seems relevant.

It is unclear when this note was made. Based on the dates recorded in the marginalia, the rental manuscript is believed to have been created around 1908.[7] *The History of the Loss of Vietnam*, published in Shanghai in literary Chinese with a preface by the famed Chinese intellectual Liang Qichao (1873–1929), arrived in Korea in 1906. First serialized in *Hwangsŏng sinmun* (Capital gazette 皇城新聞), it underwent three translations and several reprints, reaching a wide audience until it was censored in 1909. Even the newspapers of Korean expatriate communities—*Haejo sinmun* (The mainstream 海朝新聞) in Vladivostok and *Sinhan kukpo* (National herald 新韓國報) in Hawai'i—ran advertisements for it, the latter stretching its ads to 1910, even after the book's prohibition in Korea.[8] The tone of the reference to *The History of the Loss of Vietnam* suggests that it was a widely recognized novelty, so we might guess that the note was made circa 1908–1909, the time when *The History of the Loss of Vietnam* was in circulation.

Rebecca Karl has written that early twentieth-century Chinese intellectuals countered the Euro-American notion of a Darwinian world with an "uneven global spatiality" that "permitted Asia, the Pacific, Africa and other places to emerge into view, not as inert geographical designation, nor as fatally 'lost' places, but as material sites for the production and performance of new global, national and local meanings."[9] In other words, Chinese intellectuals incorporated an awareness of global anti-imperial struggle into their thinking about China's place in the world. A similar logic, it seems, guided the writer of this margin note that links the historical moment of Korea on the verge of colonization to the contexts of Vietnam and Poland, calling for self-strengthening in practical ("*sirŏp*" 實業) and moral ("*p'ungsok*" 風俗) terms. The margins of a novel that outlines a moral universe centered on the Song Empire provide a space for rethinking the structure of the world in the early twentieth century. During the eighteenth and early nineteenth century, as chapter 2 has shown, lineage novels' margins were a space for the creation of intrafamilial memories, where generations of readers left their marks.

At the same time, though, lineage novels retained some of their loyal readers. A scriber's postscript appended to a manuscript of *The Record of Two Heroes: Brothers Hyŏn* from 1914 reads:

> In the third month of the *kap'in* year when I finished my work, I copied this book bit by bit in my spare time. In the meanwhile, some parts got lost, and the text was not like it was supposed to be, which upset me a great deal. It is only now that I am awakened to the meaning of this text after having completed [copying] the entire novel. In awe, I behold the elegance of this boudoir (*kyumun* 閨門) novel and the exquisite language that like a treasure remains from the times now past. That this novel went through so many hands as a treasure makes it more valuable than a thousand gold coins. One is carried away with this novel at the very first encounter. Therefore, preserve this book well and appreciate it so it may be transmitted to posterity indefinitely. I made many mistakes, and my handwriting is clumsy, but I pray you do not hold this against me.[10]

The copyist does not sign her name, but she unmistakably is a woman: her gender is revealed by the praise she confers upon a "boudoir novel," a book clearly marked by female readership. In addition, the apology offered for the time spent producing the manuscript reflects the traditional privileging of practical tasks, such as cooking and sewing, in a woman's daily life. Lineage novels, the center of elite vernacular Korean culture within the status-conscious lineage society of Chosŏn, become decidedly antimodern at the point when Korea faces multiple challenges at home and abroad.

Although these texts continue to circulate through the first decades of the twentieth century, they slowly fall into oblivion.

At the turn of the twentieth century, in the aftermath of the expansion of Western colonial empires, the cultural logic of civilization and enlightenment was flattening and synchronizing the world along the lines of progress, conceived on the premises of Western philosophy, science, and technology. In the view held by foreign observers and Korea's intellectuals alike, cultural progress required complete renewal. Yi Kwangsu (1892–1950), a dominant figure on Korea's early twentieth-century literary scene, maintained that Korea's literature "has no past, only a future."[11] "Old" literature gradually disappears from the Korean literary scene, as if through a back door. Maurice Courant's (1865–1935) famous *Bibiographie coréenne* (1895), a survey of rental library catalogs, includes a note that most volumes are missing owing to unreliable borrowers, and most of the missing volumes appear to be lineage novels.[12] Surveying the rental libraries of Seoul in 1918, E. W. Koons identifies thirty-six businesses and notes that the books they offer are "mostly of extreme trashiness."[13] As this chapter shows, the first Korean book collectors, Yi Pyŏnggi (1891–1968) and Ch'oe Namsŏn (1890–1957), have such a faint understanding of Chosŏn-era literature that they fail to distinguish lineage novels, a core genre of elite literature, from translated Chinese texts and shorter popular fiction. In this way, the lineage novel disappears from physical circulation, vanishes from cultural memory, and is overlooked in the initial early twentieth-century articulations of a national literary canon.

Whereas the narrative of the novel's rise has been complicated by global approaches to cultural studies that have provincialized European literary modernity, the problem of disappearance has received less attention. Franco Moretti points to the loss of vitality of cultural forms that prove inadequate for the elaboration of the historical issues at hand. The demise of the bildungsroman, for instance, coincides with the modernist shattering of the psyche, when a narrative of formation (*Bildung*) metamorphoses into a narrative of fracture. As a result, the figure of Wilhelm Meister, whose journey to social fulfillment at the cost of his freedom offers a compromised vision of "happiness," is replaced with the figure of Malte Laurids Brigge, whose sensorium collapses under the weight of external reality. The European bildungsroman does not make a back-door exit. Its demise marks the quintessence of modern experience: trauma, the disintegration of the ego, and the overall perception that the hostile world offers no safe havens.[14] In figures such as Malte, the bildungsroman comes to a horrifying, aesthetically appealing, and historically significant end. The academic study of the Western novel then monumentalizes the bildungsroman as the embodiment of fundamentally human afflictions.

This chapter follows the lineage novel through the last moments of its cultural visibility, treating it as a screen on which we can observe the changes of Korean society and culture in the late nineteenth and early twentieth centuries, when the lineage system no longer guaranteed the links between social distinction, Confucian learning, and heredity. What happened to the novel when the lineage disappeared from the social and cultural stage of Korea? To answer this question, this chapter ponders the changes in the aesthetic idiom of the lineage novel and its interaction with other literary genres, the changed mode of its circulation, and, finally, the reconceptualization of the novel's historical context as it made a complicated transition from familial archives to academic classification.

Retracing the lineage novel's decline allows us to reconceive the moment that preceded Korea's colonial modernity—the country's emergence on the field of global capitalism via its status as Japan's colony[15]—from a point of indeterminacy and to account for the meaning of the cultural dynamics of the preceding period in their own time and place, much in excess of the static anteriority structured by the separation of the modern from its "pre-." Scholars of East Asia have grown increasingly wary of the future-perfect narratives of history that homogenize multidirectional vectors of cultural development under the arrow of modernity time. Pondering the metamorphoses of the lineage novel against the fading of lineage kinship in late nineteenth- and early twentieth-century Korea, this chapter maintains a conversation with such East Asia scholars as David Der-wei Wang,[16] Jonathan Zwicker,[17] Ken Ito,[18] Haiyan Lee,[19] and Grace Fong and Nanxiu Qian,[20] who use models of translation, cultural hybridity, and discursive genealogy to account for the cultural refigurations in East Asia during the late nineteenth and early twentieth centuries.

The historicization of Korea's literary culture is still dominated by the towering presence of Yi Kwangsu's novel *The Heartless* (Mujŏng 無情, 1917), which remains the ground zero of modern literary development. Yi Kwangsu's text marks the literary emergence of the individual—a self-authoring moral subject of interiority that signifies rational and affective realignment of the Confucian kinship society and genealogical subjectivity. Recent studies have added dimension to this uncritical monumentality. Jooyeon

Rhee turns to literary translations and adaptations of Western and Japanese novels that appeared in Korean newspapers at the turn of the twentieth century, which "nationalized masculinity and femininity in the novel, . . . further producing divergent visions for national progress."[21] Yoon Sun Yang approaches the emergence of the modern Korean novel not as a moment of aesthetic convergence with its Western counterpart but as a gradual "trajectory of translation" of the Western notion of the individual, which she traces from so-called "new fiction" to Yi Kwangsu's novel *The Heartless*.[22] Ellie Choi notes the zones of ambiguity and nostalgia in Yi Kwangsu's novel that complicate his political program of relentless national modernization, which encompassed literary, political, and educational renewal.[23]

In this chapter, I attempt to add nuance to the picture of the turn-of-the-twentieth-century cultural milieu of Korea by casting a glance back into the future—that is, by focusing on cultural developments that fall outside the scope of the conventional modern but that nevertheless constitute valid sites for coming to terms with historical change. The purpose of this inquiry is not to find a better, purer, earlier Korean modernity. The simple interest that guides this chapter is to think about novels and literary audiences at the time when patrilineal kinship no longer encompassed the field of aesthetic possibility and the infrastructure of book circulation in a rigidly stratified social scene. From the perspective of this waning, this chapter also attempts to cast a look back at the once essential but eroding links between the Chosŏn lineage society and the lineage novel elaborated throughout this book.

The Reading Public:
From Kinship Networks to a Literary Market

During the Chosŏn dynasty, fiction was never granted too much importance. This was especially the case with vernacular Korean fiction; in addition to being far removed from the intellectual culture that centered on Confucian philosophy, Korean fiction lacked the artistry of literary prose possessed by literary Chinese novels, which the educated men of Chosŏn valued as style guides. Although lineage novels enjoyed significant prestige during the Chosŏn dynasty, they rarely became the object of educated men's discourses; their transcribers and readers were for the most part elite women, and these texts circulated in tight, women-centered kinship networks. At the turn of the twentieth century, which marked the height of colonial politics in East Asia, East Asian intellectuals were becoming gradually invested in the development of vernacular literatures.[24] All across East Asia, vernacular writing came to be seen as the representation of an authentic national voice in the context of a phonocentric imagination that sought to effect a convergence between everyday speech and writing (K. ŏnmun ilchi; J. genbun itchi 言文一致). Korean intellectuals likewise encouraged the reading public to devote their attention to the modern novel, which promised to deliver useful cultural and historical competence. Until the 1930s, however, the majority of Korean readers favored traditional tales. Studies of Korea's modern literary beginnings often ignore this sizable cultural field, which also grappled with cultural change. The interaction of the lineage novel with the increasingly commercialized and stratified literary market produced alternative trajectories of negotiation between the culture of the Chosŏn elites and the transformed social and cultural scene, which merit examination.

After Korea's signing of the Protectorate Treaty with Japan in 1905, restrictions on publishing activity that came with the Newspaper Law of 1907 and the Publication Law of 1909 made reprints of traditional novels a viable commercial enterprise, especially because these texts appealed to already established literary sensibilities.[25] Writing about the contemporary literary scene in the late 1920s, Kim Kijin (1903–1985), a leftist author, noted that although elitist writers claimed to have invented a modern literary tradition, their "artistic novels (yesul chŏk sosŏl 藝術的小說)" were read by only a handful of educated youths. The majority of the reading public still preferred "storytales (yegich'aek)," which constituted what he called the true "popular literature (taejung munhak 大衆文學)."[26]

Popular audiences for vernacular Korean fiction were shaped by the proliferation of rental libraries and the emergence of woodblock printing, which came into being in the eighteenth and nineteenth centuries, respectively.[27] Lineage novels, with their elite audiences and close proximity to literary Chinese idiom (in terms of genre, language, and historical setting), signified the moment when literary energies coalesced around the newly aestheticized Korean vernacular in the late seventeenth century. Until then, vernacular Korean writing had a mostly technical application: it was a translation aid for technical knowledge that, until the promulgation of the Korean script, circulated in literary Chinese, and it was also used in correspondence.[28] After the lineage novel emerged in the late seventeenth century, shorter fictional prose forms in the Korean vernacular also appeared. Unlike the lineage novel, with its intrafamilial manuscript transmission, these shorter texts reached readers through commercial channels—rental libraries and woodblock publications. Lineage novels never appeared in woodblock print, but in the nineteenth century they entered rental libraries alongside other types of literature and thus reached wider, commercialized audiences. A few lineage novel titles were printed in moveable type.

Rental libraries are believed to have appeared in Korea in the eighteenth century and continued to operate until the second decade of the twentieth century.[29] These libraries carried a variegated range of books, from short popular novels to translations of Chinese fiction, such as *The Romance of the Three Kingdoms*, to lineage novels. Most of the rented volumes were manuscripts. Written on thick paper, rental novels featured sparse handwriting with significant margins, which inflated the volumes' length and increased the rental profit.[30] Scattered margin notes—mostly records of the location of the manuscript's making and that of the rental library as well as borrowing ledgers transcribed on the back leaves—point to about two dozen places around Seoul where books could be borrowed for a fee. One location cross-referenced in multiple sources is the so-called Hyangmoktong or Hyangsudong area, which coincides with the Ŭljiro ipku area of modern Seoul. Earlier references to the rental library public suggest that the majority of borrowers were women, but by the late nineteenth and early twentieth centuries most customers were low-ranking officials, merchants, commoners, and military men, with patrons of ministerial rank also occasionally making an appearance in the borrowing ledgers. Some patrons seem to have become avid readers; in many cases, a variety of checked-out items—from popular tales to Chinese historical romances to lineage novels—were recorded under the same names in the rental rosters.[31]

Lineage novels made up significant portion of rental library catalogs,[32] and these texts appear to have possessed a special status. *Vernacular Record of Master Hu* (*Ŏnmun Hu saeng rok* 諺文厚生錄) is a turn-of-the-twentieth-century Korean-script manual that covers a variety of practical advice for women. Subject areas covered include the brewing of soy sauce, childbearing, arrangements of offerings during the ancestral worship ceremonies, and appropriate wedding rituals.[33] A list of novels is recorded on the pages that precede the manual's main text. The purpose of this list is unclear, but it certainly reveals a cultural logic that guides the division of titles into "lengthy novels (*kilch'aek*)" and simply "novels (*sosŏl ch'aek* 小說冊)." The "lengthy novels" section, composed of thirteen titles, includes four Chinese novels: *The Romance of the Three Kingdoms*, *The Romance of Western Zhou*, *The Journey to the West*, and *The Water Margin*. Six titles on the list are lineage novels, including *The Record of Two Heroes: Brothers Hyŏn* and *The Remarkable Encounter of Pearls*—both of which are discussed in this book. The majority of titles in the "lengthy novels" section—Chinese historical romances and lineage novels—reflect the literary tastes of Chosŏn elites. But there are several outliers, including *The Record of the Black Dragon Year* (*Imjinnok* 壬辰錄), a popular battlefield novel situated against a mixed background of the Imjin Wars (1592–1598) and Manchu invasions into Korea (1627, 1636). A second outlier is *The Tale of Hyŏn Sumun*, which imports one of the main protagonists and some other episodes from a lineage novel, *Brothers Hyŏn*, but is devoted largely to battlefield adventures and has very little to do with the lineage novel tradition. The third outlier text, *The Tale of Ch'o Hyŏn*, has not been located.[34] The list of "novels" includes such popular tales as *The Tale of Ch'unhyang*, *The Tale of Simch'ŏng* (*Sim Ch'ŏng chŏn* 沈淸傳), *The Nine-Cloud Dream* (*Kuunmong* 九雲夢), as well as a few unidentified titles.

The list's author and purpose remain unclear,[35] and the classification of the novels is inconsistent, but the label *kilch'aek*, or "lengthy novels," certainly brings to mind the Chosŏn-era references to the lineage novel, distinguished for its length, sophistication, and prestige. If the list is meant to capture the gist of superior literary tastes at a time when readers were becoming increasingly intermixed in the commercialized literary market, the presence of several nonconforming titles is perplexing.

Several coincidences in the novels' titles point to the cause of this confusion. *The Record of the Black Dragon Year*, listed between two Chinese novels—*The Journey to the West* and *The Water Margin*—has the term *record* (*rok* 錄) in its title. As we remember, this category of vernacular Korean writing was historically associated with the elite reading tastes in contrast to "tales" (*chŏn* 傳), which were identified with simpler, popular audiences. The reference in the novel's title to the Imjin, or Black Dragon, year (1592) of the Japanese invasions, alongside the appellation *record*, jibes with the surrounding titles—Chinese romances valued for the historical information they imparted to their elite female readers. The second outlier, *The Tale of Hyŏn Sumun*, is a hybrid genre that includes a significant proportion of martial adventures. Its title, however, is derived from the name of its protagonist, who in turn is borrowed from a lineage novel, *Brothers Hyŏn*. *The Tale of Hyŏn Sumun* is listed immediately after *Brothers Hyŏn* and its sequel *Pearls*, suggesting that the compiler identified *The Tale of Hyŏn Sumun* with this sequel cluster, although in reality *The Tale of Hyŏn Sumun* shares little with the lineage novel tradition. All of this indicates that the compiler was attempting to capture the elite reading tastes but had little knowledge of them.

Another surviving nineteenth-century book list, recorded sometime between 1893 and 1910 in the volume *Affairs of the Royal Court* (*Kukcho kosa* 國朝故事), which outlines the succession order and major events during the reigns of Korean kings, is attributable to a female scriber. A margin note records the scriber's desire to transmit this knowledge of Korean history and the book list to her daughter, thus intimating that female learning was valued in this family, which probably had elite status.[36] The majority of the recorded titles on this list similarly are lineage novels, and the list stays faithful to the repertoire of the elite vernacular Korean literary canon.

Taken together, these two lists suggest that in the context of social change and commercialized urban culture, literary discernment continued to be associated with elite-status claims. If the first book list, corrupted by imprecision, appears to be aspirational in nature, the second attests to the continued relevance of traditional female learning and the elite vernacular Korean canon at the turn of the twentieth century.

In the commercialized book market of nineteenth-century Korea, elite vernacular Korean culture constituted a sought-after competence among audiences with social aspirations. Vernacular Korean letter anthologies (*ŏn'gandok* 諺簡牘), which appear in quantity in the nineteenth century, provide a case in point. Chapter 2 has shown that letter writing constituted an important skill for the elite women of Chosŏn, who acquired calligraphic and compositional proficiency by emulating well-executed letters of women in their closest kinship and social circles. Commercial letter manuals collected generalized specimens of writing that could convey the necessary skills to those who did not have a sophisticated epistolary network at their disposal. Borrowing from the elite epistolary tradition, these letter anthologies included sample epistles dispatched on occasions that no elite woman would be likely to face: commercial transactions and letters between women who were not otherwise related or acquainted.[37] Through these manuals, vernacular Korean epistolary proficiency left the space of kinship and began to circulate in broader, commercialized networks in the nineteenth century.

The lingering prestige of elite vernacular Korean culture at the turn of the twentieth century explains the fact that commercial fiction printed in moveable type, which was in wide use in Korea at that point,[38] included several lineage novels as well as newly composed texts that aspired to imitate existing lineage novel titles. The lineage novels that appeared in print were shorter texts with entertaining plotlines that could appeal to broader audience. These texts included *The Record of the Three Generations of the Cho Lineage* (*Cho ssi samdae rok* 曺氏三代錄), published in 1917; *The Record of Two Heroes: Brothers Hyŏn*, published in 1919; and *The Record of Two Households: Ha and Chin*, which appeared in print in 1915, 1927, and 1953. Other novels simply appropriated the veneer of elite literary symbolism without really providing a full-fledged study of genealogical subjectivity—the process of the socialization of the emotional self through hereditary structures of kinship obligation. The imprint of *The Record of Three Households' Marriages* (*Sammun kyuhap rok* 三門閨合錄) in 1917 verges on dramatic spectacle, which results in a rather haphazard plotline.[39] *The Remarkable Encounter of Two Beauties* (*Ssangmi kibong* 雙美奇逢), published in 1916, fuses the convention of the Chinese novel[40] with the reference to "remarkable encounter" frequently found in lineage novels that center on the affective politics of marriage within the structure of lineage kinship. This novel, however, explores the mutual attraction of the main characters outside the bounds of the social system.[41] As noted later in this chapter, *The Tale of Hyŏn Sumun* also radically departs from the lineage novel tradition from which it borrowed.

Even as lineage novels retained a measure of prestige, they underwent a variety of changes during their transition from kinship networks to a monetized book market in the form of rental manuscripts and moveable-type publications. Both rental and printed copies of these texts were significantly shortened, and the pace of the narratives was accelerated for greater entertainment. These changes, however, were hardly uniform. The rental manuscript of *Brothers Hyŏn*, created in 1909, downplays the unruly nature of both female and male protagonists and instead focuses on female virtue, melodramatic sentimentalism, and the feelings of secondary-status characters.[42] The rental manuscript of *The Record of Two Households: Ha and Chin* moves in the opposite direction, emphasizing the patriarchal authority and martial prowess of the male characters.[43]

Truncated and simplified,[44] commercialized versions of lineage novels were stripped of the multidimensional representation of emotions. As chapter 4 has shown, lineage novels exempted unruly feelings from univocal moralistic judgment and positioned them as integral to their protagonists' socialization, which unfolds through the structures of prescripted kinship. Although lineage novels retained their prestige even as they transitioned to the commercialized marketplace in the nineteenth century, they were expected to cater to a thirst for entertainment. The new audiences that accessed lineage novels through the literary marketplace were not interested in psychologically detailed descriptions of the protracted struggle to inhabit genealogical kinship. The readers of commercialized editions of lineage novels did not inhabit the structures of kinship they were reading about.

The Breakdown of the Genealogical Subject

The genealogical subject that lineage novels create embodies the confluence of the familial and the political: the moral hierarchy of human relationships is inculcated in the space of kinship and encompasses the totality of the social world, stretched to the imperial frontiers. At the turn of the twentieth century, kinship obligation and the excessive moralism of the Confucian system came under attack by Korean intellectuals. Influenced by Western philosophy, political thought, and literature—often during their studies in Japan—Korean intellectuals called for individual awakening: a shift toward a monadic, self-authoring subject of morality and rationality. Because literature came to be seen as a key agent in effecting these changes to the national psyche, the creation of a Western-inspired novel preoccupied modern writers. Yi Kwangsu's novel *The Heartless* (1917), which depicts its protagonists' awakening to interiority and national subjectivity, is accepted as the first literary expression of the modern self.

But the breaking up of the genealogical subject was also driven by fiction that could hardly be associated with this modern literary agenda. The viability of a well-ordered world sustained through generational adherence to the identical moral norm is also questioned in *The Tale of Hyŏn Sumun*. The known editions of *The Tale of Hyŏn Sumun* include two woodblock imprints, nine manuscripts (some of which are rental library copies), and eight imprints, dating from 1915 to 1952.[45] The text is believed to have been composed around the mid–nineteenth century.[46] Discussed in this chapter is the imprint made by the publishing house Sin'gu sŏrim in 1922 based on a rental library manuscript.[47] The striking hybridity of *The Tale of Hyŏn Sumun* plays out in significant plot variations in the different editions and in a motley crew of protagonists borrowed from a number of battlefield novels: *The Tale of So Taesŏng* (*So Taesŏng chŏn* 蘇大成傳) and *The Tale of Chang P'ungun* (*Chang P'ungun chŏn* 張風雲傳).[48] The main protagonist, Hyŏn Sumun, is transplanted from the lineage novel *Brothers Hyŏn*, discussed earlier in this book. Instead of kinship life, however, *The Tale of Hyŏn Sumun* deals mostly with battlefield adventures.

The narrative's genealogical structure is disrupted in the first lines of *The Tale of Hyŏn Sumun*, which begin with the vitae of Sumun's father, Hyŏn T'aekchi, and mother, Madame Chang. The family's composition is nearly identical to the one described in *The Record of Two Heroes: Brothers Hyŏn*, except that Sumun's twin brother, Kyŏngmun, does not make an appearance.[49] Unlike *Brothers Hyŏn*, *The Tale of Hyŏn Sumun* does not begin from the perspective of secured generational excellence: Hyŏn Sumun, Hyŏn T'aekchi's only heir, is born after his parents have given up all hope of having a child. In contrast, the lineage novel, *Brothers Hyŏn*, begins with the excellent officeholding record of Sumun and Kyŏngmun's grandfather, Hyŏn Hugi—who is never mentioned in *The Tale of Hyŏn Sumun*, where the hard-begotten Sumun belongs to just the second generation of his lineage.

The generational succession of family values also fails to take place in *The Tale of Hyŏn Sumun*. Despite his father's protestations, Hyŏn Sumun devotes himself to martial training rather than to a civil career, practicing in secret to forestall his father's disapproval. Furthermore, when Hyŏn Sumun reconstitutes his family, which had been dispersed during multiple rebellions, he does not rebuild it in a genealogical manner around his father; instead, Sumun himself becomes the family head.[50]

Against this fractured generational background, the home no longer constitutes the center of the narrative. Whereas the domestic realm is the central site of coming to terms with the kinship norm in the lineage novel, it remains superfluous to the plot of *The Tale of Hyŏn Sumun*. Hyŏn T'aekchi is banished for treason, and Sumun loses sight of his mother during a rebellion. As a young boy, Sumun is picked up by a magician, Master Ilgwang, who teaches him military arts. After completing his training and descending the mountain, Sumun takes a civil service examination and earns a prominent position in court, gaining power and becoming indispensable in the protection of the state. The novel briefly describes Hyŏn Sumun's marriage to Sŏk Unhye, whose vicious stepmother torments the two newlyweds, but both of them quickly flee from this temporary dwelling. The precariousness of the home space sets the stage for the ensuing narrative, which amplifies multiple instabilities in the architecture of the world into which Hyŏn Sumun has been born.

The political realm also appears to be out of joint. The tale is set during the reign of Emperor Injong of Song (Ch. Renzong, r. 1022–1063), which witnesses numerous rebellions. In the tale, one rebel king is elevated to a position of legitimate critique of the throne: he submits a respectful memorial (*p'yomun* 標文) outlining the iniquities of the Song court and presenting his rebellion as the last resort. When a second rebellion erupts at a time while Sumun is away from court, the enemy laughs at the emperor, and the civil officials pray for Sumun's speedy return and confess that they are not good at anything but "dabbling with brushes and ink."[51] What redeems Emperor Injong is that he is sincere and trusting, entirely reliant on his loyal general, Hyŏn Sumun. In gratitude for Sumun's service, Emperor Injong enfeoffs him as the king of Wi and on his deathbed solicits Sumun's support for the young crown prince. Hyŏn Sumun and his son, Hyŏn Ch'im, promise to assist the new emperor with all their power.

Hyŏn Sumun's enfeoffment as the king of Wi is, however, not the end of his story. The new emperor quickly turns to the council of corrupt officials and grows mistrustful of Sumun. The entire Song army then lays siege to Sumun's kingdom but is unable to prevail. This action takes place against the background of multiple insurrections, which Sumun quells. Sumun emphasizes his motivation: "I repelled the Hyungno [Ch. Xiongnu 匈奴] and killed their general not for the sake of the Son of Heaven but heeding the last words of the previous emperor. I am going away now."[52] The final blow to Song rule comes with the rise of the Jurchens.[53] Receiving the Song emperor's request for assistance, Hyŏn Sumun "laughs coldly and says, 'I am old, and my strength is withered. How could I be of any help in battle?'"[54] After Sumun ignores repeated entreaties, the Song is defeated, and a new empire prospers under Jurchen rule. Just before his death, Sumun holds a banquet, where he "weeps remembering the affairs of the past" and predicts the imminent rise of the Mongol Yuan dynasty.[55] After Sumun's demise, his son, Ch'im, inherits the throne in full realization that he can hold on to power only by winning the Mongols' favor.

Hyŏn Ch'im succeeds in this task, and the Yuan dynasty, with Hyŏn Ch'im's help, unites the world and reigns peacefully.

The Tale of Hyŏn Sumun seems to push a hodge-podge of half-developed generic conventions to their limit.[56] For one thing, the generational structure of this battlefield tale is uncommonly long for its genre, spanning three generations, from Hyŏn T'aekchi to Hyŏn Sumun and then to Hyŏn Ch'im. But generational succession is not the main issue. The three generations share little common ground: Hyŏn Sumun realizes the futility of civil learning championed by his father, and although he acquires a domain, he cannot pass it securely to his own son, who is forced to navigate a complex relationship with the rising Mongol Empire. The climb through social ranks habitually constitutes the problematic of the battlefield novel, but *The Tale of Hyŏn Sumun* features ceaseless assaults on the state of Song, which continue even after Hyŏn Sumun settles in the kingdom of Wi.[57] Neither the generational framework that characterizes lineage novels nor the battlefield novel's narrative of upward mobility provides a consistent narrative arc.

The transfer of the generational structure, protagonists, and plot elements from a lineage novel to a text that circulated in commercial editions—probably among nonelite readers—is intriguing. The prestige associated with elite vernacular Korean culture in nineteenth-century Korea, when status boundaries were being eroded by economic development and the rise of secondary social groups, could explain the desire to use the attributes of an elite literary genre in a largely commercial, demotic publication.[58] Indeed, the generational narrative in *The Tale of Hyŏn Sumun* amounts to little more than a claim of prestige. The ancestral example is futile, and Hyŏn Sumun is constantly left alone, attending to one crisis after another; as he moves through his life, everything behind him falls to ruin, which he recalls with regret during his last banquet.[59] *The Tale of Hyŏn Sumun* captures a sense that fundamental structures such as the generational value system and the state are in crisis.

Chu Sumin has noted that *The Tale of Hyŏn Sumun* exhibits an uncommon scope of textual variation among its known editions. In the woodblock editions, for instance, the Song dynasty manages to maintain its power, and Hyŏn Sumun is depicted as a loyal general in the service of the Song Son of Heaven. Some other editions end with the depiction of the Jurchen victory over the Song rather than with the second dynastic transition from the Jurchens to the Mongols.[60] *The Tale of Hyŏn Sumun* appears to be aimed at strikingly varied audiences, which suggests that the shattering of the Confucian world captured in some editions was not ecumenically palatable to the late Chosŏn reading public.[61] This novel simply registers the shattering of the genealogical subjectivity, without offering a creative solution. The prosperous Yuan reign that closes the tale appears to be a hard-won compromise. In short, the totalities central to the chronotope of the lineage novel—the seamless enfolding of the state, kinship, and the person—are disrupted, and the aesthetic means and agenda either of the lineage novel or of the battlefield tale are insufficient to generate a coherent symbolic perspective. This text, certainly exceptional in its hybridity, allows us to register two important moments in the mid-nineteenth-century literary culture of Korea: the interaction of the lineage novel with the commercialized literary marketplace and the aesthetic conundrum produced by the disintegration of the genealogical symbolic structures that permeated the literary field of Chosŏn and that coalesced in the massive, multigenerational narratives of lineage novels.

The Forgotten Archive of Kinship

As noted earlier, lineage novels circulated in tight kinship networks and were seldom mentioned in the male-authored sources that provide the most extensive overview of Chosŏn literary culture. The knowledge that these texts constituted the quintessence of elite women's cultural competency was perpetuated by the families that carefully transmitted the lineage novels' manuscripts to their descendants or, alternatively, created the lists of books that composed the elite vernacular Korean canon. Although the lineage novel retained some of its prestige in the newly commercialized book market in early twentieth-century Korea, the genre soon faded from cultural visibility along with its elite audience.

The first academic attempts to consolidate and nationalize Korea's cultural tradition in the early twentieth century occurred against the background of Japan's imperial discourse of Korean history. Claims of colonial primitivism articulated by Japanese scholars of Korea constructed the epistemic grid for Japan's colonial project.[62] The Korean intellectuals' search for an authentic national tradition was necessarily mediated by this discourse, and it inaugurated national culture as a counterargument to the epistemic violence of colonial claims. Vernacular Korean culture—an authentic indigenous development distinguished from "borrowed" literary Chinese scriptural practices—became a highly politicized site of historical imagination. Whereas cultural modernization dominated the agenda of Korean intellectuals in the first decade of the twentieth century, interest in Korean tradition was sparked by the aggressive assimilationist policies of the Japanese Empire in the late 1930s. Even so, lineage novels, which formed the quintessence of the elite vernacular Korean tradition, remained almost entirely unknown to the first ideologues of a national literary canon.

Ch'oe Namsŏn, a writer, scholar, and publisher whose views of cultural nationalism achieved a complex and often questioned synthesis with the agenda of Japan's colonial state, was a prominent literary and intellectual voice in colonial Korea. Ch'oe's article "Domestic Fiction in Chosŏn" ("Chosŏn ŭi kajŏng munhak" 朝鮮家庭文學, 1938) provides an overview of Chosŏn-dynasty vernacular Korean literature. Ch'oe's main concern is with domestic learning, mediated by the modern concept of "wise mother good wife (hyŏnmo yangch'ŏ 賢母良妻)," which signifies domesticity as a site of civilization, culture, and nation building. The domestic space, for Ch'oe, is also juxtaposed with elite learned men's culture in literary Chinese, and hence it includes all forms of culture excluded from that domain. This cultivated and yet demotic conception of domestic learning—comprising ethical, religious, and literary texts—allows Ch'oe to uncover broader patterns of culture, morality, and education spread among the "ordinary masses (ilban minjung 一般民衆)," which testify to the high civilizational status of Chosŏn Korea prior to colonization.[63]

In his discussion of the vernacular Korean novel, Ch'oe includes a survey of a rental library catalog compiled in the Hyangmoktong area. He records several lineage novel titles, noting the focused ideological message they convey and emphasizing the astonishing lengths of these texts, based on the number of volumes recorded in the catalog. Not having a better sense of these texts' provenance, Ch'oe groups lineage novels with Chinese fiction—in particular The Dream of the Red Chamber and its sequels, which, he notes, were read at the palace, and, "more or less center on the domestic life, portray the ups and downs of human fortunes, and teach appropriate life attitude."[64] Having acknowledged the feudal social stratification of the Chosŏn society, which led to women's oppression, Ch'oe is still impressed by the length of vernacular Korean novels he discovers. Nevertheless, the notion of a massive elite vernacular Korean novelistic tradition either eludes Ch'oe Namsŏn or is disavowed in favor of broader, demotic notion of civility. The article reaches a modest conclusion: the scarcity of vernacular Korean literary sources leaves Ch'oe with little choice but to include religious texts, which do not strictly belong to the category of literature. Ironically, the belief in the scarcity of indigenous vernacular Korean literary sources has its origins in the quest for authentic national tradition.

Just a year after Ch'oe Namsŏn's article was published, several lineage novel titles appeared on the pages of *Munjang* (Writing 文章) magazine. Much like Ch'oe Namsŏn, Yi Pyŏnggi, one of the magazine's editors, was active in a variety of fields: poetry composition, teaching, popularization of Korean tradition, and book collecting. Also like Ch'oe, Yi was invested in the construction of an authentic national literary tradition, though his vision was more elitist. Aesthetically and compositionally, *Munjang* championed the elite vernacular literary refinement as the foundation of a national literary tradition.[65] The magazine serialized two vernacular Korean texts that were, in essence, records of palace life: *Memoirs of Lady Hyegyŏng* (*Hanjungnok* 恨中錄/閑中錄) and *The True Story of Queen Inhyŏn* (*Inhyŏn wanghu chŏn* 仁顯王后傳). Admiring these texts as sophisticated examples of an essentialized vernacular Korean sensibility, Yi laments the scarcity of vernacular Korean materials, buried in oblivion. At one point, he publishes in the magazine a list of vernacular Korean books he has found in private collections. According to Yi, he put the list together very quickly, without extensive research. He records the titles of such lineage novels as *The Pledge at the Banquet of Moon-Gazing Pavilion*, which, Yi writes, can be found in Unyŏng Palace, as well as *The Record of the Three Generations of the Yu Lineage* and *The Record of the Illustrious Deeds and Righteousness*, which Yi says are translated novels in the possession of a certain Hong T'aekchu.[66] In his later work, *The Complete History of National Literature* (*Kungmunhak chŏnsa* 國文學全史, 1957), Yi Pyŏnggi describes the Naksŏn collection—a group of vernacular Korean texts, many of them lineage novels, discovered on the grounds of Ch'angdŏk Palace—in a section titled "Translated Literature and Conduct Books" ("Pŏnyŏk munhak kwa kyubŏm ryu" 飜譯文學規範類).[67] Noting that an extensive project of translating Chinese literature into vernacular Korean was under way at the palace, Yi concludes that the majority of the discovered lineage novels are also translated from Chinese. In this way, the nationalist antiquarian projects of the 1930s shape the notion that vernacular Korean culture was nearly nonexistent during the Chosŏn dynasty.

The knowledge about lineage novels stayed alive among a few royal readers, who formed a vital link between the elite readers of Chosŏn and twentieth-century scholars and collectors. An especially prominent mediating role was played by Yun Paekyŏng (1888–1986), born to Yun Yonggu (1853–1939), the posthumously adopted son of Princess Tŏkon (1822–1844). The vernacular Korean tradition was especially strong among these members of the royal family. Princess Tŏkon's brother, Prince Hyomyŏng (1809–1830), was known for his *Haksŏk Anthology* (*Haksŏk chip* 鶴石集), comprising his literary Chinese poetry translated into Korean, which is widely believed to have been produced for the benefit of his sisters. The surviving vernacular Korean brushwork of Princess Tŏkon shows that she was a superb calligrapher. She was also an avid reader who brought thousands of royal manuscript volumes—many of them lineage novels—with her to her husband's household. Although Yun Yonggu became the princess's adopted son after her death, he was probably influenced by the family tradition of vernacular Korean writing. He translated and transcribed a number of Chinese historical accounts into vernacular Korean, and his vernacular Korean brushwork reveals impressive skill.[68]

Yun Yonggu's daughter, Yun Paekyŏng (1888–1986), was also a fine calligrapher,[69] and she served as a living memory of the royal and elite culture of the late Chosŏn, making frequent media appearances and often being quoted in the first academic studies of lineage novels and vernacular Korean culture of Chosŏn. The newspaper articles that featured Yun often used the fond sobriquet "Jangseogak granny (*Changsŏgak halmŏni*)" to acknowledge the time Yun spent in the library that later housed the vernacular palace volumes. In an interview published in *Chungang ilbo* (Joongang daily 中央日報) in 1966, Yun shares her insights about lineage novels and articulates the gist of elite reading tastes prevalent in Chosŏn. She makes explicit her preference for longer texts: "A novel must be at least seventy or eighty volumes long; shorter texts are unrefined (*musikhada* 無識) and uninteresting." The long novels in the palace collection—the majority of them lineage novels—are, for Yun, defined by complex representations of emotions and finely wrought narratives that draw the reader in.[70] Yun Paekyŏng helped identify the handwriting of various palace ladies within lineage novels' manuscripts.[71] Moreover, using her own resources and time, she restored several volumes that were missing from the Jangseogak collection. The incomplete work, originally translated by Yun's father, was a compilation of Chinese history in eighty manuscript volumes. Yun restored the missing nineteenth volume, with special reverence for her father's labor and handwriting.[72] The short prefaces she wrote for several lineage novels in the royal collection are now bound together with these texts reposited in the Jangseogak Archive.[73]

In August 1966, the Nakson Pavilion of Ch'angdŏk Palace, traditionally a residence for female members of the royal family, became the site of a great "discovery." A team of scholars from the Research Institute of East Asian Culture (Tonga munhwa yŏn'guso) led by Professor Chŏng Pyŏnguk of Seoul National University located thousands of volumes of vernacular Korean novels, exquisitely transcribed and bound; a large portion of the collection comprised lineage novels. (Three of the research team's members—Kim Chinse, Yi Sang'taek, and Cho Tongil—would go on to become prominent scholars of Korean literature.) In his initial newspaper pieces about the collection, Chŏng Pyŏnguk explains that the Nakson novels were not exactly unknown. He had been introduced to the Nakson Pavilion texts in 1946 by a Seoul National University classmate and a scion of the royal family, Yi Haech'ŏng (dates not known).[74] Having been evacuated to the provisional capital of Busan during the Korean War (1951–1953), Chŏng wondered about the fate of the texts. After the novels were found in the Nakson Pavilion in 1966, neatly packed in boxes and ready to be moved, he speculated that the North Korean army had unsuccessfully attempted to transport the texts to the North but that the change in the war theater disrupted the plan.[75] In an article released just before the publicization of the collection, Chŏng also mentions that three of his female students at Seoul National University wrote their graduation theses on *The Pledge at the Banquet of Moon-Gazing Pavilion*. In what seems to be a moment of self-vindication, Chŏng adds that although the existence of palace manuscripts of vernacular Korean fiction was known, nobody had a good grasp on the extent of this realm of Korean culture.[76]

The discovery of the Nakson Library marked the starting point of the academic study of the lineage novel, although the first steps were fraught with contradiction and debate.[77] Professor Yi Pyŏngju of Tongguk University published a sarcastic article in September 1966 that derided both the media and the scholars for their bemusement over the newly discovered materials. Titled "Crooked Discovery" ("Oegoktoen sinpalgul"), Yi Pyŏngju's article emphasizes the ready availability of the Nakson Collection and the fact that Nakson novels were widely known even before 1966.[78] A number of heated debates about the new materials during this period provide a glimpse of the state of vernacular Korean studies in post-1945 South Korea in the context of national cultural reconstruction conceived in postcolonial and antifeudal terms.

The discovery of the Naksŏn Library and the early studies of vernacular Korean novels took place in the context of President Park Chung-hee's (Pak Chŏnghŭi) regime (1963–1979), which unfolded projects of national economic and cultural development. The nationalization of tradition constituted a countermeasure to the geopolitical uncertainty of the 1960s; alongside the stalemated Korean War and the prospect of a U.S. troop withdrawal, internal social volatility dramatized the need for a stable affective context.[79] In the 1970s, the state championed projects of paternalistic cultural reconstruction, which, in the words of Youngju Ryu, were "hierarchical and gendered."[80] As Hwisang Cho has noted, male Confucian culture was used "as an alternative to the resistant and subversive urban popular culture."[81] Much attention was given to such patriarchal figures as general Yi Sunsin (1545–1598), famed for his naval victories during the Japanese invasions in the late sixteenth century, and the Confucian philosophers T'oegye Yi Hwang (1501–1570) and Yulgok Yi I (1537–1584), who underpinned the aesthetics of "wholesomeness prescribed by the fascist state."[82] The women-centered domestic culture of Chosŏn Korea thus did not fit into the monumental self-presentation of the developmentalist state.

At the time of their discovery, the lineage novels in the Naksŏn collection were little understood in South Korean academic circles. A preliminary survey of the collection prompted Chŏng Pyŏnguk to outline new directions for Korean literary studies. Before the annotated catalog of the Naksŏn Library was published in 1969,[83] Chŏng Pyŏnguk summarized in 1966 his first impressions in a newspaper article with a revealing title: "Revolution in the History of National Literature" ("Kungmunhak yŏksa ka pakkwinda").[84] First, Chŏng noted that the collection challenged the commonly held belief that Korea had produced only short literary forms. These distinctively lengthy lineage novels upended the twentieth-century association of brevity attached to Chosŏn-era vernacular Korean culture. This association, no doubt, was dramatized by the well-known pronouncement by the colonial-era writer Yi T'aejun (1904–?), who had noted that the complexities of Korea's colonial experience did not yield themselves to the sustained perspective of a lengthy narrative.[85] Chŏng's preoccupation with these novels' length appears to be positioned against the projection of

Yi T'aejun's pronouncement back into the literary past. Second, Chŏng points to the elite palace audience for vernacular Korean literature, which dismantles the notion that its appeal was exclusively demotic. Third, Chŏng remarks on the novels' literary artistry and the psychological nuance of the narratives, which portray ordinary, human protagonists whose journeys through the vagaries of life unfold on a psychological rather than epic plane.[86] Chŏng dwells on this very "modern" quality of lineage novels, and in his preoccupation with native literary modernity as the articulation of naked feelings we can identify another echo of postcolonial identity politics, indebted to the phonocentric literary imagination of the turn of the twentieth century.

Despite the media attention toward and the academic promise of the Naksŏn collection, the study of lineage novels was slow to flourish in South Korea. In part, this was because in the academic and political environment of the 1970s and 1980s the national canon was configured as a duality of patriarchal elite male culture in literary Chinese and the vernacular Korean canon associated with demotic, popular practices.[87] Cultural practices centered on elite women did not easily fit into this configuration. But the slowness is also attributable to an unresolved question about the lineage novel that preoccupied Korean scholars: Were lineage novels Korean texts, or were they translations of Chinese novels?

Chŏng Pyŏnguk ultimately understood lineage novels to be domestic products. In 1973, however, Cho Hŭiung categorized several novels that are now considered original vernacular Korean compositions as either translations or adaptations of Chinese texts.[88] In 1986, Kim Chinse summarized the ongoing debates in his article "The Problem of Origin of the Naksŏn Library Novels" ("Naksŏnjae bon sosŏl kukchŏk munje") and rather cautiously suggested that the arguments made for the domestic origins of lineage novels appear more convincing. The case was backed by lineage novels' extensive use of vernacular idiomatic expressions and references to social and cultural aspects of Chosŏn society.[89] The discovery of new materials, such as Hong Hŭibok's (1794–1859) nineteenth-century survey of the literary field, which recorded titles of circulating lineage novels, further confirmed the domestic provenance of these texts. Some doubt remained, however. Yi Sangt'aek, for instance, suggested, also in 1986, that the originals could have been literary Chinese texts that were eventually translated into vernacular Korean.[90] The absence of a single literary Chinese text associated with the lineage novel tradition makes this connection highly unlikely. However, the doubts about the original script of the lineage novels' composition ultimately center on the problem of authorship.

Not a single lineage novel's author is known with certainty, but male authorship was assumed in the earliest studies of these texts. Im Hyŏngt'aek's influential essay *"The Praise of Goodness and the Admiration of Righteousness and the Rise of the Boudoir Novel in the Seventeenth Century"* ("17 segi kyubang sosŏl ŭi sŏngnip kwa *Ch'angsŏn kamŭi rok*"), published in 1988, foregrounded the notion of "boudoir literature" and drew attention to the female audiences of the lineage novel.[91] Following his lead, scholars in the 1990s who were attuned to cultural studies and feminist literary criticism focused on the centrality of female audiences, the prominence of feminine symbolism,[92] and of course the centrality of female calligraphers to the dissemination of the lineage novel tradition. Im Ch'igyun singled out the emergence of the stratum of female scribes as central to the history of the lineage novel's development.[93] Chŏng Pyŏngsŏl went as far as to propose the female authorship of some texts.[94] Pak Yŏnghŭi showed that the importance of female learning in select lineages was crucial to the cultivation of the lineage novel tradition, which marked the first instance of literarization of the Korean vernacular writing.[95]

After the disappearance of elite female audiences and the kinship framework within which lineage novels' manuscripts were created and disseminated, it took nearly a century to reassess the place of vernacular Korean lineage novels in the elite culture of Chosŏn. Why? First of all, as we have seen, the location of the lineage novel in the women-centered inner quarters and the fact that these novels were written in vernacular Korean script meant that references to these texts in elite men's writings were extremely rare. As I show in chapter 2, elite men were wont to read and to transcribe lineage novels alongside their female kin, but they were reticent about these practices, which added little to the literary fame they sought.

Second, due to their length and complexity and their transmission within families, lineage novels did not reach wide audiences. As this chapter has shown, some rental libraries in the late nineteenth century began to circulate these texts. But even after the commercialization of the literary market, lineage novels did not become widely known to novel readers, likely appealing only to select audiences.

Third, the political and cultural climate of the twentieth century did not facilitate sustained attention to the elite vernacular Korean culture of

Chosŏn. The imperial lens of Japanese scholars' view of Korean history was critiqued by Korean intellectuals, but for many it was important to locate the sources of national authenticity not in the culture of the elites—whose Confucian persuasion was often identified as the source of the country's ruin—but in the demotic, popular imagination.[96] In post-1945 South Korea and throughout the 1980s, literary scholarship was dominated by an antifeudal and anticolonial focus on popular literature and by the state-endorsed emphasis on the patriarchal culture of Chosŏn.[97] The group of scholars who worked first on the Naksŏn collection and then on the broader phenomenon of the lineage novel were unable to place themselves outside a framework within which the literary Chinese culture of elite Chosŏn men was the highest cultural standard of the time.

This extensive elite vernacular Korean archive centered on female readers and scribes was forgotten after the Chosŏn kinship system that defined the scope of domestic literary culture and women's education lost its centrality. Thus, in addition to the insights it offers into the kinship practices, everyday life, and women-centered vernacular culture of Chosŏn Korea, this archive also highlights the interstices of cultural memory and academic practice.

In Conclusion

The connection between the lineage novel and the structure of lineage kinship was set into relief when beginning around the middle of the nineteenth century a number of internal and external pressures decentered the lineage system. As the elite vernacular Korean literary tradition transitioned into the commercialized literary market, it interacted with new audiences, new questions, and new modes of circulation.

One curious feature of the lineage novel that becomes powerfully refracted from the vantage point of its closing chapter is the untenability of sophisticated, multiperspective narratives of the genealogical subject outside their immediate location within the kinship culture of Chosŏn. Women who inhabited the structures of patrilineal kinship between the late seventeenth and early nineteenth centuries were captivated by the sophisticated lineage novels' narratives, which discussed the most problematic junctures between the private self and the normative kinship structure. Lineage novels notably emphasized the distance between the person and the social norm and recognized unruly feelings as integral to the trajectory of personal life. Yun Paekyŏng, reminiscing in the 1960s of her lifelong experience of reading lineage novels, notes their complexity. Similarly, Lady Hyegyŏng fondly recalls a lineage novel she and her sister read together while mourning their mother's death, underscoring the intimate significance these texts had for women of the highest elite at moments of personal crisis.

Much too complex for extensive commercial circulation, lineage novels were modified, but these new versions had limited interaction with the literary marketplace and eventually faded altogether from circulation and broader cultural memory.

The lineage novel constituted the quintessence of elite women's domestic culture, and the history of its development intersected with the cultivation of vernacular Korean calligraphy. The meaning and value of calligraphic practice in elite women's lives was similarly determined by the repertoire of productive womanly roles articulated within the kinship system. The lineage novel allows a suggestive glimpse into the domestic culture of elite lineages of Chosŏn. Although the patrilineal kinship system of Chosŏn has been studied as the key to understanding the vagaries of culture, social politics, everyday life, political organization, and intellectual milieu of the era, lineage novels capture the most immediate affective negotiations that underlay the fashioning of this normative structure of enormous historical significance.

The gradual fading of the lineage novel—first from literary circulation in the early twentieth century and then from the cultural memory—created an aporia in the teleological construction of the national literary canon. Lineage novels remained unknown even to intellectuals, such as Yi Pyŏnggi and the coterie of *Munjang* magazine, who sought to uncover a native vernacular Korean canon conceived on elite premises. In the second half of the twentieth century, projects of national cultural reconstruction allowed no place for the study of this feminine elite tradition. Only in the 1990s did scholars gradually begin to see that vernacular Korean writing, which had been understood as a demotic, frail undertaking within the literary culture of Chosŏn dominated by elite men's literary Chinese scholarship, was in fact an aesthetic domain with considerable prestige. The emergence of the lineage novel, in fact, signifies the beginnings of the early modern Korean novel, and the literary energy that went into the creation of this elite canon of writing was to a large degree a product of the Korean kinship structure that dominated the social, cultural, and personal experience of men and women in Chosŏn.

One final moment that I want to ponder in this conclusion is the aesthetic conundrum that the nineteenth-century decentering of the Korean kinship system produced. *The Tale of Hyŏn Sumun*, a mid-nineteenth-century hybrid produced for a commercialized literary marketplace, registers the collapse of the self-certain genealogical structures that in the lineage novel signify the blending of the familial and the political. It marks the breakdown of the generational links that, as chapters 1 and 3 have shown, provided a narrative pattern for a variety of narratives—funerary genres, lineage novels, and family tales—that charted the conventions of reciprocity and the expectations of social life.

It is useful here to turn to a literary specimen that by its philosophy and design was directed at the final disarticulation of the generational structures of prescriptive kinship that in the early twentieth century came to be seen as outmoded and detrimental to Korea's national future. These few remarks on the first modern novel, Yi Kwangsu's *The Heartless*, will allow us a final glimpse of the waning of the Korean kinship structure and a sense of how fictional prose responded to the absence of the kinship context.

Yi Kwangsu's novel performs the aesthetic and ideological shift from the genealogical subject, socialized within the structures of kinship prescription, to the self-authoring individual, extricated from kinship links and instead incorporated into a national community conceived as an aesthetic and practical developmental project unfolding on the global, cosmopolitan plane and mediated, for Korea, by the colonial politics of the Japanese Empire.

To a great extent, *The Heartless* is an elaboration of multiple fissures that run through Korean society in the context of colonial modernity. The state of unfeeling, highlighted in the novel's title, refers primarily to the capitalist alienation that erodes the notion of a common humanity, and this unfeeling dialectically mediates the synthesis of national community that emerges as a utopian vision at the novel's end. The unfeeling is positioned against the background of a nostalgic social fullness that is conceived in pointedly Confucian terms. Whereas in *The Tale of Hyŏn Sumun* the crisis of the genealogical subjectivity is merely registered, in *The Heartless* it becomes a springboard for the elaboration of modern subjecthood.

The novel's three protagonists, joined by what resembles a love triangle, represent different visions of the social. Yi Hyŏngsik, an English teacher with a Western-style education, is involved with two women: Pak Yŏngch'ae, the daughter of Hyŏngsik's early benefactor and his assumed betrothed, educated in traditional womanly ways, and Kim Sŏnhyŏng, a young and beautiful woman from a wealthy family who is childishly unaware of herself or her country's affairs but full of potential. Abandoning his betrothed, Hyŏngsik marries Sŏnhyŏng and departs with her to study in the United States. This choice maps the trajectory of the country's desired future, which requires a violent shift away from the traditional past toward the modern world of science, education, and nation building that is aligned with the vision of Western modernity.

Heartlessness or unfeeling registers the fissures in the national body inflicted by capitalism and the desires it fuels, which is represented most prominently in the ubiquitous figure of a female entertainer, or *kisaeng* (妓生), signifying abjection and intense desire-objectification.[98] Yŏngch'ae is forced to become a *kisaeng* to rescue her father from debt and imprisonment. Eager but unable to buy out Yŏngch'ae shortly before she is sold to a client and raped, Hyŏngsik registers the capitalist unfeeling: "Most of the worries of modern-day people had to do with not having money. It was no surprise that people valued money in a world in which one could purchase someone's body and even their soul if one had the money."[99] The world is unfeeling in situations when money breaks down social bonds: when Yŏngch'ae's father, a selfless educator, is sent to prison for debts incurred through his school operations[100] and when money replaces the ground for human dignity. Money, which purchases women and Western clothes while fracturing the body of the nation, embodies the deterritorializing power of modernity; its consumerist, capitalist underside is a major centrifugal force in the novel.[101]

This fragmentation is juxtaposed with the Confucian moral vision of human bonds, centered on Yŏngch'ae's figure: she is a filial daughter who sacrifices herself for her father and tries to protect her chastity for Hyŏngsik's sake by attempting to take her life after the rape. Each appearance of Yŏngch'ae in the novel is marked by melodramatic sentimentality— unviable in the context of Korea's colonial modernity, she is mourned profusely in scenes of tears. Her figure stands against all those who have no notion of "morality and human bonds (*todŏk kwa illyun* 道德 人倫)"[102]—an ethical Confucian sensibility that conceives human bonds as the inalienable fusion of the familial and the social.

The dissolution of the Confucian relational structure creates a vacuum that is filled with capitalist alienation and the struggle for survival. *The Heartless* offers up various provisions to suture this national fragmentation, which appear in sequence within the novel: the melodramatic identification with tradition embodied by Yŏngch'ae; the sympathy (*tongjŏng* 同情) that Hyŏngsik feels for the most underprivileged people who surround him; and, finally, the awareness of vitalistic consanguinity, which allows Hyŏngsik to transcend moralistic judgment and to affirm instead the common destiny and nation-building project of all Koreans regardless of their ethical persuasion.[103] Leaving aside the novel's utopian modernizing vision, it is imperative to note that the disappearance of genealogical subjectivity and the kinship-based relational framework is integral to the political unconscious of Korea's first modern novel.

Ellie Choi has noted that the heartlessness in Yi Kwangsu's novel refers most prominently to the violent conversion from the affectively cognate tradition to cultural modernity. She notes the moments of nostalgia throughout Yi Kwangsu's works that identify intense affective connections with the decidedly nonmodern elements of Korean life and that call for a postcolonial project that challenges "the assumptions about capitalist modern time as a universal one" established "at the cost of forgetting what was relinquished in the same long march towards progress."[104] In *The Heartless*, this heterotopic affect is mapped onto the figure of Yŏngch'ae.[105] As Yi Kwangsu revealed in his autobiographical essay "A Journey Through Hardships, Half-Life Long" ("Tananhan pansaeng ŭi tojŏng," 1936), through the figure of Yŏngch'ae he was hoping to capture "the lingering affective memories (*chŏngtaun kiŏk*) of [his] youth."[106] And if in the novel Yŏngch'ae effects the link between tradition and modernity as she is reborn to the updated, modern identity of an educated woman who leaves her prescribed kinship role behind,[107] what were the connections that Yi Kwangsu the author held dear?

In the same essay where Yi Kwangsu fixes on the figure of Yŏngch'ae, he recalls among the strongest affective memories from his past the days he spent in his hometown in the company of his grandmother and a female cousin. These memories appear on the very first page of the text. Yi says that at about five or six years of age he learned Korean and began reading aloud to his grandmother, whose failing eyesight did not allow her to read her favorite battlefield tales, such as *The Tale of So Taesŏng* and *The Tale of Chang P'ungun*, on her own. After the death of his grandmother, Yi spent time with his female cousin, whose reading tastes were more aligned with the traditional female reading canon. She read such "boudoir novels" as *Madame Sa's Conquest of the South* and *The Praise of Goodness and the Admiration of Righteousness* during the breaks she took from embroidery. Yi recalls that he was much more captivated by the battlefield tales and that his early reading experience prompted him to write his very own first lines.[108]

Yi Kwangsu's recollection of his early vernacular Korean learning aligns almost verbatim with the Chosŏn-dynasty domestic reading scene, where boys learned and read vernacular Korean in the company of their nearest female kin. Yi Kwangsu's family did not belong to the highest elite, and his grandmother's love of battlefield tales would have been frowned upon by women of good households. And yet we see that in Yi's family vernacular Korean literacy was perpetuated through kinship structures and through the texts that trace the vagaries of kinship life. In this account, reading and writing have an irreducible aura embedded in the thickness of kinship connections and the affective contours of the domestic space. To write that Korean literature has no past, only a future—as Yi Kwangsu did in 1916—appears as an ever more dramatic gesture of conversion against the backdrop of these nostalgic recollections. Yi Kwangsu's personal story as well as his celebrated novel allow a glimpse of the affective and aesthetic weight of traditional kinship figurations that held sway over Korea's celebrated modern novelist. This testament to the lingering aura of disappearing kinship seems to be an appropriate closing sentiment for this book about the kinship novels of early modern Korea.

Notes

Introduction: The Lineage and the Novel in Chosŏn Korea, 1392–1910

1. Here and throughout the manuscript, I render Chinese personal and geographical names that appear in lineage novels in their Korean pronunciation, which is the way they would have been pronounced by the Chosŏn-dynasty readers. The only exceptions are the names of the dynasties, which are rendered in the standard romanized Chinese pronunciation in order to maintain the broader consistency of historical references.

2. Jiang Ziya was the state councilor of King Wen of Zhou (1152–1056 BCE). King Wen, seeking men of talent, found Jiang Ziya after a prophesy that presaged his encounter with a wise man.

3. Liu Bei (161–223), the founder of the Kingdom of Shu during the Three Kingdoms period in China (220–280), visited the thatched cottage of Zhuge Liang, a talented military strategist, three times before the latter agreed to join him.

4. Kim Chinse, ed., *Wanwŏl hoemaeng yŏn* [The pledge at the banquet of moongazing pavilion], 12 vols. (Seoul: Seoul National University Press, 1986–1994), 1.1:29. This is a typeface edition that renders punctuated, partially glossed original text based on the manuscript located in the Kyujanggak Archive, Seoul National University, Ko 3350-65-v.1–93. Here and in subsequent citations of novels, such as "1.1:29," the first numeral indicates the

volume number of the printed edition, followed by the manuscript volume number and then the page number in the printed volume.

5. Although genealogical openings slightly vary—with some novels focusing explicitly on the story of just one protagonist—they are common to lineage novels.

6. Following Angela Zito, I do not use the term *subject* in the Cartesian sense, which "posits an internally consistent, psychological subject who exists in tension with external society and then opposes the social order to the natural." I instead follow Zito's analysis of the culture of Qing-dynasty China (1636–1911), which uncovers the processual figuration of subjectivity mediated by Confucian ritual, in which the "metaphysics of resonant transformation underlay the simultaneous production of self and world in constant interaction" and where "subject positions (ruler, subject, father, mother, son, daughter, friend of higher status, friend of lower status, elder, younger) were practically embodied in a variety of ways that produced reciprocal hierarchical relations in a circulation of powers" ("Silk and Skin: Significant Boundaries," in *Body, Subject, and Power in China*, ed. Angela Zito and Tani Barlow [Chicago: University of Chicago Press, 1994], 104, 106; also see Angela Zito, *Of Body and Brush: Grand Sacrifice as Text/Performance in Eighteenth-Century China* [Chicago: University of Chicago Press, 1997]).

7. Maram Epstein, *Orthodox Passions: Narrating Filial Love During the High Qing* (Cambridge, MA: Harvard University Press, 2019), 48. I thank the author for making the manuscript draft available before its publication.

8. If *Confucian Transformation* focuses on the moment of "translation" of the Confucian framework to suit Korea's local sociocultural milieu, *Under the Ancestors' Eyes*—a study of remarkable scope and texture—shows how this framework served to further the socioeconomic and cultural interests of Chosŏn civil elites. See Martina Deuchler, *The Confucian Transformation of Korea: A Study of Society and Ideology* (Cambridge, MA: Harvard University Asia Center, 1992), and *Under the Ancestors' Eyes: Kinship, Status, and Locality in Premodern Korea* (Cambridge, MA: Harvard University Asia Center, 2015).

9. Deuchler, *Under the Ancestors' Eyes*, 404.

10. Kwŏn Naehyŏn usefully reminds us that the changes to women's inheritance rights, which were prompted by patrilineal reconfiguration of kinship, took change gradually and were decided on a case-by-case basis in different families. Even after the seventeenth century, women's loss of their inheritance privilege was not universal, although it certainly became more common; in some cases, women's inheritance shares were simply lower than their brothers'. See Kwŏn Naehyŏn, "17–19 segi Chosŏn ŭi chaesan sangsok kwanhaeng—chongbŏp kwa kyŏngjeryŏk pyŏndong ŭl chungsim ŭro" [The customs of property succession in Chosŏn in the seventeenth–nineteenth

centuries—focusing on the agnatic principle and changes in economic power], *Han'guksa hakpo* 70 (2018): 283–315.

11. JaHyun Kim Haboush, "Gender and the Politics of Language in Chosŏn Korea," in *Rethinking Confucianism: Past and Present in China, Korea, Japan, and Vietnam*, ed. Benjamin Elman, Asian Pacific Monograph Series (Los Angeles: University of California, 2002), 220–56; Jisoo Kim, *The Emotions of Justice: Gender, Status, and Legal Performance in Chosŏn Korea* (Seattle: University of Washington Press, 2015).

12. Deuchler, *The Confucian Transformation of Korea*, 29–88.

13. Deuchler's book *Under the Ancestors' Eyes* is an encyclopedic account of the role of kinship ideology and practice in different areas of social life.

14. As Maram Epstein has written in the context of Qing literary culture, "The tensions between *si* and *gong* expectations in traditional auto/biographical records are one of the discursive means by which the private self is expressed" (*Orthodox Passions*, 260).

15. Lauren Berlant, *Cruel Optimism* (Durham, NC: Duke University Press, 2011), 7.

16. Raymond Williams, *Marxism and Literature* (Oxford: Oxford University Press, 1977), 133–35.

17. Erich Auerbach, *Mimesis: The Representation of Reality in Western Literature* (Princeton, NJ: Princeton University Press, 1953), 16.

18. Frederic Jameson, *The Political Unconscious: Narrative as a Socially Symbolic Act* (Ithaca, NY: Cornell University Press, 1981), 79.

19. JaHyun Kim Haboush has noted the contradictions between blood-based filiations and the kinship and status system in Chosŏn. She discusses the tensions between women's filial emotions and wifely duties that are highlighted in short vernacular Korean tales, in which women are allowed to remain filial subjects even after marriage. See JaHyun Kim Haboush, "Filial Emotions and Filial Values: Changing Patterns in the Discourse of Filiality in Late Chosŏn Korea," *Harvard Journal of Asiatic Studies* 55, no. 1 (1995): 129–77.

20. I borrow the phrase "feelings of flesh and blood" from Sun Joo Kim's work, which traces elite men's elaboration of their feelings for their slave-status secondary children, who suffered social discrimination. See Sun Joo Kim, "My Own Flesh and Blood: Stratified Parental Compassion and Law in Korean Slavery," *Social History* 44, no. 1 (2019): 1–25.

21. Even though scholars have noted the multiple differences between the European novel and fictional prose that developed in other parts of the world, for the purposes of this manuscript I use the blanket term *fictional prose* to facilitate macrohistorical comparison. My use of this term is inspired by an imaginative study of the global novelistic moment: Ning Ma, *The Age of Silver: Rise of the Novel East and West* (New York: Oxford University Press, 2016).

A discussion of specific genre distinctions between the Korean novel and other fictional works across the globe remains beyond the scope of this study.

22. Ma, *The Age of Silver*, 13.

23. Nancy Armstrong, *How Novels Think: The Limits of British Individualism from 1719–1900* (New York: Columbia University Press, 2005), 4. Also see Franco Moretti, *The Way of the World: The Bildungsroman in European Culture* (London: Verso, 2000).

24. Armstrong, *How Novels Think*, 4–5.

25. See Charles Taylor, *Sources of the Self: The Making of the Modern Identity* (Cambridge, MA: Harvard University Press, 1989), 111–210; Michel Foucault, "Technologies of the Self," in *Ethics: Subjectivity and Truth*, vol. 1 of *The Essential Works of Michel Foucault, 1954–1984*, ed. Paul Rabinov (New York: New Press, 1997), 16–49, 145–62; Judith Butler, *The Psychic Life of Power: Theories in Subjection* (Stanford, CA: Stanford University Press, 1997); Judith Butler and William Connolly, "Politics, Power, and Ethics: A Discussion Between Judith Butler and William Connolly," *Theory and Event* 4, no. 2 (2000), Project Muse, https://muse.jhu.edu/article/32589; Slavoj Žižek, *The Sublime Object of Ideology* (New York: Verso, 1987).

26. Nancy Armstrong, *Desire and Domestic Fiction: A Political History of the Novel* (New York: Oxford University Press, 1987). In *The Empire of Love: Toward a Theory of Intimacy, Genealogy, and Carnality* (Durham, NC: Duke University Press, 2006), Elizabeth Povinelli coins the notion of social exfoliation advanced in the liberal politics of love.

27. Mikhail Bakhtin, *The Dialogic Imagination: Four Essays*, ed. Michael Holquist, trans. Caryl Emerson and Michael Holquist (Austin: University of Texas Press, 1981), 245–47.

28. As Nancy Armstrong has written, "The domestic novel [was] the agent and product of a cultural change that attached gender to certain kinds of writing" (*Desire and Domestic Fiction*, 28).

29. Timothy Brook, *The Confusions of Pleasure: Commerce and Culture in Ming China* (Berkeley: University of California Press, 1999), 1–14.

30. Benjamin Elman, *On Their Own Terms: Science in China, 1550–1900* (Cambridge, MA: Harvard University Press, 2009), 12.

31. Maram Epstein, *Competing Discourses: Orthodoxy, Authenticity, and Engendered Meanings in Late Imperial Chinese Fiction* (Cambridge, MA: Harvard University Asia Center, 2001), 61–79. On the entanglement of the genealogy of emotions and space in China, or so-called emotion-realms, see Ling Hon Lam, *The Spatiality of Emotion in Early Modern China: From Dreamscapes to Theatricality* (New York: Columbia University Press, 2018), 19–52.

32. Dorothy Ko, *Teachers of the Inner Chambers: Women and Culture in Seventeenth-Century China* (Stanford, CA: Stanford University Press, 1995), 29–67.

33. Epstein, *Competing Discourses*, 152–54.

34. Ko, *Teachers of the Inner Chambers*, 68–111.

35. Ellen Widmer, *The Beauty and the Book: Women and Fiction in Nineteenth-Century China* (Cambridge, MA: Harvard University Council on East Asian Studies, 2006), 137–78, 217–78.

36. See Judith Zeitlin, *Historian of the Strange: Pu Songling and the Chinese Classical Tale* (Stanford, CA: Stanford University Press, 1993).

37. Martin Huang, *Desire and Fictional Narrative in Late Imperial China* (Cambridge, MA: Harvard University Press, 2001), 58.

38. Lam, *Spatiality of Emotion*, 39, also 19–52.

39. Zito, "Silk and Skin," 117.

40. Han Myŏnggi notes that the influx of large amounts of Chinese silver into Chosŏn Korea during the Imjin Wars had a significance that exceeded its economic dimension: it paved the way for the interest in commerce and currency development that emerged in the eighteenth-century practical philosophy known as Sirhak, or Practical Learning. See Han Myŏnggi, "17 segi ch'o ŭn ŭi yut'ong kwa kŭ yŏnghyang" [The circulation of silver in the seventeenth century and its ramifications], *Kyujanggak* 15 (1992): 1–36.

41. Oh Doo Hwan notes that "when a world historical cultural diffusion was rapidly developing, Korea was alienated from contact with new civilizations" ("The Silver Trade and Silver Currency in Chosŏn Korea," trans. James Lewis, *Acta Koreana* 7, no. 1 [2004]: 97–98). On merchant activities, see also Owen Miller, "Ties of Labour and Ties of Commerce: Corvée Among Seoul Merchants in the Late 19th Century," *Journal of the Economic and Social History of the Orient* 50, no. 1 (2007): 41–71.

42. On the place of East Asia in the global economy between the 1400s and the 1800s, see Andre Gunder Frank, *ReOrient: Global Economy in the Asian Age* (Berkeley: University of California Press, 1998), 52–130.

43. On the role of Chosŏn Korea in the East Asian infrastructure of silver exchange, see Kwŏn Naehyŏn [Kwon Nae-Hyun], "Chosŏn Korea's Trade with Qing China and the Circulation of Silver," *Acta Koreana* 18, no. 1 (2015): 163–85. Although the flows of silver from Japan to China via Chosŏn had an impact on the Korean internal market, silver never became the exclusive currency in Chosŏn. See Kwŏn Naehyŏn, "17 segi–18 segi chŏnban Chosŏn ŭi ŭn yut'ong" [Circulation of silver in Chosŏn between the late seventeenth and early eighteenth centuries], *Yŏksa hakpo* 221 (2014): 19–26.

44. Ko Dong-hwan traces the urban development of Seoul to the unification of the taxation system under the rubric of the Uniform Land Tax (Taedong pŏp 大同法), which together with the circulation of metallic currency in the seventeenth century prompted the emergence of contract labor as well

as the Seoul-centered market system and the concomitant growth of the metropolitan population. See Ko Dong-hwan, "The Characteristics of the Urban Development of Seoul During the Late Chosŏn Dynasty: With a Focus on the Changes in Urban Structure," *Seoul Journal of Korean Studies* 10 (1997): 95–123; on the emergence of new literary genres and entertainment sphere, see 114–15. On the emergence of "town literature," see Im Hyŏngt'aek, "18–19 segi iyagikun kwa sosŏl ŭi paldal" [Storytellers and the development of the novel in the eighteenth to nineteenth centuries], in *Kojŏn munhak ŭl chajasŏ* [In search for traditional Korean literature], ed. Kim Yŏlgyu (Seoul: Munhak kwa chisŏngsa, 1976), 310–32; Im Hyŏngt'aek, "Yŏhang munhak kwa sŏmin munhak" [Town literature and demotic literature], in *Han'gukhak yŏn'gu immun* [Introduction to Korean studies], ed. Yi Kawŏn (Seoul: Chisik sanŏpsa, 1981), 315–30. I thank Sun Joo Kim, Hyun Jae Yoo, John Lee, and Holly Stephens for helping me understand the economic landscape of the late Chosŏn.

45. In her study of the kinship system, Martina Deuchler notes that challenges to the elite status arise from the attempts by local gentry and secondary sons to infiltrate the elite ranks as well as from wealthy commoners who purchased titles. The latter group, representing the impact of money on the status system, did not constitute a formidable threat to the traditional kinship system (*Under the Ancestors' Eyes*, 370–96).

46. Scholars contend that the lineage novel, although elaborating the values of the elite culture, registers different levels of social power in that some of the texts elaborate the issues of status loss or economic dispossession. See, for example, Han Kilyŏn, *Chosŏn sidae taeha sosŏl ŭi tach'ŭng chŏk segye* [The multilayered world of the Chosŏn-dynasty lineage novel] (Seoul: Somyŏng ch'ulp'an, 2009), 39–41, and Yi Chiha, Ogwŏn chaehap kiyŏn *yŏnjak yŏn'gu* [Study of the sequel cluster of *The remarkable encounter of jade mandarin ducks*] (Seoul: Pogosa, 2015), 170–94.

47. See JaHyun Kim Haboush, "Constructing the Center: The Ritual Controversy and the Search for a New Identity in Seventeenth-Century Korea," in *Culture and the State in Late Chosŏn Korea*, ed. Martina Deuchler and JaHyun Kim Haboush (Cambridge, MA: Harvard University Asia Center, 1999), 46–90.

48. Kwŏn Naehyŏn notes that immediately after the establishment of the Qing dynasty in 1644, Chosŏn and Qing exchanged a much greater number of annual diplomatic missions than was customary with the preceding Ming dynasty. As the Qing–Chosŏn relationship stabilized, the number of diplomatic missions decreased ("Chosŏn Korea's Trade with Qing China," 165–68). I thank Sun Joo Kim for bringing this increased Chosŏn–Qing diplomatic interaction to my attention.

49. Martina Deuchler, "Despoilers of the Way, Insulters of the Sages: Controversies Over the Classics in Seventeenth-Century Korea," in *Culture and the State in Late Chosŏn Korea*, ed. Martina Deuchler and JaHyun Kim Haboush (Cambridge, MA: Harvard University Asia Center, 1999), 131–33.

50. On the introduction of Wang Yangming's philosophy to Chosŏn, see Yu Myŏngjong, *Sŏngnihak kwa yangmyŏnghak* [Neo-Confucian orthodoxy and Wang Yangming's philosophy] (Seoul: Yonsei University Press, 1994), 173–75.

51. Ch'oe Yŏngsŏng, *Han'guk yuhak sasangsa: Chosŏn hugi p'yŏn sang* [The intellectual history of Korean Confucian scholarship: The late Chosŏn] (Seoul: Asea munhwasa, 1995), 305, 309–10, 351–54.

52. Ch'oe Yŏngsŏng, *Han'guk yuhak sasangsa*, 308.

53. Ch'oe Yŏngsŏng, *Han'guk yuhak sasangsa*, 355.

54. Wong Siu-Kit and Lee Kar-Shui, "Poems of Depravity: A Twelfth Century Dispute on the Moral Character of *The Book of Songs*," *T'oung Pao* 75, nos. 4–5 (1989): 209–25.

55. See Kim Hŭnggyu, *Chosŏn hugi* Sigyŏng *ron kwa si ŭisik* [The notion of poetry and the exegesis of *The Book of Poetry* in the late Chosŏn] (Seoul: Korea University, 1982); Sim Kyŏngho, *Chosŏn sidae hanmunhak kwa* Sigyŏng *ron* [Literary Chinese studies and the exegesis of *The Book of Poetry* in Chosŏn Korea] (Seoul: Ilchisa, 1999).

56. Yi Chiha, Ogwŏn chaehap kiyŏn *yŏnjak yŏn'gu*, 250–73.

57. Ōtani Morishige, *Chosŏn hugi sosŏl tokcha yŏn'gu* [Study of the novel audience in the late Chosŏn] (Seoul: Koryŏdae minsok munhwa yŏn'guso, 1985), 43–55, 70–74.

58. See Im Hyŏngt'aek, "17 segi kyubang sosŏl ŭi sŏngnip kwa *Ch'angsŏn kamŭi rok*" [*The praise of goodness and the admiration of righteousness* and the rise of the boudoir novel], *Tongbang hakchi* 57 (1988): 127–35. The three novels—Kim Manjung's *The Nine-Cloud Dream* (Kuunmong 九雲夢), *Madam Sa's Conquest of the South* (Sa ssi namjŏng ki 謝氏南征記), and *The Praise of Goodness and the Admiration of Righteousness* (Ch'angsŏn kamŭi rok 彰善感義錄), attributed to Cho Sŏnggi—have a significant number of literary Chinese and vernacular Korean editions. *Madame Sa's Conquest of the South* appears to have been composed in the vernacular Korean script and later translated into literary Chinese, but debates about the original script of composition of the other two novels are ongoing.

59. Min Kwandong, *Chungguk kojŏn sosŏl ŭi chŏnp'a wa suyong* [Importation and readership of Chinese classical novels] (Seoul: Asea munhwasa, 2007), 263. Sixiang Wang notes that the Korean adaptation of *The Romance of the Western Chamber*, entitled *Story of the Eastern Chamber* (Tongsang ki), turns away from the excessive romantic investment of the former text. Moreover, the

influence of Chinese vernacular fiction upon literati writing prompted a rectification of styles policy during the reign of King Chŏngjo (1752–1800). See Sixiang Wang, "*Story of the Eastern Chamber*: Dilemmas of Vernacular Language and Political Authority in Eighteenth-Century Chosŏn," *Journal of Korean Studies* 24, no. 1 (2019): 31, 34.

60. *The Praise of Goodness and the Admiration of Righteousness*—which Im Hyŏngt'aek has posited as a foundational text in the lineage novel tradition ("17 segi kyubang sosŏl")—circulated exclusively in manuscript during the Chosŏn dynasty, and the number of its manuscript editions exceeds that of any other Chosŏn-dynasty novel. See Yi Chiyŏng, "*Ch'angsŏn kamŭi rok* ŭi ibon pyŏni yangsang kwa tokcha ch'ŭng ŭi sanggwan kwan'gye" [The relationship between the audiences and variations in the editions of *The praise of goodness and the admiration of righteousness*], PhD diss., Seoul National University, 2003). Discussing various manuscripts of this text, Yi Chiyŏng notes that many of the editions contain postscripts that praise the manuscript's calligraphy and urge that it be transmitted over many generations.

61. Im Hyŏngt'aek, "17 segi kyubang sosŏl," 123–35. For a more detailed discussion of the circulation of conduct literature, see Pak Yŏnghŭi, "*So Hyŏnsŏng rok* yŏnjak yŏn'gu" [A study of *The record of So Hyŏnsŏng* and its sequels], PhD diss., Ewha Womans University, 1994, 64–70.

62. In her study of *The Record of So Hyŏnsŏng*, Pak Yŏnghŭi explicitly refines Im Hyŏngt'aek's argument, suggesting that the lineage novel rather than the so-called shorter boudoir novel constituted the beginning of vernacular Korean literary tradition ("*So Hyŏnsŏng rok* yŏnjak yŏn'gu").

63. *The Romance of the Western Zhou* is a translation of the Ming-dynasty novel *Investiture of the Gods* (Ch. *Fengshen yanyi* 封神演義), attributed to Xu Zhonglin (?–1560). On the influence of Chinese romance novels on the Korean lineage novel, see Pak Yŏnghŭi, "*So Hyŏnsŏng rok* yŏnjak yŏn'gu," 78–80; Kim Tonguk, "The Influence of Chinese Stories and Novels on Korean Fiction," in *Literary Migrations: Traditional Chinese Fiction in Asia*, ed. Claudine Salmon (Singapore: Institute of Southeast Asian Studies, 2013), 52–57.

64. On the circulation of *The Peony Pavilion* in Chosŏn, see Yu Sŭnghyŏn and Min Kwandong, "Chosŏn hugi Chungguk hŭigok ŭi suyong yangsang: *Sŏsang ki* rŭl chungsim ŭro" [Circulation of Chinese plays in the late Chosŏn: The case of *The romance of the western chamber*], *Chungguk ŏmun hakchi* 43, no. 43 (2013): 76, 82–83. On the circulation of *The Dream of the Red Chamber*, see Ch'oe Yongch'ŏl, *Honglumong* ŭi chŏnp'a wa pŏn'yŏk [The circulation and translation of *The dream of the red chamber* in Chosŏn Korea] (Seoul: Sinsŏwŏn, 2007), 20–25; and Min Kwandong, *Chungguk kojŏn sosŏl ŭi chŏnp'a wa suyong*, 264–65. On the circulation of *The Plum in the Golden Vase*, see Chŏng Okkŭn, "*Jinpingmei* zai Chaoxian chao de chuanbo yiji Chaoxian shidafu dui

Jinpingmei de jihui" [Circulation of *The plum in the golden vase* in Chosŏn and the criticism of this text by Chosŏn literati], *Chungguk munje yŏn'gu* 10 (1998): 149–56. On Chosŏn-dynasty literary adaptations of *The Plum in the Golden Vase*, see Ha Sŏngnan, "*Chŏlhwa kidam* kwa *Kŭmpyŏngmae* ŭi kwallyŏn yangsang yŏn'gu" [Study of the relationship between *The remarkable story of a plucked flower* and *The plum in the golden vase*], *Yŏlsang kojŏn yŏn'gu* 64 (2018): 253–87.

65. Jin Shengtan's (1610?–1660) edition paved the way for the popularity of *The Romance of the Western Wing* among the educated men of Chosŏn, who admired and sought to emulate the style of Jin's preface. Another important step in the popularization of the text was the wide circulation of glossaries, which explicated the Yuan-dynasty northern dialect. See Yun Chiyang, "Chosŏn ŭi *Sŏsang ki* suyong yangsang yŏn'gu" [Study of the reception of *The romance of the western wing* in Chosŏn], PhD diss., Seoul National University, 2015), 10–57, 194–223.

66. See Yi Chiyŏng, "18 segi kyŏnghwa sajok ŭi sosŏl hyangyu" [Novel readership among the metropolitan elites in the eighteenth century], *Kungmunhak yŏn'gu* 21 (2010): 67–95.

67. Kwŏn Sŏp, "Sŏnbi susa ch'aekcha punbaegi" [The roster of books handcopied and bequeathed by my late mother], in *Oksogo* [Writings of Okso], 17 vols. (Seoul: Taunsem, 2007), 8:598–99, quoted in Pak Yŏnghŭi, "Changp'yŏn kamun sosŏl ŭi hyangyu chiptan yŏn'gu" [Readership of the lineage novel], in *Munhak kwa sahoe chipdan* [Literature and society], ed. Han'guk kojŏn munhakhoe (Seoul: Chimmundang, 1995), 322. Keith McMahon, for instance, notes that *A Fortunate Union* "portrays characters who, though as determinedly in love as any elsewhere, greatly lack the passionate drives of their literary predecessors," all the while maintaining "a studious balance between ritual or propriety (*li* 禮) and feeling (*qing* 情)" (*Causality and Containment in Seventeenth-Century Chinese Fiction* [Leiden: Brill, 1988], 131–32). Maram Epstein describes it as a text "in which both the scholar and the beauty are dedicated to righting the corrupt imperial bureaucracy in order to avenge their fathers" (*Competing Discourses*, 273).

68. Ch'oe Suhyŏn and Hŏ Sunu, trans., *So Hyŏnsŏng rok* [The record of So Hyŏnsŏng], 4 vols. (Seoul: Somyŏng ch'ulp'an, 2010), 3:546.

69. Pak Ilyong, using the term *chivalric* or *hero novel*, notes the overlap between this group of texts and the lineage novel, in which the motif of a personal journey plays an important role within the teleological, moral structure of the lineage. See Pak Ilyong, "Kamun sosŏl kwa yŏngung sosŏl ŭi sosŏlsa chŏk kwallyŏn yangsang: Hyŏngsŏnggi rŭl chungsim ŭro" [The intersection between the lineage novel and the hero novel: With the focus on the formative period], *Kojŏn munhak yŏn'gu* 20 (2001): 169–206. Chŏn Sŏngun

proposes a theory that the hero novel developed out of the lineage novel. See Chŏn Sŏngun, *Chosŏn hugi changp'yŏn kungmun sosŏl ŭi chomang* [Overview of the vernacular Korean lineage novel in the late Chosŏn dynasty] (Seoul: Pogosa, 2002). South Korean scholars are wont to distinguish between the "martial" or "battlefield novel" (*kundam sosŏl* 軍談小說) and the "chivalric" or "hero novel" (*yŏngung sosŏl* 英雄小說), even as these terms overlap. In the first group of texts, the battlefield is generally depicted through war scenes, whereas the second group focuses on the rise to glory of a single distinguished individual, and the battlefield might or might not play a decisive role in this journey. These tales are often understood as social critiques: scholars see the protagonists' upward journeys through the social ranks as providing vicarious pleasure for the dispossessed. See Sŏ Taesŏk, *Kundam sosŏl ŭi kujo wa paegyŏng* [The background and structure of the battlefield novel] (Seoul: Ewha Womans University Press, 1985); Kim Kidong, *Yijo sidae sosŏl ron* [Theory of the Chosŏn-dynasty novel] (Seoul: Samusa, 1976), 253–302. Even though lineage novels are concerned mostly with the longevity of civil lineages, they abound in battlefield scenes, and their male protagonists usually combine the manners of a refined scholar with military gallantry as they champion the cause of Confucian statecraft in their numerous military expeditions. See Song Sŏnguk, *Chosŏn sidae taeha sosŏl ŭi sŏsa munpŏp kwa ch'angjak ŭisik* [The narrative grammar and outlook of Chosŏn-dynasty lineage novels] (Seoul: T'aehaksa, 2003), 204, 286–301.

70. On the traces of the storyteller's voice in the lineage novel, see Song Sŏnguk, "Chosŏn cho taeha sosŏl ŭi yuhyŏngsŏng kwa kŭ ŭimi" [Structure and meaning of the Chosŏn-dynasty lineage novel], *Kaesin ŏmun yŏn'gu* 14 (1997): 313–39. Paize Keulemans notes that in the Chinese literati fiction the storyteller's voice was utilized to redraw the boundaries between popular-oral and literati-textual novelistic forms. See Paize Keulemans, *Sound Rising from the Paper: Nineteenth-Century Martial Arts Fiction and the Chinese Acoustic Imagination* (Cambridge, MA: Harvard University Asia Center, 2014), 33–64.

71. Kim Kidong, ed., *Ogwŏn chaehap kiyŏn* [The remarkable reunion of jade mandarin ducks], vols. 27–30 of *Kojŏn sosŏl chŏnjip* [The anthology of manuscript editions of classical Korean novels] (Seoul: Asea munhwasa, 1980), 30.21:616.

72. For the context of these external references in *The Pledge*, see Kim Chinse, "Yijo hugi taeha sosŏl yŏn'gu: *Wanwŏl hoemaeng yŏn* ŭi kyŏngu" [A study of late Chosŏn lineage novels: The case of *The pledge at the banquet of moon-gazing pavilion*], in *Han'guk sosŏl munhak ŭi t'amgu* [Research in Korean fictional prose], ed. Han'guk kojŏn munhak yŏn'guhoe (Seoul: Ilchogak, 1978), 104–6. Chapter 1 shows that lineage novels often continue through sequels that extend the narrative to the lives of the new generations of the lineage. Therefore, some sequels, whose titles are recorded in the text, do in fact exist. In

other instances, such as the ones named in the introduction, the references to the outside literary space are prestige-claiming devices that connect the lineage novel to the documentary genres of kinship writing.

73. Im Hyŏngt'aek, "17 segi kyubang sosŏl," 161–62; Im Ch'igyun, *Chosŏn sidae taejangp'yŏn sosŏl yŏn'gu* [A study of the Chosŏn lineage novel] (Seoul: T'aehaksa, 1996), 345; Song Sŏnguk, *Chosŏn sidae taeha sosŏl*, 278–82.

74. Kwŏn Sŏp, "Sŏnbi susa ch'aekcha punbaegi," 8:598–99, quoted in Pak Yŏnghŭi, "Changp'yŏn kamun sosŏl ŭi hyangyu chiptan yŏn'gu," 322.

75. Kwŏn Sŏp, "Sŏnbi yusa" [In memory of my late mother], in *Oksogo*, 5:213, quoted in Pak Yŏnghŭi, "Changp'yŏn kamun sosŏl ŭi hyangyu chiptan yŏn'gu," 334–35. Surviving letters by Queen Insŏn intimate that she and her daughters frequently exchanged novels. See Kim Ilgŭn, *Ŏn'gan ŭi yŏn'gu: Han'gŭl sŏgan ŭi yŏn'gu wa charyo chipsŏng* [A study of vernacular Korean letters: Analysis and collection of materials] (Seoul: Konkuk University Press, 1986), 63. Kwŏn Sŏp's maternal granduncle Chŏng Chehyŏn (1642–1662) was married to King Hyojong's daughter, Princess Sukhwi (1642–1696), who, in Kwŏn Sŏp's own words, had been especially affectionate to him during his own numerous palace visits. See Pak Yŏnghŭi, "Changp'yŏn kamun sosŏl ŭi hyangyu chiptan yŏn'gu," 334–35.

76. Kwŏn Sŏp, "Che sŏnjobi susa *Samgukchi* hu" [A note on the text of *The romance of the three kingdoms* transcribed by my late grandmother], in *Oksogo* 8:597–98, quoted in Pak Yŏnghŭi, "Changp'yŏn kamun sosŏl ŭi hyangyu chiptan yŏn'gu," 322.

77. Kwŏn Sŏp, "Sŏnbi yusa," 5:213.

78. For the historical background of King Yŏngjo's reign and Prince Sado's death, see JaHyun Kim Haboush, *The Confucian Kingship in Korea: Yŏngjo and the Politics of Sagacity* (New York: Columbia University Press, 2001).

79. JaHyun Kim Haboush, trans., *Memoirs of Lady Hyegyŏng: The Autobiographical Writings of a Crown Princess of Eighteenth-Century Korea* (Berkeley: University of California Press, 2013), 116–17.

80. Pak Chiwŏn, *Yŏrha ilgi* [The Jehol diary], http://db.itkc.kr.

81. Hong Hŭibok, "*Cheil kiŏn sŏ*" [Preface to *The Book of Books in the vernacular*], in *Cheil kiŏn* [Flowers in the mirror], ed. Pak Chaeyŏn and Chŏng Kyubok (Seoul: Kukhak charyowŏn, 2001), 21–23.

82. Alongside the feminist reading of *Flowers in the Mirror*, scholars have also discerned the limitations of Li Ruzhen's own view of gender relations or, alternatively, have argued that the feminine in the novel is nothing more than a trope that figures in the reflections upon male literati identity. Carlos Rojas usefully reminds us that all of these readings must be considered in relation to the symbolic economy of the text, which destabilizes the signifying links, represents the issue of identity in terms of multiple slippages

and misidentifications, and thus precludes a fixed reading of its gendered logic. See Carlos Rojas, *The Naked Gaze: Reflections on Chinese Modernity* (Cambridge, MA: Harvard University Asia Center, 2008), 54–81.

83. Chŏng Kyubok, "*Cheil kiŏn* e taehayŏ" [Observations on *The Book of Books in the vernacular*], *Chunggukhak nonch'ong* 1 (1984): 79.

84. Kim Kyŏngmi, "*Kyŏnghwayŏn* ŭi pŏnyŏksŏ *Cheil kiŏn* ŭl t'onghae pon Hong Hŭibok ŭi pŏnyŏk insik" [The translator's outlook in Hong Hŭibok's *The Book of Books in the vernacular*, a translation of *Flowers in the mirror*], *Han'guk kojŏn yŏn'gu* 32 (2015): 541–68, esp. 550–52.

85. Chŏng Pyŏngsŏl [Jung Byung Sul], "Chosŏn hugi changp'yŏn sosŏlsa ŭi chŏn'gae" [The historical development of the lineage novel in the late Chosŏn], in *Han'guk kojŏn sosŏl kwa sŏsa munhak* [The traditional Korean novel and fictional prose] (Seoul: Chimmundang, 1998), 245–63.

86. For a review of terminology, see Im Ch'igyun, *Chosŏn sidae taejangp'yŏn sosŏl yŏn'gu*, 39–40. For the sake of uniformity, when citing secondary studies I translate these different terms as "lineage novel."

87. A study conducted in the 1960s among female residents of the Kyŏngsang Province revealed that in their youth women were encouraged to read narratives that were called "record" (*ki* 記), whereas the titles designated as "tale" (*chŏn* 傳) were considered unsuitable for the girls of good upbringing. See Yi Wŏnju, "Kojŏn sosŏl tokcha ŭi sŏnghyang—Kyŏngbuk pukpu chiyŏk ŭl chungsim ŭro" [The tastes of traditional novel readers—focused on the northern Kyŏngsang Province], *Han'gukhak nonjip* 1–5 (1975): 557–73.

88. Chŏng Pyŏngsŏl, "Chosŏn hugi changp'yŏn sosŏlsa ŭi chŏn'gae," 245–62.

89. This study is of course inspired by the late JaHyun Kim Haboush's work on vernacular Korean cultural production, which included shorter fiction and *The Memoirs of Lady Hyegyŏng*.

90. The three known editions of *The Pledge* are located at the Kyujanggak Archive (Ko 3350-65-v.1–93; 93 manuscript volumes), the Changsŏgak Archive (K4-6834; 180 manuscript volumes), and the Yonsei University Archive (Kosŏ (I) 811.36 wanwŏlhoe; incomplete manuscript in 5 volumes). I use the typeface edition by Kim Chinse, based on the Kyujanggak manuscript.

91. Two editions of *The Remarkable Reunion of Jade Mandarin Ducks* are known. The first one, with a slightly altered title (*Ogwŏn chunghoe yŏn* 玉鴛重會緣) is located at the Jangseogak Archive of the Academy of Korean Studies, Songnam (K4^6832; this manuscript, originally comprising 21 manuscript volumes, is missing volumes 1–5). The second manuscript, transcribed in the family of Madame Chŏng of Onyang, is located in the Kyujanggak Archive, Seoul (Ko 3350-68-v.1–21; manuscript in 21 volumes) and is the basis for the facsimile edition I use. The single extant edition of

The Commentary is located at the Kyujanggak Archive (Ko 3350-67-v.1–5; 5 manuscript volumes).

92. *The Record of Two Heroes: Brothers Hyŏn* appears to have been immensely popular, with more than seventy editions in manuscript and print formats. I use the facsimile reproduction of the ten-volume manuscript in the Jangseogak Archive (K4^6862).

93. Among the nine known manuscripts of *The Remarkable Encounter of Pearls*, I use the facsimile reproduction of the Jangseogak Archive version (K4^6804; 25 manuscript volumes).

94. The two unpublished manuscripts of *Pearls and Jade* are located at the Sŏgang University Archive (Kosŏ myŏng 77; 25 volumes) and the Yeungnam University Archive (unlisted). I examined both editions but used the Sŏgang University version (Kosŏ myŏng 77), which consists of twenty-five volumes, is of better quality, and is more easily accessible through the university library services.

1. The Structure of Kinship: Generational Narratives

1. For a discussion of terminology, see the introduction, note 69.

2. See Sŏng Hyŏn'gyŏng, "Kojŏn sosŏl kwa kamun: Ildaegi yŏngung sosŏl ŭl chungsim ŭro" [The traditional Korean novel and lineage: Focusing on the single-generation hero novels], *Inmunhak yŏn'gu* 20 (1988): 31–47.

3. Martina Deuchler, *Under the Ancestors' Eyes: Kinship, Status, and Locality in Premodern Korea* (Cambridge, MA: Harvard University Asia Center, 2015), 3, emphasis in original.

4. Deuchler, *Under the Ancestors' Eyes*, 1–14.

5. Michael Szonyi, *Practicing Kinship: Lineage and Descent in Late Imperial China* (Stanford, CA: Stanford University Press, 2002), 27–28.

6. Song Chunho, *Chosŏn sahoesa yŏn'gu: Chosŏn sahoe ŭi kujo wa sŏnggyŏk mit kŭ pyŏnch'ŏn e kwanhan yŏn'gu* [The social history of Chosŏn: The nature of the social structure and its changes] (Seoul: Ilchŏgak, 1987), 31–32.

7. Edward Wagner has noted that genealogies created before the seventeenth century reveal that women's position within kinship was much more empowered, compared to their post-seventeenth-century situation, when patrilineality became solidified. See Edward Wagner, "Two Early Genealogies and Women's Status in Early Yi Dynasty Korea," in *Korean Women: View from the Inner Room*, ed. Laurel Kendall and Mark Peterson (New Haven, CT: East Rock Press, 1983), 23–32. Women's status nevertheless remained significant: the primary wife, who was the mother of status-eligible issue, had to be an elite in order to ensure the ascriptive privilege of her children.

8. Yi Sugŏn, "Chosŏn sidae sinbunsa kwallyŏn charyo ŭi pip'an: Sŏnggwan, kagye, inmun kwallyŏn wijo charyo wa wisŏ rŭl chungsim ŭro" [Critical evaluation of the materials for the history of the Chosŏn class structure: Fabrications of ancestral seats, genealogies, and personalia], Komunsŏ yŏn'gu 14 (1998): 1–32.

9. Deuchler, Under the Ancestors' Eyes, 289–300.

10. On the encyclopedic compilations of the most powerful lineages' genealogies, see Ch'a Changsŏp, "Chosŏn sidae chokpo ŭi yuhyŏng kwa t'ŭkching" [The form and characteristics of genealogies in the late Chosŏn dynasty], Yŏksa kyoyuk nonjip 44 (2010): 239–78. Song Chunho also notes that several extant genealogies are written in the vernacular Korean script, which suggests that they were used for women's education (Chosŏn sahoesa yŏn'gu, 21–26).

11. Deuchler, Under the Ancestors' Eyes, 358–63.

12. Sun Joo Kim has shown how the visibility of northern Chosŏn elites in dynastic politics, following their examination successes after the seventeenth century, was augmented by extensive efforts in textual and architectural commemoration of notable ancestors. See Sun Joo Kim, Voice from the North: Resurrecting Regional Identity Through the Life and Work of Yi Sihang (1672–1736) (Stanford, CA: Stanford University Press, 2013), 15–54.

13. Funerary texts were certainly written for men and women alike. My emphasis on women-centered funerary texts is warranted by their ability to illuminate the contours of women-centered domestic life.

14. Hwang Hŭi, "Suwŏn Paek ssi sebo" [Preface to the genealogy of the Suwŏn Paek lineage], in Han'guk chokpo kubo sŏjip [Collection of prefaces from the Korean genealogies], ed. Chŏng Pyŏngwan (Seoul: Asea munhwasa, 1987), 3.

15. Lauren Berlant, The Female Complaint: The Unfinished Business of Sentimentality in American Culture (Durham, NC: Duke University Press, 2008), 259.

16. Yi Kyŏngha, "Mangsil haengjang yŏn'gu" [Posthumous biographies written for deceased wives], Han'guk munhwa 40 (2007): 4; Yi Subong, "Kamun sosŏl yŏn'gu" [A study of the lineage novel], Tonga nonch'ong 15, no. 1 (1978): 234.

17. Yi Kyŏngha, "Mangsil haengjang yŏn'gu," 4–7, 24.

18. See Yi Myŏnbaek, "Sŏn'gobi hapchang chi" [An inscription for my late parents' shared entombment], in 19 segi–20 segi ch'o yŏsŏng saenghwalsa charyo chip [Sources on the lives of women between the nineteenth and early twentieth centuries], 9 vols., ed. Ch'a Mihŭi., Kang Sŏngsuk, Kim Kyŏngmi, Yi Kyŏngha, Cho Hyeran, Hwang Suyŏn, Sŏ Kyŏnghŭi, Kim Hyŏnmi, Kim Kirim, and Hong Hakhŭi (Seoul: Pogosa, 2013), 2:387.

19. Kim Ch'anghyŏp, "Ŏ Yubong tap" [Reply to Ŏ Yubong], in Nongam chip [The anthology of Nongam], http://db.itkc.or.kr, quoted in An Tŭkyong,

"16 segi huban–17 segi chŏnban pijimun ŭi chŏnbŏm kwa sŏsul yangsang e taehan koch'al" [The form and narrative style of commemorative writing in the late sixteenth and early seventeenth centuries], *Han'guk munhak yŏn'gu* 39 (2007): 236.

20. Within the text of the biography, Hong Nagwŏn uses this phrase, "the worthless," to refer to himself and his younger brother, Hong Naksul.

21. Hong Nagwŏn, *Sŏnbuin kajŏn* [Biography of my late mother], Kyujanggak Archive, Seoul, Ko 813.5 Sy28, 22a–b. Although vernacular commemorative texts would most often be read within the close circle of kinship, some texts achieved wider circulation, such as the posthumous biography that the famed Chosŏn novelist Kim Manjung (1637–1692) wrote for his mother, *Posthumous Biography of My Honorable Late Mother* (*Sŏnbi chŏnggyŏng puin haengjang* 先妣貞敬夫人行狀).

22. Maram Epstein, *Orthodox Passions: Narrating Filial Love During the High Qing* (Cambridge, MA: Harvard University Press, 2019), 259.

23. Hong Nagwŏn, *Sŏnbuin kajŏn*, 16b.

24. Hong Nagwŏn, *Sŏnbuin kajŏn*, 8a.

25. JaHyun Kim Haboush, trans., *Memoirs of Lady Hyegyŏng: The Autobiographical Writings of a Crown Princess of Eighteenth-Century Korea* (Berkeley: University of California Press, 2013), 49.

26. Haboush notes that this particular memoir is written in the form of family injunction (*Memoirs of Lady Hyegyŏng*, 17–19).

27. Sŏ Yugu, "Mangsil chŏngpuin Yŏsan Song ssi myojimyŏng" [Tomb inscription for my deceased wife, Lady Song of Yŏsan], in *19 segi–20 segi ch'o*, ed. Ch'a Mihŭi et al., 2:270–74.

28. Literally in the text: "[ride] in a lofty four-horse carriage (*kogŏ sama* 高車駟馬)."

29. Sŏ Yugu, "Chosŏmo Pak yumo myomyŏng" [Tomb inscription for concubine grandmother, Matron Pak], in *19 segi–20 segi ch'o*, ed. Ch'a Mihŭi et al., 2:286–88.

30. Chŏng Yagyong, "Sŏmo Kim ssi myojimyŏng" [Tombstone inscription for my secondary mother Matron Kim], in *19 segi–20 segi ch'o*, ed. Ch'a Mihŭi et al., 2:76.

31. Hong Sŏkchu, "Che sŏjŭngjomo Kim ssi mun" [Eulogy for my concubine great-grandmother Matron Kim], in *19 segi–20 segi ch'o*, ed. Ch'a Mihŭi et al., 3:39.

32. Sŏng Haeŭng, "Sŏjomo Sŏng Hyogi ch'ŏ myoji" [Tomb inscription for secondary grandmother, concubine of Sŏng Hyogi], in *19 segi–20 segi ch'o*, ed. Ch'a Mihŭi et al., 1:195.

33. Deuchler, *Under the Ancestors' Eyes*, 130–31.

34. Kim Ch'anghyŏp, "Paekku myojimyŏng pyŏngsŏ" [Tomb inscription for my maternal uncle with an introduction], in *Nongam chip*.

35. Im Hŏnhŭi, "Sŏnbi yusa" [In memory of my late mother], in *19 segi–20 segi ch'o*, ed. Ch'a Mihŭi et al., 6:52.

36. Im Hŏnhŭi, "Sŏnyŏ Ŭnghŭi kwangji" [Tomb inscription for my secondary daughter, Ŭnghŭi], in *19 segi–20 segi ch'o*, ed. Ch'a Mihŭi et al., 6:28.

37. Alan Cole, *Mothers and Sons in Chinese Buddhism* (Stanford, CA: Stanford University Press, 1998), 2.

38. Ch'oe Kilyong originally identified ten lineage novel sequel clusters in his study *Chosŏn cho yŏnjak sosŏl yŏn'gu* [Study of the Chosŏn-dynasty sequel novels] (Seoul: Asea munhwasa, 1992), 13. Im Ch'igyun later expanded the number of clusters to thirteen in *Chosŏn sidae taejangp'yŏn sosŏl yŏn'gu* [A study of the Chosŏn-dynasty lineage novel] (Seoul: T'aehaksa, 1996), 175.

39. *Myŏngju ogyŏn kihap rok* [The remarkable encounter of pearls and jade], 25 vols., Sŏgang University Archive, Seoul, Kosŏ myŏng 77, 25:38a (denoting manuscript volume and manuscript page).

40. *Myŏngju kibong* [The remarkable encounter of pearls], 25 vols., Jangseogak Archive, K4^6804; *Myŏngju kibong* [The remarkable encounter of pearls], 2 vols. (Seoul: Munhwajae kwalliguk Changsŏgak, 1978), 1.2:37 (denoting print volume, manuscript volume, and print page).

41. The closing lines of the parent novel, *Jade Mandarin Ducks*, intimate that the story of the lineage will continue in another text, *The Remarkable Account of Ten Phoenixes* (*Sippong kiŏn* 十鳳奇言), tracing the life of So Segyŏng's son, Ponghŭi. Although no copies have been found, *The Remarkable Account of Ten Phoenixes* appears to be an actual composition, given other extant references to this title. See Yi Chiha, Ogwŏn chaehap kiyŏn *yŏnjak yŏn'gu* [Study of the sequel cluster of *The remarkable encounter of jade mandarin ducks*] (Seoul: Pogosa, 2015), 26 n. 23.

42. *Ogwŏn chŏnhae* [Commentary to jade mandarin ducks], 5 vols., Kyujanggak Archive, Seoul, Ko 3350-67, 1:6a–b.

43. *Ogwŏn chŏnhae*, 4:3b.

44. James Legge, trans., *Li Chi: The Book of Rites*, 2 vols. (New York: New York University, 1966), 2:266.

45. *Myŏngju ogyŏn kihap rok*, 13:26b.

46. *Myŏngju ogyŏn kihap rok*, 15:3a.

47. For more on the monetary policy toward the late Chosŏn dynasty, see James Palais, *Politics and Policy in Traditional Korea* (Cambridge, MA: Harvard University Asia Center, 1975), 160–76; Sun Joo Kim, *Marginality and Subversion in Korea: The Hong Kyŏngnae Rebellion of 1812* (Seattle: University of Washington Press, 2007), 66–88.

48. In her study of the Hyŏn lineage novels' sequence, Yi Chiha similarly suggests that the sequels were written by different authors. She notes that in the third novel the protagonists are more standardized, with men becoming more

heroic and women much more domesticated than in the parent text. See Yi Chiha, *"Hyŏn ssi yangung ssangnin ki* yŏnjak yŏn'gu" [Study of the sequel cluster of *The record of two heroes: Brothers Hyŏn*], MA thesis, Seoul National University, 1992.

49. Yi Chiha notes that between *The Remarkable Reunion of Jade Mandarin Ducks* and *The Commentary to Jade Mandarin Ducks* the characters do not undergo any significant changes, and the plots are tightly aligned (Ogwŏn chaehap kiyŏn *yŏnjak yŏn'gu*, 27–28).

50. *Ogwŏn chŏnhae*, 3:39a.

51. Keith McMahon, "Eliminating Traumatic Antinomies: Sequels to *Honglou meng*," in *Snakes' Legs: Sequels, Continuations, Rewritings, and Chinese Fiction*, ed. Martin Huang (Honolulu: University of Hawai'i Press, 2004), 111; Ellen Widmer, *The Beauty and the Book: Women and Fiction in Nineteenth-Century China* (Cambridge, MA: Harvard University Council on East Asian Studies, 2006), 181–247.

52. Cho Hŭiung, *Kojŏn sosŏl ibon mongnok* [Catalog of extant editions of traditional novels] (Seoul: Chimmundang, 1999), 831–39.

53. Yi Tawŏn notes that *Brothers Hyŏn*'s drastically reduced volume and the emphasis on the more dramatic twists of the plot point to the commercial provenance of this manuscript. See Yi Tawŏn, ed., *Hyŏn ssi yangung ssangnin ki* [The record of two heroes: Brothers Hyŏn], 2 vols. (Seoul: Kyŏngin munhwasa, 2006), 1:xii.

54. Ch'oe Suhyŏn, *"Myŏngju kibong* ibon yŏn'gu" [A study of various editions of *The remarkable encounter of pearls*], *Han'guk kojŏn yŏn'gu* 32 (2015): 569–602.

55. Yi Chiha, Ogwŏn chaehap kiyŏn *yŏn'gu*, 24.

56. Generational succession within a sequel group is not the only way in which cross-textual filiation operates in lineage novels. *Pearls and Jade*, for instance, establishes its relation not only with the novels that precede it in its group but with completely extraneous texts as well. In particular, this novel records marriages between its male protagonists and the female heroines of two other novels—*The Record of So Hyŏnsŏng*, believed to be the earliest known lineage novel, and *The Record of Virtuous Lord Ku Rae* (*Ku Rae kong chŏngch'ung chikchŏl ki* 寇萊公貞忠直節記), a war romance about the well-known Song-dynasty official Kou Zhun (961–1023) and his descendants. In this way, the lineage novel circumscribes the domain that it shares with other novels—such as historical romances—applying the logic of kinship, sustained with marriage ties, to the literary space, where novels of similarly elevated cultural register develop affinal ties through their protagonists.

57. *Oksugi* [Record of the jade tree], vol. 11 of *P'ilsabon kojŏn sosŏl chŏnjip* [Compendium of manuscript editions of classical Korean novels], ed. Kim Kidong (Seoul: Asea munhwasa, 1982), 747.

58. *Ch'oe Hyŏn chŏn* [The tale of Ch'oe Hyŏn], National Library of Korea, Seoul, Kojo 48-134, copyist's note.

59. For a longer list of claims of textual filiation in novels that are not, strictly speaking, part of a lineage novel cluster, see Ch'oe Kilyong, *Chosŏn cho yŏnjak sosŏl yŏn'gu*, 61.

60. Although there is no standard rendition of the term *family tale* in contemporary Chosŏn sources, my use of the term is inspired by Ying Zhang's work on Qing-dynasty family tales, which I reference in the ensuing discussion.

61. Kim Sangch'ae, quoted in Chŏng Pyŏngsŏl [Jung Byung Sul], "Changp'yŏn taeha sosŏl kwa kajoksa sosŏl ŭi yŏn'gwan mit kŭ ŭimi—kojŏn sosŏl ŭi ch'angjak sigi wa ch'angjak kwajŏng e taehan kasŏl" [The generic connections between the lineage novel and family tales: Hypothesis on the period and process of composition of traditional novels], *Kojŏn munhak yŏn'gu* 12 (1997): 243 n. 38.

62. Yi Subong, "Kamun sosŏl yŏn'gu," 252–53, 327–28.

63. Ying Zhang, *Confucian Image Politics: Masculine Morality in Seventeenth-Century China* (Seattle: University of Washington Press, 2017), 15.

64. Professor Yi Subong discovered this text in a private home in Togok hamlet, Ch'uksan Township, Yŏngdŏk County, North Kyŏngsang Province. He notes that he has encountered many more copies of the text, although he does not specify their number and location ("Kamun sosŏl yŏn'gu," 358).

65. Deuchler, *Under the Ancestors' Eyes*, 311.

66. Yi Subong reconstructs these facts from interviews with the surviving members of the Chinsŏng Yi lineage. See Yi Subong, "*Haedong Yi ssi samdae rok* yŏn'gu" [A study of *The record of the three generations of the Yi lineage from the East of the sea*], in *Han'guk kamun sosŏl yŏn'gu nonch'ong* [Studies of the Korean lineage novel], 3 vols., ed. Yi Subong (Seoul: Kyŏngin munhwasa, 1992), 1:337.

67. *Haedong Yi ssi samdae rok* [The record of the three generations of the Yi lineage from the East of the sea], JaHyun Kim Haboush Archive, IDBoo2b, http://www.habousharchives.org, 88. This note is not in the actual manuscript in the Haboush Archive; it is appended to the transcribed version of the text. The Haboush Archive contains a manuscript and a transcription of *Haedong Yi ssi samdae rok*. The transcription appears to have been made from a different manuscript than the one contained in the archive. The transcription is divided into chapters that are accompanied by abbreviated content descriptions, whereas the manuscript contains an undivided text. In the transcription, parts of the text appear in different order than in the manuscript. Rather than being mistakes or redactions, these dissimilarities point to a different original.

68. Deuchler, *Under the Ancestors' Eyes*, 114, 150, 169.

69. *Sunjo sillok* [The veritable records of Sunjo's reign], 25:8b (1822/3/25).

70. *Haedong Yi ssi samdae rok* [The record of the three generations of the Yi lineage from the East of the sea], JaHyun Kim Haboush Archive, IDB002a, http://www.habousharchives.org, 1a. This is a facsimile of an undated manuscript, executed in well-trained cursive vernacular brushwork. Here and in the subsequent references to the text I am using the manuscript facsimile version from the Haboush archive. The original text is unpaginated, and I assign leaf numbers starting with the first page of text.

71. *Haedong Yi ssi samdae rok*, IDB002a, 12a. "Yŏngnam" is another name for the Kyŏngsang Province. *Sunjo sillok* records the fact that Yi Ŏnsun, along with other officials, received promotions and gifts in 1823, although the nature of the gifts is not specified (*Sunjo sillok*, 26:16a [1823/3/6]). As a result of factional disputes and local unrest, the position of Yŏngnam elites in central court was significantly weakened in the early eighteenth century; they were partially rehabilitated in the late eighteenth century. See Deuchler, *Under the Ancestors' Eyes*, 319–38.

72. *Haedong Yi ssi samdae rok*, IDB002a, 33a.

73. *Haedong Yi ssi samdae rok*, IDB002a, 29a.

74. *Haedong Yi ssi samdae rok*, IDB002a, 31a–31b.

75. *Haedong Yi ssi samdae rok*, IDB002a, 46a–47a.

76. Deuchler, *Under the Ancestors' Eyes*, 382.

77. "Kyonam" is another name for Kyŏngsang Province.

78. The text merely gives 某 (*mo*), meaning "someone." *The Yi Lineage* rarely uses first names, possibly due to the reverential refusal to directly name one's immediate ancestors. Yi Ŏnsun (1774–1845) is identifiable by his nom de plume "Nongwa."

79. Yi Kuyong (1730–1815).

80. Yi Sehyŏp (dates unknown).

81. Yi Kyesun (1764–1830).

82. *Haedong Yi ssi samdae rok*, IDB002a, 1a–2a.

83. Curiously, the story of the milk debt that Yi Ŏnsun acquires from his cousin Yi Kyesun's (1764–1830) wife receives further elaboration in the sphere of ritual. After his wife's death, Yi Kyesun wonders if Yi Ŏnsun should mourn her as his mother. Chŏng Chongno (1738–1816), to whose judgment Yi Kyesun appeals, suggests that such mourning performance would be extravagant, given that Yi Ŏnsun was not formally adopted. See Chŏng Chongno, "Tap Yi Kyesun munmok" [Responding to Yi Kyesun's inquiry], in *Ipchae chip* [The Ipchae anthology], http://db.itkc.or.kr.

84. Other family narratives also emulate lineage novels' titles. See Song Sŏnguk, *Chosŏn sidae taeha sosŏl ŭi sŏsa munbŏp kwa ch'angjak ŭisik* [The narrative

grammar and outlook of Chosŏn-dynasty lineage novels] (Seoul: T'aehaksa, 2003), 219.

85. The affinity of *The Yi Lineage* with the novelistic narrative prompted Yi Subong to suggest that this text embodied the transition from biographic narratives to the lineage novel ("Kamun sosŏl yŏn'gu"). However, as Im Ch'igyun points out, reverse influence is more likely (*Chosŏn sidae taejangp'yŏn sosŏl yŏn'gu*, 17–18). The earliest lineage novels date to the late seventeenth century, whereas the events described in *The Yi Lineage* date to the late nineteenth century

86. Song Sŏnguk notes that whereas other family tales are closer to episodic accounts typical for funerary writing, *The Yi Lineage* is much more narrative in nature (*Chosŏn sidae taeha sosŏl ŭi sŏsa munbŏp kwa ch'angjak ŭisik*, 220–21).

87. *Haedong Yi ssi samdae rok*, IDB002a, 50a–51a.

88. *Haedong Yi ssi samdae rok*, IDB002a, 6a–b.

89. *Haedong Yi ssi samdae rok*, IDB002a, 7b.

90. *Haedong Yi ssi samdae rok*, IDB002a, 48a.

91. Ellen Widmer, *Fiction's Family: Zhan Xi, Zhan Kai, and the Business of Women in Late-Qing China* (Cambridge, MA: Harvard University Asia Center, 2016), 249, 251.

92. *Haedong Yi ssi samdae rok*, IDB002a, 32b.

93. *Haedong Yi ssi samdae rok*, IDB002a, 52b.

94. In the introduction, I show how *The Pledge* constantly refers the reader to allegedly extant documentary records: *The Record of the Rewarded Filial Piety of the Chŏng Lineage* (*Chŏng ssi hyohaeng poŭng rok* 鄭氏孝行報應錄), *The Pledge That Fulfills the Good Connection* (*Maengsŏng hoyŏn* 盟成好因), and the like.

2. The Texture of Kinship: Vernacular Korean Calligraphy

1. For a study of paper and book prices in the late Chosŏn, see Chŏng Pyŏngsŏl [Jung Byung Sul], *Chosŏn sidae sosŏl ŭi saengsan kwa yut'ong* [The production and circulation of novels in Chosŏn] (Seoul: Seoul National University Press, 2016), 53–59.

2. Kim Pyŏngmok, "T'aegyo e taehan mundap" [Observations on prenatal education], in *19 segi–20 segi ch'o yŏsŏng saenghwalsa charyo chip* [Sources on the lives of women between the nineteenth and early twentieth centuries], 9 vols., ed. Ch'a Mihŭi, Kang Sŏngsuk, Kim Kyŏngmi, Yi Kyŏngha, Cho Hyeran, Hwang Suyŏn, Sŏ Kyŏnghŭi, Kim Hyŏnmi, Kim Kirim, and Hong Hakhŭi (Seoul: Pogosa, 2013), 6:277.

3. Sŏng Haeŭng, "Sŏnbi haengjang" [Posthumous biography of my late mother], in *19 segi–20 segi ch'o*, ed. Ch'a Mihŭi et al., 1:188.

4. Hŏ Chŏn, "Sukpuin Hanyang Cho ssi yujŏk" [In memory of Lady Cho of Hanyang], in *19 segi–20 segi ch'o*, ed. Ch'a Mihŭi et al., 5:152.

5. John Hay, "The Human Body as a Microcosmic Source of Macrocosmic Values in Calligraphy," in *Theory of the Arts in China*, ed. Susan Bush and Christian Murck (Princeton, NJ: Princeton University Press, 1983), 74–102.

6. Sixiang Wang, "*Story of the Eastern Chamber*: Dilemmas of Vernacular Language and Political Authority in Eighteenth-Century Chosŏn," *Journal of Korean Studies* 24, no. 1 (2019): 40, 42.

7. Sheldon Pollock, *The Language of the Gods in the World of Men: Sanskrit, Culture, and Power in Premodern India* (Berkeley: University of California Press, 2006).

8. Patrick Hanan, *The Chinese Vernacular Story* (Cambridge, MA: Harvard University Press, 1981), 4.

9. Haruo Shirane, "Canon Formation in Japan: Genre, Gender, Popular Culture, and Nationalism," in *Reading East Asian Writing: The Limits of Literary Theory*, ed. Michel Hockx and Ivo Smits (London: Routledge Curzon, 2014), 22–38.

10. Caroline Levine, *Forms: Whole, Rhythm, Hierarchy, Network* (Princeton, NJ: Princeton University Press, 2015), 6.

11. Wang, "*Story of the Eastern Chamber*," 44.

12. Yi Tŏngmu, "Tongguk puin nŭngsŏ" [Women calligraphers of the eastern country], in *Ch'ŏngjanggwan ch'ongsŏ* [The complete works of Ch'ŏngjanggwan], vols. 257–59 of *Han'guk munjip ch'onggan* [The complete compendium of Korean literary collections], ed. Minjok munhwa ch'ujinhoe (Seoul: Minjok munhwa ch'ujinhoe, 2000), 259:4.

13. On the elite vernacular epistolary practice, see Ksenia Chizhova, "Vernacular Itineraries: Korean Letters from Family to National Archive," *Journal of Korean Studies* 24, no. 2 (2019): 345–71.

14. The best-known text of a father's advice to his daughter is Song Siyŏl's *Instruction to My Daughter* (*Kyenyŏsŏ* 戒女書).

15. Yŏngho Ch'oe, trans., "King Sejong: Preface to *Correct Sounds to Instruct the People*," in *Sourcebook of Korean Civilization*, 2 vols., ed. Peter H. Lee (New York: Columbia University Press, 1993), 1:295.

16. Chŏng Taham suggests that the Korean alphabet was not so much a nativist impulse to capture and communicate the spoken language as a more effective means of reflecting the changes in the Chinese language—the linguistic manifestation of Korea's place in the Sinocentric world order. The creation of the Korean alphabet would solidify Chosŏn's place within the Sinosphere rather than strengthen its autonomy therein. See Chŏng Taham, "Yŏmal

Sŏnch'o ŭi Tongasia chilsŏ wa Chosŏn eso ŭi han'ŏ, hansamun, hunmin chŏngŭm" [The East Asian world order, the literary Chinese culture, and vernacular Korean during the late Koryŏ and early Chosŏn], *Han'guksa hakpo* 36 (2009): 269–305.

17. See Young-Key Kim-Renaud, ed., *Creative Women of Korea: The Fifteenth Through the Twentieth Centuries* (New York: M. E. Sharpe, 2004).

18. It is important to note that despite their enforced domesticity, women were active in the legal space, submitting vernacular Korean petitions on behalf of their family members. See Jisoo Kim, *The Emotions of Justice: Gender, Status, and Legal Performance in Chosŏn Korea* (Seattle: University of Washington Press, 2015), 54–73.

19. For the politics of gender in the scriptural field of Chosŏn Korea, see JaHyun Kim Haboush, "Gender and Politics of Language in Chosŏn Korea," in *Rethinking Confucianism: Past and Present in China, Japan, Korea, and Vietnam*, ed. Benjamin A. Elman, John B. Duncan, and Herman Ooms, Asian Pacific Monograph series (Los Angeles: University of California, 2002), 220–56.

20. The passage refers to the letter (ŭng) of the Korean alphabet. This letter could be written either as a simple circle or as a circle crowned with a vertical stroke, the latter representing a more elaborate writing style.

21. Yi Ok, "Yiŏn" [Maxims], quoted in Im Hyŏngt'aek, "17 segi kyubang sosŏl ŭi sŏngnip kwa *Ch'angsŏn kamŭi rok*" [*The praise of goodness and the admiration of righteousness* and the rise of the boudoir novel], *Tongbang hakchi* 57 (1988): 125.

22. Yun Paekyŏng (1888–1986), a scion of the royal family of Chosŏn, provided a great amount of information about the practice of vernacular Korean calligraphy in the royal palace. Yun distinguished "male" and "female" styles in palace calligraphy. In an article published in the *Chungang ilbo* in 1966, Yun noted that male and female hands are easily distinguishable, but she did not lay out their characteristic differences. She pointed to the manuscript of a vernacular Korean novel, *The Best Vernacular Text That Puts Other Fanciful Tales to Shame* (*Pyŏkhŏdam kwanje ŏllok* 碧虛談關帝言錄), as an example of the male hand. See Yi Chongsik, "T'ongdokcha Yun Paekyŏng yŏsa mal hanŭn kŭ naeryŏk kwa ilhwa tŭl—Naksŏnjae mun'go wa pansegi" [Recollections of an avid reader, Madame Yun Paekyŏng—half a century at the Naksŏn Library], *Chungang ilbo*, August 25, 1966.

23. See JaHyun Kim Haboush, "The Vanished Women of Korea: The Anonymity of Texts and the Historicity of Subjects," in *Servants of the Dynasty: Palace Women in World History*, ed. Ann Walthall (Berkeley: University of California Press, 2008), 280–98; and Yesul ŭi chŏndang, ed., *Chosŏn sidae han'gŭl sŏye* [Vernacular Korean calligraphy of the Chosŏn dynasty] (Seoul: Mijinsa, 1994).

24. See Haboush, "The Vanished Women of Korea," and Kim Yongsuk, *Chosŏnjo kungjung p'ungsok yŏn'gu* [Customs of the Chosŏn court] (Seoul: Ilchisa, 1987). For the archival transmission of royal vernacular Korean materials, see Kim Pongjwa, "Wangsil han'gŭl p'ilsabon ŭi chŏnsŭng hyŏnhwang kwa kach'i" [The transmission and value of royal vernacular manuscripts], *Kug'ŏsa yŏn'gu* 20 (2015): 39–64. The Jangseogak (Changsŏgak) Archive, now located at the Academy of Korean Studies in Songnam, is the largest repository of vernacular Korean materials that circulated in the royal palace. See Kim Mokhan, Kim Sŏnggyu, Nam Yunjin, Pak Puja, Pak Chinho, Yi Raeho, Yi Hyŏnju, Chŏng Sŭnghye, Chŏng Yunja, Chŏng Chaeyŏng, Hwang Munhwan, Hwang Sŏnyŏp, and Hong Ŭnjin, eds., *Changsŏgak han'gŭl charyo haeje* [Annotated catalog of vernacular Korean materials of the Jangseogak Archive] (Songnam: Academy of Korean Studies Press, 2000).

25. Im Hyŏngt'aek, "17 segi kyubang sosŏl," 125.

26. *The Veritable Records of the Chosŏn Dynasty* (*Chosŏn wangjo sillok* 實錄, http://sillok.history.go.kr) mentions the circulation of vernacular Korean letters between the royal palace and the outside world already in the sixteenth century. See *Yŏnsan'gun ilgi* [The daily records of King Yŏnsan], 52:27b (1504/4/1), and *Chungjong sillok* [The veritable records of Chungjong's reign], 74:56b (1533/5/20), quoted in Kim Ilgŭn, *Ŏn'gan ŭi yŏn'gu: Han'gŭl sŏgan ŭi yŏn'gu wa charyo chipsŏng* [A study of vernacular Korean letters: Analysis and collection of materials] (Seoul: Konkuk University Press, 1986), 27. A later example of letters exchanged between a palace woman, Matron Ha, and the wife of Yun Yonggu (1853–1937) can be found in JaHyun Kim Haboush, ed., *Epistolary Korea: Letters in The Communicative Space of the Chosŏn, 1392–1910* (New York: Columbia University Press, 2009), 223.

27. On the inclusion of lineage novels in royal dowries, see Kim Tonguk, "Yijo sosŏl ŭi chŏja wa tokcha e taehayŏ" [Readership and authorship of Chosŏn-dynasty novels], in *Changam Chi Hŏnyŏng sŏnsaeng hwagap kinyŏm nonch'ong* [Papers offered to Changam Professor Chi Hŏnyŏng on his sixtieth anniversary] (Seoul: Hosŏ munhwasa, 1971), 40. One of the margin notes in the manuscript of *The Record of Two Heroes: Brothers Hyŏn* from 1880 states that it was transcribed from a volume produced at the royal palace. See Yi Tawŏn, "*Hyŏn ssi yangung ssangnin ki* yŏn'gu: Yŏndae bon *Hyŏn ssi yangung ssangnin ki* chungsim ŭro" [Study of *The record of two heroes: Brothers Hyŏn*, with a focus on the Yonsei University manuscript], MA thesis, Yonsei University, 2001, 39.

28. Francesca Bray, *Technology and Gender: Fabrics of Power in Late Imperial China* (Berkeley: University of California Press, 1997), 2.

29. Yi Chae, "Paekkumo chŏnggyŏng puin Yŏn'an Yi ssi haengjang" [The posthumous biography of my aunt, Lady Yi of Yŏnan], in *18 segi yŏsŏng saenghwalsa charyo chip* [Sources on the lives of women in the eighteenth century], 8 vols.,

ed. Hwang Suyŏn, Yi Kyŏngha, Kim Kyŏngmi, Kim Kirim, Kim Hyŏnmi, Cho Hyeran, Kang Sŏngsuk, Sŏ Kyŏnghŭi, and Kim Nam'i (Seoul: Pogosa, 2010), 6:107.

30. Song Siyŏl, "Yuin Kim ssi myojimyŏng" [Tombstone inscription for Kim ssi], in *17 segi yŏsŏng saenghwalsa charyo chip* [Sources on the lives of women in the seventeenth century], 4 vols., ed. Chŏng Hyŏngji, Kim Kyŏngmi, Hwang Suyŏn, Kim Kirim, Cho Hyeran, and Yi Hyŏngha (Seoul: Pogosa, 2006), 1:227, also cited in Yi Kyŏngha, "17 segi sangch'ŭng yŏsŏng ŭi kungmun saenghwal e kwanhan munhŏn chŏk koch'al" [Overview of sources on women's use of vernacular Korean script in the seventeenth century], *Han'guk munhak nonch'ong* 39 (2005): 227. Yi Kyŏngha similarly notes the connection between women's embodied skills and vernacular Korean handwriting.

31. An Chŏngbok, "Sŏnbi Kongin Yi ssi haengjang kyŏngin" [The posthumous biography of my late mother, Madame Yi of Kongin, the kyŏngin year," in *18 segi*, ed. Hwang Suyŏn et al., 8:284.

32. Kim Chusin, "Paengmo sugin Hansan Yi ssi myoji" [Tomb inscription for my aunt, Lady Yi of Hansan], in *18 segi*, ed. Hwang Suyŏn et al., 7:84, also cited in Yi Kyŏngha, "17 segi sangch'ŭng yŏsŏng kungmun saenghwal e kwanhan munhŏn chŏk ilgoch'al," 228.

33. See Sixiang Wang, "The Filial Daughter of Kwaksan—Finger Severing, Confucian Virtues, and Envoy Poetry in Early Chosŏn," *Seoul Journal of Korean Studies* 25, no. 2 (December 2012): 175–212.

34. Min Usu, "Komo yuin Min ssi myoji" [Tomb inscription for my deceased aunt, Madame Min], in *18 segi*, ed. Hwang Suyŏn et al., 1:501.

35. Kim Manjung, "Sŏnbi chŏnggyŏng puin haengjang" [Posthumous biography of my honorable late mother], in *17 segi*, ed. Chŏng Hyŏngji et al., 1:364.

36. Kim Chin'gyu, "Chobi haengjang sŭp" [The posthumous biography of my late grandmother], in *18 segi*, ed. Hwang Suyŏn et al., 1:446.

37. Pak Sedang, "Yi Tŏkpu ch'ŏ myojimyŏng" [Tomb inscription for the wife of Yi Tŏkpu], in *17 segi*, ed. Chŏng Hyŏngji et al., 3:99.

38. Yi Tŏngmu, "Che ajae sohak cha kwŏnmi" [Postscript to the book from which my younger brother learned letters], in *Ch'ŏngjanggwan ch'ongsŏ*, vols. 257–59 of *Han'guk munjip ch'onggan*, 258:135.

39. Yi Tŏngmu, "Chokchil Pokch'o" [To my nephew, Pokch'o], in *Ch'ŏngjanggwan ch'ongsŏ*, vols. 257–59 of *Han'guk munjip ch'onggan*, 258:237.

40. Yi Insuk, "Chosŏn sidae hanmun kanch'al ŭi sŏyesa chŏk ŭiŭi" [The calligraphic significance of literary Chinese epistles during the Chosŏn dynasty], *Sŏyehak yŏn'gu* 6 (2005): 57–60.

41. Sim Hyŏnsŏp, "Chosŏn sŏnbi tŭl ŭi sŏye insik kwa kyoyuk" [Calligraphy in the life of Chosŏn scholars: Its significance and training practices], *Sŏyehak yŏn'gu* 15 (2009): 66–73.

42. Yi Tŏngmu, "Sasojŏl," in *Ch'ŏngjanggwan ch'ongsŏ*, vols. 257–59 of *Han'guk munjip ch'onggan*, 257:485.

43. Yi Tŏngmu, "Humok yŏn'gap myŏng" [Ode to the ink-stone case of old wood], in *Ch'ŏngjanggwan ch'ongsŏ*, vols. 257–59 of *Han'guk munjip ch'onggan*, 257:86–87.

44. Sin Kyŏng, "Sŏnbi yusa" [In memory of my late mother], in *18 segi*, ed. Hwang Suyŏn et al., 3:221.

45. *Yun ssi haengjang* [Posthumous biography of Madame Yun], Kyujanggak Archive, Seoul National University, Karam ko 920.7-G422y. This sketchbook lacks any coherent organization, and the archive title is given after the first copied text, which happens to be Kim Manjung's "Posthumous Biography of My Honorable Late Mother."

46. Quoted in Chŏng Poktong, "Osukche Song Ikhŭm ŏn'gan sŏch'e ŭi hyŏngsŏng kwa chohyŏngsŏng koch'al" [The formation and style of Osukche Song Ikhŭm's calligraphy in his vernacular Korean letters], *Sŏyehak yŏn'gu* 22 (2013): 142.

47. Hong Hŭibok, "*Cheil kiŏn sŏ*" [Preface to *The Book of Books in the vernacular*], in *Cheil kiŏn* [Flowers in the mirror], ed. Pak Chaeyŏn and Chŏng Kyubok (Seoul: Kukhak charyowŏn, 2001), 22.

48. Kwŏn Chinŭng, quoted in Pak Yŏnghŭi, "Changp'yŏn kamun sosŏl ŭi hyangyu chiptan yŏn'gu" [Readership of the lineage novel], in *Munhak kwa sahoe chipdan* [Literature and society], ed. Han'guk kojŏn munhakhoe (Seoul: Chimmundang, 1995), 324–25.

49. Kim Kidong, ed., *Ogwŏn chaehap kiyŏn* [The remarkable reunion of jade mandarin ducks], vols. 27–30 of *Kojŏn sosŏl chŏnjip* [The anthology of manuscript editions of classical Korean novels] (Seoul: Asea munhwasa, 1980), 27.5:574 (denoting print volume, manuscript volume, and print page number), also quoted in Sim Kyŏngho, "Naksŏnjae bon sosŏl ŭi sŏnhaengbon e kwanhan ilkoch'al: Onyang Chŏng ssi p'ilsabon *Ogwŏn chaehap kiyŏn* kwa Naksŏnjae bon *Ogwŏn chunghoeyŏn* ŭi kwan'gye rŭl chungsim ŭro" [A study of the manuscripts of the Nakson Library novels: The relationship between *The remarkable reunion of jade mandarin ducks* copied by Madame Chŏng of Onyang and the Naksŏn Library manuscript], *Chŏngsin munhwa yŏn'gu* 38 (1990): 178. Sim Kyŏngho was the first to study the margin notes of this novel and link it to the scribal activity of Madame Chŏng of Onyang and her kinswomen.

50. Sim Kyŏngho, "Naksŏnjae bon sosŏl," 181.

51. Reginald Jackson, *Textures of Mourning: Calligraphy, Mortality, and* The Tale of Genji *Scrolls* (Ann Arbor: University of Michigan Press, 2018), 64.

52. Quoted in Yi Tawŏn, "*Hyŏn ssi yangung ssangnin ki* yŏn'gu," 16.

53. Quoted in Chŏng Pyŏngsŏl [Jung Byung Sul], Wanwŏl hoemaeng yŏn *yŏn'gu* [A study of *The pledge at the banquet of moon-gazing pavilion*] (Seoul: T'aehaksa, 1998), 175.

54. *The Miscellaneous Records of Songnam* misattributes the two novels written by Kim Manjung, *Nine-Cloud Dream* and *Madame Sa's Conquest of the South*, to the author's nephew, Kim Ch'unt'aek.

55. Drawing on extant sources, Han Kilyŏn shows that in the Chŏnju Yi branch, to which Madame Yi belonged, women indeed possessed sufficient knowledge and training to make their collective authorship of *The Pledge* plausible. See Han Kilyŏn, "*Paek Kye yangmun sŏnhaeng rok* ŭi chakka wa kŭ chubyŏn: Chŏnju Yi ssi kamun yŏsŏng ŭi taehasosŏl ch'angjak kanŭngsŏng ŭl chungsim ŭro" [The author and the social context of *The record of good deeds of two households: Paek and Kye*: Women of the Chŏnju Yi lineage as potential authors of lineage novels], *Kojŏn munhak yŏn'gu* 27 (2005): 329–61.

56. *Ogwŏn chaehap kiyŏn*, 30.22:620.

57. This note generated several theories of *Jade Mandarin Ducks'* authorship. Ch'oe Kilyong suggested that the author is Yi Kwangsa (1705–1777), Madame Chŏng's male relative on her husband's side. See Ch'oe Kilyong, *Chosŏn cho yŏnjak sosŏl yŏn'gu* [Study of Chosŏn-dynasty sequel novels] (Seoul: Asea munhwasa, 1992), 430–58. Chŏng Pyŏngsŏl, however, cites a family connection between the alleged author of *The Pledge*, Madame Yi of Chŏnju, and Madame Chŏng of Onyang, in whose family *Jade Mandarin Ducks* circulated, and alleges that the former is also the author of this text. See Chŏng Pyŏngsŏl [Jung Byung Sul], "*Ogwŏn chaehap kiyŏn* chakka chaeron: Chosŏn hugi yŏsŏng sosŏlga ŭi han kŏn'ye" [Reconsidering the authorship of *The remarkable reunion of jade mandarin ducks*: The case of one late-Chosŏn female author], *Kwan'ak ŏmunhak yŏn'gu* 22 (1997): 317–32.

58. After circulating exclusively in family-transmitted manuscripts for most of their history, lineage novels entered rental libraries around the turn of the twentieth century. This phase in the history of the lineage novel's development is discussed in chapter 5.

59. See, for instance, such titles as Yesul ŭi chŏndang, *Chosŏn sidae han'gŭl sŏye*.

60. See Andre Schmid, *Korea Between Empires, 1895–1919* (New York: Columbia University Press, 2002), 55–138.

61. See Thomas Lamarre, *Uncovering Heian Japan: An Archaeology of Sensation and Inscription* (Durham, NC: Duke University Press, 2000), 1–12, 116–42.

62. Hui-shu Lee, *Empresses, Art, & Agency in Song Dynasty China* (Seattle: University of Washington Press, 2010), 56–57.

63. John Guillory, *Cultural Capital: The Problem of Literary Canon Formation* (Chicago: University of Chicago Press, 1993), 16.

3. Feelings and the Space of the Novel

1. I use the terms *feelings, emotions,* and *sentiments* as well as the adjective *affective* interchangeably. Although scholars have noted theoretical distinctions among these concepts, I use these terms in a historical not theoretical perspective that aligns with Barbara Rosenwein's vision, as outlined in the text and note 2.

2. Barbara Rosenwein has suggested that emotions are to the study of history what gender once was: "The ideal history, which seems far away right now— will not be a history of the emotions but rather an integration of the history of emotions into 'regular' history. Nowadays, no one would think of writing a history of, say, Germany between the wars without dealing with the issues of gender and the roles and images of men and women" (in Jan Plamper, "The History of Emotions: An Interview with William Reddy, Barbara Rosenwein, and Peter Stearns," *History and Theory* 49 [2010]: 260).

3. Barbara Rosenwein, *Emotional Communities in the Early Middle Ages* (Ithaca, NY: Cornell University Press, 2006), 25.

4. Catherine Lutz, *Unnatural Emotions: Everyday Sentiments on a Micronesian Atoll and Their Challenge to Western Theory* (Chicago: University of Chicago Press, 1988), 83.

5. Mencius, *The Works of Mencius,* trans. James Legge (New York: Dover, 1970), 295.

6. Mencius, *Mencius,* 2 vols., trans. D. C. Lau (Hong Kong: Chinese University Press, 1984), 1:107.

7. On the Confucian rhetoric of imperial inclusion during the Qing dynasty, see James Hevia, *Cherishing Men from Afar: Qing Guest Ritual and the Macartney Embassy of 1793* (Durham, NC: Duke University Press, 1995), 116–33, esp. 116–21. Hevia notes in particular that the power of the sovereign's attraction was supposed to bring the lesser lords closer to the center of empire through a guest ritual that included them in the manner of *qin* (K. *ch'in* 親), or love for one's kin.

8. Martina Deuchler, *The Confucian Transformation of Korea: A Study of Society and Ideology* (Cambridge, MA: Harvard University Asia Center, 1992), 107, 24–25, 127–38, 237.

9. Deuchler, *The Confucian Transformation of Korea,* 288.

10. As noted in the introduction, I borrow the phrase "feelings of flesh and blood" from Sun Joo Kim, "My Own Flesh and Blood: Stratified Parental Compassion and Law in Korean Slavery," *Social History* 44, no. 1 (2019): 1–25.

11. In her study of the Chosŏn kinship system, Martina Deuchler notes that two versions of kinship were practiced side by side. The ritual lineage (*tangnae* 堂內) included vertical, genealogically fixed relationships of those who

participated in ancestral worship. In contrast, the "associational" group (*munjung* 門中) was characterized by kinship through lateral connection: this larger, fraternal kinship group benefitted from ancestral prestige and shared economic resources. As a result, "two principles of kinship—primogeniture and fraternal solidarity—conjoined in a way that offered a descent group, in a localized setting, a high degree of cohesion and continuance" (*Under the Ancestors' Eyes: Kinship, Status, and Locality in Premodern Korea* [Cambridge, MA: Harvard University Asia Center, 2015], 287). Following in the lines of Deuchler's argument, I designate as "ritual kinship" those aspects of lineage practice—heir adoption and wives' virilocal residence—that were designed to streamline the verticality of the patriline. I define "blood kinship" as a conditional, culturally determined vision of consanguinity. As anthropologist Robin Fox suggests, "In its commonest definition, 'kinship' is simply the relations between 'kin,' i.e., persons related by real, putative, or fictive consanguinity. 'Real' consanguinity is difficult to pin down of course, and our own scientific notions of genetic relationship are not shared by all peoples and cultures. Who does, and who does not, count as 'blood' kin, varies considerably" (*Kinship and Marriage: An Anthropological Perspective* [Cambridge: Cambridge University Press, 1967], 33).

12. Nicola di Cosmo, *Ancient China and Its Enemies: The Rise of Nomadic Power in the East Asian History* (Cambridge: Cambridge University Press, 2002), 94.

13. Franco Moretti, *Atlas of the European Novel, 1800–1900* (London: Verso, 1999), 5.

14. In "Encountering the Other: Identity, Culture, and the Novel in Late Imperial China" (PhD diss., University of California at Irvine, 2010), Huili Zheng offers a captivating account of the imagination of the barbarians that unfolds in late imperial vernacular fiction.

15. Kim Chinse, ed., *Wanwŏl hoemaeng yŏn* [The pledge at the banquet of moon-gazing pavilion], 12 vols. (Seoul: Seoul National University Press, 1986–1994), 1.1:50 (denoting print volume, manuscript volume, and print page number).

16. *Wanwŏl hoemaeng yŏn*, 1.2:70.

17. Eugene Park suggests that "the status boundary separating the aristocracy from the rest of society was far clearer and more rigid than any of the differentiations between various *yangban* subgroups in terms of their branch affiliation or extent of participation in the central political structure" (*Between Dreams and Reality: The Military Examination in Late Chosŏn Korea, 1600–1894* [Cambridge, MA: Harvard University Asia Center, 2007], 119; also see 117–42). Park suggests that the three branches of aristocracy that were fleshed out in the seventeenth century—central civil official, military official, and local kinship groups—in fact continued to be related to each other through ties of adoption and marriage, which underscored elite cohesiveness, especially on

the level of economic privileges (the shared desire to protect their tax-exempt status). Contrary to historical evidence, lineage novels propagate the idea of the civil elites' distinctness from the military elites.

18. In *The Pledge*, for instance, Chŏng Insŏng saves a certain Sŏk ssi from captivity. Impressed by his gallantry, Sŏk ssi immediately professes her love for Insŏng. When she is rebuked for her indecorous declaration, Sŏk ssi attributes her lack of refinement to her upbringing in a military household (*Wanwŏl hoemaeng yŏn*, 5.62:52). Similarly in *Pearls and Jade*, one of Hŭimun's wives, Ko ssi, is a woman of vigorous stature and little reserve. When Hŭimun attempts to counter her refusal to comply with one of his requests by using force, Ko ssi quickly responds in kind, and she nearly topples Hŭimun with her strength. The novel mentions suggestively that Ko ssi comes from a military lineage (*Myŏngju ogyŏn kihap rok* [The remarkable encounter of pearls and jade], 25 vols., Sŏgang University Archive, Seoul, Kosŏ myŏng 77, 16:36–39 [denoting manuscript volume and page numbers]).

19. For the details of Chosŏn-dynasty wedding ceremony, see Deuchler, *The Confucian Transformation of Korea*, 251–56.

20. The lineage novel shares with the late imperial Chinese novel an anxiety over the boundaries of the home that represents Confucian culture, which Huili Zheng calls the anxiety over the boundary between heterodoxy and Confucian orthodoxy ("Encountering the Other," 15).

21. *Wanwŏl hoemaeng yŏn*, 1.5:180.

22. *Myŏngju ogyŏn kihap rok*, 18:14–16.

23. Parhae (698–926) was established in northern Manchuria after the kingdom of Koguryŏ (37 BCE–668 CE) was conquered by Silla, the kingdom that ruled over the unified Korean Peninsula (668–935).

24. *Wanwŏl hoemaeng yŏn*, 10.141:139.

25. References to the Warring States country Yue (越) in the sources from the Warring States and Han dynasties (ca. 400–350 BCE) do not use the name "Yue" to designate a homogeneous political, cultural, or ethnical entity; the name instead applies to inhabitants in what would be present-day China's Southeast, who are perceived as barbarians. See Erica Brindley, "Barbarians or Not? Ethnicity and Changing Conceptions of the Ancient Yue (Viet) Peoples ca. 400–50 BCE," *Asia Major* 16, no. 1 (2003): 1–32. During the Ming dynasty, "Yue" was one of the names used (although rarely) to refer to Vietnam, which the Ming attempted and failed to incorporate into its empire. Kathleen Baldanza notes that the Ming's unsuccessful attempt to recolonize Vietnam in the early 1400s led to a reconceptualization of the Ming–Vietnam relationship after this point. Vietnam was part of the Chinese Empire until the tenth century; from the Ming onward, however, it was discursively fashioned as an uncivilized realm. See Kathleen Baldanza, "De-civilizing

Ming China's Southern Border: Vietnam as Lost Province or Barbarian Culture," in *Chinese History in Geographical Perspective*, ed. Jeff Kyong-McClain and Yongtao Du (Lanham, MD: Lexington, 2013), 55–70. In geographic terms, eastern Yue could not border Parhae, which is in northern Manchuria, but *The Pledge* replaces geographical fact with cultural geography: the proximity of the two states suggests their parity as uncivilized places.

26. *Wanwŏl hoemaeng yŏn*, 10.142:138.

27. *Wanwŏl hoemaeng yŏn*, 10.142:141.

28. *Myŏngju kibong* [The remarkable encounter of pearls], 2 vols. (Seoul: Munhwajae kwalliguk Changsŏgak, 1978), 1.21:254–56.

29. The borderland sensibilities in the lineage novel do not easily compare to those in China's context. The trope of bitter journey that marks the boundaries of the civilized empire appears in the Tang frontier poetry. But, as Timothy Chan has written, Tang poets transform geography into the experience of "textual and scholastic frontier" that marks their attachment to cultural tradition, not kinship. See Timothy Chan, "Beyond Border and Boudoir: The Frontier in the Poetry of the Four Elites of Early Tang," in *Reading Medieval Chinese Poetry: Text, Context, and Culture*, ed. Paul W. Kroll (Leiden: Brill, 2015), 130–68.

30. This line comes from *The Book of Poetry* (*Shijing* 詩經), in James Legge, trans., *The Chinese Classics*, vol. 4 (Hong Kong: Hong Kong University Press, 1960), 55.

31. *Wanwŏl hoemaeng yŏn*, 10.149:317–18.

32. *Wanwŏl hoemaeng yŏn*, 1.12:379.

33. *Wanwŏl hoemaeng yŏn*, 5.61:23.

34. *Wanwŏl hoemaeng yŏn*, 1.10:324.

35. The motif of refusing the barbarians' food is reminiscent of the story of Boyi and Shuqi that appears in various Chinese sources. I thank Maram Epstein for bringing this similarity to my attention. On the historical appropriations of this story in China, see Aat Vervoorn, "Boyi and Shuqi: Worthy Men of Old?," *Papers on Far Eastern History* 28 (1983): 1–22.

36. *Wanwŏl hoemaeng yŏn*, 1.12:392.

37. *Wanwŏl hoemaeng yŏn*, 2.25:288.

38. Martin Huang, *Desire and Fictional Narrative in Late Imperial China* (Cambridge, MA: Harvard University Press, 2001), 58–59.

39. *Wanwŏl hoemaeng yŏn*, 3.40:323. This novelistic statement echoes the social politics of kinship that underlay the Chosŏn-dynasty status system. As Martina Deuchler has noted, "The slave was conceptualized as [the] elite's social antipode—as a 'kinless' person, to whom the concept of an enduring descent group did not apply" (*Under the Ancestors' Eyes*, 5).

40. *Wanwŏl hoemaeng yŏn*, 11.128:44.

41. *Wanwŏl hoemaeng yŏn*, 7.95:118.

42. Sun Joo Kim, "My Own Flesh and Blood," esp. 13–23.

43. *Wanwŏl hoemaeng yŏn*, 1.1:50.

44. *Wanwŏl hoemaeng yŏn*, 1.7:209.

45. *Wanwŏl hoemaeng yŏn*, 2.22:175.

46. *Wanwŏl hoemaeng yŏn*, 2.27:333.

47. *Wanwŏl hoemaeng yŏn*, 3.38:242.

48. *Wanwŏl hoemaeng yŏn*, 8.117:250.

49. *Wanwŏl hoemaeng yŏn*, 3.38:242.

50. *Wanwŏl hoemaeng yŏn*, 3.38:257.

51. Hwisang Cho, "Feeling Power in Chosŏn Korea: Popular Grievances, Royal Rage, and the Problem of Human Sentiments," *Journal of Korean Studies* 20, no. 1 (2015): 7–32.

52. For the legal understanding of feelings, see the following two works: JaHyun Kim Haboush, "Gender and the Politics of Language in Chosŏn Korea," in *Rethinking Confucianism Past and Present in China, Japan, Korea, and Vietnam*, ed. Benjamin Elman, John B. Duncan, and Herman Ooms, Asian Pacific Monograph series (Los Angeles: University of California, 2002), 220–57; and Jungwon Kim, "'You Must Avenge on My Behalf': Widow Chastity and Honour in Nineteenth-Century Korea," *Gender & History* 26, no. 1 (2014): 128–46.

53. Dorothy Ko, "Thinking About Copulating: An Early-Qing Confucian Thinker's Problem with Emotion and Words," in *Remapping China: Fissures in Historical Terrain*, ed. Gail Hershatter, Emily Honig, Jonathan N. Lipman, and Randall Stross (Stanford, CA: Stanford University Press, 1996), 66.

54. *Wanwŏl hoemaeng yŏn*, 1.3:125.

55. *Wanwŏl hoemaeng yŏn*, 1.4:125.

56. *Wanwŏl hoemaeng yŏn*, 1.6:209.

57. *Wanwŏl hoemaeng yŏn*, 2.26:298.

58. Mencius, *The Works of Mencius*, trans. Legge, 294.

59. Confucius, *The Analects*, in *The Life and Teaching of Confucius*, trans. James Legge (London: N. Trübner, 1895), 137.

60. "Of charges, which is the greatest? The charge of one's self is the greatest. That those who do not fail to keep themselves are able to serve their parents is what I have heard. But I have never heard of any, who, having failed to keep themselves, were able notwithstanding to serve their parents" (Mencius, *The Works of Mencius*, trans. Legge, 309).

61. *Wanwŏl hoemaeng yŏn*, 3.21:22.

62. *Wanwŏl hoemaeng yŏn*, 4.53:236.

63. *Wanwŏl hoemaeng yŏn*, 3.31:18.

64. *Wanwŏl hoemaeng yŏn*, 3.26:38.

65. *Wanwŏl hoemaeng yŏn*, 4.51:181.

66. *Wanwŏl hoemaeng yŏn*, 7.95:120.

67. Nancy Armstrong writes in her study of the British novel that the modern novel and modern subjectivity are coeval events structured through the emergence of interiority—a form of self-enclosure of the subject, distinguished against the "outside" world. See Nancy Armstrong, *How Novels Think: The Limits of British Individualism from 1719–1900* (New York: Columbia University Press, 2005). Tracing the emergence of modern Japanese literature shaped by its encounter with Western philosophy and the Western novel, Karatani Kojin singles out the appearance of interiority as the most profound psychosocial transformation of Japan's modernity. See Karatani Kōjin, *The Origins of Modern Japanese Literature*, trans. Brett de Bary (Durham, NC: Duke University Press, 1993), 45–75. Kwŏn Podŭrae traces the process of emergence of literary interiority in the modern Korean novel at the level of grammatical adjustments, pronoun use, and the distinction drawn between fiction that describes essential, psychological truths and the newspaper, oriented toward the cowitnessing of contemporary historical events. See Kwŏn Podŭrae, *Han'guk kŭndae sosŏl ŭi kiwŏn* [The origins of the modern Korean novel] (Seoul: Somyŏng ch'ulp'an, 2012), 199–284.

68. David Lawton, *Voice in Later Medieval English Literature: Public Interiorities* (Oxford: Oxford University Press, 2017), 8, 74.

69. William Theodore de Bary, in a similar vein, distinguishes between "private" and "negative" individuality in the Confucian context. In his view, " 'negative' individualism . . . has no effect on the status of other individuals. It makes no positive claim within society. . . . By contrast, there is a more 'positive' and public individualism which seeks to establish the place of the individual or self in relation to others, to secure his rights or status in some institutional framework or on the basis of widely declared and accepted principles" ("Individualism and Humanism in Late Ming Thought," in *Self and Society in Ming Thought*, ed. William Theodore de Bary [New York: Columbia University Press, 1970], 147).

70. De Bary notes that Confucian selfhood is founded upon the exercise of the moral will, which has reciprocity as its major imperative ("Individualism and Humanism," 149).

71. Although the term *interiority* is certainly imbricated with the Western genealogy of this concept, my use of it is consistent with the vocabulary of the lineage novel that describes Madame So as a person with striking differences between her "inside" and "outside."

72. Angela Zito, "Silk and Skin: Significant Boundaries," in *Body, Subject, and Power in China*, ed. Angela Zito and Tani Barlow (Chicago: University of Chicago Press, 1994), 119, 106. Zito writes: "The subject constituted within

[Confucian ritual discourse] has little in common with our modern Western idea of the disembodied Cartesian subject, a unitary consciousness that has found social expression in the ideology of possessive individualism. Instead, in eighteenth-century China human consciousness as agent constantly performed itself into being through actions of (social) significance, the set of practices called *wen*. These signifying practices produce both bodies and texts simultaneously" ("Silk and Skin," 120).

4. Feelings and the Conflicts of Kinship

1. See Pak Ilyong, *Chosŏn sidae ŭi aejŏng sosŏl: Sasil kwa nangman ŭi sosŏlsa chŏk chŏn'gae yangsang* [Love novels of Chosŏn: Novelistic development between reality and romanticism] (Seoul: Chimmundang, 1993), 14.

2. Song Sŏnguk was the first one to point out that the relationship between father-in-law and son-in-law is problematized only in the lineage novel (*Chosŏn sidae taeha sosŏl ŭi sŏsa munbop kwa ch'angjak ŭisik* [The narrative grammar and outlook of Chosŏn-dynasty lineage novels] [Seoul: T'aehaksa, 2003], 200).

3. Jungwon Kim, "Between Morality and Crime: Filial Daughters and Vengeful Violence in Eighteenth-Century Korea," *Acta Koreana* 21, no. 2 (2018): 481–502.

4. Hong Hŭibok, "*Cheil kiŏn sŏ*" [Preface to *The book of books in the vernacular*], in *Cheil kiŏn* [Flowers in the mirror], ed. Pak Chaeyŏn and Chŏng Kyubok (Seoul: Kukhak charyowŏn, 2001), 22–23.

5. Kim Chinse, ed., *Wanwŏl hoemaeng yŏn* [The pledge at the banquet of moon-gazing pavilion], 12 vols. (Seoul: Seoul National University Press, 1986–1994), 4.51:161–62 (denoting print volume, manuscript volume, and print page numbers). On the motif of marriage in lineage novels, see Yang Hyeran, *Chosŏn cho kibong ryu sosŏl yŏn'gu* [Study of Chosŏn-dynasty novels focused on the remarkable encounter] (Seoul: Ihoe munhwasa, 1995).

6. On the cult of chastity in Chosŏn, see Jungwon Kim, " 'You Must Avenge on My Behalf': Widow Chastity and Honour in Nineteenth-Century Korea," *Gender & History* 26, no. 1 (2014): 130–33.

7. For a discussion of the love-sickness motif in Chosŏn literature, see Janet Lee, "Dilemma of the Lovesick Hero: Masculine Images and Politics of the Body in Seventeenth-Century Korean Love Tales," *Journal of Korean Studies* 21, no. 1 (2016): 45–69.

8. Writing about the motif of cross-dressing in scholar–beauty novels of late imperial China, Martin Huang notes: "A maiden's adventures outside the confines of her boudoir are 'transgressions' that are often needed to make a

romantic story more dramatic and exciting. At the same time, cross-dressing makes such transgressions less liable to moral censorship at the time when sex segregation was the norm" (*Negotiating Masculinities in Late Imperial China* [Honolulu: University of Hawai'i Press, 2006], 137; also see 66–71, 135–37). On the fluidity of gender in the fiction of late imperial China, see Judith Zeitlin, *Historian of the Strange: Pu Songling and the Chinese Classical Tale* (Stanford, CA: Stanford University Press, 1993), 98–131.

9. Keith McMahon, *Misers, Shrews, and Polygamists: Sexuality and Male–Female Relations in Eighteenth-Century Chinese Fiction* (Durham, NC: Duke University Press, 1995), 1–16, 28–54.

10. Martin Huang, *Desire and Fictional Narrative in Late Imperial China* (Cambridge, MA: Harvard University Press, 2001), 5–22.

11. *Hyŏn ssi yangung ssangnin ki* [The record of two heroes: Brothers Hyŏn], 2 vols. (Seoul: Sŏngmunsa, 1979), 1.3:267.

12. *Hyŏn ssi yangung ssangnin ki*, 2.10:481.

13. *Hyŏn ssi yangung ssangnin ki*, 2.10:491.

14. *Hyŏn ssi yangung ssangnin ki*, 2.10:494, 495.

15. *Hyŏn ssi yangung ssangnin ki*, 2.10:496.

16. On the rape motif in the lineage novel, see Chang Sigwang, "Kojŏn taeha sosŏl ŭi kanggan mot'ip'ŭ yŏn'gu" [A study of the rape motif in lineage novels], *Kug'ŏ kungmunhak* 170 (2015): 353–89.

17. *Myŏngju kibong* [The remarkable encounter of pearls], 2 vols. (Seoul: Munhwajae kwalliguk Changsŏgak, 1978), 1.1:32–33.

18. *Myŏngju kibong*, 1.3:67.

19. *Myŏngju kibong*, 1.5:151–52.

20. *Myŏngju kibong*, 1.5:152.

21. *Myŏngju kibong*, 2.9:266.

22. *Myŏngju kibong*, 2.10:388–89.

23. *Myŏngju ogyŏn kihap rok* [The remarkable encounter of pearls and jade], 25 vols., Sŏgang University Archive, Seoul, Kosŏ myŏng 77, 25:8–9 (denoting manuscript volume and page numbers).

24. *Myŏngju ogyŏn kihap rok*, 12:23.

25. *Myŏngju ogyŏn kihap rok*, 12:30.

26. Huang, *Desire and Fictional Narrative*, 107.

27. Ch'oe Kilyong, "Kososŏl e nat'ananŭn aenghyŏl hwaso ŭi sŏsa silsang kwa ŭimi" [The motif of nightingale blood in the traditional Korean novel], *Kososŏl yŏn'gu* 29 (2010): 50; Donald Harper, "The Sexual Arts of Ancient China as Described in a Manuscript of the Second Century B.C," *Harvard Journal of Asiatic Studies* 47, no. 2 (1987): 557–58.

28. See Ch'oe Kilyong, "Kososŏl e nat'ananŭn aenghyŏl hwaso"; Cho Hyeran, "Kososŏl e nat'anan namsŏng seksyuŏllit'i ŭi chaehyŏn yangsang"

[Reproduction of male sexuality in the traditional Korean novel], *Kosos̆ol yŏn'gu* 20 (2005): 387–89.

29. According to a former palace lady's testimony recorded in the twentieth century, nightingale blood was used to certify the virginity of palace ladies when they entered service (Kim Yongsuk, *Chosŏnjo kungjung p'ungsŏk yŏn'gu* [Customs of the Chosŏn court] [Seoul: Ilchisa, 1987], 37, quoted in Ch'oe Kilyong, "Kosos̆ol e nat'ananŭn aenghyŏl hwaso," 45). Ch'oe Kilyong notes that outside this record no extant sources suggest that nightingale blood was widely used in Chosŏn society.

30. *Hyŏn ssi yangung ssangnin ki*, 2.7:174–76.

31. The phrase *sunyang*, "fully a man," refers to the loss of virginity, which is not yet Kyŏngmun's case.

32. *Hyŏn ssi yangung ssangnin ki*, 2.8:303–4.

33. *Hyŏn ssi yangung ssangnin ki*, 2.8:319.

34. Also see Cho Hyeran, "Kosos̆ol e nat'anan namsŏng seksyuŏllit'i."

35. Kim Kidong, ed., *Ogwŏn chaehap kiyŏn* [The remarkable reunion of jade mandarin ducks], vols. 27–30 of *Kojŏn sosŏl chŏnjip* [The anthology of manuscript editions of classical Korean novels] (Seoul: Asea munhwasa, 1980), 27.1:78–80.

36. An almost identical amorous encounter between father-in-law and son-in-law occurs in *The Pledge*. Chŏng In'gwang first appears before his future father-in-law, Chang Hŏn, in the guise of a female maid. During the funeral procession for the Chŏng lineage patriarch, Chŏng Han, In'gwang and his sister, Wŏlyŏm, break away from the family train and begin a series of peregrinations. Along the way, the word of Wŏlyŏm's beauty reaches the ears of Chang Hŏn, who has been looking for a concubine. To save his sister's honor, In'gwang dons a woman's dress and enters Chang Hŏn's house in her stead. For the bedroom rendezvous between father-in-law and son-in-law, see *Wanwŏl hoemaeng yŏn*, 2.18:77–78.

37. *Ogwŏn chaehap kiyŏn*, 27.6:86–88.

38. *Ogwŏn chaehap kiyŏn*, 29.14:439.

39. *Ogwŏn chaehap kiyŏn*, 29.14:449–50.

40. *Ogwŏn chaehap kiyŏn*, 29.14:451.

41. *Myŏngju kibong*, 2.24:352–53.

42. The *Tale of Simch'ŏng* (Sim Ch'ŏng chŏn 沈清傳) depicts a blind man's daughter who is preoccupied with the care of her disabled father. Even after she miraculously survives an effort to sacrifice her life for him and goes on to marry the emperor of China, she retains her identity as daughter; in lavishly honoring her father and mourning his eventual death for three years, she assumes the ritual role reserved for a son. JaHyun Kim Haboush has thus noted that this story assumes "the reciprocity and untransferrability of

emotion" ("Filial Emotions and Filial Values: Changing Patterns in the Discourse of Filiality in Late Chosŏn Korea," *Harvard Journal of Asiatic Studies* 55, no. 1 [1995]: 175).

43. On succession and adoption practices, see Martina Deuchler, *The Confucian Transformation of Korea: A Study of Society and Ideology* (Cambridge, MA: Harvard University Asia Center, 1992), 212–13. The position of the lineage heir was ultimately linked to his ritual role as he officiated the ancestral worship ceremonies as the oldest living male descendant.

44. *Wanwŏl hoemaeng yŏn*, 1.3:118.

45. *Wanwŏl hoemaeng yŏn*, 5.68:217.

46. *Wanwŏl hoemaeng yŏn*, 5.54:258–59.

47. In Chosŏn Korea, women legally kept their natal last name after marriage, and Madame So is usually referred to by her natal last name. In rare instances, however, she is called by her husband's last name, "Madame Chŏng," as in the given excerpt. Other lineage novels also refer to married women by their husbands' surnames, which suggests that this might have been a common practice.

48. *Wanwŏl hoemaeng yŏn*, 7.91:29–30.

49. *Wanwŏl hoemaeng yŏn*, 1.2:42.

50. *Wanwŏl hoemaeng yŏn*, 1.6:207.

51. *Wanwŏl hoemaeng yŏn*, 1.6:207.

52. *Wanwŏl hoemaeng yŏn*, 1.6:209, my emphasis.

53. *Wanwŏl hoemaeng yŏn*, 9.129:139. The capping ceremony (K.: *kwallye*, C.: *guanli* 冠禮) for boys took place any time between five and twenty years of age, marking their initiation into adulthood. It was common for the capping ceremony to take place right before a boy's wedding. See Deuchler, *Confucian Transformation of Korea*, 244–45.

54. *Wanwŏl hoemaeng yŏn*, 3.41:354.

55. Lauren Berlant, "Intimacy: A Special Issue," *Critical Inquiry* 24, no. 2 (1998): 282.

56. *Wanwŏl hoemaeng yŏn*, 12.180:305.

57. *Myŏngju kibong*, 1.11:333.

58. *Wanwŏl hoemaeng yŏn*, 9.133:208.

59. *Wanwŏl hoemaeng yŏn*, 12.180:313.

60. As discussed in chapter 1, lineage novels often claim that the lives of their protagonists are recorded in external textual sources—posthumous biographies, family histories, and so on. This gesture makes a claim for the prestige of documentary genres.

61. Lila Abu-Lughod, *Veiled Sentiments: Honor and Poetry in a Bedouin Society* (Berkeley: University of California Press, 1999), 238. Abu-Lughod draws the distinction between value and norm from Ralf Turner, "The Real Self: From

Institution to Impulse," *American Journal of Sociology* 81, no. 5 (1976): 989–1016.

62. Haiyan Lee, *Revolution of the Heart: A Genealogy of Love in China, 1900–1950* (Stanford, CA: Stanford University Press, 2006), 30, 33.

63. Ning Ma, *The Age of Silver: Rise of the Novel East and West* (New York: Oxford University Press, 2016).

64. I thank Maram Epstein for suggesting this idea.

65. *Wanwŏl hoemaeng yŏn*, 12.173:157.

66. *Ogwŏn chŏnhae* [Commentary to jade mandarin ducks], 5 vols., Kyujanggak Archive, Seoul, Ko 3350-67, 5:8b.

5. The Novel Without the Lineage

1. Yumi Moon, *Populist Collaborators: The Ilchinhoe and the Japanese Colonization of Korea, 1896–1910* (Stanford, CA: Stanford University Press, 2015), 22–46. Moon notes that the two visions converge after the Tonghaks convert to the Japanese ideas of civilization and enlightenment and merge with the elite reformers in the formation of the organization called the Ilchinhoe (74–78). For a study of the Tonghak beliefs, see George Kallander, *Salvation Through Dissent: Tonghak Heterodoxy and Early Modern Korea* (Honolulu: Hawai'i University Press, 2013), 28–57.

2. Kyung Moon Hwang, *Beyond Birth: Social Status in the Emergence of Modern Korea* (Cambridge, MA: Harvard University Press, 2004), 329–44. Hwang notes that advancement through the bureaucratic ranks and other realms of society rarely occurred in the group of commoners and slaves (337).

3. Martina Deuchler, *Under the Ancestors' Eyes: Kinship, Status, and Locality in Premodern Korea* (Cambridge, MA: Harvard University Asia Center, 2015), 370–96.

4. Hwang, *Beyond Birth*, 337.

5. Deuchler, *Under the Ancestors' Eyes*, 391.

6. *Ha Chin yangmun rok* [The record of two households: Ha and Chin], 25 vols., Tōyō bunko, Tokyo, VII-4-234, 2:1–9, 3:1–27 (denoting manuscript volume and page numbers).

7. Pak Sungnye, "*Ha Chin yangmun rok* yŏn'gu: P'ilsabon kwa hwaljabon ŭi taebi rŭl chungsim ŭro" [A study of *The record of two households: Ha and Chin*, focused on the comparison between manuscript and printed editions], MA thesis, Academy of Korean Studies, 1998, 14.

8. Kang Yŏngsim, "1900 nyŏndae Tongasia ŭi *Wŏllam mangguk sa* yut'ong kwa suyong: Han'guk, Chungguk, Wŏllam chungsim ŭro [Circulation of *The*

history of the loss of Vietnam in the East Asia of the 1900s: The cases of Korea, China, and Vietnam], *Ihwa sahak yŏn'gu* 49 (2014): 93–102.

9. Rebecca Karl, *Staging the World: Chinese Nationalism at the Turn of the Twentieth Century* (Durham, NC: Duke University Press, 2002), 16; on Liang Qichao and Phan Bội Châu, see 164–65.

10. *Hyŏn ssi yangung ssangnin ki* [The record of two heroes: Brothers Hyŏn], National Library of Korea, Seoul, Ko 3636-223, scriber's postscript.

11. Yi Kwangsu, "What Is Literature?," trans. Jooyeon Rhee, *Azalea* 4 (2011): 312.

12. Maurice Courant, *Bibliographie coréenne: Tableau littéraire de la Corée, contenant la nomenclature des ouvrages publiés dans ce pays jusqu'en 1890 ainsi que la description et l'analyse détaillées des principaux d'entre ces ouvrages* [Korean bibliography: The catalog of Korean literature, containing the classification of works published in this country until 1890 as well as the detailed description and analysis of the main works] (Paris: Ernest Leroux, 1894), xxiv–xxvi. Chŏng Pyŏngsŏl argues that the missing volumes are lineage novels because their descriptions are absent in Courant's bibliography, which supplies summaries of volumes that he was able to recover. See Chŏng Pyŏngsŏl [Jung Byung Sul], "Chosŏn hugi changp'yŏn sosŏlsa ŭi chŏn'gae" [The historical development of the lineage novel in the late Chosŏn], in *Han'guk kojŏn sosŏl kwa sŏsa munhak* [The traditional Korean novel and fictional prose] (Seoul: Chimmundang, 1998), 257.

13. E. W. Koons, "The House Where Books Are Given for Rent," *Korea Mission Field*, July 1918, 150, quoted in Michael Kim, "Literary Production, Circulating Libraries, and Private Publishing: The Popular Reception of Vernacular Fiction Texts in the Late Chosŏn Dynasty," *Journal of Korean Studies* 9, no. 1 (2004): 30.

14. Franco Moretti, *The Way of the World: The Bildungsroman in European Culture* (London: Verso, 2000), 229–45.

15. On colonial modernity, see Tani Barlow, "Introduction: On Colonial Modernity," in *Formations of Colonial Modernity in East Asia,* ed. Tani Barlow (Durham, NC: Duke University Press, 1997), 1–20.

16. David Der-wei Wang traces the changes in decidedly nonmodern genres of the post-Taiping era to decenter Western literary development as the central moment of change in the development of Chinese fiction. As Wang contends, "The late Qing was already engaged in a reworking of Chinese traditions when it confronted the additional task of understanding European traditions" (*Fin-de-Siècle Splendor: Repressed Modernities of Late Qing Fiction, 1848–1911* [Stanford, CA: Stanford University Press, 1997], 8).

17. Discursive shift as a connecting mode allows Jonathan Zwicker, in his study of the long nineteenth century in Japan's history, to link Edo and Meiji

literature into a "genealogy of sentimental and melodramatic fiction" that traces shifts in the function of tears in literature. See Jonathan Zwicker, *Practices of the Sentimental Imagination: Melodrama, the Novel, and the Social Imaginary in Nineteenth-Century Japan* (Cambridge, MA: Harvard University Press, 2006).

18. Ken Ito has traced the concept of Meiji family, a cross-breed of Western discourses of domesticity and traditional *ie* ideology, in the literary works of turn-of-the-twentieth-century Japanese fiction, which mediate anxieties over the redistribution of gender and family roles. See Ken Ito, *An Age of Melodrama: Family, Gender, and Social Hierarchy in the Turn-of-the-Century Japanese Novel* (Stanford, CA: Stanford University Press, 2008).

19. In the *Revolution of the Heart: A Genealogy of Love in China, 1900–1950* (Stanford, CA: Stanford University Press, 2006), Haiyan Lee follows the trajectory of ideological reformulation of feelings through different historical regimes, identifying "the Confucian structure of feelings," "the Enlightenment structure of feelings," and "the revolutionary structure of feelings."

20. The collected volume *Different Worlds of Discourse* construes the late Qing not as a simple transition "between two worlds" but as "a world unto itself—one of cultural vitality and experimentation" (Nanxiu Qian, Grace S. Fong, and Richard J. Smith, introduction to *Different Worlds of Discourse: Transformation of Gender and Genre in Late Qing and Early Republican China*, ed. Nanxiu Qian, Grace S. Fong, and Richard J. Smith [Leiden: Brill, 2008], 7).

21. Jooyeon Rhee, *The Novel in Transition: Gender and Literature in Early Colonial Korea* (Ithaca, NY: Cornell University Press, 2019), 50–51.

22. Yoon Sun Yang, *From Domestic Women to Sensitive Young Men: Translating the Individual in Early Colonial Korea* (Cambridge, MA: Harvard University Asia Center, 2017), 4.

23. Ellie Choi, "Memories of Korean Modernity: Yi Kwangsu's *The Heartless* and New Perspectives in Colonial Alterity," *Journal of Korean Studies* 77, no. 3 (2018): 659–91.

24. See Atsuko Ueda, *Concealment of Politics, Politics of Concealment: The Production of "Literature" in Meiji Japan* (Stanford, CA: Stanford University Press, 2006); and Lydia Liu, *Translingual Practice: Literature, National Culture, and Translated Modernity, China, 1900–1937* (Stanford, CA: Stanford University Press, 1995).

25. Ch'ŏn Chŏnghwan suggests that in terms of the mode of circulation— serialization and type print—and even audience, old and new novels were practically indistinguishable throughout the first two decades of the twentieth century (*Kŭndae ŭi ch'aek ilkki: Tokcha ŭi t'ansaeng kwa Han'guk kŭndae munhak* [Reading the books of modernity: The birth of readers and modern Korean literature] [Seoul: P'urŭn yŏksa, 2014], 66–68).

26. Kim Kijin, "Taejung sosŏl ron" [The popular novel], *Tonga ilbo*, 1929.

27. Chŏng Pyŏngsŏl [Jung Byung Sul], "Chosŏn hugi insoae ŭi paljŏn, sŏjŏk ŭi pogŭp kŭrigo Sirhak chisik ŭi sot'ong: Chosŏn hugi han'gŭl panggak sosŏl ŭi chŏn'guk chŏk yu'tong kanŭngsŏng e taehayŏ" [Development of printing in the late Chosŏn, dissemination of books, and circulation of Sirhak knowledge: On the possibility of country-wide circulation of woodblock print novels], *Tasan kwa hyŏndae* 3 (2010): 115–33. On woodblock printing during the Chosŏn dynasty, see Kim Tonguk, "Han'gŭl sosŏl panggakbon ŭi sŏngnip e taehayŏ" [The development of woodblock publishing of vernacular novels], in *Hyangt'o Sŏul* [The city of Seoul], ed. Sŏul t'ŭkpyŏlsi sap'yŏnch'an wiwŏnhoe (Seoul: Sŏul t'ŭkpyŏlsi sap'yŏnch'an wiwŏnhoe, 1960), 38–67, and Chŏng Pyŏngsŏl [Jung Byung Sul], "Chosŏn hugi han'gŭl sosŏl ŭi sŏngjang kwa yut'ong: Sech'aek kwa panggakbon chungsim ŭro" [The rise and circulation of vernacular Korean novels in the late Chosŏn: Rental and woodblock editions], *Kug'ŏ kungmunhak* 100 (2005): 263–97. On the development of novels' circulation, see Chŏng Pyŏngsŏl [Jung Byung Sul], *Chosŏn sidae sosŏl ŭi saengsan kwa yut'ong* [The production and circulation of novels in Chosŏn] (Seoul: Seoul National University Press, 2016), 111–34.

28. See Ksenia Chizhova, "3. Korean," in *How Literatures Begin*, ed. Joel Lande and Denis Feeney (Princeton, NJ: Princeton University Press, forthcoming); and Paek Tuhyŏn, *Han'gŭl munhŏnhak* [Korean bibliography] (Seoul: T'aehaksa, 2015).

29. Although the majority of extant datable rental library book editions come from the late nineteenth and early twentieth centuries, extant references to rental libraries by Ch'ae Chaegong (1720–1799) and Yi Tŏngmu (1741–1793) from the mid–eighteenth century point to the earlier boundaries of this practice. See Chŏng Myŏnggi, " 'Sech'aek p'ilsabon kososŏl' e taehan sŏsŏl chŏk ihae: Ch'ongnyang, kanso (kan'gi), yut'ong yangsang ŭl chungsim ŭro" [Introductory remarks on the "rental manuscript editions of traditional novels": Total volume of works, places of their production (production records), and mode of circulation], *Kososŏl yŏn'gu* 12 (2001): 445–80; and Chŏng Pyŏngsŏl [Jung Byung Sul], "Sech'aek sosŏl yŏn'gu ŭi chaengjŏm kwa panghyang" [Problems and directions in the study of rental library novels], *Kungmunhak yŏn'gu* 10 (2003): 27–57. Chŏng Pyŏngsŏl notes that in the 1920s rental libraries changed their collections from manuscript volumes, which included a great number of lineage novels, to shorter, moveable-type imprints (*Chosŏn sidae sosŏl ŭi saengsan kwa yut'ong*, 210).

30. See Chŏng Myŏnggi, "'Sech'aek p'ilsabon kososŏl' e taehan sŏsŏl chŏk ihae," 445–47; and Yu Ch'undong, "Ilbon Tongyang mun'go sojang sech'aek kososŏl ŭi sŏnggyŏk kwa ŭimi" [The character and significance of rental novels located in Tōyō bunko in Japan], *Minjok munhwa yŏn'gu* 64 (2014): 287–90.

31. See Chŏng Myŏnggi, "Sech'aekbon sosŏl ŭi yut'ong yangsang: Tongyang mun'go sojang sech'aekbon sosŏl e nat'anan sech'aek changbu rŭl chungsim ŭro" [Circulation of rental novels: Rental rosters recorded in rental novels in the Tōyō bunko collection], *Kososŏl yŏn'gu* 16 (2003): 71–99; Chŏn Sanguk, "Sech'aek taech'ulja ŭi t'ŭksŏng e taehan yŏn'gu: Tongyang mungo bon taech'ul changbu rŭl chungsim ŭro" [Rental libraries' readers: Rental rosters from the Tōyō bunko manuscripts], *Kososŏl yŏn'gu* 26 (2008): 239–74; Chŏn Sanguk, "Hyangmoktong sech'aek ŭi taech'ul changbu ŭi taehan koch'al" [Overview of the rosters of rental library borrowers in the Hyangmoktong area], *Yŏlsang kojŏn yŏn'gu* 37 (2013): 535–63.

32. Chŏng Myŏnggi, "'Sech'aek p'ilsabon kososŏl' e taehan sŏsŏl chŏk ihae"; Chŏng Pyŏngsŏl, "Sech'aek sosŏl yŏn'gu ŭi chaengjŏm kwa panghyang," 51–54; Chŏng Pyŏngsŏl, *Chosŏn sidae sosŏl ŭi saengsan kwa yut'ong*, 199–240; Kim Hyogyŏng and Yu Ch'undong, *Saech'aek kwa panggakbon: Chosŏn sidae tŏksŏ yŏlp'ung kwa mannada* [Rental and woodblock novels: The reading trends of the Chosŏn dynasty] (Seoul: National Library of Korea, 2016).

33. See Pak Hyŏnmo, Yi Wanu, Im Ch'igyun, and Hwang Munhwan, eds., *Han'gŭl: Sot'ong kwa paeryŏ ŭi munja* [Han'gŭl: The script of communication and care] (Songnam: Academy of Korean Studies, 2016), 144–45; Chŏng Myŏnggi, "Sech'aekbon sosŏl e taehan sae charyo ŭi sŏnggyŏk yŏn'gu: Ŏnmun Hu saeng rok sojae mongnok ŭl chungsim ŭro" [New discoveries in the studies of rental novels: Book catalog in *The vernacular record of Master Hu*], *Kososŏl yŏn'gu* 19 (2005): 227–54.

34. Chŏng Myŏnggi suggests that the mistakenly recorded title in *Vernacular Record of Master Hu* might refer to either *Ch'oe Hyŏn chŏn* or *Ch'o Han chŏn* ("Sech'aekbon sosŏl e taehan sae charyo ŭi sŏnggyŏk yŏn'gu," 239 n. 27).

35. Chŏng Myŏnggi speculates that the list might have been created by a rental library owner with the purpose of advertising his catalog ("Sech'aekbon sosŏl e taehan sae charyo ŭi sŏnggyŏk yŏn'gu," 239 n. 26). Chŏng Pyŏngsŏl and Kim Tonguk, however, dispute the rental provenance of this manuscript (Chŏng Pyŏngsŏl, *Chosŏn sidae sosŏl ŭi saengsan kwa yut'ong*, 224–25; Kim Tonguk, "Sŏuldae bon *Ogwŏn chaehap kiyŏn* sojae sosŏl mongnok e taehan koch'al" [Observations on the book list recorded in the Seoul National University manuscript of *The remarkable encounter of jade mandarin ducks*], *Kojŏn munhak yŏn'gu* 47 [2015]: 297).

36. Yu Ch'undong, "'Ch'aek yŏl mongnok' e taehayŏ" [Study of "A book roster"], *Munhŏn kwa haesŏk* 34 (2006): 187–204.

37. See Kim Chongch'ŏl, "Ŏn'gandok yŏn'gu—chakmun kyojae ŭi kwanjŏm esŏ" [A study of the *Vernacular letter manual* as composition primer], *Kug'ŏ kyoyuk yŏn'gu* 25 (2015): 237–81.

38. See U K'waeje, "Kuhwaljabon kososŏl ŭi ch'ulp'an mit yŏn'gu hyŏnhwang kŏmt'o" [State of the field: Studies of novels in old movable type], *Kojŏn munhak yŏn'gu* 0 (1985): 113–43. Moveable-type publications of traditional novels were often unchanged renditions of rental library and woodblock copies. See Yu Ch'undong, "Hwaljabon kososŏl ŭi ch'ulp'an kwa yut'ong e taehan myŏt kaji munje tŭl" [Traditional fiction in moveable type: Some observations on its publication and circulation], *Hanminjok munhwa yŏn'gu* 50 (2015): 292–93; also see Yu Ch'undong, "Ilbon Tongyang mun'go sojang sech'aek kososŏl ŭi sŏnggyŏk kwa kŭ ŭimi," 286–87.

39. See Cho Chaehyŏn, "*Sammun kyuhap rok* yŏn'gu" [Study of *The record of three households' marriages*], *Ŏmun yŏn'gu* 152 (2011): 211–37.

40. *The Remarkable Encounter of Two Beauties* is considered an adaptation of the Qing-dynasty novel *A Short Story of a Sojourn in a Spring Garden* (Ch. *Zhu chunyuan xiaoshi* 駐春園小史). See Ch'oi Yunhŭi, "*Ssangmi kibong* pŏn'an yangsang yŏn'gu" [Study of the adaptation manner of *The remarkable encounter of two beauties*], *Kososŏl yŏn'gu* 11 (2001): 265–92.

41. Hwang Hyejin, "*Ssangmi kibong* e hyŏngsanghwatoen aejŏng ŭi yangsang kwa ŭimi yŏn'gu" [Figuration of love in *The remarkable encounter of two beauties* and its significance], *Kojŏn munhak kwa kyoyuk* 8 (2004): 301–37.

42. Yi Tawŏn, "*Hyŏn ssi yangung ssangnin ki* yŏn'gu: Yŏndae bon *Hyŏn ssi yangung ssangnin ki* chungsim ŭro" [Study of *The record of two heroes: Brothers Hyŏn*, with a focus on the Yonsei University manuscript], MA thesis, Yonsei University, 2001, 67–86. Yi Tawŏn explains the novel's softened character by the fact that, according to margin notes in this rental manuscript, it was circulated in the Tongho area (modern-day Oksu-dong area of Seoul); the historically more demotic population of this area could have favored a more downplayed, comforting narrative.

43. Yi Taehyŏng, "19 segi changp'yŏn sosŏl *Ha Chin yangmun rok* ŭi taejung chŏk pyŏnmo" [Popular transformation of a lineage novel, *The record of two households: Ha and Chin*, in the nineteenth century," *Minjok munhwasa yŏn'gu* 39 (2008): 28–56.

44. The imprint of *The Record of Two Heroes: Brothers Hyŏn* appears to be the closest to a rental library manuscript, now contained at the Yonsei University library, although the latter text is not its direct prototype. Compared to this rental manuscript, the printed version is shortened roughly by half, with some episodes omitted and the overall clarity of the narrative affected by these redactions. See Yi Tawŏn, "*Hyŏn ssi yangung ssangnin ki* yŏn'gu," 58–63. However, it appears that when *The Record of Two Households: Ha and Chin* was converted to moveable type, it was smoothed out compared to the extant rental editions. On the comparison between the rental manuscript and the first printed edition of *The Record of the Two Households*, see Yu Kwangsu,

"Hwalp'an bon *Ha Chin yangmun rok* Tongmisŏsi bon e taehayŏ" [On the Tongmisŏsi moveable-type imprint of *The record of two households: Ha and Chin*], *Ilsang kojŏn yŏn'gu* 42 (2014): 379–417. Yi Tawŏn writes that while undergoing moveable-type reprinting, *The Record of Two Heroes: Brothers Hyŏn* was shortened by about half, whereas *The Record of the Two Households: Ha and Chin* was shortened by only 10 percent, with the printed text attempting to remedy the inconsistencies of the narrative. This difference, Yi claims, might explain the fact that the latter text had many more reprints in the twentieth century ("*Hyŏn ssi yangung ssangnin ki* yŏn'gu," 60).

45. Chu Sumin, "*Hyŏn Sumun chŏn* ibon yŏn'gu" [A study of different editions of *The tale of Hyŏn Sumun*], *Chŏngsin munhwa yŏn'gu* 37, no. 1 (2014): 230–35.

46. Chu Sumin notes that the earliest recorded transcription date for *The Tale of Hyŏn Sumun* is 1859, which suggests that the text was composed somewhat earlier ("*Hyŏn Sumun chŏn* ibon yŏn'gu," 247–49).

47. Chu Sumin, "Han'gŭl kososŏl ibon hwaksan ŭi il kyŏnghyang kwa kŭ ŭimi—*Hyŏn Sumun chŏn* chungsim ŭro" [The proliferation of different versions of traditional Korean novels: The case of *The tale of Hyŏn Sumun*], *Kososŏl yŏn'gu* 42 (2016): 86 n. 5.

48. Chu Sumin, "*Hyŏn Sumun chŏn* ŭi ch'angjak pangsik yŏn'gu: Taejangp'yŏn sosŏl *Hyŏn ssi yangung ssangnin ki* wa ŭi kwan'gye chungsim ŭro" [The composition of *The tale of Hyŏn Sumun*: Its relationship with a lineage novel, *The record of two heroes: Brothers Hyŏn*], *Kojŏn kwa haesŏk* 17 (2014): 151–71.

49. Chu Sumin notes that besides the nearly identical genealogical credentials, *The Tale of Hyŏn Sumun* adopts some of the narrative episodes from the parent text ("*Hyŏn Sumun chŏn* ŭi ch'angjak pangsik yŏn'gu," 151–62).

50. Chu Hyŏngye, "Tongyang mun'go bon *Hyŏn Sumun chŏn* ŭi sŏsa chŏk t'ukching kwa ŭimi" [The narrative characteristics of the Tōyō bunko edition of *The tale of Hyŏn Sumun*], *Yŏlsang kojŏn yŏn'gu* 15 (2002): 232.

51. *Hyŏn Sumun chŏn* [The tale of Hyŏn Sumun] (Seoul: Sin'gu sŏrim, 1922), National Library of Korea, Seoul, 3634-2-68(2), 41.

52. *Hyŏn Sumun chŏn*, 92.

53. The wars between the Jurchen Jin (1115–1234) and the Song dynasty (960–1279) resulted in the significant territorial losses for the Song; the weakened dynasty suffered its final defeat at the hands of the Mongols, who proclaimed the Yuan dynasty (1271–1368).

54. *Hyŏn Sumun chŏn*, 101.

55. *Hyŏn Sumun chŏn*, 112.

56. Chu Hyŏngye remarks that *The Tale of Hyŏn Sumun* is simply an amalgamation of established genre forms, strung together through the matrix of constant barrier taking, typical of the marital novel ("Tongyang mun'go bon *Hyŏn Sumun chŏn*," 233).

57. See Chu Sumin, "*Hyŏn Sumun chŏn* ŭi ch'angjak pangsik yŏn'gu," 152, 173.

58. Another curious reference to elite genres is made in a eulogy that Hyŏn Sumun offers at the grave of his benefactor and father-in-law, Master Sŏk. The text of the eulogy includes the habitual formulaic expressions, such as "As it comes to pass (*yusech'a* 維歳次)" used in the opening lines, or expressions of sorrow, such as "Woe! (*hot'ongjae* 呼痛哉)" (*Hyŏn Sumun chŏn*, 53). The diction in this section uses significantly Sinographic loan words than the rest of the text.

59. Along similar lines, Chu Hyŏngye suggests that Hyŏn Sumun is a lone figure who always needs to make an independent choice about the direction of his life ("Tongyang mun'go bon *Hyŏn Sumun chŏn*," 241–42).

60. Chu Sumin notes that there is hardly ever such vast variation between different editions of a single work, even when the number of extant editions is significantly higher than that of *The Tale of Hyŏn Sumun* ("Han'gŭl kososŏl ibon hwaksan ŭi il kyŏnghyang," 102).

61. In a study that looks at Chosŏn novels set in the Yuan and Qing dynasties, traditionally considered barbaric in Chosŏn Korea, Chu Sumin notes that these works are in fact outliers, representing nonstandard literary tastes and illuminating the fact that although attitudes toward the Qing in particular started to become more positive during the late Chosŏn, these attitudes did not constitute a majority opinion. See Chu Sumin, "Kojŏn sosŏl e nat'anan Chungguk insik yŏn'gu: Wŏn Ch'ŏng paegyŏng chakp'um chungsim ŭro" [Attitudes toward China reflected in traditional Korean novels, focused on the texts set in the Yuan and Qing dynasties], PhD diss., Academy of Korean Studies, 2016, 178–81.

62. Andre Schmid, *Korea Between Empires, 1895–1919* (New York: Columbia University Press, 2002), 23–54; Jun Uchida, *Brokers of Empire: Japanese Settler Colonialism in Korea, 1876–1945* (Cambridge, MA: Harvard University Asia Center, 2011), 188–226.

63. Ch'oe Namsŏn, "Chosŏn ŭi kajŏng munhak" [Domestic fiction in Chosŏn], in *Yuktang chŏnjip* [The complete anthology of Yuktang], 15 vols., ed. Asea munje yŏn'guso (Seoul: Hyŏn'amsa, 1973–1975), 9:429–44.

64. Ch'oe Namsŏn, "Chosŏn kajŏng munhak," 9:441. Although Chinese historical romances were read by elite women of Chosŏn, it does not appear that *Dream of the Red Chamber* reached wide female audiences outside the palace.

65. On the aesthetic program of *Munjang* magazine, see Janet Poole, *When the Future Disappears: The Modernist Imagination in Late Colonial Korea* (New York: Columbia University Press, 2014), 85–113. I discuss Yi Pyŏnggi's interest in elite vernacular Korean culture in "Vernacular Itineraries: Korean Letters from Family to National Archive," *Journal of Korean Studies* 24, no. 2 (2019): 356–58.

66. Yi Pyŏnggi, "Chosŏn munhŏn myŏngjak haeje" [Overview of the Chosŏn-dynasty literary masterpieces], *Munjang* 8 (1940): 230. Hong T'aekchu's identity remains unclear, but Yi Pyŏnggi also mentions this name on the pages of his diary in conjunction with book borrowing. These entries appear under the dates October 4, 1940, February 16, 1942, and December 11, 1944 (Yi Pyŏnggi, *Karam ilgi* [The diary of Karam], 2 vols. [Seoul: Sin'gu munhwasa, 1976], 2:516, 531, 551).

67. Yi Pyŏnggi and Paek Ch'ŏl, *Kungmunhak chŏnsa* [The complete history of national literature] (Seoul: Sin'gu munhwasa, 1957), 182.

68. See Pak Myŏnguk, Chŏng Hayŏn, Pang Kŏnch'un, Shinohara Hirokata, Yi Chaejŏng, Ko Ŭnsuk, Ŏm T'aeyong, and Im Chŏngyŏn, eds., *Kongjyu kŭlsi tyŏkŭsini: Tŏkon kongju chipan samdae han'gŭl yusan* [Handwriting of a princess: Vernacular Korean heritage in the three generations of Princess Tŏkon's family] (Seoul: National Hangeul Museum, 2019). I thank Professor Pak Chŏngsuk for alerting me to the familial legacy of vernacular Korean learning in Yun Paekyŏng's immediate family.

69. For a study of Yun Paekyŏng's calligraphic practice, see Pak Chŏngsuk, "Sahudang Yun Paekyŏng ŭi ŏpchŏk mit han'gŭl sŏye chakp'um t'ŭkching punsŏk" [The analysis of Sahudang Yun Paekyŏng's work and calligraphy], *Kuhyŏng kyoyuk* 61 (2017): 85–115.

70. Yi Chongsik, "T'ongdokcha Yun Paekyŏng yŏsa ka mal hanŭn kŭ naeryŏk kwa ilhwa tŭl—Naksŏnjae mun'go wa pansegi" [Recollections of an avid reader, Madame Yun Paekyŏng—half a century at the Naksŏn Library], *Chungang ilbo*, August 25, 1966.

71. Yun Paekyŏng, for instance, records the names of the palace ladies who created the manuscript of *The Remarkable Reunion of Pearls and Jade*, which is contained at the Yeungnam University in Taegu. See Kim Chinse, "*Myŏngju ogyŏn kihap rok ko*" [Overview of *The remarkable reunion of pearls and jade*], *Kwan'ak ŏmun yŏn'gu* 12 (1987): 1–19.

72. "Yŏgi san in'gan munhwajae: 77 se halmŏni ka Chungguksa pŏnyŏk p'yŏnch'an" [The cultural treasure living here: A 77-year-old granny compiles the translation of Chinese history], *Sŏul sinmun*, May 8, 1964, in *Kongjyu kŭlsi tyŏkŭsini*, ed. Pak Myŏnguk et al., 149.

73. Also known by her courtesy name, Sahudang, Yun Paekyŏng left a total of ten handwritten prefaces that are now bound into the novels located at the Jangseogak Archive. For the most part, the prefaces summarize the novels' content, make note of the sequel relations between different novels, and remark on the texts' alternative titles. The prefaces were written in 1970 and 1971, when Yun Paekyŏng was eighty-three or eighty-four years old. See Hong Hyŏnsŏng, "Sahudang i namgin Naksŏnjae bon sosŏl haeje ŭi charyo

chŏk sŏnggyŏk" [The character of Yun Paekyŏng's annotations to Naksŏn Library novels], *Changsŏgak* 32 (2014): 207–9.

74. Chŏng Pyŏnguk notes that Yi Haech'ŏng was the illegitimate son (*saja* 私子) of Yi Kiyong (1889–1961). Yi Kiyong's grandfather, Yi Ch'angŭng (1809–1828), was the oldest brother of Yi Haŭng, known as Hŭngsŏn T'aewŏn'gun (1820–1898), father and regent (r. 1863–1873) to King Kojong (r. 1863–1897) and a powerful political figure in late nineteenth-century Korea. See Chŏng Pyŏnguk, "Aksŏnjae [*sic*] mun'go" [The Aksŏn Library], *Chungang ilbo*, August 27, 1966. In a later retelling of the story, Kim Chinse writes that Yi Haech'ŏng was the direct fourth-generation descendant of Hŭngsŏn T'aewŏn'gun. See Kim Chinse, "Naksŏnjae bon sosŏl ŭi t'ŭksŏng" [The distinctive features of the Naksŏn Library novels], *Chsŏngsin munhwa yŏn'gu* 44 (1991): 3–20.

75. Chŏng Pyŏnguk, "Aksŏnjae mun'go."

76. Chŏng Pyŏnguk, "Naksŏnjae mun'go esŏ ŏdŭn charyo" [Materials discovered at the Naksŏn Library], *Tonga ilbo*, August 30, 1966.

77. Chŏng Pyŏngsŏl usefully reminds us that the Naksŏn Pavilion did not serve as a royal library per se. It was simply a residence for the female members of the royal family (*Chosŏn sidae sosŏl ŭi saengsan kwa yut'ong*, 156). The title "Naksŏn Library" (Naksŏnjae mun'go, Naksŏnjae bon sosŏl) has to be understood to designate a collection of books rather than a physical space for reading.

78. Yi Pyŏngju, "Oegoktoen sinpalgul" [Crooked discovery], *Kyŏnghyang sinmun*, September 5, 1966.

79. See Kim Wŏn, "The Race to Appropriate 'Koreanness': National Restoration, Internal Development, and Traces of Popular Culture," in *The Cultures of Yushin*, ed. Youngju Ryu (Ann Arbor: University of Michigan Press, 2018), 22–23.

80. Youngju Ryu, introduction to *The Cultures of Yushin*, ed. Ryu, 14.

81. Hwisang Cho, "[De]popularizing a Confucian Master: Yushin and the Birth of T'oegye Studies," in *The Cultures of Yushin*, ed. Ryu, 60.

82. Ryu, introduction to *The Cultures of Yushin*, 13.

83. Chŏng Pyŏnguk, "Naksŏnjae mun'go mongnok mit haeje rŭl naemyŏnsŏ" [Toward an annotated catalog of the Naksŏn Library], *Kug'ŏ kungmunhak* 44 (1969): 2–65.

84. Chŏng Pyŏnguk, "Kungmunhak yŏksa ka pakkwinda" [Revolution in the history of national literature], *Chungang ilbo*, August 22, 1966.

85. Yi T'aejun, *Eastern Sentiments*, trans. Janet Poole (New York: Columbia University Press, 2009), 61; also see 59–63.

86. Chŏng Pyŏnguk also revisits these qualities of the lineage novel in his later article "Yijo malgi sosŏl ŭi yuhyŏng chŏk t'ŭkching" [Structural characteristics of the late Chosŏn novel], *Munhwa pip'yŏng* 1 (1969): 30–60.

87. Chizhova, "Vernacular Itineraries," 358–59.

88. Cho Hŭiung, "Naksŏnjae bon pŏnyŏk sosŏl yŏn'gu" [A study of translated novels of the Naksŏn collection], *Kug'ŏ kungmunhak* 62–63 (1973): 257–73.

89. Kim Chinse, "Naksŏnjae bon sosŏl ŭi kukchŏk munje" [The problem of origin of the Naksŏn library novels], in *Han'guk munhaksa ŭi chaengjŏm* [Issues in Korean literary history], ed. Memorial Publication Committee for Sŏngsan Chang Tŏksun's Retirement (Seoul: Chimmundang, 1986), 361–67.

90. Yi Sangt'aek, "Chosŏn taeha sosŏl ŭi chakchach'ŭng e taehan yŏn'gu" [Study of the social background of the Korean lineage novels' authors], *Kojŏn munhak yŏn'gu* 3 (1986): 236.

91. Im Hyŏngt'aek, "17 segi kyubang sosŏl ŭi sŏngnip kwa *Ch'angsŏn kamŭi rok*" [*The praise of goodness and the admiration of righteousness* and the rise of the boudoir novel in the seventeenth century], *Tongbang hakchi* 57 (1988): 103–76.

92. See Chŏng Ch'anggwŏn, "Kungmun changp'yŏn sosŏl kwa yŏsŏng" [Vernacular lineage novels and women], *Han'gukhak yŏn'gu* 16 (2002): 202–10.

93. Im Ch'igyun, "Chosŏn hugi sosŏl ŭi chŏn'gae wa yŏsŏng ŭi yŏkhal" [The proliferation of the novel in the late Chosŏn and the role of women], in *Han'guk sŏsa munhaksa ŭi yŏn'gu* [History of Korean fictional prose literature], ed. Sa Chaedong (Seoul: Chungang munhaksa, 1995), 1591–610.

94. Chŏng Pyŏngsŏl [Jung Byung Sul], *Wanwŏl hoemaeng yŏn yŏn'gu* [A study of *The pledge at the banquet of moon-gazing pavilion*] (Seoul: T'aehaksa, 1998); Chŏng Pyŏngsŏl [Jung Byung Sul], "*Ogwŏn chaehap kiyŏn* chakka chaeron: Chosŏn hugi yŏsŏng sosŏlga ŭi han kŏn'ye" [Reconsidering the authorship of *The remarkable reunion of jade mandarin ducks*: The case of one late Chosŏn female author], *Kwan'ak ŏmunhak yŏn'gu* 22 (1997): 317–32.

95. Pak Yŏnghŭi, "Changp'yŏn kamun sosŏl ŭi hyangyu chiptan yŏn'gu" [Readership of the lineage novel], in *Munhak kwa sahoe chipdan* [Literature and society], ed. Han'guk kojŏn munhakhoe (Seoul: Chimmundang, 1995), 319–62.

96. See Henry Em, "Minjok as a Modern and Democratic Construct: Sin Ch'aeho's Historiography," in *Colonial Modernity in Korea*, ed. Gi-Wook Shin and Michael Robinson (Cambridge, MA: Harvard University Asia Center, 1999), 336–62.

97. See Chŏng Ch'anggwŏn, "Kungmun changp'yŏn sosŏl kwa yŏsŏng."

98. Other *kisaeng* figures include Sŏnhyŏng's mother, described as a striking beauty; Yŏngch'ae's bosom friend Wŏlhyang, who figures prominently in Yŏngch'ae's memories; and the young *kisaengs* in P'yŏngyang, whom Hyŏngsik encounters in the second half of the novel.

99. Yi Kwangsu, *Parojapŭn* Mujŏng [*The heartless*: A corrected edition], ed. Kim Ch'ol (P'aju: Munhak tongne, 2004), 171; Yi Kwangsu, *Yi Kwangsu and Modern Korean Literature*: Mujŏng, trans. and ed. Ann Sung-hi Lee (Ithaca, NY:

Cornell University Press, 2005), 131. I use Lee's translation and indicate my modifications.

100. Yi Kwangsu, *Parojapŭn* Mujŏng, 63; Yi Kwangsu, *Yi Kwangsu*, 90.

101. Described from the perspective of the numerous female entertainers in the novel, the world is full of men "with money and lust" (Yi Kwangsu, *Parojapŭn* Mujŏng, 206; Yi Kwangsu, *Yi Kwangsu*, 145).

102. Ann Sung-hi Lee translates *todŏk kwa illyun* as "morality and ethics" (Yi Kwangsu, *Yi Kwangsu*, 101).

103. On the convergence of cosmopolitanism and national biopolitics in Yi Kwangsu, see Travis Workman, *Imperial Genus: The Formation and Limits of the Human in Modern Korea and Japan* (Oakland: University of California Press, 2016), 62–96.

104. Choi, "Memories of Korean Modernity," 661.

105. For the characterization of the novel's affect as "heterotopic," see Choi, "Memories of Korean Modernity," 663 n. 10.

106. Yi Kwangsu, "Tananhan pansaeng ŭi tojŏng" [A journey through hardships, half-life long], in *Yi Kwangsu chŏnjip* [The complete anthology of Yi Kwangsu], 10 vols. (Seoul: Samjongdang, 1963), 8:452. Ellie Choi calls these lingering affects "northerly memories" of Yi Kwangsu's hometown P'yŏngyang, "covered over by the veil of capitalist modernity" ("Memories of Korean Modernity," 680).

107. Ryu Suyŏn, "'Yŏngch'ae chŏn,' kyemong chŏk yŏljŏng kwa pongintoen yukch'e" ["The tale of Yŏngch'ae," enlightened passions and contained carnality], *Hyŏndae sosŏl yŏn'gu* 34 (2007): 7–21.

108. Yi Kwangsu, "Tananhan pansaeng ŭi tojŏng," 8:445.

References

Abu-Lughod, Lila. *Veiled Sentiments: Honor and Poetry in a Bedouin Society*. Berkeley: University of California Press, 1999.

An Tŭkyong. "16 segi huban–17 segi chŏnban pijimun ŭi chŏnbŏm kwa sosul yangsang e taehan koch'al" [The form and narrative style of commemorative writing in the late sixteenth and early seventeenth centuries]. *Han'guk munhak yŏn'gu* 39 (2007): 223–59.

Armstrong, Nancy. *Desire and Domestic Fiction: A Political History of the Novel*. Oxford: Oxford University Press, 1987.

——. *How Novels Think: The Limits of British Individualism from 1719–1900*. New York: Columbia University Press, 2005.

Auerbach, Erich. *Mimesis: The Representation of Reality in Western Literature*. Princeton, NJ: Princeton University Press, 1953.

Bakhtin, Mikhail. *The Dialogic Imagination: Four Essays*. Edited by Michael Holquist. Translated by Caryl Emerson and Michael Holquist. Austin: University of Texas Press, 1981.

Baldanza, Kathleen. "De-civilizing Ming China's Southern Border: Vietnam as Lost Province or Barbarian Culture." In *Chinese History in Geographical Perspective*, edited by Jeff Kyong-McClain and Yongtao Du, 55–70. Lanham, MD: Lexington, 2013.

Barlow, Tani. "Introduction: On Colonial Modernity." In *Formations of Colonial Modernity in East Asia*, edited by Tani Barlow, 1–20. Durham, NC: Duke University Press, 1997.

Berlant, Lauren. *Cruel Optimism*. Durham, NC: Duke University Press, 2011.

———. *The Female Complaint: The Unfinished Business of Sentimentality in American Culture*. Durham, NC: Duke University Press, 2008.

———. "Intimacy: A Special Issue." *Critical Inquiry* 24, no. 2 (1998): 281–88.

Bray, Francesca. *Technology and Gender: Fabrics of Power in Late Imperial China*. Berkeley: University of California Press, 1997.

Brindley, Erica. "Barbarians or Not? Ethnicity and Changing Conceptions of the Ancient Yue (Viet) Peoples ca. 400–50 BCE." *Asia Major* 16, no. 1 (2003): 1–32.

Brook, Timothy. *The Confusions of Pleasure: Commerce and Culture in Ming China*. Berkeley: University of California Press, 1999.

Butler, Judith. *The Psychic Life of Power. Theories in Subjection*. Stanford, CA: Stanford University Press, 1997.

Butler, Judith, and William Connolly. "Politics, Power, and Ethics: A Discussion Between Judith Butler and William Connolly." *Theory and Event* 4, no. 2 (2000). Project Muse, https://muse.jhu.edu/article/32589.

Ch'a Changsŏp. "Chosŏn sidae chokpo ŭi yuhyŏng kwa t'ŭkching" [The form and characteristics of genealogies in the late Chosŏn dynasty]. *Yŏksa kyoyuk nonjip* 44 (2010): 239–78.

Ch'a Mihŭi, Kang Sŏngsuk, Kim Kyŏngmi, Yi Kyŏngha, Cho Hyeran, Hwang Suyŏn, Sŏ Kyŏnghŭi, Kim Hyŏnmi, Kim Kirim, and Hong Hakhŭi, eds. *19 segi–20 segi ch'o yŏsŏng saenghwalsa charyo chip* [Sources on the lives of women between the nineteenth and early twentieth centuries]. 9 vols. Seoul: Pogosa, 2013.

Chan, Timothy. "Beyond Border and Boudoir: The Frontier in the Poetry of the Four Elites of Early Tang." In *Reading Medieval Chinese Poetry: Text, Context, and Culture*, edited by Paul W. Kroll, 130–68. Leiden: Brill, 2015.

Chang Sigwang. "Kojŏn taeha sosŏl ŭi kanggan mot'ip'ŭ yŏn'gu" [A study of the rape motif in lineage novels]. *Kug'ŏ kungmunhak* 170 (2015): 353–89.

Chizhova, Ksenia. "3. Korean." In *How Literatures Begin*, edited by Joel Lande and Denis Feeney. Princeton, NJ: Princeton University Press, forthcoming.

———. "Vernacular Itineraries: Korean Letters from Family to National Archive." *Journal of Korean Studies* 24, no. 2 (2019): 345–71.

Cho Chaehyŏn. "*Sammun kyuhap rok* yŏn'gu" [Study of *The record of three households' marriages*]. *Ŏmun yŏn'gu* 152 (2011): 211–37.

Cho Hŭiung. *Kojŏn sosŏl ibon mongnok* [Catalog of extant editions of traditional novels]. Seoul: Chimmundang, 1999.

———. "Naksŏnjae bon pŏnyŏk sosŏl yŏn'gu" [A study of translated novels of the Naksŏn Collection]. *Kug'ŏ kungmunhak* 62–63 (1973): 257–73.

Cho, Hwisang. "[De]popularizing a Confucian Master: Yushin and the Birth of T'oegye Studies." In *The Cultures of Yushin*, edited by Youngju Ryu, 59–88. Ann Arbor: University of Michigan Press, 2018.

——. "Feeling Power in Chosŏn Korea: Popular Grievances, Royal Rage, and the Problem of Human Sentiments." *Journal of Korean Studies* 20, no. 1 (2015): 7–32.

Cho Hyeran. "Kososŏl e nat'anan namsŏng seksyuŏllit'i ŭi chaehyŏn yangsang" [Reproduction of male sexuality in the traditional Korean novel]. *Kososŏl yŏn'gu* 20 (2005): 381–411.

Ch'oe Hyŏn chŏn [The tale of Ch'oe Hyŏn]. National Library of Korea, Seoul. Kojo 48-134.

Ch'oe Kilyong. *Chosŏn cho yŏnjak sosŏl yŏn'gu* [Study of Chosŏn-dynasty sequel novels]. Seoul: Asea munhwasa, 1992.

——. "Kososŏl e nat'ananŭn aenghyŏl hwaso ŭi sŏsa silsang kwa ŭimi" [The motif of nightingale blood in the traditional Korean novel]. *Kososŏl yŏn'gu* 29 (2010): 41–84.

Ch'oe Namsŏn. "Chosŏn ŭi kajŏng munhak" [Domestic fiction in Chosŏn]. In *Yuktang chŏnjip* [The complete anthology of Yuktang], 15 vols., edited by Asea munje yŏn'guso, 9:429–44. Seoul: Hyŏn'amsa, 1973–1975.

Ch'oe Suhyŏn. "*Myŏngju kibong* ibon yŏn'gu" [A study of various editions of *The remarkable encounter of pearls*]. *Han'guk kojŏn yŏn'gu* 32 (2015): 569–602.

Ch'oe Suhyŏn and Hŏ Sunu, trans. *So Hyŏnsŏng rok* [The record of So Hyŏnsŏng]. 4 vols. Seoul: Somyŏng ch'ulp'an, 2010.

Ch'oe Yongch'ŏl. Honglumong *ŭi chŏnp'a wa pŏn'yŏk* [The circulation and translation of *The dream of the red chamber* in Chosŏn Korea]. Seoul: Sinsŏwŏn, 2007.

Ch'oe, Yŏngho, trans. "King Sejong: Preface to *Correct Sounds to Instruct the People*." In *Sourcebook of Korean Civilization*, 2 vols., edited by Peter H. Lee, 1:295. New York: Columbia University Press, 1993.

Ch'oe Yŏngsŏng. *Han'guk yuhak sasangsa: Chosŏn hugi p'yŏn sang* [The intellectual history of Korean Confucian scholarship: The late Chosŏn]. Seoul: Asea munhwasa, 1995.

Choi, Ellie. "Memories of Korean Modernity: Yi Kwangsu's *The Heartless* and New Perspectives in Colonial Alterity." *Journal of Asian Studies* 77, no. 3 (2018): 659–91.

Ch'oi Yunhŭi. "*Ssangmi kibong* pŏn'an yangsang yŏn'gu" [Study of the adaptation manner of *The remarkable encounter of two beauties*]. *Kososŏl yŏn'gu* 11 (2001): 265–92.

Ch'ŏn Chŏnghwan. *Kŭndae ŭi ch'aek ilkki: Tokcha ŭi t'ansaeng kwa Han'guk kŭndae munhak* [Reading the books of modernity: The birth of readers and modern Korean literature]. Seoul: P'urŭn yŏksa, 2014.

Chŏn Sanguk. "Hyangmoktong sech'aek ŭi taech'ul changbu e taehan koch'al" [Overview of the rosters of rental library borrowers in the Hyangmoktong area]. *Yŏlsang kojŏn yŏn'gu* 37 (2013): 535–63.

———. "Sech'aek taech'ulja ŭi t'ŭksŏng e taehan yŏn'gu: Tongyang mungo bon taech'ul changbu rŭl chungsim ŭro" [Rental libraries' readers: Rental rosters from the Tōyō bunko manuscripts]. *Kososŏl yŏn'gu* 26 (2008): 239–74.

Chŏn Sŏngun. *Chosŏn hugi changp'yŏn kungmun sosŏl ŭi chomang* [Overview of the vernacular Korean lineage novel in the late Chosŏn dynasty]. Seoul: Pogosa, 2002.

Chŏng Ch'anggwŏn. "Kungmun changp'yŏn sosŏl kwa yŏsŏng" [Vernacular lineage novels and women]. *Han'gukhak yŏn'gu* 16 (2002): 193–213.

Chŏng Chongno. *Ipchae chip* [The Ipchae anthology]. http://db.itkc.or.kr.

Chŏng Hyŏngji, Kim Kyŏngmi, Hwang Suyŏn, Kim Kirim, Cho Hyeran, and Yi Hyŏngha, eds. *17 segi yŏsŏng saenghwalsa charyo chip* [Sources on the lives of women in the seventeenth century]. 4 vols. Seoul: Pogosa, 2006.

Chŏng Kyubok. "*Cheil kiŏn* e taehayŏ" [Observations on *The book of books in the vernacular*]. *Chunggukhak nonch'ong* 1 (1984): 73–100.

Chŏng Myŏnggi. "Sech'aekbon sosŏl e taehan sae charyo ŭi sŏnggyŏk yŏn'gu: *Ŏnmun Hu saeng rok* sojae mongnok ŭl chungsim ŭro" [New discoveries in the studies of rental novels: Book catalog in *The vernacular record of Master Hu*]. *Kososŏl yŏn'gu* 19 (2005): 227–54.

———. "Sech'aekbon sosŏl ŭi yut'ong yangsang: Tongyang mun'go sojang sech'aekbon sosŏl e nat'anan sech'aek changbu rŭl chungsim ŭro" [Circulation of rental novels: Rental rosters recorded in rental novels in the Tōyō bunko collection]. *Kososŏl yŏn'gu* 16 (2003): 71–99.

———. "'Sech'aek p'ilsabon kososŏl' e taehan sŏsŏl chŏk ihae: Ch'ongnyang, kanso (kan'gi), yut'ong yangsang ŭl chungsim ŭro" [Introductory remarks on "the rental manuscript editions of traditional novels": Total volume of works, places of their production (production records), and mode of circulation]. *Kososŏl yŏn'gu* 12 (2001): 445–80.

Chŏng Okkŭn. "*Jinpingmei* zai Chaoxian chao de chuanbo yiji Chaoxian shidafu dui *Jinpingmei* de jihui" [Circulation of *The plum in the golden vase* in Chosŏn and the criticism of this text by Chosŏn literati]. *Chungguk munje yŏn'gu* 10 (1998): 149–56.

Chŏng Poktong. "Osukche Song Ikhŭm ŏn'gan sŏch'e ŭi hyŏngsŏng kwa chohyŏngsŏng koch'al" [The formation and style of Osukche Song Ikhŭm's calligraphy in his vernacular Korean letters]. *Sŏyehak yŏn'gu* 22 (2013): 134–68.

Chŏng Pyŏngsŏl [Jung Byung Sul]. "Changp'yŏn taeha sosŏl kwa kajoksa sosŏl ŭi yŏn'gwan mit kŭ ŭimi—kojŏn sosŏl ŭi ch'angjak sigi wa ch'angjak kwajŏng e taehan kasŏl" [The generic connections between the lineage novel and family tales: Hypothesis on the period and process of composition of traditional novels]. *Kojŏn munhak yŏn'gu* 12 (1997): 221–48.

———. "Chosŏn hugi changp'yŏn sosŏlsa ŭi chŏn'gae" [The historical development of the lineage novel in the late Chosŏn]. In *Han'guk kojŏn sosŏl kwa sŏsa munhak* [The traditional Korean novel and fictional prose], 245–63. Seoul: Chimmundang, 1998.

——. "Chosŏn hugi han'gŭl sosŏl ŭi sŏngjang kwa yut'ong: Sech'aek kwa panggakbon chungsim ŭro" [The rise and circulation of vernacular Korean novels in the late Chosŏn: Rental and woodblock editions]. *Kug'ŏ kungmunhak* 100 (2005): 263–97.

——. "Chosŏn hugi insoae ŭi paljŏn, sŏjŏk ŭi pogŭp kŭrigo Sirhak chisik ŭi sot'ong: Chosŏn hugi han'gŭl panggak sosŏl ŭi chŏn'guk chŏk yu'tong kanŭngsŏng e taehayŏ" [Development of printing in the late Chosŏn, dissemination of books, and circulation of Sirhak knowledge: On the possibility of country-wide circulation of woodblock print novels]. *Tasan kwa hyŏndae* 3 (2010): 115–33.

——. *Chosŏn sidae sosŏl ŭi saengsan kwa yut'ong* [The production and circulation of novels in Chosŏn]. Seoul: Seoul National University Press, 2016.

——. "*Ogwŏn chaehap kiyŏn* chakka chaeron: Chosŏn hugi yŏsŏng sosŏlga ŭi han kŏn'ye" [Reconsidering the authorship of *The remarkable reunion of jade mandarin ducks*: The case of one late Chosŏn female author]. *Kwan'ak ŏmunhak yŏn'gu* 22 (1997): 317–32.

——. "Sech'aek sosŏl yŏn'gu ŭi chaengjŏm kwa panghyang" [Problems and directions in the study of rental library novels]. *Kungmunhak yŏn'gu* 10 (2003): 27–57.

——. *Wanwŏl hoemaeng yŏn yŏn'gu* [A study of *The pledge at the banquet of moongazing pavilion*]. Seoul: T'aehaksa, 1998.

Chŏng Pyŏnguk. "Aksŏnjae [*sic*] mun'go" [The Aksŏn Library]. *Chungang ilbo*, August 27, 1966.

——. "Kungmunhak yŏksa ka pakkwinda" [Revolution in the history of national literature]. *Chungang ilbo*, August 22, 1966.

——. "Naksŏnjae mun'go esŏ ŏdŭn charyo" [Materials discovered at the Naksŏn Library]. *Tonga ilbo*, August 30, 1966.

——. "Naksŏnjae mun'go mongnok mit haeje rŭl naemyŏnsŏ" [Toward an annotated catalog of the Naksŏn Library]. *Kug'ŏ kungmunhak* 44 (1969): 2–65.

——. "Yijo malgi sosŏl ŭi yuhyŏng chŏk t'ŭkching" [Structural characteristics of the late Chosŏn novel]. *Munhwa pip'yŏng* 1 (1969): 30–60.

Chŏng Taham. "Yŏmal Sŏnch'o ŭi Tongasia chilsŏ wa Chosŏn eso ŭi han'ŏ, hansamun, hunmin chŏngŭm" [The East Asian world order, the literary Chinese culture, and vernacular Korean during the late Koryŏ and early Chosŏn]. *Han'guksa hakpo* 36 (2009): 269–305.

Chosŏn wangjo sillok [Veritable records of the Chosŏn dynasty]. http://sillok.history .go.kr.

Chu Hyŏngye. "Tongyang mun'go bon *Hyŏn Sumun chŏn* ŭi sŏsa chŏk t'ukching kwa ŭimi" [The narrative characteristics of the Tōyō bunko edition of *The tale of Hyŏn Sumun*]. *Yŏlsang kojŏn yŏn'gu* 15 (2002): 221–49.

Chu Sumin. "Han'gŭl kososŏl ibon hwaksan ŭi il kyŏnghyang kwa kŭ ŭimi—*Hyŏn Sumun chŏn* chungsim ŭro" [The proliferation of different versions of traditional Korean novels: The case of *The tale of Hyŏn Sumun*]. *Kososŏl yŏn'gu* 42 (2016): 83–109.

——. "*Hyŏn Sumun chŏn* ibon yŏn'gu" [A study of different editions of *The tale of Hyŏn Sumun*]. *Chŏngsin munhwa yŏn'gu* 37, no. 1 (2014): 227–56.

——. "*Hyŏn Sumun chŏn* ŭi ch'angjak pangsik yŏn'gu: Taejangp'yŏn sosŏl *Hyŏn ssi yangung ssangnin ki* wa ŭi kwan'gye chungsim ŭro" [The composition of *The tale of Hyŏn Sumun*: Its relationship with a lineage novel, *The record of two heroes: Brothers Hyŏn*]. *Kojŏn kwa haesŏk* 17 (2014): 147–79.

——. "Kojŏn sosŏl e nat'anan Chungguk insik yŏn'gu: Wŏn Ch'ŏng paegyŏng chakp'um chungsim ŭro" [Attitudes toward China reflected in traditional Korean novels, focused on the texts set in the Yuan and Qing dynasties]. Ph.D. diss., Academy of Korean Studies, 2016.

Cole, Alan. *Mothers and Sons in Chinese Buddhism.* Stanford, CA: Stanford University Press, 1998.

Confucius. *The Analects.* In *The Life and Teaching of Confucius.* Translated by James Legge. London: N. Trübner, 1895.

Courant, Maurice. *Bibliographie coréenne: Tableau littéraire de la Corée, contenant la nomenclature des ouvrages publiés dans ce pays jusqu'en 1890 ainsi que la description et l'analyse détaillées des principaux d'entre ces ouvrages* [Korean bibliography: The catalog of Korean literature, containing the classification of works published in this country until 1890 as well as the detailed description and analysis of the main works]. Paris: Ernest Leroux, 1894.

De Bary, William Theodore. "Individualism and Humanism in Late Ming Thought." In *Self and Society in Ming Thought*, edited by William Theodore de Bary, 145–247. New York: Columbia University Press, 1970.

Deuchler, Martina. *The Confucian Transformation of Korea: A Study of Society and Ideology.* Cambridge, MA: Harvard University Asia Center, 1992.

——. "Despoilers of the Way, Insulters of the Sages: Controversies Over the Classics in Seventeenth-Century Korea." In *Culture and the State in Late Chosŏn Korea*, edited by Martina Deuchler and JaHyun Kim Haboush, 91–133. Cambridge, MA: Harvard University Asia Center, 1999.

——. *Under the Ancestors' Eyes: Kinship, Status, and Locality in Premodern Korea.* Cambridge, MA: Harvard University Asia Center, 2015.

Di Cosmo, Nicola. *Ancient China and Its Enemies: The Rise of Nomadic Power in the East Asian History.* Cambridge: Cambridge University Press, 2002.

Elman, Benjamin. *On Their Own Terms: Science in China 1550–1900.* Cambridge, MA: Harvard University Press, 2009.

Em, Henry. "Minjok as a Modern and Democratic Construct: Sin Ch'aeho's Historiography." In *Colonial Modernity in Korea*, edited by Gi-Wook Shin and

Michael Robinson, 336–62. Cambridge, MA: Harvard University Asia Center, 1999.

Epstein, Maram. *Competing Discourses: Orthodoxy, Authenticity, and Engendered Meanings in Late Imperial Chinese Fiction.* Cambridge, MA: Harvard University Asia Center, 2001.

——. *Orthodox Passions: Narrating Filial Love During the High Qing.* Cambridge, MA: Harvard University Press, 2019.

Foucault, Michel. "Technologies of the Self." In *Ethics: Subjectivity and Truth,* vol. 1 of *The Essential Works of Michel Foucault, 1954–1984,* edited by Paul Rabinov, 16–49, 145–62. New York: New Press, 1997.

Fox, Robin. *Kinship and Marriage: An Anthropological Perspective.* Cambridge: Cambridge University Press, 1967.

Frank, Andre Gunder. *ReOrient: Global Economy in the Asian Age.* Berkeley: University of California Press, 1998.

Guillory, John. *Cultural Capital: The Problem of Literary Canon Formation.* Chicago: University of Chicago Press, 1993.

Ha Chin yangmun rok [The record of two households: Ha and Chin]. 25 vols. Tōyō bunko, Tokyo. VII-4-234.

Ha Sŏngnan. "*Chŏlhwa kidam* kwa *Kŭmpyŏngmae* ŭi kwallyŏn yangsang yŏn'gu" [Study of the relationship between *The remarkable story of a plucked flower* and *The plum in the golden vase*]. *Yŏlsang kojŏn yŏn'gu* 64 (2018): 253–87.

Haboush, JaHyun Kim. *The Confucian Kingship in Korea: Yŏngjo and the Politics of Sagacity.* New York: Columbia University Press, 2001.

——. "Constructing the Center: The Ritual Controversy and the Search for a New Identity in Seventeenth-Century Korea." In *Culture and the State in Late Chosŏn Korea,* edited by Martina Deuchler and JaHyun Kim Haboush, 46–90. Cambridge, MA: Harvard University Asia Center, 1999.

——, ed. *Epistolary Korea: Letters in the Communicative Space of the Choson, 1392–1910.* New York: Columbia University Press, 2009.

——. "Filial Emotions and Filial Values: Changing Patterns in the Discourse of Filiality in Late Chosŏn Korea." *Harvard Journal of Asiatic Studies* 55, no. 1 (1995): 129–77.

——. "Gender and the Politics of Language in Chosŏn Korea." In *Rethinking Confucianism: Past and Present in China, Korea, Japan, and Vietnam,* edited by Benjamin Elman, John B. Duncan, and Herman Ooms, 220–56. Asian Pacific Monograph series. Los Angeles: University of California, 2002.

——, trans. *Memoirs of Lady Hyegyŏng: The Autobiographical Writings of a Crown Princess of Eighteenth-Century Korea.* Berkeley: University of California Press, 2013.

——. "The Vanished Women of Korea: The Anonymity of Texts and the Historicity of Subjects." In *Servants of the Dynasty: Palace Women in World History,* edited by Ann Walthall, 280–98. Berkeley: University of California Press, 2008.

Haedong Yi ssi samdae rok [The record of the three generations of the Yi lineage from the East of the sea]. JaHyun Kim Haboush Archive, IDB002a. http://www .habousharchives.org.

Haedong Yi ssi samdae rok [The record of the three generations of the Yi lineage from the East of the sea]. JaHyun Kim Haboush Archive, IDB002b. http://www .habousharchives.org.

Han Kilyŏn. *Chosŏn siade taeha sosŏl ŭi tach'ŭng chŏk segye* [The multilayered world of the Chosŏn-dynasty lineage novel]. Seoul: Somyŏng ch'ulp'an, 2009.

——. "*Paek Kye yangmun sŏnhaeng rok* ŭi chakka wa kŭ chubyŏn: Chŏnju Yi ssi kamun yŏsŏng ŭi taehasosŏl ch'angjak kanŭngsŏng ŭl chungsim ŭro" [The author and the social context of *The record of good deeds of two households*: *Paek and Kye*: Women of the Chŏnju Yi lineage as potential authors of lineage novels]. *Kojŏn munhak yŏn'gu* 27 (2005): 329–61.

Han Myŏnggi. "17 segi ch'o ŭn ŭi yut'ong kwa kŭ yŏnghyang" [The circulation of silver in the seventeenth century and its ramifications]. *Kyujanggak* 15 (1992): 1–36.

Hanan, Patrick. *The Chinese Vernacular Story*. Cambridge, MA: Harvard University Press, 1981.

Harper, Donald. "The Sexual Arts of Ancient China as Described in a Manuscript of the Second Century B.C." *Harvard Journal of Asiatic Studies* 47, no. 2 (1987): 539–93.

Hay, John. "The Human Body as a Microcosmic Source of Macrocosmic Values in Calligraphy." In *Theory of the Arts in China*, edited by Susan Bush and Christian Murck, 74–102. Princeton, NJ: Princeton University Press, 1983.

Hevia, James. *Cherishing Men from Afar: Qing Guest Ritual and the Macartney Embassy of 1793*. Durham, NC: Duke University Press, 1995.

Hong Hŭibok. "*Cheil kiŏn sŏ*" [Preface to *The book of books in the vernacular*]. In *Cheil kiŏn* [Flowers in the mirror], edited by Pak Chaeyŏn and Chŏng Kyubok, 21–24. Seoul: Kukhak charyowŏn, 2001.

Hong Hyŏnsŏng. "Sahudang i namgin Naksŏnjae bon sosŏl haeje ŭi charyo chŏk sŏnggyŏk" [The character of Yun Paekyŏng's annotations to Naksŏn Library novels]. *Changsŏgak* 32 (2014): 198–224.

Hong Nagwŏn. *Sŏnbuin kajŏn* [Biography of my late mother]. Kyujanggak Archive, Seoul. Ko 813.5 Sy28.

Huang, Martin. *Desire and Fictional Narrative in Late Imperial China*. Cambridge, MA: Harvard University Press, 2001.

——. *Negotiating Masculinities in Late Imperial China*. Honolulu: University of Hawai'i Press, 2006.

Hwang Hŭi. "Suwŏn Paek ssi sebo" [Preface to the genealogy of Suwŏn Paeks]. In *Han'guk chokpo kubo sŏjip* [Collection of prefaces from the Korean genealogies], edited by Chŏng Pyŏngwan, 3–4. Seoul: Asea munhwasa, 1987.

Hwang Hyejin. "*Ssangmi kibong* e hyŏngsanghwatoen aejŏng ŭi yangsang kwa ŭimi yŏn'gu" [Figuration of love in *The remarkable encounter of two beauties* and its significance]. *Kojŏn munhak kwa kyoyuk* 8 (2004): 301–37.

Hwang, Kyung Moon. *Beyond Birth: Social Status in the Emergence of Modern Korea.* Cambridge, MA: Harvard University Press, 2004.

Hwang Suyŏn, Yi Kyŏngha, Kim Kyŏngmi, Kim Kirim, Kim Hyŏnmi, Cho Hyeran, Kang Sŏngsuk, Sŏ Kyŏnghŭi, and Kim Nam'i, eds. *18 segi yŏsŏng saengwalsa charyo chip* [Sources on the lives of women in the eighteenth century]. 8 vols. Seoul: Pogosa, 2010.

Hyŏn ssi yangung ssangnin ki [The record of two heroes: Brothers Hyŏn]. 10 vols. Jangseogak Archive, Songnam. K4^6862.

Hyŏn ssi yangung ssangnin ki [The record of two heroes: Brothers Hyŏn]. 2 vols. Seoul: Sŏngmunsa, 1979.

Hyŏn ssi yangung ssangnin ki [The record of two heroes: Brothers Hyŏn]. National Library of Korea, Seoul. Ko 3636-223.

Hyŏn Sumun chŏn [The tale of Hyŏn Sumun]. Seoul: Sin'gu sŏrim, 1922. National Library of Korea, Seoul. 3634-2-68.

Im Ch'igyun. "Chosŏn hugi sosŏl ŭi chŏn'gae wa yŏsŏng ŭi yŏkhal" [The proliferation of the novel in the late Chosŏn and the role of women]. In *Han'guk sŏsa munhaksa ŭi yŏngu* [History of Korean fictional prose literature], edited by Sa Chaedong, 1591–610. Seoul: Chungang munhaksa, 1995.

——. *Chosŏn sidae taejangp'yŏn sosŏl yŏn'gu* [A study of the Chosŏn lineage novel]. Seoul: T'aehaksa, 1996.

Im Hyŏngt'aek. "17 segi kyubang sosŏl ŭi sŏngnip kwa *Ch'angsŏn kamŭi rok*" [*The praise of goodness and the admiration of righteousness* and the rise of the boudoir novel in the seventeenth century]. *Tongbang hakchi* 57 (1988): 103–76.

——. "18–19 segi iyagikun kwa sosŏl ŭi paldal" [Storytellers and the development of the novel in the eighteenth to nineteenth centuries]. In *Kojŏn munhak ŭl chajasŏ* [In search for traditional Korean literature], edited by Kim Yŏlgyu, 310–32. Seoul: Munhak kwa chisŏngsa, 1976.

——. "Yŏhang munhak kwa sŏmin munhak" [Town literature and demotic literature]. In *Han'gukhak yŏn'gu immun* [Introduction to Korean studies], edited by Yi Kawŏn, 315–30. Seoul: Chisik sanŏpsa, 1981.

Ito, Ken. *An Age of Melodrama: Family, Gender, and Social Hierarchy in the Turn-of-the-Century Japanese Novel.* Stanford, CA: Stanford University Press, 2008.

Jackson, Reginald. *Textures of Mourning: Calligraphy, Mortality, and* The Tale of Genji *Scrolls.* Ann Arbor: University of Michigan Press, 2018.

Jameson, Frederic. *The Political Unconscious: Narrative as a Socially Symbolic Act.* Ithaca, NY: Cornell University Press, 1981.

Kallander, George. *Salvation Through Dissent: Tonghak Heterodoxy and Early Modern Korea.* Honolulu: Hawai'i University Press, 2013.

Kang Yŏngsim. "1900 nyŏndae Tongasia ŭi *Wŏllam mangguk sa* yut'ong kwa suyong: Han'guk, Chungguk, Wŏllam chungsim ŭro [Circulation of *The history of the loss of Vietnam* in the East Asia of the 1900s: The cases of Korea, China, and Vietnam]. *Ihwa sahak yŏn'gu* 49 (2014): 93–102.

Karatani, Kōjin. *The Origins of Modern Japanese Literature.* Translated by Brett de Bary. Durham, NC: Duke University Press, 1993.

Karl, Rebecca. *Staging the World: Chinese Nationalism at the Turn of the Twentieth Century.* Durham, NC: Duke University Press, 2002.

Keulemans, Paize. *Sound Rising from the Paper: Nineteenth-Century Martial Arts Fiction and the Chinese Acoustic Imagination.* Cambridge, MA: Harvard University Asia Center, 2014.

Kim Ch'anghyŏp. *Nongam chip* [The anthology of Nongam]. http://db.itkc.or.kr.

Kim Chinse. "*Myŏngju ogyŏn kihap rok* ko" [Overview of *The remarkable reunion of pearls and jade*]. *Kwan'ak ŏmun yŏn'gu* 12 (1987): 1–19.

——. "Naksŏnjae bon sosŏl ŭi kukchŏk munje" [The problem of origin of the Naksŏn Library novels]. In *Han'guk munhaksa ŭi chaengjŏm* [Issues in Korean literary history], edited by Memorial Publication Committee for Sŏngsan Chang Tŏksun's Retirement, 361–67. Seoul: Chimmundang, 1986.

——. "Naksŏnjae bon sosŏl ŭi t'ŭksŏng" [The distinctive features of the Naksŏn Library novels]. *Chsŏngsin munhwa yŏn'gu* 44 (1991): 3–20.

——, ed. *Wanwŏl hoemaeng yŏn* [The pledge at the banquet of moon-gazing pavilion]. 12 vols. Seoul: Seoul National University Press, 1986–1994.

——. "Yijo hugi taeha sosŏl yŏn'gu: *Wanwŏl hoemaeng yŏn* ŭi kyŏngu" [A study of late Chosŏn lineage novels: The case of *The pledge at the banquet of moon-gazing pavilion*]. In *Han'guk sosŏl munhak ŭi t'amgu* [Research in Korean fictional prose], edited by Han'guk kojŏn munhak yŏn'guhoe, 101–48. Seoul: Ilchogak, 1978.

Kim Chongch'ŏl. "*Ŏn'gandok* yŏn'gu—chakmun kyojae ŭi kwanjŏm esŏ" [A study of the *Vernacular letter manual* as composition primer]. *Kugŏ kyoyuk yŏn'gu* 25 (2015): 237–81.

Kim Hŭnggyu. *Chosŏn hugi* Sigyŏng *ron kwa si ŭisik* [The notion of poetry and the exegesis of *The Book of Poetry* in the late Chosŏn]. Seoul: Korea University, 1982.

Kim Hyogyŏng and Yu Ch'undong. *Saech'aek kwa panggakbon: Chosŏn sidae tŏksŏ yŏlp'ung kwa mannada* [Rental and woodblock novels: The reading trends of the Chosŏn dynasty]. Seoul: National Library of Korea, 2016.

Kim Ilgŭn. *Ŏn'gan ŭi yŏn'gu: Han'gŭl sŏgan ŭi yŏn'gu wa charyo chipsŏng* [A study of vernacular Korean letters: Analysis and collection of materials]. Seoul: Konkuk University Press, 1986.

Kim, Jisoo. *The Emotions of Justice: Gender, Status, and Legal Performance in Chosŏn Korea.* Seattle: University of Washington Press, 2015.

Kim, Jungwon. "Between Morality and Crime: Filial Daughters and Vengeful Violence in Eighteenth-Century Korea." *Acta Koreana* 21, no. 2 (2018): 481–502.

——. "'You Must Avenge on My Behalf': Widow Chastity and Honour in Nineteenth-Century Korea." *Gender & History* 26, no. 1 (2014): 128–46.

Kim Kidong, ed. *Ogwŏn chaehap kiyŏn* [The remarkable reunion of jade mandarin ducks]. Vols. 27–30 of *Kojŏn sosŏl chŏnjip* [The anthology of manuscript editions of classical Korean novels]. Seoul: Asea munhwasa, 1980.

——. *Yijo sidae sosŏl ron* [Theory of the Chosŏn-dynasty novel]. Seoul: Samusa, 1976.

Kim Kijin. "Taejung sosŏl ron" [The popular novel]. *Tonga ilbo*, 1929.

Kim Kyŏngmi. "*Kyŏnghwayŏn* ŭi pŏnyŏksŏ *Cheil kiŏn* ŭl t'onghae pon Hong Hŭibok ŭi pŏnyŏk insik" [The translator's outlook in Hong Hŭibok's *The Book of Books in the vernacular*, a translation of *Flowers in the mirror*]. *Han'guk kojŏn yŏn'gu* 32 (2015): 541–68.

Kim, Michael. "Literary Production, Circulating Libraries, and Private Publishing: The Popular Reception of Vernacular Fiction Texts in the Late Chosŏn Dynasty." *Journal of Korean Studies* 9, no. 1 (2004): 1–31.

Kim Mokhan, Kim Sŏnggyu, Nam Yunjin, Pak Puja, Pak Chinho, Yi Raeho, Yi Hyŏnju, Chŏng Sŭnghye, Chŏng Yunja, Chŏng Chaeyŏng, Hwang Munhwan, Hwang Sŏnyŏp, and Hong Ŭnjin, eds. *Changsŏgak han'gŭl charyo haeje* [Annotated catalog of vernacular Korean materials of the Jangseogak Archive]. Songnam: Academy of Korean Studies Press, 2000.

Kim Pongjwa. "Wangsil han'gŭl p'ilsabon ŭi chŏnsŭng hyŏnhwang kwa kach'i" [The transmission and value of royal vernacular manuscripts]. *Kug'ŏsa yŏn'gu* 20 (2015): 39–64.

Kim, Sun Joo. *Marginality and Subversion in Korea: The Hong Kyŏngnae Rebellion of 1812*. Seattle: University of Washington Press, 2007.

——. "My Own Flesh and Blood: Stratified Parental Compassion and Law in Korean Slavery." *Social History* 44, no. 1 (2019): 1–25.

——. *Voice from the North: Resurrecting Regional Identity Through the Life and Work of Yi Sihang (1672–1736)*. Stanford, CA: Stanford University Press, 2013.

Kim Tonguk. "Han'gŭl sosŏl panggakbon ŭi sŏngnip e taehayŏ" [The development of woodblock publishing of vernacular novels]. In *Hyangt'o Sŏul* [The city of Seoul], edited by Sŏul t'ŭkpyŏlsi sap'yŏnch'an wiwŏnhoe, 38–67. Seoul: Sŏul t'ŭkpyŏlsi sap'yŏnch'an wiwŏnhoe, 1960.

——. "The Influence of Chinese Stories and Novels on Korean Fiction." In *Literary Migrations: Traditional Chinese Fiction in Asia*, edited by Claudine Salmon, 52–57. Singapore: Institute of Southeast Asian Studies, 2013.

——. "Sŏuldae bon *Ogwŏn chaehap kiyŏn* sojae sosŏl mongnok e taehan koch'al" [Observations on the book list recorded in the Seoul National University manuscript of *The remarkable encounter of jade mandarin ducks*]. *Kojŏn munhak yŏn'gu* 47 (2015): 279–309.

——. "Yijo sosŏl ŭi chŏja wa tokcha e taehayŏ" [Readership and authorship of Chosŏn-dynasty novels]. In *Changam Chi Hŏnyŏng sŏnsaeng hwagap kinyŏm nonch'ong* [Papers offered to Changam Professor Chi Hŏnyŏng on his sixtieth anniversary], 39–57. Seoul: Hosŏ munhwasa, 1971.

Kim, Wŏn. "The Race to Appropriate 'Koreanness': National Restoration, Internal Development, and Traces of Poplular Culture." In *The Cultures of Yushin*, edited by Youngju Ryu, 21–58. Ann Arbor: University of Michigan Press, 2018.

Kim Yongsuk. *Chosŏnjo kungjung p'ungsok yŏn'gu* [Customs of the Chosŏn court]. Seoul: Ilchisa, 1987.

Kim-Renaud, Young-Key, ed. *Creative Women of Korea: The Fifteenth Through the Twentieth Centuries*. New York: M. E. Sharpe, 2004.

Ko, Dong-hwan. "The Characteristics of the Urban Development of Seoul During the Late Chosŏn Dynasty: With a Focus on the Changes in Urban Structure." *Seoul Journal of Korean Studies* 10 (1997): 95–123.

Ko, Dorothy. *Teachers of the Inner Chambers: Women and Culture in Seventeenth-Century China*. Stanford, CA: Stanford Unviersity Press, 1995.

——. "Thinking About Copulating: An Early-Qing Confucian Thinker's Problem with Emotion and Words." In *Remapping China: Fissures in Historical Terrain*, edited by Gail Hershatter, Emily Honig, Jonathan N. Lipman, and Randall Stross, 59–96. Stanford, CA: Stanford University Press, 1996.

Koons, E. W. "The House Where Books Are Given for Rent." *Korea Mission Field*, July 1918, 150.

Kwŏn Naehyŏn. "17 segi–18 segi chŏnban Chosŏn ŭi ŭn yut'ong" [Circulation of silver in Chosŏn between the late seventeenth and early eighteenth centuries]. *Yŏksa hakpo* 221 (2014): 3–31.

——. "17–19 segi Chosŏn ŭi chaesan sangsok kwanhaeng—chongbŏp kwa kyŏngjeryŏk pyŏndong ŭl chungsim ŭro" [The customs of property succession in Chosŏn in the seventeenth–nineteenth centuries—focusing on the agnatic principle and economic change]. *Han'guksa hakpo* 70 (2018): 283–315.

—— [Kwon Nae-Hyun]. "Chosŏn Korea's Trade with Qing China and the Circulation of Silver." *Acta Koreana* 18, no. 1 (2015): 163–85.

Kwŏn Podŭrae. *Han'guk kŭndae sosŏl ŭi kiwŏn* [The origins of the modern Korean novel]. Seoul: Somyŏng ch'ulp'an, 2012.

Kwŏn Sŏp. *Oksogo* [Writings of Okso]. 17 vols. Seoul: Taunsem, 2007.

Lam, Ling Hon. *The Spatiality of Emotion in Early Modern China: From Dreamscapes to Theatricality*. New York: Columbia University Press, 2018.

Lamarre, Thomas. *Uncovering Heian Japan: An Archaeology of Sensation and Inscription*. Durham, NC: Duke University Press, 2000.

Lawton, David. *Voice in Later Medieval English Literature: Public Interiorities.* Oxford: Oxford University Press, 2017.

Lee, Haiyan. *Revolution of the Heart: A Genealogy of Love in China, 1900–1950.* Stanford, CA: Stanford University Press, 2006.

Lee, Hui-shu. *Empresses, Art, & Agency in Song Dynasty China.* Seattle: University of Washington Press, 2010.

Lee, Janet. "Dilemma of the Lovesick Hero: Masculine Images and Politics of the Body in Seventeenth-Century Korean Love Tales." *Journal of Korean Studies* 21, no. 1 (2016): 45–69.

Legge, James, trans. *The Chinese Classics.* Vol. 4. Hong Kong: Hong Kong University Press, 1960.

——, trans. *Li Chi: The Book of Rites.* 2 vols. New York: New York University, 1966.

Levine, Caroline. *Forms: Whole, Rhythm, Hierarchy, Network.* Princeton, NJ: Princeton University Press, 2015.

Liu, Lydia. *Translingual Practice: Literature, National Culture, and Translated Modernity, China, 1900–1937.* Stanford, CA: Stanford University Press, 1995.

Lutz, Catherine. *Unnatural Emotions: Everyday Sentiments on a Micronesian Atoll and Their Challenge to Western Theory.* Chicago: University of Chicago Press, 1988.

Ma, Ning. *The Age of Silver: Rise of the Novel East and West.* New York: Oxford University Press, 2016.

McMahon, Keith. *Causality and Containment in Seventeenth-Century Chinese Fiction.* Leiden: Brill, 1988.

——. "Eliminating Traumatic Antinomies: Sequels to *Honglou meng.*" In *Snakes' Legs: Sequels, Continuations, Rewritings, and Chinese Fiction*, edited by Martin Huang, 98–115. Honolulu: University of Hawai'i Press, 2004.

——. *Misers, Shrews, and Polygamists: Sexuality and Male–Female Relations in Eighteenth-Century Chinese Fiction.* Durham, NC: Duke University Press, 1995.

Mencius. *Mencius.* 2 vols. Translated by D. C. Lau. Hong Kong: Chinese University Press, 1984.

——. *The Works of Mencius.* Translated by James Legge. New York: Dover, 1970.

Miller, Owen. "Ties of Labour and Ties of Commerce: Corvée Among Seoul Merchants in the Late 19th Century." *Journal of the Economic and Social History of the Orient* 50, no. 1 (2007): 41–71.

Min Kwandong. *Chungguk kojŏn sosŏl ŭi chŏnp'a wa suyong* [Importation and readership of Chinese classical novels]. Seoul: Asea munhwasa, 2007.

Moon, Yumi. *Populist Collaborators: The Ilchinhoe and the Japanese Colonization of Korea, 1896–1910.* Stanford, CA: Stanford University Press, 2015.

Moretti, Franco. *Atlas of the European Novel, 1800–1900.* London: Verso, 1999.

——. *The Way of the World: The Bildungsroman in European Culture.* London: Verso, 2000.

Myŏngju kibong [The remarkable encounter of pearls]. 25 vols. Jangseogak Archive, Songnam. K4^6804.

Myŏngju kibong [The remarkable encounter of pearls]. 2 vols. Seoul: Munhwajae kwalliguk Changsŏgak, 1978.

Myŏngju ogyŏn kihap rok [The remarkable encounter of pearls and jade]. 25 vols. Sŏgang University Archive, Seoul. Kosŏ myŏng 77.

Ogwŏn chaehap kiyŏn [The remarkable reunion of jade mandarin ducks]. 21 vols. Kyujanggak Archive, Seoul, Ko 3350-68.

Ogwŏn chŏnhae [Commentary to jade mandarin ducks]. 5 vols. Kyujanggak Archive, Seoul. Ko 3350-67.

Oh, Doo Hwan. "The Silver Trade and Silver Currency in Chosŏn Korea." Translated by James Lewis. *Acta Koreana* 7, no. 1 (2004): 97–98.

Oksugi [Record of the jade tree]. Vol. 11 of *P'ilsabon kojŏn sosŏl chŏnjip* [Compendium of manuscript editions of classical Korean novels], edited by Kim Kidong. Seoul: Asea munhwasa, 1982.

Ōtani Morishige. *Chosŏn hugi sosŏl tokcha yŏn'gu* [Study of the novel audience in the late Chosŏn]. Seoul: Koryodae minsok munhwa yŏn'guso, 1985.

Paek Tuhyŏn. *Han'gŭl munhŏnhak* [Korean bibliography]. Seoul: T'aehaksa, 2015.

Pak Chiwŏn. *Yŏrha ilgi* [The Jehol diary]. http://db.itkc.kr.

Pak Chŏngsuk. "Sahudang Yun Paekyŏng ŭi ŏpchŏk mit han'gŭl sŏye chakp'um t'ŭkching punsŏk" [The analysis of Sahudang Yun Paekyŏng's work and calligraphy]. *Kuhyŏng kyoyuk* 61 (2017): 85–115.

Pak Hyŏnmo, Yi Wanu, Im Ch'igyun, and Hwang Munhwan, eds. *Han'gŭl: Sot'ong kwa paeryŏ ŭi munja* [Han'gŭl: The script of communication and care]. Songnam: Academy of Korean Studies Press, 2016.

Pak Ilyong. *Chosŏn sidae ŭi aejŏng sosŏl: Sasil kwa nangman ŭi sosŏlsa chŏk chŏn'gae yangsang* [Love novels of Chosŏn: Novelistic development between reality and romanticism]. Seoul: Chimmundang, 1993.

———. "Kamun sosŏl kwa yŏngung sosŏl ŭi sosŏlsa chŏk kwallyŏn yangsang: Hyŏngsŏnggi rŭl chungsim ŭro" [The intersection between the lineage novel and the hero novel: With the focus on the formative period]. *Kojŏn munhak yŏn'gu* 20 (2001): 169–206.

Pak Myŏnguk, Chŏng Hayŏn, Pang Kŏnch'un, Shinohara Hirokata, Yi Chaejŏng, Ko Ŭnsuk, Ŏm T'aeyong, and Im Chŏngyŏn, eds. *Kongjyu kŭlsi tyŏkŭsini: Tŏkon kongju chipan samdae han'gŭl yusan* [Handwriting of a princess: Vernacular Korean heritage in the three generations of Princess Tŏkon's family]. Seoul: National Hangeul Museum, 2019.

Pak Sungnye. "*Ha Chin yangmun rok* yŏn'gu: P'ilsabon kwa hwaljabon ŭi taebi rŭl chungsim ŭro" [A study of *The record of two households: Ha and Chin*, focused on the comparison between manuscript and printed editions]. MA thesis, Academy of Korean Studies, 1998.

Pak Yŏnghŭi. "Changp'yŏn kamun sosŏl ŭi hyangyu chiptan yŏn'gu" [Readership of the lineage novel]. In *Munhak kwa sahoe chipdan* [Literature and society], edited by Han'guk kojŏn munhakhoe, 319–62. Seoul: Chimmundang, 1995.

——. "*So Hyŏnsŏng rok* yŏnjak yŏn'gu" [A study of *The record of So Hyŏnsŏng* and its sequels]. PhD diss., Ewha Womans University, 1994.

Palais, James. *Politics and Policy in Traditional Korea*. Cambridge, MA: Harvard University Asia Center, 1975.

Park, Eugene. *Between Dreams and Reality: The Military Examination in Late Chosŏn Korea, 1600–1894*. Cambridge, MA: Harvard University Asia Center, 2007.

Pettid, Michael, Gregory N. Evon, and Chan E. Park, eds. *Premodern Korean Literary Prose: An Anthology*. New York: Columbia University Press, 2018.

Plamper, Jan. "The History of Emotions: An Interview with William Reddy, Barbara Rosenwein, and Peter Stearns." *History and Theory* 49 (2010): 237–65.

Pollock, Sheldon. *The Language of the Gods in the World of Men: Sanskrit, Culture, and Power in Premodern India*. Berkeley: University of California Press, 2006.

Poole, Janet. *When the Future Disappears: The Modernist Imagination in Late Colonial Korea*. New York: Columbia University Press, 2014.

Povinelli, Elizabeth A. *The Empire of Love: Toward a Theory of Intimacy, Genealogy, and Carnality*. Durham, NC: Duke University Press, 2006.

Qian, Nanxiu, Grace S. Fong, and Richard J. Smith, eds. *Different Worlds of Discourse: Transformation of Gender and Genre in Late Qing and Early Republican China*. Leiden: Brill, 2008.

Rhee, Jooyeon. *The Novel in Transition: Gender and Literature in Early Colonial Korea*. Ithaca, NY: Cornell University Press, 2019.

Rojas, Carlos. *The Naked Gaze: Reflections on Chinese Modernity*. Cambridge, MA: Harvard University Asia Center, 2008.

Rosenwein, Barbara. *Emotional Communities in the Early Middle Ages*. Ithaca, NY: Cornell University Press, 2006.

Ryu Suyŏn. "'Yŏngch'ae chŏn,' kyemong chŏk yŏljŏng kwa pongintoen yukch'e" ["The tale of Yŏngch'ae," enlightened passions and contained carnality]. *Hyŏndae sosŏl yŏn'gu* 34 (2007): 7–21.

Ryu, Youngju. Introduction to *The Cultures of Yushin*, edited by Youngju Ryu, 1–20. Ann Arbor: University of Michigan Press, 2018.

Schmid, Andre. *Korea Between Empires, 1895–1919*. New York: Columbia University Press, 2002.

Shirane, Haruo. "Canon Formation in Japan: Genre, Gender, Popular Culture, and Nationalism." In *Reading East Asian Writing: The Limits of Literary Theory*, edited by Michel Hockx and Ivo Smits, 22–38. London: Routledge Curzon, 2014.

Sim Hyŏnsŏp. "Chosŏn sŏnbi tŭl ŭi sŏye insik kwa kyoyuk" [Calligraphy in the life of Chosŏn scholars: Its significance and training practices]. *Sŏyehak yŏn'gu* 15 (2009): 37–77.

Sim Kyŏngho. *Chosŏn sidae hanmunhak kwa* Sigyŏng *ron* [Literary Chinese studies and the exegesis of *The Book of Poetry* in Chosŏn Korea]. Seoul: Ilchisa, 1999.

———. "Naksŏnjae bon sosŏl ŭi sŏnhaengbon e kwanhan ilkoch'al: Onyang Chŏng ssi p'ilsabon *Ogwŏn chaehap kiyŏn* kwa Naksŏnjae bon *Ogwŏn chunghoeyŏn* ŭi kwan'gye rŭl chungsim ŭro" [A study of the manuscripts of the Nakson Library novels: The relationship between *The remarkable reunion of jade mandarin ducks* copied by Madame Chŏng of Onyang and the Naksŏn Library manuscript]. *Chŏngsin munhwa yŏn'gu* 38 (1990): 169–88.

Sŏ Taesŏk. *Kundam sosŏl ŭi kujo wa paegyŏng* [The background and structure of the battlefield novel]. Seoul: Ewha Womans University Press, 1985.

Song Chunho. *Chosŏn sahoesa yŏn'gu: Chosŏn sahoe ŭi kujo wa sŏnggyŏk mit kŭ pyŏnch'ŏn e kwanhan yŏn'gu* [The social history of Chosŏn: The nature of the social structure and its changes]. Seoul: Ilchŏgak, 1987.

Sŏng Hyŏn'gyŏng. "Kojŏn sosŏl kwa kamun: Ildaegi yŏngung sosŏl ŭl chungsim ŭro" [The traditional Korean novel and lineage: Focusing on the single-generation hero novels]. *Inmunhak yŏn'gu* 20 (1988): 31–47.

Song Sŏnguk. "Chosŏn cho taeha sosŏl ŭi yuhyŏngsŏng kwa kŭ ŭimi" [Structure and meaning of the Chosŏn-dynasty lineage novel]. *Kaesin ŏmun yŏn'gu* 14 (1997): 313–39.

———. *Chosŏn sidae taeha sosŏl ŭi sŏsa munbŏp kwa ch'angjak ŭisik* [The narrative grammar and outlook of Chosŏn-dynasty lineage novels]. Seoul: T'aehaksa, 2003.

Szonyi, Michael. *Practicing Kinship: Lineage and Descent in Late Imperial China.* Stanford, CA: Stanford University Press, 2002.

Taylor, Charles. *Sources of the Self: The Making of the Modern Identity.* Cambridge, MA: Harvard University Press, 1989.

Turner, Ralf. "The Real Self: From Institution to Impulse." *American Journal of Sociology* 81, no. 5 (1976): 989–1016.

U K'waeje. "Kuhwaljabon kososŏl ŭi ch'ulp'an mit yŏn'gu hyŏnhwang kŏmt'o" [State of the field: Studies of novels in old movable type]. *Kojŏn munhak yŏn'gu* 0 (1985): 113–43.

Uchida, Jun. *Brokers of Empire: Japanese Settler Colonialism in Korea, 1876–1945.* Cambridge, MA: Harvard University Asia Center, 2011.

Ueda, Atsuko. *Concealment of Politics, Politics of Concealment: The Production of "Literature" in Meiji Japan.* Stanford, CA: Stanford University Press, 2006.

Vervoorn, Aat. "Boyi and Shuqi: Worthy Men of Old?" *Papers on Far Eastern History* 28 (1983): 1–22.

Wagner, Edward. "Two Early Genealogies and Women's Status in Early Yi Dynasty Korea." In *Korean Women: View from the Inner Room*, edited by Laurel Kendall and Mark Peterson, 23–32. New Haven, CT: East Rock Press, 1983.

Wang, David Der-wei. *Fin-de-Siècle Splendor: Repressed Modernities of Late Qing Fiction, 1848–1911*. Stanford, CA: Stanford University Press, 1997.

Wang, Sixiang. "The Filial Daughter of Kwaksan—Finger Severing, Confucian Virtues, and Envoy Poetry in Early Chosŏn." *Seoul Journal of Korean Studies* 25, no. 2 (December 2012): 175–212.

———. "*Story of the Eastern Chamber*: Dilemmas of Vernacular Language and Political Authority in Eighteenth-Century Chosŏn." *Journal of Korean Studies* 24, no. 1 (2019): 29–62.

Wanwŏl hoemaeng yŏn [The pledge at the banquet of moon-gazing pavilion]. Kyujanggak Archive, Seoul National University, Ko 3350-65-v.1–93.

Widmer, Ellen. *The Beauty and the Book: Women and Fiction in Nineteenth-Century China*. Cambridge, MA: Harvard University Council on East Asian Studies, 2006.

———. *Fiction's Family: Zhan Xi, Zhan Kai, and the Business of Women in Late-Qing China*. Cambridge, MA: Harvard University Asia Center, 2016.

Williams, Raymond. *Marxism and Literature*. Oxford: Oxford University Press, 1977.

Wong, Siu-Kit, and Lee Kar-Shui. "Poems of Depravity: A Twelfth Century Dispute on the Moral Character of *The Book of Songs*." *T'oung Pao* 75, nos. 4–5 (1989): 209–25.

Workman, Travis. *Imperial Genus: The Formation and Limits of the Human in Modern Korea and Japan*. Oakland: University of California Press, 2016.

Yang Hyeran. *Chosŏn cho kibong ryu sosŏl yŏn'gu* [Study of Chosŏn-dynasty novels focused on the remarkable encounter]. Seoul: Ihoe munhwasa, 1995.

Yang, Yoon Sun. *From Domestic Women to Sensitive Young Men: Translating the Individual in Early Colonial Korea*. Cambridge, MA: Harvard University Asia Center, 2017.

Yesul ŭi chŏndang, ed. *Chosŏn sidae han'gŭl sŏye* [Vernacular Korean calligraphy of the Chosŏn dynasty]. Seoul: Mijinsa, 1994.

Yi Chiha. "*Hyŏn ssi yangung ssangnin ki* yŏnjak yŏn'gu" [Study of the sequel cluster of *The record of two heroes: Brothers Hyŏn*]. MA thesis, Seoul National University, 1992.

———. *Ogwŏn chaehap kiyŏn yŏnjak yŏn'gu* [Study of the sequel cluster of *The remarkable encounter of jade mandarin ducks*]. Seoul: Pogosa, 2015.

Yi Chiyŏng. "18 segi Kyŏnghwa sajok ŭi sosŏl hyangyu" [Novel readership among the metropolitan elites in the eighteenth century]. *Kungmunhak yŏn'gu* 21 (2010): 67–95.

——. "*Ch'angsŏn kamŭi rok* ŭi ibon pyŏni yangsang kwa tokcha ch'ŭng ŭi sang-gwan kwan'gye" [The relationship between the audiences and variations in the editions of *The praise of goodness and the admiration of righteousness*]. PhD diss., Seoul National University, 2003.

Yi Chongsik. "T'ongdokcha Yun Paekyŏng yŏsa ka mal hanŭn kŭ naeryŏk kwa ilhwa tŭl—Naksŏnjae mun'go wa pansegi" [Recollections of an avid reader, Madame Yun Paekyŏng—half a century at the Naksŏn Library]. *Chungang ilbo*, August 25, 1966.

Yi Insuk. "Chosŏn sidae hanmun kanch'al ŭi sŏyesa chŏk ŭiŭi" [The calligraphic significance of literary Chinese epistles during the Chosŏn dynasty]. *Sŏyehak yŏn'gu* 6 (2005): 51–81.

Yi Kwangsu. *Parojapŭn* Mujŏng [*The heartless*: A corrected edition]. Edited by Kim Ch'ol. P'aju: Munhak tongne, 2004.

——. "Tananhan pansaeng ŭi tojŏng" [A journey through hardships, half-life long]. In *Yi Kwangsu chŏnjip* [The complete anthology of Yi Kwangsu], 10 vols., 8:445–57. Seoul: Samjongdang, 1963.

——. "What Is Literature?" Translated by Jooyeon Rhee. *Azalea* 4 (2011): 312.

——. *Yi Kwangsu and Modern Korean Literature*: Mujŏng. Translated and edited by Ann Sung-hi Lee. Ithaca, NY: Cornell University Press, 2005.

Yi Kyŏngha. "17 segi sangch'ŭng yŏsŏng ŭi kungmun saenghwal e kwanhan munhŏn chŏk koch'al" [Overview of sources on women's use of vernacular Korean script in the seventeenth century]. *Han'guk munhak nonch'ong* 39 (2005): 217–41.

——. "Mangsil haengjang yŏn'gu" [Posthumous biographies written for deceased wives]. *Han'guk munhwa* 40 (2007): 1–26.

Yi Pyŏnggi. "Chosŏn munhŏn myŏngjak haeje" [Overview of the Chosŏn-dynasty literary masterpieces]. *Munjang* 8 (1940): 230.

——. *Karam ilgi* [The diary of Karam]. 2 vols. Seoul: Sin'gu munhwasa, 1976.

Yi Pyŏnggi and Paek Ch'ŏl. *Kungmunhak chŏnsa* [The complete history of national literature]. Seoul: Sin'gu munhwasa, 1957.

Yi Pyŏngju. "Oegoktoen sinpalgul" [Crooked discovery]. *Kyŏnghyang sinmun*, September 5, 1966.

Yi Sangt'aek. "Chosŏn taeha sosŏl ŭi chakchach'ŭng e taehan yŏn'gu" [Study of the social background of the Korean lineage novels' authors]. *Kojŏn munhak yŏn'gu* 3 (1986): 228–49.

Yi Subong. "*Haedong Yi ssi samdaerok* yŏn'gu" [A study of *The record of the three generations of the Yi lineage from the East of the sea*]. In *Han'guk kamun sosŏl yŏn'gu nonch'ong* [Studies of the Korean lineage novel], 3 vols., edited by Yi Subong, 1:335–55. Seoul: Kyŏngin munhwasa, 1992.

——. "Kamun sosŏl yŏn'gu" [A study of the lineage novel]. *Tonga nonch'ong* 15, no. 1 (1978): 226–491.

Yi Sugŏn. "Chosŏn sidae sinbunsa kwallyŏn charyo ŭi pip'an: Sŏnggwan, kagye, inmun kwallyŏn wijo charyo wa wisŏ rŭl chungsim ŭro" [Critical evaluation of the materials for the history of the Chosŏn class structure: Fabrications of ancestral seats, genealogies, and personalia]. *Komunsŏ yŏn'gu* 14 (1998): 1–32.

Yi Taehyŏng. "19 segi changp'yŏn sosŏl *Ha Chin yangmun rok* ŭi taejung chŏk pyŏnmo" [Popular transformation of a lineage novel, *The record of two households: Ha and Chin*, in the nineteenth century]. *Minjok munhwasa yŏn'gu* 39 (2008): 28–56.

Yi T'aejun. *Eastern Sentiments.* Translated by Janet Poole. New York: Columbia University Press, 2009.

Yi Tawŏn, ed. *Hyŏn ssi yangung ssangnin ki* [The record of two heroes: Brothers Hyŏn]. 2 vols. Seoul: Kyŏngin munhwasa, 2006.

——. "*Hyŏn ssi yangung ssangnin ki* yŏn'gu: Yŏndae bon *Hyŏn ssi yangung ssangnin ki* chungsim ŭro" [Study of *The record of two heroes: Brothers Hyŏn*, with a focus on the Yonsei University manuscript]. MA thesis, Yonsei University, 2001.

Yi Tŏngmu. *Ch'ŏngjanggwan ch'ongsŏ* [The complete works of Ch'ŏnggjangwan]. Vols. 257–59 of *Han'guk munjip ch'onggan* [The complete compendium of Korean literary collections], edited by Minjok munhwa ch'ujinhoe. Seoul: Minjok munhwa ch'ujinhoe, 2000.

Yi Wŏnju. "Kojŏn sosŏl tokcha ŭi sŏnghyang—Kyŏngbuk pukpu chiyŏk ŭl chungsim ŭro" [The tastes of traditional novel readers—focused on the northern Kyŏngsang Province]. *Han'gukhak nonjip* 1–5 (1975): 557–73.

"Yŏgi san in'gan munhwajae: 77 se halmŏni ka Chungguksa pŏnyŏk p'yŏnch'an" [The cultural treasure living here: A 77-year-old granny compiles the translation of Chinese history]. *Sŏul sinmun*, May 8, 1964.

Yu Ch'undong. "'Ch'aek yŏl mongnok' e taehayŏ" [Study of "A book roster"]. *Munhŏn kwa haesŏk* 34 (2006): 187–204.

——. "Hwaljabon kososŏl ŭi ch'ulp'an kwa yut'ong e taehan myŏt kaji munje tŭl" [Traditional fiction in moveable type: Some observations on its publication and circulation]. *Hanminjok munhwa yŏn'gu* 50 (2015): 289–315.

——. "Ilbon Tongyang mun'go sojang sech'aek kososŏl ŭi sŏnggyŏk kwa ŭimi" [The character and significance of rental novels located in Tōyō bunko in Japan]. *Minjok munhwa yŏn'gu* 64 (2014): 283–309.

Yu Kwangsu. "Hwalp'an bon *Ha Chin yangmun rok* Tongmisŏsi bon e taehayŏ" [On the Tongmisŏsi moveable-type imprint of *The record of two households: Ha and Chin*]. *Ilsang kojŏn yŏn'gu* 42 (2014): 379–417.

Yu Myŏngjong. *Sŏngnihak kwa yangmyŏnghak* [Neo-Confucian orthodoxy and Wang Yangming's philosophy]. Seoul: Yonsei University Press, 1994.

Yu Sŭnghyŏn and Min Kwandong. "Chosŏn hugi Chungguk hŭigok ŭi suyong yangsang: *Sŏsang ki* rŭl chungsim ŭro" [Circulation of Chinese plays in the late

Chosŏn: The case of *The romance of the western wing*]. *Chungguk ŏmun hakchi* 43, no. 43 (2013): 57–96.

Yun Chiyang. "Chosŏn ŭi *Sŏsang ki* suyong yangsang yŏn'gu" [Study of the reception of *The romance of the western chamber* in Chosŏn]. PhD diss., Seoul National University, 2015.

Yun ssi haengjang [Posthumous biography of Madame Yun]. Kyujanggak Archive, Seoul National University. Karam ko 920.7-G422y.

Zeitlin, Judith. *Historian of the Strange: Pu Songling and the Chinese Classical Tale.* Stanford, CA: Stanford University Press, 1993.

Zhang, Ying. *Confucian Image Politics: Masculine Morality in Seventeenth-Century China.* Seattle: University of Washington Press, 2017.

Zheng, Huili. "Encountering the Other: Identity, Culture, and the Novel in Late Imperial China." PhD diss., University of California at Irvine, 2010.

Zito, Angela. *Of Body and Brush: Grand Sacrifice as Text/Performance in Eighteenth-Century China.* Chicago: University of Chicago Press, 1997.

——. "Silk and Skin: Significant Boundaries." In *Body, Subject, and Power in China,* edited by Angela Zito and Tani Barlow, 103–30. Chicago: University of Chicago Press, 1994.

Žižek, Slavoj. *The Sublime Object of Ideology.* New York: Verso, 1987.

Zwicker, Jonathan. *Practices of the Sentimental Imagination: Melodrama, the Novel, and the Social Imaginary in Nineteenth-Century Japan.* Cambridge, MA: Harvard University Press, 2006.

Index

grandmothers, 45–46; concubines, 53, 64, 130; in the family tale, 64; funerary writings and, 45–46; in the lineage novel, 53, 130–32; milk family and, 46, 47; property and, 48

Confucianism, 10, 13; attack on, 174, 178; culture and men, 183; father-son bond and, 47–48; human feelings and, 97; Kabo Reforms and, 162; kinship system and, 3; lineage and, 3–4; with marriage as moral bond, 102–3, 128–29; moralism of, 156, 174; negative individualism and, 224n69

Confucian ritual, 194n6, 224n72; in the lineage novel, 102

Confucian scholarship, 10, 39

Confucius, 118–19

Courant, Maurice, 166, 230n12

cross-dressing, 129, 225n8

cult of *qing. See* desire

Daoguang (Emperor), 58–59

De Bary, William Theodore, 224nn69–70

desexualized couples, 137

desire: in Chinese novels, 11, 18, 110; containment of, 135; cult of qing and, 9, 11–13, 17, 154; as dangerous, 115, 130, 156; domestic surveillance and, 130, 136–37; gender and, 129–33, 137, 140; marriage and, 125, 128–38, 140; narrative desire, 8, 49, 53–54, 65, 154

Deuchler, Martina, 3–4, 97, 194n8, 195n13, 198n45, 219n11, 222n39, 228n43

discernment, 47, 117, 118, 172

Discourse That Dispels Illusion, 26

divorce, 4, 69, 125

domestic novel, 196n28

domestic space: bodies of women in, 69–70; culture and, 179; family tales and, 62, 65; funerary writings and, 40–48; the lineage novel and, 122–23, 187; vernacular Korean script and, 39–40

doubleness and dissimulation, 117, 119, 120, 121, 150

dowries, 76, 102, 215n27

Dream of the Jade Kirin, 26

Dream of the Red Chamber, The (Cao Xueqin), 11, 17–18, 54, 110, 179, 200n64, 236n64

education: men and, 80; women and, 75, 76

Elementary Learning, 52

emotional reciprocity, 116, 117, 122–24

emotions. *See* feelings

epistolary calligraphy, 77, *78*

Epstein, Maram, 42–43, 194n7, 195n14, 196n31, 197n3, 201n67, 207n22

eulogies, 41, 45, 47, 236n58

European novels, 9, 11, 166–67, 195n21

families: with calligraphy training, 80–81; funerary writings and, 40–48; Mencius on, 119; milk, 46, 47; tale, 56–65, 59. *See also* feelings, conflicts of kinship and; marriage

family tales, 210n60; Confucian, 57, 58; domestic space and, 62, 65; funerary texts and, 56, 64–65

father-in-law and son-in law, 3, 7, 225n2; with feelings and conflicts of kinship, 139–40, 143, 145, 156, 158, 227n36; as problem in the lineage novel, 225n2; sexuality and, 139–40

fathe-son bond, 3, 47–48, 96, 111–12, 150

father-to-son succession, property and, 39

Confucian moral bond, 102–3; consummation of, 130, 131–32, 135, 137–38, 139, 156, 158; desire and, 128–38; divorce and, 4, 69, 125; dowry, 76, 102, 215n27; lineage perpetuity and, 124, 125; maternal kin and, 97, 125, 138–45; paternal kin and, 125, 138–45; patriarchal authority and, 7, 130, 134, 137–38, 139; polygamy, 128, 130; rape and, 131–33; sexuality and, 128; titles referencing, 125; unruly feelings and, 103; virilocal, 5, 97; women and last names after, 228n47. *See also* rape

Master Im and His Three Wives, 26, 55

maternal and paternal kin, 125, 138–45; mourning grades, 97

McMahon, Keith, 54, 201n67

Memoirs of Lady Hyegyŏng, 21, 180, 204n90, 207n26

men: Confucianism and culture, 183; with conjugal unions and patriarchy, 130, 134, 137–38; education and, 80; with feelings of flesh and blood, 111, 195n20; love sickness and, 129, 134; male sexuality and, 128–29, 138; vernacular Korean calligraphy and, 79–83; vernacular Korean fiction and, 16, 72, 82; vernacular Korean script and, 16, 39–40, 72, 74, 83, 185; women separated from, 128; writing about women, 78–79, 92

Mencius, 96, 118, 119, 223n60

milk family, 46, 47. *See also* breast milk

Min (Queen), 162

Ming dynasty (1368–1644), 9, 198n48, 200n63

Min Usu, 77–78

modernity, 156, 167–68, 179, 184, 190, 230n15; in East Asian literary studies,

8, 167; the end of bildungsroman and, 166–67; the global rise of the novel and, 8, 224n67; in *The Heartless*, 188–89

money: cultural influence of, 8, 53, 198n45, 240n101; global infrastructure of, 12, 155; metallic currency, 197n44; paper prices, 68; social bonds and, 189

Moon, Yumi, 229n1

Moretti, Franco, 100, 166

mother–daughter relationship, 157

mother-in-law and daughter-in-law, 146–47

mother–son bond, 48, 157

Munjang (Writing) magazine, 180, 187

Naksŏn collection, 180, 182–83, 184, 186

Naksŏn Pavilion, 182, 238n77

Nam Yunwŏn, 55

narrative desire, 8, 11, 49, 53–55, 65, 154; narrative expansion and, 55

negative individualism, 224n69

negative interiority, 116–22

Newspaper Law of 1907, 169

nightingale blood, 150, 227n29. *See also* parrot blood; red mark

Nine-Cloud Dream, The (Kim Manjung), 171, 199n58, 218n54

novels: battlefield, 19, 37–38, 171, 175, 177, 201n69, 202; bildungsroman, 166–67; boudoir, 16, 165, 185, 191, 200n62, 214n21, 239n91; domestic, 196n28; early modern world and rise of, 8–15; European, 9, 11, 195n21; hero, 37–38, 201n69; negative interiority and space of, 116–22; scholar–beauty, 12, 18, 129, 155, 225n8; sources and chapters, 30–34. *See also* lineage novel, the; vernacular Korean novels